NOSE ART
OF THE AIR FORCE
Pin-Ups and More
1942–1947

DAVID VINCENT

Schiffer
Military History
4880 Lower Valley Road
Atglen, PA 19310

Other Schiffer books on related subjects

Combat Recon: 5th Air Force Images from the SW Pacific 1943–45
Robert Stava
978-0-7643-2777-3

Protect & Avenge: The 49th Fighter Group in World War II
Steve W. Ferguson and William K. Pascalis
978-0-88740-750-5

Copyright © 2025 by David Vincent

Library of Congress Control Number: 2024941474

All rights reserved. No part of this work may be reproduced or used in any form or by any means—graphic, electronic, or mechanical, including photocopying or information storage and retrieval systems—without written permission from the publisher.
 The scanning, uploading, and distribution of this book or any part thereof via the Internet or any other means without the permission of the publisher is illegal and punishable by law. Please purchase only authorized editions and do not participate in or encourage the electronic piracy of copyrighted materials.
 "Schiffer," "Schiffer Publishing, Ltd.," and the pen and inkwell logo are registered trademarks of Schiffer Publishing, Ltd.

Designed by Beth Oberholtzer
Cover design by BMac
Type set in Boton/Helvetica Now/Garamond Premerier Pro

ISBN: 978-0-7643-6921-6
Printed in India
10 9 8 7 6 5 4 3 2 1

Published by Schiffer Publishing, Ltd.
4880 Lower Valley Road
Atglen, PA 19310
Phone: (610) 593-1777; Fax: (610) 593-2002
Email: Info@schifferbooks.com
Web: www.schifferbooks.com

For our complete selection of fine books on this and related subjects, please visit our website at www.schifferbooks.com. You may also write for a free catalog.
 Schiffer Publishing's titles are available at special discounts for bulk purchases for sales promotions or premiums. Special editions, including personalized covers, corporate imprints, and excerpts, can be created in large quantities for special needs. For more information, contact the publisher.
 We are always looking for people to write books on new and related subjects. If you have an idea for a book, please contact us at proposals@schifferbooks.com.

Contents

Introduction		5
Chapter 1	**Some of the Better-Known Artists**	23
Chapter 2	**Bomber and Long-Range Photo Recon Beauties**	35
Chapter 3	**Fighter and Photo Recon Fillies**	189
Chapter 4	**Cargo Cuties**	221
Chapter 5	**Other Types**	257
Chapter 6	**Fearsome Nose Art**	265
Chapter 7	**What Happened to Them All?**	295
Chapter 8	**Postwar Postscript**	319

Appendixes

Appendix 1	**P-39 Door Art**	329
Appendix 2	**Far East Air Service Command Nose Art**	331
Appendix 3	**"The Painted Ladies of Nadzab"**	337

Bibliography 341
Index of Named Airplanes 345

Introduction

The photos that appear in this volume were purchased over more than twenty years and represent the author's interest in aircraft of the Second World War and their official and unofficial markings, which spans more than six decades.

Aircraft designed for military use are designed to undertake specific roles. In times of conflict, these planes generally start out camouflaged in military paint schemes and bear official markings designed to identify them and the unit to which they belong. Yet, once in the hands of their crews and in action, unofficial markings are often added. In World War II this was particularly the case with the frontline aircraft of the US Army Air Forces (USAAF), the noses of which, more often than not, became the focal point for largely unapproved artistic endeavors. To begin with, this artwork was mostly lighthearted and anti-Axis in nature, but once the idea of adding scantily clad or nude representations of the female form took hold, competition arose to come up with more and more risqué works. As a result, these aircraft, which reflected pop culture of the day on such a grand scale, became in all probability the most photographed of World War II.

In January and February 1942, soon after America's entry into World War II, USAAF established the first of its separately numbered combat air forces for service in different theaters of war: the 5th Air Force (AF), based in the Philippine Islands; the 6th AF, in the Panama Canal Zone; the 7th AF, in the South Pacific; the 8th AF, in England; the 10th AF, in India-Burma; and the 11th AF, in the North Pacific. The 9th AF was activated soon after, and others followed. The original 5th AF, however, had virtually disappeared by the time that surviving personnel and airplanes made it to Australia by April 1942, and it was only after the arrival of Lt. Gen. George C. Kenney as commanding general of Allied Air Forces in late July 1942 that a new 5th AF came into being from September 3, 1942.

This project does not attempt to catalog all artworks, named or unnamed, applied to aircraft of the 5th AF; the large number of units involved and the sometimes brief periods that some planes (and crews) served make a complete collection of photos nearly impossible, but, nevertheless, the widest-possible net has been cast over the subject over many years to capture the diversity and extent of what many readers see as the most-interesting aspects of this unofficial art genre; namely, pin-up and fearsome animal-based representations. Three appendixes provide additional images and information that the author feels will be of interest to most readers.

Following Japan's seemingly unstoppable southward advances commencing on December 7, 1941, Australia

Photographed in France, probably in January 1940, the difficult-to-make-out picture adjacent to the nose glasshouse on this Bristol Blenheim Mk. IV light bomber may well have been the first pin-up on an Allied aircraft in World War II. This is not a painting, though, but a page featuring a nude female form cut from an unidentified book or magazine and taped to the side of the plane. Such publications of the day published in Britain, though, emphasized artistic form and the portrayal of classic figure poses, nothing else. *British Official*

It is difficult to find dated photos of camouflaged USAAF aircraft wearing unit insignia immediately prior to the Pacific war, but here is one of a Douglas B-18 photographed in Dutch Guiana on December 5, 1941, with its pilot, Maj. (later colonel) Gerald E. Williams. Note the positioning of the insignia; in this case the charging American Buffalo of the 99th Bomb Squadron (BS). With the commencement of hostilities only days later and the subsequent removal of existing unit insignia, it was still the nose of the bomber that remained the focal point for later unofficial names or artworks. *US Army Signal Corps*

Boeing B-17, 41-24403, artist MSgt. Peter C. Culp, 65th and 63rd BSs, 43rd BG, later 5th AF Headquarters (HQ). The fact that there was approval of nose art in principle in the 5th AF can be seen from this photo of the deputy commander, subsequently (from June 1944) commanding general of the 5th AF, Maj. Gen. Ennis C. Whitehead (*back row, far left*), with his crew in front of their VIP B-17 with its picture of "Uncle Sam." The artwork and name (the latter originally in more-ornate script) seem to have been applied in the first quarter of 1943, when this B-17 was in frontline use with the 65th BS before being passed to the 63rd BS (it had earlier carried the name *BLITZ BUGGY*). Subsequently converted for Whitehead's use (nonstandard features included a bed and refrigerator), it is thought that the B-17 retained this look (keeping not only the nose art and name but camouflage as well) until war's end.

The Army Air Forces in World War II authors note that by September 1943, some 175 B-25s had been converted to strafers at the Townsville Air Depot in northern Queensland. Here are three of them, photographed in June 1943 by a depot official photographer. From the point of view of nose art history, however, they are also representative of the time before the rise in popularity of pin-ups on planes. Of these three B-25s, only the story behind *ROSE IN BLOOM* is currently known; this was an original 498th BS, 345th BG ship (serial number 41-30063) assigned to squadron commander, then captain, Bert S. Rosenbaum, the name he gave to it being simply a play on his own name. This nose art, added en route to Australia at McClelland Field, Sacramento, California, was short lived, though, since a fierce-looking bird's head, an early attempt at a squadron insignia, subsequently covered the entire nose. Nothing is currently known of the history of either *LI'L ROXIE RAE* or *"Strokem Dodie"*, but both B-25s were probably from the same production batch as *ROSE IN BLOOM*.

became the only safe refuge for US forces, both those that had seen action in the Philippines and the Dutch East Indies and new arrivals sent from home. Gen. Douglas MacArthur assumed command of the Southwest Pacific Area (SWPA) of operations (from the Philippines down to and including Australia, west as far as Borneo and Java, and east to New Guinea and New Britain) on April 18, 1942, and while a good number of dive-bombers (subsequently used sparingly due to heavy losses) plus some light and medium bombers had arrived in Australia by this time, the number of available heavy bombers, Boeing B-17s, was something of the order of only twelve, and, unsurprisingly, this situation improved only slowly to begin with (two B-17s a day were to be flown from the US after March 20, 1942, but by the end of the month only nine had arrived in Australia, and the delivery rate was cut back to one a day in April). So meager were the available resources that plans were made to add Royal Australian Air Force (RAAF) units to the mix, but, while after the arrival of Kenney this all changed, RAAF and USAAF personnel continued to work closely together.

Few would disagree that men in forward areas needed morale boosters at a time when there was little good news, and, clearly, a liberal attitude toward unofficial markings on US planes helped, but they were limited to begin with.

Although some exceptions have been noted, it was not until the United States entered the war in December 1941 that the idea of decorating military aircraft with personal names or artwork (or both) gained any traction. It is true that such artwork had first appeared in World War I, but only in a limited way. The German Legion Condor sent to fight in the Spanish Civil War in the late 1930s dabbled with a variety of personal markings too, but the official view was that squadron emblems were the only approved insignia. The air forces of other European powers continued to use squadron badges to identify units as well at this time, although Britain's Royal Air Force was an exception here, doing away with them altogether prior to the start of the war against Germany. After this time, a few RAF squadron badges slipped back into use, although, apparently, without official approval. In America, however, it was, again, unit badges that primarily decorated Army Air Corps / Army Air Forces aircraft (Maj. Gen. Henry H. "Hap" Arnold was appointed chief, Army Air Forces, on June 20, 1941) right up to and immediately after President Roosevelt's declaration of war against the Axis powers. In fact, unit badges continued to be big business during the war (243 had been approved up to some point in 1943), but applying unit insignia in the early post–Pearl Harbor era was outlawed. This, together with news of the emergence of unofficial emblems on the aircraft of RAF squadrons,[1] undoubtedly stimulated the notion among USAAF airmen, certainly those destined for overseas service, that the addition of unofficial names or artworks to their airplanes would be seen in a positive light.

How 5th AF pin-up nose art had grown in three years of war is graphically seen in these two views of right-hand side (RHS) artwork on 5th AF Consolidated B-24s. At top is *BOMBS TO NIP ON* of the 90th Bomb Group (BG), serial number 41-23942, which was, perhaps, the first 5th AF B-24 nose art to feature a topless pin-up, while the photo below is of an unnamed B-24 of the 43rd BG, serial number 44-41256, photographed in 1945. What was probably considered quite risqué in 1942 (*BOMBS TO NIP ON* was lost in a takeoff accident at Iron Range, Queensland, on November 16, 1942) had paled into insignificance by 1945! It is also important to note that nose art featuring pin-up girls in 1942 was relatively uncommon; yet, by 1945, broadly speaking, bomber nose art was almost entirely pin-up-based, proving so popular that, predictably, some artists wanted to make their artworks bigger and more extreme than what was around at the time. *THE DRAGON AND HIS TAIL*, seen on the cover, remains the most extravagant nose artwork in the 5th AF and, in fact, the war in the Pacific, but the unnamed nude seen here (a work in progress at the time that the photo was taken) may have been the largest ever attempted on any USAAF plane in World War II. Again, the who, what, when, and where are not known, and there is some doubt, in fact, about whether it was completed. On that basis, it may have simply been an early postwar art project while the unit was in limbo; late-war bombers such as this one were generally candidates for return to the US postwar, but if that did occur, it is suspected that the artwork was removed before it arrived. *BOMBS TO NIP ON* via Bob Tupa / Michael Musumeci

An early dated example of this (most personal snaps of nose art are undated) was the unofficial markings added to the North American B-25 bombers destined for the famous carrier-based surprise attack against Japan carried out on April 18, 1942. Of the sixteen B-25s that were loaded aboard the carrier USS *Hornet* (CV-8) on March 31 and April 1, 1942, more than half had had either a personal name or artwork added.

So it was that names without accompanying artwork or simple, small artworks became common sights on bombers transferred overseas in 1942–43; this freedom of expression was regarded as a sign of the positive attitude being demonstrated not only by the young men involved in flying the aircraft, but those maintaining them as well. Right from the early days, when troops were being sent overseas they were told that the war was about "the freedom of your lives." As an official US poster issued in July 1942 told readers: "We are of one mind—Hitler, Mussolini, and Hirohito shall *never* take from us the Freedom for which our forefathers sacrificed *their* lives and fortunes."[2] That the American way of life was considered, by many, to be in jeopardy, particularly during the war in the Pacific, was confirmed immediately after the war ended by the 5th AF's then commanding general, Lt. Gen. Ennis C. Whitehead. In a circular printed in the thousands and distributed widely to 5th AF personnel, he began by saying, "Three years ago we commenced our campaigns against a vicious, arrogant enemy determined to destroy our way of living."[3] It is little wonder, then, that unofficial artworks on government property, particularly planes, became an accepted demonstration of that "way of living."

In more-recent years, it has been suggested that such artworks (which, on heavy bombers, were added mostly prior to the planes being ferried overseas) were approved by an Army Air Forces regulation, but that document (said to have been dated August 1944 but first issued in August 1943 and revised two years later) referred specifically to squadron insignia.[4] When it came to pin-up nose art, a 1943 article by an Associated Press staff writer claimed that there was an order that curbed "the boys' more ribald inclinations," but not only is there no record of that document now, but at best it must have been short lived.[5]

INTRODUCTION

As the Army Air Forces saw it, the unofficial names applied to aircraft, the nicknames, as they were sometimes called, were fine (even the VIP Boeing B-17 used by Gen. Kenney carried a nickname, *Sally*, bestowed upon it by Maj. Clarence "Kip" Chase when he was Kenney's aide). This was confirmed in December 1943, when the practice came under urgent review. A crew member from an 8th AF B-17 shot down over Germany a month earlier and taken prisoner had been found to have had his aircraft's name, *Murder, Inc*, painted on the back of his flying jacket, photos of which were subsequently published in the German press. Headquarters Allied Air Force, Southwest Pacific Area, wrote to Royal Australian Air Force (RAAF) Command advising that

> this is a matter of grave concern, and it is desired that immediate steps be taken to ensure that nothing is painted on an airplane, clothing or equipment which might be used as propaganda material by the enemy or which might tend to bring action against captured Air Force personnel.

On the subject of other named aircraft, however, it was pointed out that there was "no objection to painting a name such as 'Marie Louise' on an airplane."[6]

By December 1943, though, it was the unofficial artworks, mostly named, that upstaged just names that had been added to airplanes. All over the world, USAAF planes, medium and heavy bombers particularly, were having artworks, in some cases not insignificant in size, added to them. Many of the pictures were based on comic book or cartoon characters, others on birds and animals, but by the second half of 1943 the most popular theme was representations of women, sometimes just a face, but generally copies of the nearly nude pin-up paintings that appeared mainly in magazines or calendar art of the day, so pin-ups were to play an important part in the nose art story.

The term "pin-up" is not so well known today but was in common use in World War II, when it referred to any cutting, photo, or artwork of any young lady that was pinned up or otherwise affixed to an accepting surface. It can be imagined that collections of such pictures were better suited to firmly constructed buildings than life under canvas, which is how most soldiers lived in forward areas, but somehow pin-ups were to be found everywhere that Allied soldiers served, their popularity supported by base newspapers and readily available magazines such as the famed *Yank* and the *Army Weekly*, written "by the men . . . for the men in the service." Building up a collection of pin-up pictures or cuttings from magazines, or photos (many of which were of film stars of the day), required, as with any collecting "bug," some effort; around the

The fact that not all 5th AF bombers featured nose art is well represented by these photos of North American B-25s of the 345th BG. The vast majority of this group's planes featured either personal or squadron insignia nose art (see chapter 6 for the latter), but here are two exceptions. *THE JADED SAINT*, serial number 41-30076, had been assigned to the 501st BS in April 1943 and was transferred out only following damage caused by an enemy bombing attack on September 1, 1944; yet, despite that lengthy service, no artwork was ever added. The 498th BS adopted a falcon head as a nose insignia, and the squadron is widely remembered as the "Falcons," but *LITTLE NEL*, serial number 41-30188, was one B-25 that escaped the artist's brush except for the name, which appeared on both sides of the nose. Assigned to the squadron in August 1943, she was transferred out following the forced landing seen here (which was due to enemy action) at Port Moresby on December 22, 1943.

One of the most important uses of pin-ups in the SWPA and elsewhere was to grab soldiers' attention to remind them to take precautions against the transmission of malaria by the (female) *Anopheles* mosquito. These photos, all of which are believed to have been taken in New Guinea, show how pin-ups helped. The reference to "612" (*top right*) is to the Formula No. 612 synthetic insect repellent. The bottles seen in this and the "USE YOUR REPELLANT" photo (*above*) were those produced by the National Carbon Co. under their Eveready trade name. Both pin-ups in these two photos, probably painted by the same artist, were based on *Esquire* magazine's September 1943 Varga Girl.

INTRODUCTION

Cartoon by Pvt. (later corporal) Frank G. Farina taken from the 89th BS's wartime souvenir book, *Altitude Minimum* (Farina was also a contributor to the later souvenir book *The Reaper's Harvest*, produced for members of the 3rd Attack Group). The reference to "Benson" is to fellow 89th BS member and artist Sgt. Tony Benson, who was possibly also a squadron nose art painter.

This cartoon, drawn by an unidentified artist and taken from the 8th Air Service Group 1945 souvenir book, was purely wishful thinking but suggests how attached servicemen became to these often life-sized—sometimes larger—airplane artworks.

time of the end of the war or shortly afterward, a member of the RAAF wrote to the editor of *Wings* magazine, a widely distributed fortnightly journal published by the service's directorate of public relations, claiming that while based in New Guinea, he and a tentmate had collected more than 1,700![7]

The same Australian magazine had early on published a center spread of official photos of nose art on US aircraft in North Africa, but a RAAF medical officer expressed his displeasure on seeing a close-up photo of nose art on a 9th AF B-24 named *The Vulgar Virgin* (copied from a 1941 George Petty artwork) by writing to the magazine's editor, complaining about the adverse affect that such artworks may have on servicemen in general. "A healthy attitude to sex is most necessary," he wrote, "and pictures such as the Vulgar Virgin do not help in this vital national need."[8]

No doubt the same officer would have taken exception to the use of pin-up style art to promote the use of insect repellent and the importance of taking Atabrine tablets to combat malaria, as seen in these photos below. Like it or not, even in World War II, the adage of "sex sells" rang true.

What did help to legitimize pin-up art, particularly pin-up nose art, for the USAAF was the publicity given to the twenty-five-mission B-17 *"MEMPHIS BELLE"*, which was flown back to the US from England for a public-relations tour in June 1943. In July 1943, the AAF's Training Aids Division even published a small booklet about the bomber, but this placed no emphasis on the unofficial markings (apart from the name and mission symbols, there was a tasteful but nonetheless unauthorized artwork of a bathing beauty copied from a 1941 George Petty pin-up calendar on both sides of the nose), just the fact that the plane and her crew had survived twenty-five missions. The public-relations tour was followed by a forty-one-minute Technicolor documentary, another product of the AAF, centered on this B-17's combat tour. Released in April 1944, the film gave audiences an idea of the work the crews of the 8th AF were doing bombing targets in Germany and occupied Europe from its British bases.

While the *"MEMPHIS BELLE"* was touring the US, an article titled "Nudes Names and Numbers" about 8th AF bombers appeared in the US service newspaper *Stars and Stripes*. Written by journalist Andrew A. "Andy" Rooney (1919–2011), by 1943 a *Stars and Stripes* staff writer, Rooney noted that "most of the Eighth Air Force bombers operating from England have fantastic names scrawled across their elongated noses," photos accompanying the article including two of B-17s that featured "informally undressed gals" as nose art. By this time, such was the popularity of AAF bomber nose art featuring pin-ups that the craze had spread all over the world, the only difference being that not all AAF combat air forces were receiving the same publicity as the 8th AF. Rooney again: "In the early days of US bombing in the ETO [European theater of operations], the Eighth Air Force was small and correspondents from US news services and major newspapers could give adequate coverage to the few operational [air]fields." As a result, named aircraft became easily recognizable and popular with reporters, which, in turn, led to them also becoming "well known at home."[9]

Other examples of nose art photos of the day can be found in other contemporaneous magazines and newspapers, but close-ups of pin-ups appear to have been relatively rare at this stage.

The already-mentioned concern over a healthy attitude toward sex was real, particularly given the fact that pin-up art (and, therefore, most nose art paintings) was inspired by male erotic fantasies,[10] but as former 312th BG Douglas A-20 pilot Joseph W. Rutter saw it, looking back on his 5th AF service, "These artistic decorations were innocent enough and denoted no great moral breakdown by the valiant troops."[11]

Former 49th Fighter Group (FG) member and keen photographer James P. Gallagher agrees. In his memoir of wartime 5th AF service, he wrote that the nose art he saw in New Guinea, the Philippines, and Japan, much of which he subsequently photographed, demonstrated "the bravado, the humor, and, of course, the loneliness of the airmen in the Pacific War."[12]

This page of photos (together with that opposite, *top*) provides some idea of the affect that the absence of women had on men on active service in the SWPA, where women were few and far between. As Col. Charles Lindbergh noted in a September 1944 diary entry while serving there, "The men out here don't see a white woman for months at a time, and when they do see one, many simply stand and stare." The upper row of photos consists of contact prints from a roll of negatives and contrasts the apparent glamour offered by a nose art painting on a relatively new B-24 against the obvious drabness of life under canvas. In the next photo, taken at Gusap in New Guinea, five sergeants from an unidentified unit advertise the fact that they are single with a professional-looking sign. No internet in those days! Base visits by beautiful single, young white ladies were the stuff of dreams, but dancer Patty Thomas, who toured with Bob Hope's entertainment troupe, made a memorable contribution to morale wherever she went; note the wartime caption on this photo taken on Biak Island. For the rank and file, though, apart from artworks around their campsites (including airplane nose art), they had to be content with pin-up girls in magazines, even in the serviceman's magazine *Yank*, as seen in the photo at bottom right. In this case, an unidentified member of the 312th BG looks wistfully away from the August 4,

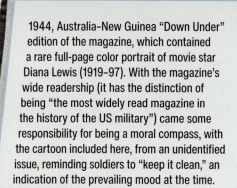

1944, Australia–New Guinea "Down Under" edition of the magazine, which contained a rare full-page color portrait of movie star Diana Lewis (1919–97). With the magazine's wide readership (it has the distinction of being "the most widely read magazine in the history of the US military") came some responsibility for being a moral compass, with the cartoon included here, from an unidentified issue, reminding soldiers to "keep it clean," an indication of the prevailing mood at the time.

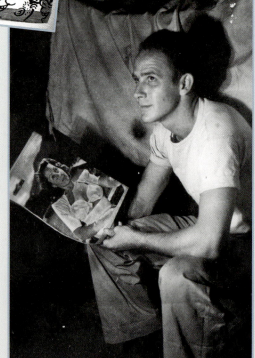

For officers, though, camp life was without doubt a little better; this was the elaborate mural painted by an unidentified artist that was to be found in the 475th FG's officers' club, "Club 38," an open-sided, T-shaped raised tent at Dobodura.

"I'm thinking of you" was a much-used expression in wartime correspondence and is repeated here in an amusing look at the rise of the popularity of pin-ups during World War II. The document is a preprinted V-Mail (Victory Mail) letter sheet that was sent home by a member of the 118th Naval Construction Battalion (NCB), then based at Mindanao. Artist Albert J. Andersen was a talented, popular wartime artist (and perhaps a nose art painter) who was a member of the Guam-based 4th NCB, so evidently the "Seabees" distributed these letter sheets widely. V-Mail, a complicated system that used standard-sized sheets with limited space that were subsequently microfilmed prior to transmission and later, prior to delivery, printed on special paper in smaller form, saved a lot of wartime shipping space when compared with usual letter mail.

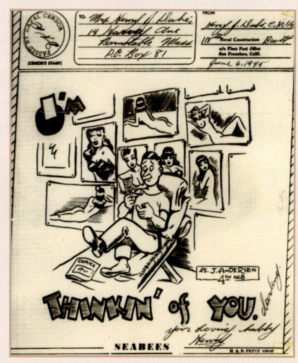

Perhaps more concerned about risqué nose art than medical officers were military chaplains. Rutter recalled that his unit's Catholic priest "deplored the practice," and commented that he

mentioned his disfavour at several Sunday services for his Catholic flock and finally wrote a strong editorial against the art form in his "Chaplain Chatter" newsletter. He argued that our heathen enemy did not decorate his planes in such a manner and said he feared some of us might go to our deaths with those obscene paintings and worse slogans [i.e., names] as our epitaph. The chaplain inadvertently used "Hot Box" as an example of the nose art to which he objected, only to learn that the plane and its crew had been lost, causing him some remorse and embarrassment. The good father's views may have been sincere, but most of us failed to see the connection between mildly risqué cartoons or slogans [names] and damnation. We called such artistic efforts "chaplain shockers."[13]

There were other detractors as well; famed veteran flier Col. Charles A. Lindbergh, who was serving in the SWPA in an advisory capacity at the time, wrote in his diary on June 20, 1944, while at Nadzab, New Guinea, that he drove to No. 3

Airdrome with Gen. Paul B. Wurtsmith, commander of V Fighter Command, subsequently driving the latter's jeep back to headquarters past "long lines of planes parked in revetments. The cheapness of the emblems and names painted on the bombers and fighters nauseates me at times—mostly naked women or "Donald Ducks"—names such as "Fertile Myrtle" under a large and badly painted figure of a reclining nude."[14]

Such comments were typical of authority figures, but they were not representative, agewise, of the younger generation of men who flew in and worked on the planes and painted the nose art. An Australian-born British war correspondent who visited the SWPA earlier and later wrote of his travels told of waiting at a Port Moresby airfield in the early hours of December 9, 1943, with a B-24 crew that he had been authorized to fly with on a bombing mission. They all sat aboard a truck for three hours, waiting for a weather report before the mission was canceled. "Two topics only in their talk," he wrote, "flying and sex."[15] Unsurprisingly, it has been stated that wartime soldiers tended "to feel a freedom from civilian society's taboos and controls," even more so, no doubt, when those soldiers were in frontline areas or out-of-the way places. In such a climate as that, it can be seen how pin-up art, unless controlled in some way, thrived.

The problem was, of course, the overabundance of men and absence of women. As one SWPA soldier put it in a poem set in Port Moresby:

> We sat by the beach at Moresby,
> Neath a moon of romance by a cocoa-palm tree,
> Neath a tropical sky by the surf and the sea.
> And beside me—to share this rare sight with a sigh,
> Entranced, too, with romance by the night and by
>   the sky—
> Sat . . . only another G.I.
> Dammit! Only another G.I.[16]

As to why so much of this artwork was based on color paintings of beautiful women (the vast majority of poses of whom still left a lot to the imagination when this craze began) rather than photos, the answer is simple: color photography in the early 1940s was still in its infancy, color photographic film was not readily available, nor was it inexpensive, and for most popular magazines of the day, black-and-white photography was the staple. Other pin-up inspirations were taken from calendars, arcade cards, and mail-order photos.[17]

The most popular magazine of the day that provided readers with beautiful color pin-ups was *Esquire*, a classy periodical that first appeared in October 1933 and quickly shifted from quarterly to a monthly publication. Made up of 116 oversized pages on glossy paper with much color content, the magazine had originally promoted high-end men's fashion. Previously mentioned George Petty (1894–1975) had been *Esquire*'s first pin-up artist, but his early offerings, a series called the "Petty Girl," were little more than elaborate colorful cartoons featuring scantily dressed young ladies. They quickly developed a following, however, and led to the better-known lifelike pin-ups by Petty, which eventually appeared on foldout pages (now often called gatefolds). In 1940, the magazine took on another talented artist, the then-unemployed Alberto Vargas (1896–1982), and this was to change everything. Initially both men shared the spotlight, but gradually the emphasis swung from Petty to Vargas and by the end of 1941 (by chance, around the same time that America entered World War II), the "Varga Girl"—it had been *Esquire*'s decision to drop the last letter of Vargas's name—had replaced the "Petty Girl" as a regular feature of the magazine. As will be seen in this comprehensive study, it was more often than not as the war progressed the Varga Girls that became the source of inspiration for airplane nose art artists. They were beautiful works that were suggestive in nature but always beautifully executed, and, in fact, every pin-up was clothed to some degree.[18]

There have been reports of original "nose art," but most pin-ups on planes were based primarily on existing published illustrations and scaled up from there. There were some instances of actual photos being used as artwork on smaller planes (for example, Dick Bong's Lockheed P-38 *Marge*; see chapter 3), but on heavy bombers affixing a photo or magazine or calendar cutting on any part of the plane's exterior would tend to be lost on such a large background.

Around the same time that Col. Lindbergh was at Nadzab, Paramount News in the US was putting together official footage taken in the Southwest Pacific to give bomber nose art in the war against Japan an airing via a newsreel for the general public back home (this was soon after the D-Day landings in France, and no doubt stories on a lighter note were seen necessary as "fillers"). As already mentioned, thanks in part, no doubt, to the widespread publicity given to the work of the *"MEMPHIS BELLE"* both in real life and on film, the premise that many famous USAAF bombers, particularly, featured nose art was well established, the commentator beginning his voiceover with "You've all seen them, the girls on our bombers," before going on to describe them as "symbols of good luck and happy landings," and later as "swell morale builders."

While Army (USAAF) crews were certainly mainly responsible for bomber nose art, it should be kept in mind that by the time the perhaps stricter United States Navy (USN) had grown to be equipped with land-based bombers, crews of which, in some cases, shared the same airfields as their AAF counterparts, they also often added pin-up nose art to their charges. In fact, while theatergoers would not have realized it, *BALES' BABY*, which had the starring role in the newsreel just mentioned, was one such airplane, a Consolidated PB4Y, the USN version of the B-24.[19]

It was not all pin-up nose art, of course, and the wide diversity of personal markings was finding itself in more mainstream media by mid-1944 if not earlier. The July 10, 1944, issue of *Life* magazine, for example, featured a photo of the 15th AF B-24 named after the magazine, as well as some of the first Boeing B-29s used in bombing raids against Japan, two of which were bedecked both with names and pin-up nose art. The same issue even included a Glenn L. Martin Co. aircraft advert with artwork based on photos of nine of the company's aircraft

INTRODUCTION

"Miss January"

After much checking, the author believes that the most copied pin-up used for airplane nose art was the January offering from the 1944 *Esquire Varga Calendar*. Here are seven examples from more than seventy worldwide examples found. Note that none of these examples are on planes of the 5th AF; in fact, two are on RAF bombers, a Lancaster and a Halifax. The other aircraft types represented here are a B-24, B-25, B-26, B-29, and C-47.

NOSE ART OF THE 5TH AIR FORCE

"Other Women"

Occasionally (very occasionally, it seems), nose art featured women for reasons other than their perceived beauty. In this group of photos, *I'll Be Seeing You* (at top) acknowledged the importance of female companionship. With artwork by Raymond A. Hafner, this Consolidated B-24, serial number 44-40923, flew with the 529th BS, 380th BG, from August 1944 until the end of the war and was subsequently returned to the US but later salvaged. It might seem that the name of this B-24 was taken from the popular wartime film of the same name, but that, however, was not released until January 4, 1945. Two of the other three named planes here, though, were definitely also film names: *"TUGBOAT ANNIE"* was a smash hit movie from 1933 that starred Marie Dressler (1868–1934) in the title role as a tough waterfront character. The artwork, artist unknown, was applied to North American B-25, 41-12998, which originally served with the 405th BS and 71st BS, 38th BG, prior to strafer conversion ca. June 1943. This photo was taken while *"ANNIE"* was in 71st Squadron's hands, squadron commander Maj. Robert H. McCutcheon in the cockpit. After strafer conversion, this B-25 was assigned to the 8th BS, 3rd BG, but was lost in action on November 2, 1943. *The Powers Girl* (Consolidated B-24, 42-72807, artist unknown, 400th BS, 90th BG) seems to have been a reflection of the general military audience opinion of the 1943 musical comedy film of the same name (seen in New Guinea in July 1943 if not earlier), a story supposedly about girls employed by the then-famous John Robert Powers modeling agency. One soldier spectator commented that the inclusion of stars Carole Landis (1919–48) and Anne Shirley (1918–93) was the film's "only redeeming feature." A similar pin-up appeared on the RHS, but the accompanying name was in capital letters. As to the unnamed C-46 with field number XA118 or 119 (unidentified serial number, artist unknown, 55th TCS, 375th TCG), this artwork appears to have been a tongue-in-cheek reference not only to pin-ups in general but also to the shape of the airplane.

unofficial markings was widely accepted in official circles. In an effort to keep those men and women involved in building warplanes interested in the results of their labors, the government even produced a small, stapled pamphlet providing stories and photos of thirteen "famous" planes (including five from the 5th AF), all but one with individual names if not nose art (but again, no pin-ups, not even shark's-teeth markings!). The publication, titled *In the Eyes of the Flyers Your Planes Are Alive*, explained:

> On the assembly line one plane is very much like another.
>
> But once a plane gets into the air with a fighting crew aboard, something happens; a change takes place.
>
> To airmen the ship becomes a "she." To them, feeling the quiver of power in her frame and the lift as she takes the air, she seems alive, real, one with themselves—almost able to think and feel as they do—certainly able, like themselves, to surpass her best in an emergency.
>
> They give her a name. And immediately she begins to collect a personality around that name. They get a thrill out of her performance. When, as so often happens, she brings them safely through a tight spot, they pat her affectionately, as one would pat a faithful horse. They exult in her feats of arms, boast of her speed and endurance, carrying power, adorn her with little painted swastikas or Rising Sun flags to show how many enemies she has destroyed.
>
> So it often happens that a plane acquires a reputation, even a measure of fame in the stories airmen swap, talking through the night in the ready rooms of far-off flying fields.[20]

That reputation was more often than not enhanced by nose art of some sort or another, whether it be a pin-up, anti-Axis sentiment, cartoon characters, or fearsome markings, but the accent of this promotional publication was named planes only, with two photos used in it rather oddly apparently having been cropped on purpose to exclude unofficial fearsome unit markings (both were from 5th AF squadrons; B-25 *Tokyo Sleeper* and P-38 *REGINA II*, photos of which can be found in chapter 6).

As far as bombers were concerned, it was generally the aircraft captain who decided on the name for his plane, but other members of the crew often had involvement in the process as well, which, as Ann Elizabeth Pfau in *Miss Yourlovin* (the book's title was taken from the name of a 15th AF B-24) notes, augmented group cohesion.

Pin-up nose art was, in fact, so common by 1944 that it was even being featured in official training films. *Land and Live in the Desert*, produced by the AAF's First Motion Picture Unit, for example, features a B-24 that was said to have made a forced landing named *"THE PIPPIN"* with nose art of a scantily clad dark-haired beauty. After the crew, all of whom survived the first incident, were found and rescued and returned to their squadron, they are seen to be flying in another B-24 named *"PIPPIN II"* with similar artwork.

A great variety of RAF bombers were "wearing" pin-up nose art by this time; popular Australian travel writer Frank Clune (1893–1971) noted that in the course of a visit to India in 1944, when he was given permission to visit what he described as a "Royal Australian Air Force Bomber Squadron" but was, in fact, No. 355 Squadron RAF, that "most of the aircraft [the squadron was Liberator equipped] had nicknames, such as 'Body Urge,' 'Calamity Jane,' or 'Jumping Juggernaut.'" Each had a row of yellow drawings of bombs painted on its fuselage, denoting the number of raids it had been in. Some had artistic decorations—a pink pig, a Mexican bullfighter, Dick Turpin,[21] more examples of the widespread influence of US popular culture at the time.

Risqué artwork on American aircraft became more and more common in the final year of the war, as the artwork on which the nose art was based also became bolder. British aviation writers O. G. Thetford and C. B. Maycock noted in 1945, somewhat reservedly, that "all variety of personal insignia and emblems" were appearing on USAAF planes by then, and while this comment was based on observations carried out in Britain, the same situation then existed worldwide. These paintings, which had, in the meantime, also became a lot bigger than they had been in 1942–43, were now being seen not just as morale boosters but as welcome diversions from monotony. As the AAF Pacific Oceans Area magazine *Brief* tried to explain Pacific island life in early 1945:

> A long time ago an anonymous military expert remarked that war was 10 percent action and 90 percent waiting. Nobody understands this profound and unhappy truth better than the Air Force men who seem—to themselves at least—to be hopelessly stranded on little islands in the big Pacific. After the back-breaking, heart-tearing work that follows the Air Forces' occupation of an island is finished, men settle down to something like garrison life.
>
> But it isn't the garrison life of the old Army, or that of the new Army back on the Mainland. It's a deadly dull routine, with a job to do every day—and nothing to do when the job is over. In most places there are movies and radios, and sports are more popular than ever before. But those things don't take care of all the spare time that every man finds hanging heavy on his hands.
>
> So a lot of them invent diversions of their own. Back home, some of them might say these off-duty occupations were hobbies; a lot of them would call it just plain work. Whatever you call it, it's one way to lick the deadly monotony of waiting out that 90 per cent of the war that isn't action.[22]

With the war getting closer to Japan and, as stated, a lot more free time available (for other than frontline personnel certainly), there is little wonder that some of the largest and most-complicated nose artworks of all were created at this time; *THE DRAGON AND HIS TAIL* (see chapter 2) won this category hands down. The coming together of USAAF and, for that matter, USN bomber squadrons, from late 1944 onward was undoubtedly another reason why nose art paintings flourished at this time.

Regardless of the shape of an airplane, once the pin-up nose art concept took hold, there seems to have been no real problems in finding the materials and an artist prepared to give any aircraft type his attention; hence, nose art appeared not only on the relatively flat-sided bomber types such as the Douglas A-20, Consolidated B-24, and North American B-25, but, as far as bombers go, the more "curvy" Boeing B-17s as well as the smaller fighter plane types used by the 5th AF, particularly Lockheed P-38s and Republic P-47s. Nose art on all these aircraft types, as well as oft-overlooked cargo planes and other types, will be found in this study.

Wherever possible, detailed photo captions attempt to summarize the history of every identified plane and the origins of the nose art, while around eighty photos in chapter 7 show readers what happened to some of them following career changes or accidents, or in aircraft dumps, particularly in New Guinea and the Philippines. Readers may also be interested to know that where nose art was changed along the way, as many as possible of the known alterations, some major, some minor, have also been documented.

World War II aircraft nose art can be seen now to have been, for the most part, a temporary aberration, a freedom of expression by servicemen for servicemen that was tolerated by the authorities for the sake of morale, but, essentially, short lived.[23] The process, however, lacked any official ruling as to the subject matter, positioning, and size, and consequently the floodgates well and truly opened up to personal interpretation. Apart from the already-mentioned concern by chaplains in forward areas as to what they saw, the only other control mechanism in play was that airplanes being returned to the United States were, generally speaking, "cleaned up"— if considered necessary—en route. This practice appears to have begun in 1943 and continued until after the war ended; *Playboy* magazine's publisher, Hugh M. Hefner (1926–2017), noted in the 1990s: "What was considered appropriate for boys in the service was dismissed as smut on the homefront."[24]

The craze—that is what it was, a craze—to decorate planes like this reached a crescendo by 1945, as the Allies tightened the grip on victory in Europe and the war in the Pacific dragged on until the dropping of two atomic bombs on Japan in August 1945 (the widely remembered B-29 that dropped the atomic bomb on Hiroshima, named *ENOLA GAY*, did not feature any artwork—not surprising, given that this plane was named after pilot Paul Tibbets's mother—but other aircraft involved in weather and photographic flights or held in reserve did).

Some 5th Air Force planes did go to Japan postwar with nose art in place (see chapter 8 for brief coverage of postwar 5th AF nose art to around 1947), but certainly the boldness of the World War II artworks had, it seems, all but died out by 1948–49. With the commencement of the Korean War in 1950, though, what can be said is that a new chapter in the history of aircraft nose art began—one, though, that owed much to what had become a major reflection of the American way of life only a few years earlier.

Unless otherwise stated, all pictorial material presented in this history is from the author's own collection both of original prints and, in some cases, original negatives, in the main purchased from internet auction websites commencing in 2004 (one of the challenges of this work has been to get the best-quality images possible, a challenge that, the author trusts, has been, for the most part, successfully met). A special mention goes to my two closest friends, Malcolm Long and Ken Merrick, who not only inspired me by their dedication to their own historical aviation interests over decades but enthusiastically helped me with this project right from its outset. Sadly, however, neither lived to see its completion. Special thanks must also go to Yvonne Kinkaid, formerly senior research historian, Air Force Historical Research Division, Joint Base Anacostia/Bolling, Washington, DC, for her ever-helpful responses to my many questions concerning USAAF World War II units and airplanes. Additionally, I would also like to thank the Air Force Historical Research Agency, the Australian War Memorial, Ian K. Baker, Mrs. Joan Barlow, John Bennett, Steve Birdsall, Gordon Birkett, Trevor Boughton, Max Brand, Rick Breithaupt, Ron Burchett, David Bussey, Stewart Campbell, Tom Cleary, Raymond and Wayne Crawford, Ron Cuskelly, Nigel Daw, Mrs. Dina DeCristofaro, Gordon De'Lisle, David Devenish, Douglas Doe (digital archivist, Rhode Island School of Design), John Dorsett, the Embassy of the Philippines, Brian Featherstone, Susie Fields, Neil Follett, Darryl Ford, Craig Fuller, Eric Geddes, Kevin Gogler, Geoff Goodall, Neville and Shane Heatlie, Peter Helson, R. E. "Dusty" Hensel, David

With many new fathers serving in the armed forces by 1944–45, it was hardly surprising that their children also became nose art subjects, either by name or name and artwork. Here is one such example in the latter category, Consolidated B-24, *the Bobby Anne of Texas* (serial number 44-40727, artist unknown, 319th BS, 90th BG). Like many other personally connected nose art forms, children were seen as potential good-luck charms, something that seems to have worked for this B-24, since the bomb log went on to show close to or in excess of one hundred mission markers.

INTRODUCTION

Toward the end of World War II, the great variety of nose art that existed on airplanes belonging to 5th AF units made new arrivals without nose art stand out as being different, and it seems likely that the crew of this 6th Emergency Rescue Squadron (ERS) Boeing B-17 of the 5th Emergency Rescue Group (ERG), serial number 43-39270, resorted to applying this perhaps makeshift name to show that the matter was under consideration, but within a few months the war ended, probably before any changes were made. More photos of 5th AF ASR B-17s appear in chapters 5 and 8.

Hopton, Bruce Hoy, Graham Hustings, Martin Jackson, C. H. "Con" Keally, the Lake Boga Flying Boat Museum, William T. Larkins, John Lascelles, John Lever, Ted Liefman, Ken B. Lloyd Jr., Ian Madden, Damien Mardon, John "Puss" McDonnel, A. H. "Strawb" McEgan, John V. Miller, Wayne Miller, Michael Musumeci, John Naumann, Mark Nelson, Doug and R. P. "Ron" Nicholas, John O'Leary, the No. 2 Operational Training Unit Air Museum, Ian Parker, Bert Peake, A. A. "Bill" Penglase, Claude Phoenix, Bob and Misako Piper, Mrs. Barbara Prime, the Queensland Aviation Museum, the RAAF Museum, the RAAF Townsville Museum, Maurice Ritchie, Pete Roberts, Edward Rogers, Haydn Roy, Jack Ryan, Judi and Kevin Ryan, Frank Ryland, Dr. Richard Saffro, Chas Schaedel, Denis Shackell, Frank F. Smith, Frank P. Smith, the South Australian Aviation Museum, Les Sullivan, Les Sutton, Bob Talbot, Ron Taylor, Deane Tietzel, Colin Tigwell, Jim Trevor, Bob Tupa, Chuck Varney, the Venning family, Dorothy and Jack Vincent, Mark Vincent, Bob Wiseman, Tom Wood, and Fred Woolcock for their assistance along this long journey. Finally, to my own pin-up girl, Claire, who once jokingly said that a book that somehow combined sex and planes "might work"; that was not the reason why I went ahead with this project, but here's hoping that she's right!

David Vincent
Highbury, South Australia
April 2024

Notes and sources

1. Britain's *Flight* magazine devoted a page to such markings on RAF aircraft in the issue of February 12, 1942. Prior to this, popular British flying magazines had devoted space to publicizing German airplane markings, although these were mostly unit insignia; see, for example, "Enemy Emblems" in *Aeronautics* (April 1940), and "German Squadron Crests" in *The Aeroplane* (April 25, 1941).

2. Joseph T. Hamrick, who served in the FEAF's Technical Air Intelligence Unit SWPA late in the war, has commented on this topic: "A noticeable difference between the Japanese and US Air Forces [during World War II] was evident in the way Americans ornamented their airplanes [with nose art]. There probably is nothing that depicts more graphically the difference in a military force of a democratic country and one led by a military dictatorship than those decorated airplanes. The individuality of the airplane and its crew is well advertised." Joseph T. Hamrick, *Technical Air Intelligence in the Pacific, World War II* (Cassville, MO: Joseph T. Hamrick, 2007), 75–6.

3. Lt. Gen. Ennis C. Whitehead, "To the Men of the Fifth Air Force," circular, August 19, 1945; author's collection. A popular song from 1942 that featured in Universal Picture's musical *When Johnny Comes Marching Home* was "This Is Worth Fighting For," and at least one USAAF bomber, a North American B-25 of the 12th AF, later featured nose art of a pin-up named WORTH FIGHTING FOR.

4. This was AAF Regulation No. 35-22, apparently stemming from the 1942 authorization, a small extract from which was included in the article "Aircraft Insignia, Spirit of Youth" by Gerard Hubbard that appeared in the June 1943 issue of *National Geographic*. Suggesting, incorrectly, that the regulation approved personal airplane nose art came much later, by way, it seems, of an article written by Jeffrey L. Ethell and published in *FlyPast* magazine in February 1996, it being here where the 1944 date appears. This error has been picked up by others since; see, for example, Jane Mersky Leder, *Thanks for the Memories: Love, Sex, and World War II* (Washington, DC: Potomac Books, 2009), 108.

5. John Frye, "Plane Names Are Strictly American," *US Air Services* (magazine), November 1943, 30.

6. Headquarters Allied Air Force, Southwest Pacific Area, to

RAAF Command, "Painting on Aircraft, Clothing and Equipment," December 31, 1943, in "RAAF Command Headquarters—Recognition Marking on Allied Aircraft," NAA A11093 Item 452/D2. In fact, there had been two B-26s operated by the 22nd BG in the SWPA with the same name as the B-17, but the first had come to grief in February 1943, and the second was flown to Amberley, Queensland, for scrapping in January 1944.

7. "Let's Open the Hangar Door," [RAAF Directorate of Public Relations] *Wings* 5, no. 13 (October 2, 1945): 22–23.

8. "Let's Open the Hangar Door," *Wings*, January 18, 1944, 30. Raising "the cultural level," as the medical officer (MO) put it, of men from different backgrounds thrown together by war was always going to be extremely difficult. For example, there were, on occasion, complaints about the moral standard of concerts performed by and for unit personnel, but as another RAAF MO later recalled of his time in New Guinea "A few bawdy songs were sung lustily and often. They did much for morale and no harm to anyone." W. Deane-Butcher, *Fighter Squadron Doctor: 75 Squadron RAAF New Guinea, 1942* (Gordon, Australia: W. Deane-Butcher, 1989), 200.

9. Andrew A. "Andy" Rooney, "Nudes, Names, and Numbers," *Stars and Stripes*, "Feature Special Supplement," August 5, 1943. This opportunity to connect servicemen with one aircraft that normally looked like another would not have otherwise been possible, since identification of individual planes and units by their official numbering as well as airfields by name during wartime all were strictly forbidden.

10. See, for example, Joan Nicholson's foreword to Mark Gabor's *The Pin-Up: A Modest History* (London: Pan Books, 1973).

11. Joseph W. Rutter, *Wreaking Havoc: A Year in an A-20* (College Station: Texas A & M University Press, 2004), 102.

12. James P. Gallagher, *With the Fifth Army Air Force: Photos from the Pacific Theater* (Baltimore: Johns Hopkins University Press, 2001), 124.

13. Rutter, *Wreaking Havoc*, 102. Douglas A-20 *Hot Box*, of the 386th Bomb Squadron (BS), 312th BG, was lost on August 11, 1944.

14. Charles A. Lindbergh, *The Wartime Journals of Charles A. Lindbergh* (New York: Harcourt, Brace, 1970), 853.

15. Alan Wood, *Flying Visits* (London: Dennis Dobson, 1946), 47.

16. Cpl. C. M. Stewart, "Soldier in the South Seas," taken from an unidentified wartime publication and added to the scrapbook of Pvt. Ford A. Reynolds.

17. It interesting to note that at least one 5th AF unit, and probably others as well, got to see color movie footage of "local" nose art. The diary of the 8th Photo Reconnaissance Squadron (PRS) notes on December 29, 1943: "Last night's movie—'Hi Diddle Diddle' [a musical comedy released earlier in the year]—was the cat's undies and all enjoyed it, mainly because it was unusual and because there was some toe curling kissing in it. After the regular movie a short reel of color photos showing the sexy pictures on the noses of bombers was shown, with the last few shots [being] of the late B-17 RFD Tojo [this B-17, which featured nose art of a bomb-carrying stork, had been used by the squadron since January 1943, but it had crashed on December 26 soon after takeoff, with the loss of two lives]. See *The Diary of 8th Photo Squadron New Guinea* (Privately published, 1945), 215.

18. See Dian Hanson, *The Little Book of Pin-Up, Vargas: The War Years, 1940–1946* (Cologne: Taschen, 2015).

19. This newsreel, which was in black and white, titled *Bomber Girls!*, excerpts from which were first seen by the author in a pin-up documentary aired on TV in the 1990s, is now held by the Sherman Grinberg Library and can be seen in its brief entirety online via Getty Images as clip no. 504412223. For more details on USN land-based bomber nose art, see William Tate and Jim Meehan, *Paint Locker Magic: A History of Naval Aviation Special Markings and Artwork* (Stroud, UK: Fonthill Media, 2015).

20. US War Department [?], *In the Eyes of the Flyers Your Planes Are Alive* (Washington, DC: US Government Printing Office, 1944), 3; the airplanes that feature in this small PR offering were an A-20, A-36s of the "Train Busters" group [27th FG], two B-17s, two B-24s, two B-25s, and a B-26, F-5, P-40, and P-47, airplane types built in the factories of the USAAF's main combat airplane manufacturers of the day—Boeing, Consolidated, Curtiss, Douglas, Lockheed, Martin, and North American. The concept that military aircraft, under certain circumstances, took on "individual human characteristics" was reported for perhaps the first time in an official restricted handbook published in September 1943 titled *War Neuroses in North Africa*, compiled by two USAAF doctors, Lt. Col. Roy R. Grinker and Capt. John P. Spiegel.

21. Frank Clune, *Song of India* (Sydney, Australia: Invincible, 1946), 274; Clune spent five days with the squadron, commencing on March 28, 1944. The absence of mention of pin-ups on any of these planes may have been intentional on his part. Late-war full-page-sized AAF recruiting adverts that appeared in popular magazines of the day similarly promoted the fact that the AAF's bombers flew, for the most part, with "pet" names, although, again, if there was accompanying artwork, that appears to have received no publicity!

22. "Ninety Percent Waiting," *Brief*, March 13, 1945, 19; photos accompanying the article show "a few of the spare time occupations of a few men on a few of the Pacific's countless islands," including a 7th AF nose art artist at work. The 7th AF worked with the 5th AF from June 1945, and this connection no doubt stimulated some friendly rivalry when it came to airplane nose art.

23. Highly respected and best known of 8th AF researchers and writers, the late Roger A. Freeman neatly described USAAF wartime nose art in an early assessment as "an infectious form of unauthorised paintwork"; Roger A. Freeman, "US Eighth and Ninth A.F. Aircraft Paintwork Part 3: Personal Insignia," *Air Pictorial*, July 1966, 254. It is interesting to note that the existence of the extremes of aircraft nose art was virtually unknown (or certainly virtually unreported) outside military circles for ten or more years after the end of World War II; a rare general-interest article on the subject published in that time was "Fun Helped Them Fight," written by Stuart E. Jones, which appeared in the January 1948 issue of *National Geographic*. The article included twelve Kodachrome color images of US wartime nose art, three of which were pin-up based.

24. From Hugh Hefner's introduction to Gretchen Edgren, *The Playmate Book: Five Decades of Centerfolds* (Santa Monica, CA: General Publishing Group, 1996).

Abbreviations

AA	antiaircraft
AAF	Army Air Forces
ACG	air cargo group
AF	Air Force
AFB	Air Force base
ARU(F)	aircraft repair unit (floating)
ASAC	Air Service Area Command
ASR	air-sea rescue
BG	bomb group
BS	bomb squadron
CCG	cargo-carrying group
CCS	cargo-carrying squadron
CMS	combat mapping squadron
CRTC	Combat Replacement & Training Center
ERG	emergency rescue group
ERS	emergency rescue squadron
FEAF	Far East Air Force
FEASC	Far East Air Service Command
FG	fighter group
FS	fighter squadron
LS	liaison squadron
MGM	Metro-Goldwyn-Mayer
NARA	National Archives & Records Administration
NMF	natural metal finish
OD	olive drab
OTU	operational training unit
PRG	photographic reconnaissance group
PRS	photographic reconnaissance squadron
RAF	Royal Air Force
RAAF	Royal Australian Air Force
RCM	radar countermeasures
SWPA	Southwest Pacific Area
TCG	troop-carrying group
TCS	troop-carrying squadron
TCW	troop carrier wing
TRG	tactical reconnaissance group
TRS	tactical reconnaissance squadron
USAAF	United States Army Air Force
USN	United States Navy

CHAPTER 1
Some of the Better-Known Artists

Today it is generally the work of only the outstanding nose art artists that is most widely remembered, thanks largely to the "exposure" given to them by other aviation enthusiasts, commencing with Steve Birdsall in the 1970s. These artists came from various backgrounds such as drafting, sign painting, and other commercial art, but it should be remembered that painting pin-ups on planes began for most as a sideline to other work such as servicing or flying them. Just how many artists there were from unit to unit with an interest in or talent for illustrating is impossible to know, but it is likely to have been a handful at most (Carl Mann, whose book *Air Heraldry*, published in 1944, was the first available to the public to discuss World War II USAAF unit insignia, considered that "in virtually every squadron in the Air Force there will be from one to a half-dozen crew members or officers who have at one time or another dabbled in professional artwork."[1]). Some artwork was signed off, but more often than not this did not happen. As a result, most artists remain unidentified, but, as a starting point, photos of and brief details on eight of the better-known men follow. Photos of non-pin-up nose art and other artworks by them are also included.

Many readers will know already that the best-known 5th AF nose art artist was Al G. Merkling, who served with the 20th Combat Mapping Squadron. He is seen here at work on *PATCHED UP PIECE*, probably his first SWPA nose artwork. Two more photos of this popular work follow in chapter 2.

Sarkis E. Bartigian (1906–55)

This artist produced the largest and, arguably, the most-complicated nose art paintings of World War II, but his star shone brightly for only a matter of months, cut short by the war's end.

The fact that he never signed off his artworks, together with his early death, added to the mystery of identifying who had painted these large and colorful works (as late as 1972, when *Air Combat 1939–1945* magazine published three photos of Bartigian's artwork in sensational color, all that could be said of the then-unidentified artist was that "he seems to have faded into anonymity since 1945"). Just who it was that identified the artist is not known to this author, but to confuse matters further, the computerized records of World War II army enlistments available through US National Archives & Records Administration (NARA) show his name as Bartigan rather than Bartigian!

Bartigian graduated from his technical high school class in 1924 after taking classes in the Rhode Island School of Design's Department of Painting and Freehand Drawing as an evening student

Sarkis and Mabel Bartigian, probably photographed ca. 1944. *Via Mrs. Dina DeCristofaro*

IT AINT SO FUNNY, Consolidated B-24, 44-49853, 64th BS, 43rd BG. This late-war B-24L (the record card for which indicates it left the United States on Christmas Day 1944) saw frontline service from March to August 1945 but is best remembered now for being the backdrop for Bartigian's tribute to so many contemporaneous American cartoon characters. Not all of them are known to this author around seventy-five years later, but Dick Tracy (with accompanying text "I THINK I'LL JOIN THE MPs") can be seen at far left by the bomber's wing root, looking down on Li'l Abner, who is striking an unidentified character, presumably a "crook." Below Li'l Abner (*in shadow here*) are Dagwood Bumstead, an unidentified cook, and J. Wellington Wimpy, apparently discussing bully beef hamburgers. The next grouping of characters is difficult to separate, but the nearest to the right of Wimpy is the bald Henry, while a little farther over it appears to be the head of Goofy. Letting out the "OOF" sound after falling flat on his face appears to be Jiggs from *Bringing Up Father*, and above the catapulted top hat is Olive Oyl, who is kissing boyfriend Popeye the Sailor. Slipping over on her roller skates may be Nancy, but that is only a suggestion based on the character's hairstyle! Above Nancy, if that is who she is, may be Lord Plushbottom of *Moon Mullins* fame, while above the nosewheel is a more obvious Donald Duck adjacent to Miss Fury, who is holding up Denny Dimwit (a character from the *Winnie Winkle* cartoon strip). Assessing the situation from his jungle hideaway at far right is Tarzan. All in all a very complicated artwork, it may easily have taken weeks to complete. This B-24 did survive the war but was salvaged afterward; location not currently known.

LAST HORIZON, Consolidated B-24, 44-40865, 64th BS, 43rd BG. It was natural, given the end of the war in Europe in May 1945, that thoughts of servicemen in the Pacific turned to wondering when the war against Japan would likewise end, which, in turn, gave rise to a widely repeated comment that they, like their European-based counterparts, hoped to be "Home alive in '45." Given the track record of an enemy that refused to surrender, however, the war could easily go on for years, and so if not "Home alive" in 1945, soldiers serving in the Pacific hoped to be "Out of the sticks in '46," "From hell to heaven in '47," or, at the very least, to see the "Golden Gate by '48," followed by the expectation that, owing to lack of work, one could be on the "Bread Line in '49." Of these five catchcries, at least three were added, in one way or another, to the noses of 5th AF B-24s (one of which follows in this chapter), but here we see Bartigian's *LAST HORIZON* (the name probably borrowed from Frank Capra's popular 1937 film *Lost Horizon*), based on the artist's expectation at the time (before the dropping of two atomic bombs) that, evidently, the war could go on for another three years. The close-up view shows the detail in this work well, while the nose view shows more of the area adjacent to the nose turret. While the war did, thankfully, end soon after, this B-24 failed to ever return to the US, being flown instead to Biak, where it was later scrapped.

in 1922–23. Later, in 1929–31, he returned to the school as a day student. NARA records confirm that he enlisted in the army in 1942, and while it is known that he had been stationed at Lowry Field, Denver, Colorado, as a camouflage instructor at one stage, he was later posted to the SWPA, where he joined the 64th BS, 43rd BG (probably after the squadron had moved to the Philippines), his background as a commercial artist quickly giving rise to nose art requests. By August–September 1945, he had completed six fantastic paintings on B-24s.

Only two works did not feature pin-up art as some part of a bigger picture; *IT AINT SO FUNNY* and *LAST HORIZON* (his least complicated work), seen here, while photos of the balance (*COCKTAIL HOUR*, *THE DRAGON AND HIS TAIL*, *MABEL'S LABELS*, and *MICHIGAN*) can be found in the following chapter.

Bartigian returned to Providence, Rhode Island, to his wife after his discharge and resumed work as a commercial artist, painting "many murals in Rhode Island business establishments," his obituary later noted. His death at the young age of forty-nine was due to a motor vehicle accident.

Charles R. Chesnut (1921–2008)

Chesnut was born in Amarillo, Texas, and spent his formative years in Missouri before enlisting in the US Army in 1942. Like the other artists profiled in this chapter, his movements within the army after his enlistment are largely unknown, but it is known that he was sent to the SWPA, where he joined the 33rd BS, 22nd BG, in 1944, his name appearing in the group's souvenir book, *Marauder*, published that year, as a contributing artist. Subsequently Chesnut became noted for his pin-up artwork, photos of all but one of which follow in chapter 2 under the following names: *DADDY'S GIRL*, *th' Duchess*, *KANSAS-CITY KITTY*, *LIBERTY BELLE II*, *Ole' Tomato*, *Our Gal III*, *PATIENT KITTEN*, *RED-HOT*

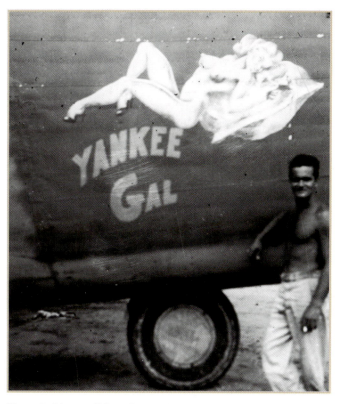

Chesnut with one of his earliest works, *YANKEE GAL*, on 33rd BS B-24 42-10073.

RIDEN-HOOD II/III, *Redhot Ridinhood*, *Round Trip Ticket*, *ROUND TRIP Ticket*, *SLEEPY-TIME GAL*, *Slightly DANGEROUS*, *SWEET RACKET*, *Tail Wind / TAIL WIND*, and two different *YANKEE GAL*s.

Daughter Toni wrote, following her father's death, that postwar "he traveled the United States before settling down in Fresno, California":

> Dad worked in commercial art while he continued his education at Fresno State College, where he earned his master's degree in art. After receiving his master's degree, he taught the fine art of lithography at Fresno State College and was considered a master lithographer.
>
> Dad was also an inventor. He created an artist worktable known as the RotoTilt Artist Table. Because of the design ingenuity that allows the artist's piece to be held in unlimited positions, Dad obtained a US patent [this was issued in 1979]. He designed, produced, marketed, and sold his RotoTilt Artist Table to artists, sculptors, studios, manufacturers, and universities that still appreciate the uniqueness and application today.[2]

Chesnut, obviously an innovator, holds a special place in World War II 5th AF history not only for his beautiful artwork, but as the most prolific of the 5th's bomber nose art artists.

Joseph A. DiLorenzo (1920–2001?)

Little is known of this artist, but he hailed from New Jersey and enlisted in the US Army in 1942, finding his way to the 389th BS in New Guinea in 1944. Here he became particularly well known for his beautiful sign painting on the sides of the squadron's A-20s, such as *Lak-a-Nuki*, seen over the page. He

A rare view of Chesnut painting the pin-up on the 22nd BG's VIP B-25 that was subsequently named *Fast Lady*; the location is Guiuan airfield, Samar, Philippines, and the date is early 1945. The identity of this B-25 is currently not known; the 22nd BG had been equipped with B-25s prior to receiving B-24s, but all had been transferred out by February 1944.

DiLorenzo is seen in the adjacent photo with one of his works, *The Queen of Spades*. In the second photo, 389th BS line chief M/Sgt. Vernon E. "Buddy" Powell stands by *Lak-a-Nuki*, Douglas A-20, serial no. 43-9404, that shows off DiLorenzo's sign painting skills. While the name may sound vaguely "native" it was, in fact, a thinly-disguised version of lack of "nookie," i.e., a lack of sexual intercourse, a common complaint of men kept separated from women! This A-20, which featured an unnamed pin-up on the RHS (see photo chapter 2), was only on the 389th BS's "books" from March to June 1944.

completed at least three pin-up works on A-20s: *The Queen of Spades* plus MISS POSSUM MY TEXAS GAL (for the 8th BS, 3rd BG) and SLEEPY TIME GAL (all three works carry his name in very neat capital letters), photos of which can be found in the following chapter. Another squadron A-20 for which DiLorenzo provided the sign painting was named *Miss Clair McQuillen*, after a top swimsuit model of the day. While it has been suggested that DiLorenzo was engaged to Miss McQuillen, it seems unusual that, if that was the case, he would have misspelled her Christian name; an internet check suggests that it was actually Claire.

The death of a Joseph A. DiLorenzo in Fort Lauderdale, Florida, in 2001 has been noted, and it may be that this was the 389th BS's former talented sign painter.

Richard A. ("Dick") Ebbeson (1912–2001)

For most of his life, Ebbeson was never far away from a pencil, pen, or brush and some kind of surface on which to apply these essential artist's tools. In 1985, he self-published a collection of his *Bonnie*, the "World Famous Cow" cartoons, and nine years later a second book appeared under his name, this time a selection of the thousands of daily sketches he had made that covered the first eighteen years of his youngest daughter's life. In this book, *Gretel: Eighteen Year Sketch*, Ebbeson had the foresight to include a very readable autobiography (he called it his "art-o-biography"), from which the following is taken:

> I was born with a pencil in my skinny fist, and it wasn't long before it was worn down to a stub. Another replaced it and it too was reduced to a stub, and so on, and so on thru the years. I have made stub after stub after stub from countless perfectly good pencils.

> Enough paper to satisfy my needs was hard to come by in my early days. I drew pictures on most everything and almost as soon as I found a new supply it was covered with scribbles and scrawls and scrambles.

> In third grade while all the other boys planned to be policemen or firemen when they grew up, I was going to be a cartoonist and draw "The Captain and the Kids." I copied from the funny papers . . . "Billy the Boy Artist" was one of my favourites, but mostly I drew my own characters.

> The kids in school thot I was pretty good and laughed at my attempts at cartooning[,] which gave me encouragement.

> As I grew older the *Saturday Evening Post* was a favourite source of material to copy, especially Norman Rockwell's work. When a new Norman Rockwell cover arrived in the mail I would sit and study it for about half an hour before even opening the magazine.

> After graduating from high school in 1930, start of the great depression, jobs were scarce. My parents allowed me to sit in an attic room and draw cartoons, sketch, and paint day after day, for a big part of several years. I consider that time spent as my college education with Norman Rockwell along with many other magazine illustrators as my teachers.

Dick Ebbeson in the eastern suburbs of Adelaide, South Australia, in 1944. *Venning family*

A Wing an' 10 Prayers, Consolidated B-24, 44-42378, 528th BS, 380th BG. The expression "coming in on a wing and a prayer," used in popular culture since 1942 if not earlier, spawned a film (*Wing and a Prayer*), a song, and various other examples (see cartoon below taken from an unidentified wartime magazine) and was undoubtedly the inspiration for this Ebbeson work "commissioned" by Lt. Otis Ray Hill ca. May 1945, featuring his crew (a B-24 crew comprised ten men; hence the "10 Prayers"). The B-24 flew around thirty missions and survived the war, although this photo shows that a replacement nose panel had been added late in the piece that affected the artwork. This was one of the 380th BG B-24s selected to be returned to the US postwar, and as part of that process a list of names of targets was stenciled on the other side of the nose (the list included Tokyo, which was never bombed by the 380th), and 5th AF and squadron insignia were added. Following some time in open-air storage at Kingman Army Air Field, Arizona, though, "378" went the way of all other former World War II planes at this location, and after it was salvaged, what was left was cut up and melted down.

". COMING IN ON A WING AND A PRAYER."
—Cpl. Hugh E. Kennedy

Bread Line in '49, Consolidated B-24, 44-42201, 528th BS, 380th BG. Even if the war did finish as late as 1948, as considered likely by some (see the caption to Bartigian's *LAST HORIZON* above), in many cases prospects for future employment in postwar US did not seem particularly good. This gave rise to the pessimistic thought that even if soldiers did return from the war, then they would be on the "Bread line in '49." Here is Ebbeson's version of how he thought that might look. As to this B-24's fate, it suffered damage while landing at Yontan, Okinawa, ca. August 1945 and was subsequently salvaged there; a last photo of this fantastic nose art can be found in chapter 7.

Around this time, I started submitting my work to the magazines and syndicates, and eventually collecting enough rejection slips to paper the walls of an average-sized room, then started on a second room.

I was interested in the outdoors, fishing, hunting, etc, and my cartoons gravitated pretty much to those subjects.

One day I received a rejection from *Hunting and Fishing* magazine published in Boston. The editor, William H. Foster, liked my drawing but not my gags. He gave me some pointers and criticisms and a better idea of what was wanted. A new batch landed me with three accepted cartoons at four bucks each. Hooray!! I was a cartoonist!

I continued to sell to *Hunting and Fishing* for several years while collecting more and more rejection slips from my other markets. In the meantime, I worked at a number of jobs: work in the woods, on farms, orchards, carpentry, pick and shovel, school bus driver, etc, etc. I needed the money to buy fishing and hunting equipment to gain experience to produce believable or unbelievable cartoons.

Time marches on—it is now 1942 with World War II and I find myself in the Army Air Force: nine days basic training, about two months Airplane Armament School, then overseas in the South[west] Pacific with the famous 380th Bomb Group with the B-24 "Flying Boxcars." Big flat-sided planes—great places to paint pictures. So besides being an armorer, I am the 528th Squadron artist and paint pictures on our planes, mostly pin-up girls with little or no clothes, but also some original cartoon paintings. The combat crews paid me for these paintings.

I meet a girl while on rest leave in Adelaide, South Australia, and before I know it I'm engaged [the engagement, to Miss Barbara Rae Venning, was announced in November 1944] so get very serious about painting to make some money to get married on. Now I'm painting during most of my time off from working on the planes plus a big chunk of my sack time.

Beside[s] the pictures on the planes, I'm painting squadron and group insignias on kangaroo hide to sell to the boys. Then one of the flying fellers came to me with his leather flight jacket—wants a big painting of a B-24 on the back. After finishing his painting, the jobs start coming in right and left, and I have paint coming out of my ears. I'm making more money in a week spare time than I get per month with my sergeant's pay.

In the meantime, our outfit has moved to the Philippines and on up to Okinawa. The war ends and soon after my painting jobs end also. I'm shipped back to the States, and after discharge from the Army, I hitch-hike to San Francisco, board a ship and head back to Australia for my girl—get married and take her home to Maine.

Now I settle down to married life—work in the woods, apple orchards, freelance a few cartoons. Then I buy a dairy farm thinking I would have a lot of time in winter to push my cartooning but had to go back to woodcutting in the winter to keep the wolf away from the door.

Gave up the farm after two years. Then attended sign school in Boston under the GI Bill. Sign painting wasn't cartooning, but it was closer to it than shovelling manure was.

During and after finishing sign school I painted signs along with raising a young family.

I have lettered about everything from greeting cards for Gibson Card Co. to 40-foot trailers, store fronts and big circus canvases—also sho-cards, posters, paper signs, display work, murals, silk screen etc. Picture work was my specialty.

In 1958, I quit sign painting—moved to Pembroke, Maine, and went full-time freelance cartooning. The first year I made only $1,200. But as I gained experience I began selling to more and more magazines and publications. Now I have sold to more than 150 different publications. I also ghosted the syndicated comic strip "Mutt and Jeff" in 1971 and 1972. At one time I painted many oil portraits for people.

In January 1960, Gretel, our youngest, was born and that started me off on another venture tho I didn't realize it for a long time—I had no idea of publishing a book. It was just one sketch today—one tomorrow—at least one each day and they piled up to quite a stack.[3]

In common with so many other artists, Ebbeson's apprenticeship had been long and difficult but evidently worth it in the long run. His local newspaper, the *Bangor Daily News*, reported after his death that "he lived life to the fullest."

Apart from the cartoon nose art mentioned above (these were *A Wing an' 10 Prayers* and *Bread Line in '49*, photos of which are seen here), Ebbeson created ten beautiful pin-up nose art paintings, nine for the 528th BS and one for the 529th. Of these, photos of the following nine can be found spread over the following chapter: *Beautiful Beast*, *Fire Power*, *Flak Fed Flapper*, *Gypsy*, *Heavenly Body*, *MISS GIVING*, *Net Results*, *Queerdeer*, and *Rangy Lil*.

Raymond A. Hafner (1919–88)

The 529th BS's best-known artist, Ray Hafner hailed from Rochester, New York. While the author has been unable to find out anything of Hafner's early life, the partial record available about him online from NARA confirms that he was married when he enlisted in the US Army in July 1942. As in Ebbeson's case, Hafner was also trained as an aircraft armorer (by chance, both men enlisted in the military around the same time), but it seems unlikely that they got to know each other until their assignments to the 380th BG. In Hafner's case that was around May 1943. Altogether he is known to have completed eleven nose art paintings, making him, perhaps, the most prolific of all the 380th BG artists (the 530th's Bill McBroom may have completed twelve, but his full catalog has not been confirmed). Of Hafner's eleven, a photo of one, *I'll Be Seeing You*, has already been seen at the end of the introduction, and nine of the remaining ten featured pin-up art. Photos of these (*ADELAIDE FEVER, LIBERTY BElIE,*

A slightly indistinct rear view of Hafner working on *"Six Bitts"* at Fenton. The bomb log (twenty-four missions) dates this photo as ca. June 1944. A photo of the RHS version of this artwork can be found in the following chapter. *RAAF Museum*

'*Luvablass*', The MISS HAP, PEACE OFFERING, "*Queen Hi*", "*QUEEN OF THE STRIP*", "*Six Bitts*", and SQUAW PEAK) can be found in the next chapter. Hafner passed away in 1988 in Rochester at the relatively young age of sixty-nine.

Artists worked not only on airplanes but signage as well. This view of parachute riggers Lucien E. Kostrewski and Leonard B. Mungia outside the entrance to the 529th's parachute department, probably at Fenton, displays a sign suspected to have been painted by Hafner. *From The History of the 380th Bomb Group (H) AAF, Affectionately Known as the Flying Circus.*

Carl W. ("Bill") Hankey (1915–99)

While the author could not find a summary page of World War II enlistment records on the NARA website for this artist, this deficiency was more than made up by chance contact with Hankey's daughter, Susie, in 2013. She told the author that "he was born in Ohio in 1915 and died just before his eighty-fourth birthday in 1999 after a long struggle with Parkinson's disease (possibly a result of being exposed to all the paint and its associated chemicals all his life). Though he worked for a couple of brief stints in Florida, he started his own sign-painting business as a very young man in the very small town of Jackson, Ohio, and continued it there upon his return from the war until his disease made his once-steady hands tremble and he was unable to paint any longer. He was truly exceptionally talented, and anyone who has lived in southern Ohio for a long time could probably spot his work at a glance."[4] Hankey's early army history is currently unknown, but it is known that he joined the 8th Photographic Reconnaissance Squadron (PRS) in 1944, serving in the squadron's tech supply area. Here he undertook all manner of signage required for the unit, including on vehicles and pet names for the Lockheed F-5s, such as *Harriett* (see photo

Two views of Bill Hankey, back and front; the back view shows him at work adding the finishing touches to a beautiful copy of a pin-up by K. O. Munson (1900–67; that is Munson's *Artist's Sketch Pad Calendar* for 1945 that Hankey is holding) onto an 8th PRS Lockheed F-5. The work was subsequently named *LOUISE!* In the second photo, probably taken after one of Hankey's first diving-hawk 6th PRG insignias was added to the vertical fin of an 8th PRS F-5, he is seen at right with Capt. Robert Spence, engineering officer, and Lt. Murray E. Walker, technical supply officer.

Two more examples of Hankey's 6th PRG / 6th Reconnaissance Group artwork, on a unit "fat cat" B-25 and as a road sign. "Fat cat" planes (the serial number of *"The HAWKEYE EXPRESS"* is not currently known), named after the first of the type, were stripped of combat equipment and used for the transportation of "essential materials," most famously fresh produce and alcohol! Photos of some other of these planes can be found later in this work.

in chapter 3), *Kay*, and *Little 't' III*. Perhaps most famously, he painted the eight-ball squadron insignia used around the squadron's campsites (this comprised an enlarged eight ball being held up by an angry-looking Indian brave armed with a war ax and wearing a camera around his neck), and, after it was decided that all units of the 6th PRG (photo reconnaissance group) would wear the diving-hawk group insignia, he added those to 8th PRS planes too. Pin-up art by Hankey seems to have been limited to two works, *Little Lorraine* (see photo in chapter 3) and *LOUISE!* (see preceding page and chapter 3), but clearly his overall work was widespread and apparently extended to requests from the 6th PRG, as suggested by the impressive group sign, bearing his name, seen below (the 6th PRG officially became 6th Reconnaissance Group in May 1945).

Al G. Merkling (1909–91)

As already noted, Merkling was the 5th AF's best-known nose art artist. He is remembered mostly for his works on the widely traveled Consolidated F-7s of his squadron, the 20th Combat Mapping Squadron (CMS), and his paintings were generally large in format and very popular, given not only the artist's attention to detail but the amusing names that were provided for them. Additionally, all fifteen of his airplane artworks are readily identifiable, since each carried his name. This connection between man and machine was not lost on aviation enthusiasts, but it was not, it seems, until 1978 when Steve Birdsall's book on the 5th AF, *Flying Buccaneers: An Illustrated History*, was published that something of Merkling's story became known to a wide readership after contact between the two men. Merkling was a native of Philadelphia who, showing an artistic flair from a young age, began his career sketching people in the street for a quick cash return. One of those he sketched led to his first regular work as an artist/illustrator, for Embree Manufacturing Co. of Elizabeth, New Jersey. That was ca. 1937. He enlisted in the army in 1942 and appears to have been an early member of the 20th Squadron, contributing drawings to an early (and modest, at only forty-six pages) squadron history apparently published at Peterson Field, Colorado Springs, in 1943. The 20th Squadron, then officially the 20th Photo Squadron (Heavy), was at that time part of

BOURBON BOXCAR, Consolidated F-7, 42-73048, 20th CMS, 6th PRG. This clear close-up view picks up a lot of detail not easily seen in other photos, but 20th CMS researcher Chuck Varney has established that this F-7 flew only two missions, after which it dropped out of unit records. It is possible, therefore, that *BOURBON BOXCAR* became just that, a freight hauler, to and from Australia, and certainly the artwork suggests that. Merkling's name is missing from his artistry in this photo but was added later and can be seen in views of the nose art after the camouflage paint was stripped away. Following the end of the war, this F-7 was scrapped on Biak Island.

SOME OF THE BETTER-KNOWN ARTISTS

Left and below left: "hangover haven" II, Consolidated F-7, 42-64053, 20th CMS, 6th PRG. Two views of the end result of a night at Smilin' Joe's bar and one pink elephant (a type of cocktail) later. Note in the photo taken after the camouflage paint had been stripped back how bolder text replaced the original lettering and how the first quotation mark was, apparently unintentionally, omitted. This F-7 was in squadron use from April 1944 to January 1945 and, according to research by Chuck Varney, flew thirty-eight missions, but when subsequently flown to Biak to await its fate still displayed only the twelve mission symbols as shown in the second photo.

Below: ST LOUIS BLUES, Consolidated F-7, 42-64172, 20th CMS, 6th PRG. The popular US jazz number of the same name made famous by the Glenn Miller Orchestra was the inspiration for this artwork (note the musical symbols used in the artwork). Airplane captain Dave Ecoff constantly hummed this tune on combat missions according to his crew, so it was an easy and recognizable choice, particularly since Ecoff did not want a pin-up, in case a photo of the finished product might have offended his mother. On that score, Ecoff would seem to have been a lot more concerned about such things than most of his 5th AF contemporaries. ST LOUIS BLUES was not in service long, participating in sixteen missions between May and September 1944. Unfortunately, the location and date of this beautiful photo are not known.

the 4th Photographic Group (PG) and was yet to see overseas service, but that changed in September 1943, when the unit, redesignated the 20th CMS a month earlier, was transferred from Peterson Field to Camp Stoneman for movement to the SWPA. Ground personnel arrived in Sydney, New South Wales, on October 10, 1943, and were subsequently sent to Port Moresby two months later, by which time the 20th CMS had been assigned to the 6th Group, now redesignated the 6th PRG. The air echelon of the 20th CMS began arriving at Nadzab in March 1944, and it was one of its first F-7s—the first to leave for New Guinea, in fact, delayed from arriving after flying through bad weather, necessitating repairs at the New Caledonia Air Depot—that provided Merkling's first "canvas." These repairs led to the suggestion that the plane be named "Patched Up Piece," and after it arrived at Nadzab, Merkling was approached regarding nose art for it. As he told another Australian author,

the WANGO WANGO BIRD, Consolidated F-7, 42-64048, 20th CMS, 6th PRG. Despite the fame this F-7 achieved by virtue of its artwork, the *BIRD* completed only four missions before it was destroyed in a landing accident. A postaccident photo of it can be found in chapter 7.

Any reluctance I may have had was quickly dispelled when the spokesman said that each crew member would chip in an Australian Pound note [one Australian pound was worth about USD3.20 at the time; thus, to paint this early F-7, with a crew of eleven, would have netted Merkling the equivalent of about USD35]. I started painting in my own time but was soon relieved from my photo-lab duties, which I found boring, and spent full time painting the planes. When people saw what I was doing, that first job got me a lot of orders.[5]

Altogether Merkling completed eleven artworks on 20th CMS F-7s, as follows: *BOURBON BOXCAR*, *"hangover haven" II*, *ST LOUIS BLUES*, and *the WANGO WANGO BIRD*, photos of which appear in this chapter, and *American Beauty*, *CHEROKEE STRIP*, *Little Joe*, *PATCHED UP PIECE*, *PHOTO QUEEN!*, *the RIP SNORTER*, and *UNDER EXPOSED*, photos of which appear in the next chapter.

It is interesting to note that all these works were completed in a short space of time—by August 1944, it seems, the latest probably being *CHEROKEE STRIP* (first mission flown August 10). Aside from his nose art paintings (which also required some touching up when camouflage paint was stripped away), Merkling was probably kept busy on other artwork for the squadron, although only one photo has come to this author's attention showing a Merkling artwork other than an example of one of his famous airplane nose art paintings.

A factor here may have been that later commanding officers did not share the unit's general enthusiasm for Merkling's nose art, or it may have been that the squadron's later F-7s were on the ground for shorter periods of time (Maj. Gen. Hugh J. Casey, in his *Engineer Intelligence* volume, stated that the 20th CMS's early F-7s, A models, "contained many mechanical defects"). Merkling did, however, also complete works for other units: *HARD TO GET* on an A-20 for the 8th BS, and *QUEEN MAE* on a 319th BS B-24 (photos of these two can be found in the following chapter), as well as two artworks on C-47s of the 55th Troop Carrier Squadron (TCS). The last named were probably the last of the fifteen he completed (a photo of one of these, *HOT PANTS*, appears in chapter 4).

Merkling returned home to Philadelphia postwar and resumed mostly commercial work, from which he retired in 1971.

Ernest J. Vandal (1917–95)

There is no doubt that Vandal was an accomplished artist. Although his primary role was airplane mechanic (he told Steve Birdsall in 1991 that he prepared 63rd BS planes for missions on eighty-one occasions in 1942–43), his design of the 63rd's unit leather patch led to nose art requests, his recollection being that he completed thirteen or fourteen (my count is fourteen or fifteen) of these in his spare time "as the planes weren't flying all the time and I wasn't working all the time."[6] Much of the work was done at Mareeba, Queensland, where the 63rd was based from August 1942 to January 1943, making Vandal the most prolific of early 5th AF nose art

SOME OF THE BETTER-KNOWN ARTISTS

This photo of Vandal was enlarged from a group image that appeared in the 43rd BG's wartime souvenir book, *Down Under*.

The JOKER'S WILD, Boeing B-17, 41-24521, 63rd BS, 43rd BG. Vandal completed both LHS (seen here) and RHS nose (named *BLACK JACK*) artworks on this B-17; note that the Joker is a representation of the devil, crushing an enemy fighter in his left hand and thumbing his nose with the other. The idea for this artwork came from the B-17's crew chief, Sgt. Tony DeAngelis, and is suspected to have been completed by early 1943. By then the B-17 had already been in service for some months, but it had to be ditched off the north coast of New Guinea following a raid on Rabaul on the night of July 10–11, 1943, after encountering both mechanical problems and bad weather (fortunately all the crew, some of whom were injured, survived). Found in 1987 at a depth of around 450 feet, the remarkably intact B-17 has become a major drawcard for recreational divers and, as such, even featured on a postage stamp issued by Papua New Guinea in 2011.

MONKEY BIZZ-NEZZ, Boeing B-17, 41-2417, 63rd BS, 43rd BG. While this B-17 had earlier seen service with the 19th BG and for reasons unknown remained on their books until February 1943 (the bomber group left Australia to return to the US ca. October 1942), after which it passed through the 403rd and 65th BSs briefly before being transferred to the 63rd BS. It served with this squadron from around March to July 1943, and it seems likely that this is when the nose art was added (an earlier photo shows that the artwork was done first prior to the addition of the name). Subsequently, the B-17 remained in New Guinea until pensioned off and converted for VIP use, becoming the personal airplane of Gen. Clements McMullen, commanding general of the Far East Air Service Command, in 1944–45. By then the plane had been stripped of camouflage paint and this artwork and was renamed *NANCY* as a tribute to Gen. McMullen's wife. *Orville K. Coulter via Steve Birdsall*

artists. In keeping with the more varied requests of those earlier days, only five featured pin-ups: B-24 *ART'S CART*, B-17 *The LAST STRAW*, B-17 *The MUSTANG* (RHS), B-17 *PANAMA HATTIE*, and B-25 *RED HEADED GAL*. Photos of each of these can be found in the following chapter. His other nine or ten nose art paintings, all on B-17s, were as follows: *BLACK JACK, CRAPS FOR THE JAPS, Fightin SWEDE, The JOKER'S WILD, Lulu Belle* (thought to have been one of his, but by 1991 Vandal could not recall with certainty whether or not it was), *MONKEY BIZZ-NESS, The MUSTANG* (left-hand side [LHS]), *Talisman*, an unnamed artwork of cartoon character Dumbo, and an unnamed artwork of cartoon character "Pluto," based on a similar work on an earlier B-17 lost on March 26, 1943.

After his service with the 63rd BS, Vandal was appointed crew chief on Gen. Whitehead's B-17, *The Old Man*, the nose art on which was, however, the work of another artist (see photo in the introduction).

Vandal was born in North Dakota, enlisted in the army in 1941 in Minnesota, and later resided in California.

Notes and sources

1. Carl Mann, *Air Heraldry* (New York: Robert M. McBride, 1944), 27.
2. From the findagrave.com entry for Charles Richard Chesnut, accessed June 8, 2012.
3. Dick Ebbeson, *Gretel: Eighteen Year Sketch* (Pembroke, ME: East Wind, 1994), courtesy of Damien Mardon.
4. Susie Fields, email to author, July 11, 2013.
5. Merkling, quoted by Michael John Claringbould in *Forty of the Fifth: The Life, Times and Demise of Forty US Fifth Air Force Aircraft*, vol. 1 (Melbourne, Australia: Aerothentic, 1999), 44.
6. Ernest Vandal, letter to Steve Birdsall, September 18, 1991, courtesy of Steve Birdsall.

CHAPTER 2
Bomber and Long-Range Photo Recon Beauties

A wonderfully clear and appealing photo of *Heavenly Body* (Consolidated B-24, 42-73116, artist Dick Ebbeson, 528th BS, 380th BG) at rest, this image was probably taken at RAAF Station Darwin, where the 380th BG (unofficially known as "the Flying Circus") was based from August 1944 until it left for the Philippines in early 1945. Although this B-24 was received in Australia well before the end of 1943, when camouflaged bombers were the norm, no photos of *Heavenly Body* in camouflage seem to be known. A closer view of the nose art can be found a little later in this chapter.

Of all World War II airplane pin-up nose art, it is the paintings on US bombers that remain best remembered. This is not surprising, given the fact that World War II bomber types, particularly the heavy bombers such as the Boeing B-17 and Consolidated B-24 (the most widely produced US airplane of World War II), are well known for their widespread usage and the wartime publicity that accompanied them. In addition, the space available for artworks, particularly on B-24s, was, as Dick Ebbeson has said, "great places to paint pictures." For the 5th AF, though, while B-24s were to become symbolic of its strength and bombing power (B-24s eventually equipping four 5th AF bomb groups), the bomber's operational service in the SWPA began in only a small way in November 1942.

It has already been mentioned that the B-17 was the first heavy bomber to serve in the SWPA (the first heavy bomber groups in Australia were the 19th and 43rd BGs, but the early hectic days of the former Philippine-based 19th BG provided little opportunity in undertaking anything unessential such as adding unofficial markings). Another early type of bomber made available to the 5th AF to fight the Japanese was the Douglas A-24, but this dive-bomber had but a short and unsuccessful combat career in New Guinea, and whether there had been any time for elaborate nose art to be added is unknown. In the medium-bomber class, the North American B-25 and Martin B-26 were two other early additions to the 5th AF's armory, while the smaller Douglas A-20 was, like the B-25, a successful low-level attacker that was to build up a great track record in the Pacific. So successful were B-25s and A-20s in action that both types continued in 5th AF service in numerous bomb squadrons until the end of the war. Both the B-17 and B-26 were phased out in 1943, the former replaced by the B-24, the latter by more B-25s. Toward the end of the war, Gen. Kenney was keen for the 5th AF to receive the first of the US very heavy bombers (VHBs), the Boeing B-29, and while this did not happen, late in the piece a few VHB Consolidated B-32s were received. The vast majority of these types of bombers, particularly B-24s, featured nose art of varying shapes and sizes, mostly named, but not all pin-up related (as an indication of the extent of nose art in one B-24 bomb group, the 380th, see "History Project: WE WENT TO WAR, 380th Aircraft—Listing by Aircraft" on website 380th.org, which lists 229 B-24s known to have been used by the group, of which 184 are identified as having been named, most of which featured artwork, an 80 percent uptake rate).

NOSE ART OF THE 5TH AIR FORCE

Over this chapter, more than five hundred images document 5th AF pin-up art on these and other planes of the 5th AF's bomb groups; the 3rd, 22nd, 38th, 43rd, 90th, 312th, 345th, 380th, and 417th. Pin-up nose art featured on Consolidated F-7s (the reconnaissance version of the B-24) of the 20th Combat Mapping Squadron (CMS; renamed 20th Reconnaissance Squadron [Long Range, Photographic-RCM] in the second quarter of 1945) and 4th Photo Charting Squadron (PCS; renamed Reconnaissance Squadron [Long Range, Photographic]), which was attached to the 5th AF from May 1945 onward, are also included. For bombers that featured fearsome nose art, for the most part squadron markings, see chapter 6.

Medium and heavy bombers were ferried overseas by combat crews, and it has been noted earlier that artworks were added mostly in the US before the long ferry flights. This was particularly the case in the early days because the crews responsible for the deliveries thought that they would stay with their charges after being assigned to a squadron, something that only rarely occurred as far as B-24 deliveries were concerned (an exception in the 5th AF was specially modified B-24s—equipped with radar and a low-altitude bombsight—destined for the 63rd BS since their crews were specially trained for nighttime shipping attacks using these bombers). Thus, if other crews assigned to these planes later wanted a piece of artwork changed, it would be up to them to arrange for the new work to be added, and for the most part this would have to be done in the field. We have already seen in chapter 1 that there were enough artists and, apparently, enough resources available to make this happen, but we have also seen that this was generally a spare-time activity for artists (Merkling was one artist who has noted that he was taken off his normal duties to concentrate on nose art, but this may not have lasted for long). Even so, the practice of repainting or making alterations to nose art was still able to flourish. Certainly, there were paint shops in Australian depots used by the 5th AF in 1942–44 that could assist; the editors of the

ACE O' SPADES, Consolidated B-24, 42-40945, artist unknown, 404th BS, 43rd BG. Nose art was sometimes changed along the way, and here we have an example of that where the artwork was altered from a skull, to a rather flamboyant dancer, but the original name and background were retained. Fortunately, both photos were taken from an almost identical spot, and while the second is a little blurred, note that a considerable number of operations had already been flown (in the course of which five enemy planes were claimed as shot down) before the decision was made to change the artwork. Not all airplanes had art on both sides of the nose, but this was an example of one that did. However, the pin-up that replaced the skull on the RHS was different from that on the LHS. This B-24 was condemned and salvaged ca. November 1944.

1944 yearbook of the Brisbane-based 81st Air Depot Group commented that the group's Paint Department comprised ten enlisted men whose "work consisted of serious and frivolous paintings on planes."

While personal cameras were not uncommon in World War II, not everyone had one, but pin-up nose art was so alluring to soldiers that there was plenty of demand for copies of nose art photos, particularly on bombers. Given the number of duplicated high-quality prints of some nose art that has been found, it is clear that some units in the field made photos taken by their photographers openly available to their personnel, but where this did not occur, entrepreneurial "types" could, more often than not, be relied on to provide poorer-quality prints at a cost (some wartime photos of 380th BG nose art were printed so often that they have been found in photo collections both in the US and Australia).

As mentioned in the introduction, the end of the war saw an abrupt end to many of the 5th AF's "war-winning" planes, A-20s being among the first of the bombers to be taken out of service, followed by the vast majority of B-24s. Some B-25s went on to serve briefly in Japan, but their days were also numbered, as with all the 5th AF's airplanes, due to such factors as age, hours flown, serviceability, and even availability of servicing personnel. All the images that follow in this chapter are of, or relate to, 5th AF bomber (and F-7) nose art to August 1945, while more photos can be found later in this volume of some of the same airplanes, plus others, in later markings or at the end of their service life. For a few examples of 5th AF B-25 and F-7 pin-up nose art that existed in Japan after August 1945, see chapter 8.

A Touch of "Texas", Douglas A-20, 43-21424, artist unknown, 672nd BS, 417th BG. Although overshadowed to a large degree by the medium and heavy bombers used in the SWPA, the A-20 filled an important role as a tough, fast, and very effective low-level light bomber/attack airplane. It equipped three 5th AF bomb groups, with the 417th BG being the last to enter the fray, in March 1944. As this name suggests, the assigned pilot, Lt. McCoy E. Palmer, was from Texas. For other 417th BG A-20 nose art in this chapter, see *Betty's Best*, *"Contented Lady"*, *In the Mood*, *"Little Butch"*, *MY JOY*, *THE ROARING TWENTIES*, and *SNIPER*. Some currently unidentified/unconfirmed A-20 photos may also be of 417th group planes.

ADELAIDE FEVER, Consolidated B-24, 42-41247, artist Raymond A. Hafner, 529th BS, 380th BG. For more than twelve months, when members of the 380th BG went on leave in Australia, Adelaide, the capital city of the southern state of South Australia, more than 1,500 miles south of their Northern Territory bases (at Fenton and later Darwin), was the destination. Soft drinks, alcohol, dairy, and other fresh produce were also sourced from Adelaide and flown north in unit airplanes, and it was this particular B-24's claim to fame that it lost part of such a load over an Adelaide suburb (fortunately without any personal injury to residents) while doing a low pass south of the city prior to heading northward on August 22, 1944. This plane had already been named ADELAIDE FEVER before this event, one suggestion being that the name was a euphemism for a locally sourced sexually transmitted disease, but more likely is that it was an indication of how eager 380th crews were to visit there. This B-24 flew her first mission in November 1943, her last in June 1944, after which she was modified to carry supplies (an investigation into the August incident found that the failure of a "non-standard rack" had been the cause of the load loss, plus bomb bay door damage), which enabled this B-24 to be returned to the squadron for so-called "fat cat" duties (see photo of The *HAWKEYE EXPRESS* in the previous chapter) until later in the year. Fifty-two bomb symbols show in the photo, representing missions flown (the addition of the star above the bomb signified mission accomplished), dating it as taken after June 29, 1944.

After Hours, Consolidated B-24, 44-41030, artist unknown, 400th BS, 90th BG. Based on a Roy Best calendar art illustration titled *Sleepy Time Gal*, but with some different features from the waist up and an alarm clock replacing the original candle and candlestick holder, here are two views of what was, in the author's opinion, one of the 90th BG's most beautiful nose art paintings. What a pity the artist's identity is not known. As shown in the second photo, this B-24 went on to complete more than a hundred missions before the war ended (the possible gold mission symbol in the third row marks this B-24's 101st mission). *After Hours* was subsequently salvaged, location unknown.

AIR POCKET, Consolidated B-24, 44-41479, artist unknown, 320th BS, 90th BG. Late-war nose art was much bolder (in size if nothing else) than earlier efforts, and here is another example of that, this one featuring a very elaborate crumpled parachute. At lower right can be seen part of the exposed teeth markings that identified the fact that, as far as 5th AF B-24s are concerned, this example came from the "Moby Dick Squadron," the 320th. While the story behind this in-theater marking is covered in chapter 6, for other late-war "Moby Dick Squadron" B-24s that combined teeth markings with a pin-up, see *Cherrie*, *DISPLAY OF ARMS*, *"GRRR"*, *LIVE WIRE*, and *QUEEN OF HEARTS* in this chapter. This B-24 was returned to the USA postwar, but whether with or without the nose art in place is not currently known.

ALL ALONE—AND LONELY, North American B-25, unidentified serial number, artist unknown, unit(s) unidentified. Although it has been said that this B-25 was operated by the 92nd Airdrome Squadron, such special-maintenance units had no aircraft of their own. In a short story published first in 2008, former 92nd Airdrome Squadron member Alfred Kern does describe a detachment that he was a member of that was equipped with three B-25s that operated from Angaur Island in support of 7th AF B-24 missions; perhaps this was one of those aircraft. A photo of another B-25, named *TUG-O-WAR*, from the same source and featuring the same two men, would seem likely to have been from the same unit.

American Beauty, Consolidated F-7, 42-73045, artist Al G. Merkling, 20th CMS, 6th PRG. Another example of Merkling's majestic artworks, this one was his version of a famous illustration said to be reflecting "what's on a man's mind." For other such illusionary illustrations that appeared on 5th AF planes, see B-24 *Big Chief Cockeye*, which follows, and an unnamed P-39 in appendix 1. This F-7 was in squadron use from May to September 1944, completing, according to squadron records, only nineteen missions during this time. It ended the war at Nadzab, where it continued to draw a lot of attention until her remains were eventually scrapped (see photo in chapter 7). For Merkling's other F-7 pin-ups, see *CHEROKEE STRIP*, *Little Joe*, *PATCHED UP PIECE*, *PHOTO QUEEN!*, the *RIP SNORTER*, and *UNDER EXPOSED!* in this chapter.

AMOROUS AMAZON, Douglas A-20, unidentified serial number, artist unknown, 90th BS, 3rd BG. As suggested by the nose number, this A-20 is suspected to have been one of the early long-barrel, 20 mm, cannon-armed A-20Gs (also equipped with two forward-firing machine guns; later A-20Gs were equipped with six machine guns) sent to the SWPA for the 5th AF. Later photos of the RHS of the *AMAZON* (it is thought that the pin-up and name were only on the RHS, but in this view the name is a little hard to read) show her with the pin-up retained and 90th BS's trademark shark's teeth added. The squadron's transition from B-25s to A-20s had occurred by early December 1943, but without an airplane serial number, more-specific detail is not currently available.

APACHE PRINCESS, North American B-25, 43-28152, artist George M. Blackwell, 501st BS, 345th BG. This was one of more than a dozen new B-25J-11 airplanes assigned to the 501st BS in October 1944, five of which received nose art soon after, all by Blackwell, with names painted by Cpl. Joseph Merenda. The others were *Cactus Kitten*, *LAZY DAISY MAE*, *Reina del PACIFICO*, and *WHITE WING*, photos of all of which can also be found in this chapter. *APACHE PRINCESS* was lost on a mission to Formosa on May 27, 1945, but four of the crew survived the war as prisoners of war.

Baby Blitz, Douglas A-20, 43-9115, artist unknown, 386th BS, 312th BG. This A-20, named by and assigned to Lt. Joseph B. Bilitzke, was in service with the 386th from February to August 1944. Bilitzke, promoted to major, later commanded the 388th BS and then flew another A-20 that he named *Baby Blitz II*. After he left the squadron and returned to the US, *Baby Blitz II* was renamed *RIDIN' HIGH* (q.v.)

BOMBER AND LONG-RANGE PHOTO RECON BEAUTIES

ART'S CART, Consolidated B-24, 42-40896, artist Ernie Vandal, 63rd BS, 43rd BG. One of the original twelve radar-equipped night attack B-24s led by Lt. Col. Edward W. Scott that arrived at Port Moresby ca. October 1943 to replace the 63rd BS's remaining B-17s, this plane was assigned to Lt. Arthur H. Millard, and the name, in cursive script, was added to each side of the nose before the crew left Hamilton Field for Hawaii. Vandal added the artwork at Dobodura in January 1944, on the basis of a popular pin-up picture by another great pin-up artist of the day, Gil Elvgren (1914–80), named "Sport Model", substituting a cart for what originally had been a car, on the RHS of the nose. Some weeks later, Millard added a shellac sealer over Vandal's work that, he noted, "brought out the colors even better." The original cursive-script version of the name remained on the LHS, but Vandal overpainted the RHS version so that the pin-up could be added. He then repainted the name in capital letters as shown in the two close-up photos here. *ART'S CART*, which flew the first B-24 mission for the 63rd, stayed with the squadron until August 1944, after which it was transferred out as war weary. See *LIBERTY BELLE*, which follows, for another photo of one of these 63rd BS B-24s with a deeper chin position than normal, as shown in the above photo. The required modification work was carried out during the second half of 1943 at a stateside air depot.

ATOM SMASHER / "ATOM SMASHER", Consolidated B-24, 42-64045, artist unknown, 63rd BS, 43rd BG and 530th BS, 380th BG, and also reported to have been used by 90th BG. Scientists knew about "smashing the atom" long before World War II, but given this particular artwork, the name, in this case, possibly referred to something else. There had been some radar countermeasures (RCM) B-24s in Australia in 1943, but they had been converted in theater. *ATOM SMASHER*, however, is understood to have been one of the first fully fitted-out RCM B-24s to be sent to the SWPA (see also *The Duchess of Paducah*), and it was because of this that it was moved around (with separately provided specially trained RCM operators) as required. Just where and when the nose art (apparently by two different artists—perhaps from different units) was added is not known, but note the exaggerated leg length of the artwork on the RHS; pin-up art did not usually promote the normal or natural figures of women, with one *Life* magazine reader commenting on pin-up pictures that "I trust the boys on return home will not be disappointed by the real thing." This B-24 had been stricken from USAAF records by March 1945.

ATOMIC BLONDE, Consolidated B-24, 44-51414, artist J. Oetienna (?), 531st BS, 380th BG. According to the very useful 380th BG website, 380th.org, this B-24 flew its first mission on June 25, 1945, but her next was not until August 28, well after when the atomic bombs were dropped. The close-up of the artist's name reveals that the artwork is dated, but it is too indistinct to confirm what that date is other than August 1945. Certainly, though, this was a very late example of 5th AF wartime nose art (the surrender of Japanese forces occurred on September 2). The artist responsible for this beautiful painting (based on the September pin-up in K. O. Munson's *Artist's Sketch Pad Calendar* for 1945) has been identified as a Mindoro local. He also painted the nose art on *BACHELOR'S BROTHEL*, *FREE FOR ALL!!!*, and *POM POM EXPRESS* (photos of which all follow) for the 531st. This particular *ATOMIC BLONDE* (there was at least one other 5th AF bomber, a B-25, so named; see photo in chapter 8) was subsequently flown back to the US later in the year, where it was later salvaged.

"BABY", Consolidated B-24, 42-72798, artist unknown, 400th BS, 90th BG. Photos of this artwork are not uncommon, but these two views display some interesting differences that are worth pointing out. In the first photo, it can be seen that the artist has left an unpainted section in about the middle of his pin-up. Subsequently, a diaper held together by a safety pin was added to this area, but part of the unpainted section remained (see second photo), giving a hint of "nether regions" not normally included in 5th AF nose art of this ca. 1943 period. Other points of interest in these photos are that in the first photo there is a newly added nose turret, the fitting of which caused the second quotation mark to be overpainted, but it was subsequently replaced. Note too in the second photo the ball-mounted machine gun added to what had been originally the navigator's window and, not seen before, the inclusion of odd mission symbols (*at left*): a bottle (eighth mission) and parachute drop (tenth mission). These symbols appear to have been short lived. This B-24 is believed to have survived 400th BS service to subsequently be sent to the 5th Bomber Command Replacement Pool at Nadzab.

BACHELOR MADE, North American B-25, 41-30597, artist unknown, 2nd BS, 22nd BG, later 500th BS, 345th BG. Research for the 22nd BG history *Revenge of the Red Raiders* concluded that this B-25 flew fifty-seven combat missions with that bomb group. That being the case, then this photo must have been taken while it served with the 345th BG, since more than sixty mission symbols can be seen here. Like the nose art (which appeared on both sides of the nose), the nose number, "6," was a leftover from its 2nd BS service. After roughly a year in frontline service with these two units, *BACHELOR MADE* was converted for second-line duties and assigned to the 38th BG in September 1944, subsequently being renamed *HARDSHIPS 2nd* (see photo in chapter 7).

BACHELOR'S BROTHEL, Consolidated B-24, 44-50927, artist J. Oetienna (?), 531st BS, 380th BG. Assigned to the 531st in June 1945, this B-24 remained in squadron hands for about four months and was the first airplane from the 380th to land in Japan, an action that was unplanned but necessary due to the receipt of a typhoon warning while airborne for the flypast following the surrender of the Japanese forces aboard USS *Missouri* in Tokyo Bay. Note three of the last four digits of the serial numbers visible in this photo, which materially assisted in correctly identifying the airplane, and the fact that it has been disarmed, indicating that the photo was taken after hostilities had ended. The same artist, a Mindoro local, was also responsible for three other nose art paintings for the 531st—*ATOMIC BLONDE*, *FREE FOR ALL!!!*, and *POM POM EXPRESS*, photos of all of which are included in this chapter.

"Bachelor's Den", Consolidated B-24, unidentified serial number, artist unknown, unit(s) unidentified. Given the increased interest in heavy-bomber nose art, in particular, over the last two decades (most notably demonstrated by the numerous websites that have sprung up in that time that link heavy-bomber names and nose art with their serial numbers and units with which these planes served), it would not come as a surprise to most readers that the author would be hard-pressed to find a new example of 5th AF heavy-bomber nose art to include in this work, but here is one. This photo (since uploaded to the internet) was taken at the Townsville Air Depot ca. February 1944; below the fire extinguisher panel appears a chalked-on note "Engines Pickled 2/6/44." This was some sort of treatment that was carried out following arrival of the plane from the US; photos taken of other newly received B-24s at Garbutt feature the same two-word notation.

BAIL-OUT Belle, Consolidated B-24, 42-72951, artist unknown, 529th BS, 380th BG. The men in this photo are from Flt. Lt. Ron Dixon's RAAF crew: they flew *Belle*'s fifty-seventh mission, which was from Darwin, on November 30, 1944. This artwork had originally been applied to both sides of the airplane when camouflaged and was retained after the paint was stripped off by mid-1944 (the standard 380th practice by then, though, seems to have been that unofficial artworks appeared on the RHS of the nose, while squadron insignia usually appeared on the LHS, so this was an exception to that rule). A photo of the LHS nose of this airplane (taken while in the process of being scrapped) showing the pin-up together with the squadron insignia that was added later can be found in chapter 7. *Ian Parker*

BARBARA JEAN, Consolidated B-24, 44-40980, artist unknown, 65th BS, 43rd BG. Another of the large late-war 43rd BG paintings (inspired, perhaps, by the work of the 64th BS's Bartigian) was this work, a copy of the Varga Girl that appeared in the February 1941 *Esquire* magazine. This B-24 had been assigned to the 65th BS ca. September 1944 and was lost on June 3, 1945, when it crashed into Mount Arayat following an early morning takeoff on a Formosa raid from Clark Field. None of the eleven-man crew survived.

Bashful, North American B-25, 41-30772, artist unknown, 33rd and 408th BSs, 22nd BG. *Bashful* served with the 33rd BS from September 1943 to January 1944, and it was probably during this time that the nose art was added. The pin-up appeared first, while the name came later. When this photo was taken, the airplane had flown at least twenty-five missions (note the number 25 adjacent to what can be seen of the bomb log). After the 33rd BS, *Bashful* was passed to the 408th BS for a matter of a few weeks and from there transferred to the 823rd BS, 38th BG, where the pin-up was probably replaced with the "Terrible Tigers" squadron insignia (for examples of which, see chapter 6). Later this B-25 was converted for "fat cat" duties, becoming the second B-25 to carry that name (see photo in chapter 7).

Battle Weary, Consolidated B-24, 42-41243, artist Sgt. Wheatley, 528th BS, 380th BG. Glenn R. Horton Jr. in his comprehensive study of the 380th BG, *The Best in the Southwest*, provides some great background information on this B-24, noteworthy being that it was originally named *Fascinating Bitch* and was renamed *Battle Weary* after a run-in with a Japanese fighter over Wewak's Boram airfield on the night of March 7–8, 1944, when two crew members were wounded in action, one of whom subsequently died. Given that the artwork seen here was based on the Vargas gatefold pin-up from the April 1944 edition of *Esquire* magazine, then the pin-up was added sometime after April. Horton also established that this B-24 flew sixty-two missions (website 380th.org lists sixty-one) prior to her being considered war weary, and identified artist Wheatley, who was also responsible for at least one other 380th BG pin-up, *"Lady Luck"* (q.v.), as a member of "one of the service squadrons supporting the [380th] units at Fenton." This B-24 was assigned to the 380th in November 1943, and the last known mission flown by it occurred on New Year's Day 1945. *Battle Weary* did not make the move to the Philippines but, instead, remained in Darwin until salvaged postwar. *Ken Crane via Bob Wiseman / Nigel Daw*

BAYBEE, Consolidated B-24, 42-109978, artist Harold H. Heighton, 2nd BS, 22nd BG. Heighton was this B-24's original second pilot, and after he completed the artwork he added the name only in chalk; it was never added permanently. As shown in the second photo, the background was eventually "framed" in a much-darker color, and Heighton's "hhh" sign-off was painted over. A later photo of the nose of this B-24 published in Michael Musumeci's *Iron Range Airbase* history shows it with what was probably another chalked-on name, MERRY MAX. Another photo of the nose art, following the 1945 demise of this B-24 (revealing no trace of any name), can be found in chapter 7.

THE BEAST, North American B-25 41-30606, artist unknown, 408th BS, 22nd BG. Despite the sixty-seven-mission bomb log (added over the period September 1943–January 1944), few photos of this impressive artwork, paradoxically of a beauty despite the name, have survived (the subtext below this B-25's name reads *"RED-HEADED & LONELY"*). Four 408th Squadron B-25s, including *Bashful* (*see previous page*) and *THE BEAST*, were, early in 1944, transferred to the 822nd BS, 38th BG, but it seems likely that the artwork was replaced at that stage by the squadron's "Black Panthers" unit markings. The B-25 did, subsequently, have a brief third life as a "fat cat" plane for the 345th BG. Stripped of camouflage and bearing the name *CHOW HOUND JUNIOR* and another impressive artwork, this time showing cartoon character "Pluto" walking on a sidewalk carrying a loaded basket of food between his teeth while passing a fire hydrant, this was another short-lived painting, since the war ended within three months of "606" being received. It is likely that the former bomber was scrapped soon after.

THE BEAUTIFUL BEAST / *Beautiful Beast*, Consolidated B-24, 42-73167, second artwork artist Dick Ebbeson, 528th BS, 380th BG. Seen here both in early and later guises, this B-24 arrived at Townsville in October 1943 and was assigned to the 380th, subsequently flying her first mission in December. The earlier artwork was based on a George Petty pin-up, while, following the stripping back of camouflage and markings, the new artwork (now on the RHS only), was, it seems, a mirror image of the March pin-up from the 1944 *Esquire Varga Calendar*. In the second photo here, Arch Dunne's RAAF crew clown around with some machine guns beside the *Beast* ca. August 1944. It was this crew that made the last operational flight in this airplane; that was on August 13, 1944. Later in the month it was involved in a taxiing accident and was subsequently stripped of parts, but the bare fuselage remained in situ for years until removed for scrapping. A later wartime photo of the nose of *Beautiful Beast* can be found in chapter 7. *Below, courtesy of R. E. "Dusty" Hensel*

"Belle Wringer", Consolidated B-24, 42-109859, artist unknown, 400th BS, 90th BG. The name and artwork for this B-24 were taken from a 1940 Gil Elvgren pin-up named *Belle Ringer*, but what is interesting (hence the inclusion of the second photo) is that sometime after the first photo was taken, subtle changes were made to the artwork. Most notably, the dark edging evident in the twenty-five-missions photo has been painted out, but also the clothing (including the bow) worn by the pin-up has been given a new coat of paint and a higher neckline! With a bomb log of sixty-two missions, *"Belle Wringer"* ended her days on Biak, where the 90th BG was based from August 1944 to January 1945.

Bette, North American B-25, 41-30017, artist unknown, 499th BS, 345th BG. This B-25 featured similar pin-ups on both sides of its nose, which were based on the August 1942 *Esquire Varga Calendar* artwork, but that on the LHS, named *"FLYING GINNY"* (q.v), was devoid of clothing. The differences in appearances and names were because the LHS artwork was carried out under the directions of the plane's original pilot, Lt. Jack L. Broadhurst, while the RHS artwork, seen here, was completed under the instructions of the copilot, Lt. Chandler S. Whipple (Whipple's girlfriend's name was Bette). Broadhurst left the squadron in September 1943, and Whipple took over as pilot (it seems likely that the squadron's new "Bats Outa Hell" nose insignia replaced any personal nose art by then), and this B-25 along with her five-man crew was lost on a mission not far from the northern coast of Papua New Guinea on October 5, 1943. These were still early days for the 499th, and this B-25 became just the second lost to the squadron in New Guinea.

BETTY and *Betty's Best*, Douglas A-20s, unidentified serial numbers, artists unknown, 673rd BS, 417th BG. BETTY was assigned to Lt. (later captain) Raymond N. Pollitt and featured a pin-up based on the April offering from the 1943 *Esquire Varga Calendar*. This A-20 had completed nineteen missions at the time the photo was taken, but was later transferred to the 3rd BG, where she saw further service after being renamed *madame Guillotine* and the bathing-suit color was changed. As for *Betty's Best*, the artwork was based on the November page from the *Artist's Sketch Pad Calendar* for 1944 of another great pin-up artist, Earl MacPherson (1910–93), but apart from the fact that she was assigned to Capt. Norman G. Patterson, no other particulars are currently known.

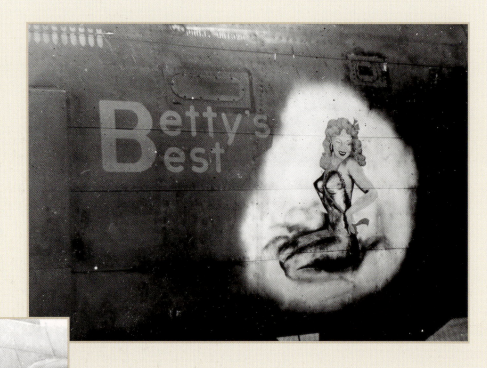

"Black Widow", Consolidated B-24, 42-40967, artist Bill McBroom, 528th BS, 380th BG. Younger readers will know this name as being that of a comic character that first appeared in a 1964 issue of *Tales of Suspense*, but clearly the connection between the black widow spider and women of bad character goes back to the 1940s if not earlier (the Urban Dictionary defines the nickname as referring to "a female who feeds off of the mental, physical and material means of a male and then leaves him for dead"). The B-24 was received by the 380th BG with an earlier black widow nose art (and name in block letters) in place, probably having been added prior to the bomber leaving the States. According to 380th researcher Glenn R. Horton Jr., Maurice Beller's crew, assigned to this plane in September 1943, considered the first artwork of poor quality and called on 530th Squadron artist McBroom to paint something better. This was done but was short lived, since the B-24 was shot down over Manokwari in Dutch New Guinea on November 21, 1943. Lost with *"Black Widow"* were Beller's crew plus a RAAF RCM operator. *Ed Crabtree from Radar Gunner* [see bibliography].

Big Chief Cockeye / BIG CHIEF COCKEYE, Consolidated B-24, 42-40351, artist unknown, 403rd BS, 43rd BG, later 529th BS, 380th BG. Research by authoritative website pacificwrecks.com indicated that this B-24 was assigned first to the 90th BG in April 1943 and next to the 43rd BG in July 1943, finally being transferred to the 380th BG in May 1944. The artwork, based on the "what's on a man's mind" illusionary illustration, however, seems to have been added only while the airplane was with the 43rd BG. It was retained after it was transferred to the 380th, though, but the style and positioning of the name were changed. The photos used here show the artwork and the two styles of lettering, the first, at lower right, in original cursive style with a bomb log showing thirty-three missions, the second with the repositioned name in block lettering. It seems from another photo, not used here, that a cumulative bomb log was subsequently added and the symbol for destroyed enemy aircraft was reapplied. Postwar it was established that this B-24, which had failed to return from a routine weather reconnaissance flight on July 5, 1944 (its eighth mission with the 529th BS), had carried out an attack on an enemy vessel and subsequently crashed into mountainous Seram (then spelled Ceram) Island. Four of the eleven men aboard that day survived the loss of the B-24, but all died as prisoners of war: three on nearby Ambon Island, the fourth after transfer to Japan.

BLACK MAGIC, North American B-25, unidentified serial number, artist unknown, unidentified BS, 3rd BG (unconfirmed). This author has seen only a handful of photos of this nose art, at least one of which was probably taken in Townsville, Queensland, late in 1943. Apart from the fact that the artwork is based on the *Arabian Nights* tale of the genie in the bottle, further details are currently not known. The name, however, was popular in other combat theaters and on other bomber types, notably B-24s.

Blonde Bomber, Boeing B-17, 41-24357, artist unknown, 65th BS, 43rd BG. *Blonde Bomber* had served originally in the 63rd BS as *Tojo's Nite Mare*, without any accompanying artwork. It was damaged on January 19, 1943, in a ground collision, though, and it was only after it was repaired and assigned to the 65th BS (ca. April 1943) that this name and artwork were added. A number of B-17s of this squadron featured pin-ups, and while details are lacking, it seems likely that there were only one or two artists responsible. Certainly, the similarity of the presentation of the names *Blonde Bomber* and *Caroline* (q.v.) would suggest that the same artist was involved in some way. By November 1943, *Blonde Bomber* had been transferred to the 41st TCS, 317th TCG, but this particular identity was short lived since the pin-up was painted out and the name changed to *the SUPER CHIEF*.

"The Blonde Bomber", Consolidated B-24, 42-40942, artist unknown, 320th BS, 90th BG. Photographing pin-ups on planes often led to images such as this, where the artwork and bomb log were captured but not the full name. Authoritative website pacificwrecks.com states that this plane was assigned to the 320th BS, but also mentions that it was possibly assigned to the 321st too. For what is probably the last view of this nose art, see chapter 7.

BLONDE BOMBER, North American B-25, 41-30768, artist unknown, 408th BS, 22nd BG. Proof that artists in the US sometimes duplicated pin-ups on bombers before their dispatch overseas is afforded by the two views seen here, taken from virtually identical vantage points on two different aircraft. That on the left is of BLONDE BOMBER, while that on the right is of MILLIE, also sent to the Pacific but not to the 5th AF. The paintings are virtually identical and seem likely to have been the work of the same stateside artist (MILLIE may well have been from the same production batch; her serial number also begins 41-30xxx). From the 408th, BLONDE BOMBER was transferred to the 38th BG ca. January 1944, where the pin-up was probably replaced by either "Black Panthers" or "Terrible Tigers" squadron markings, depending on which squadron it was assigned to.

An undated but rarely seen air-to-air view of the RHS of *BLONDE BOMBER*. One of the many popular names for US bomber nose art, "Blonde Bomber" would seem to be a wartime version of the earlier "Blonde Bombshell" nickname given to actress Jean Harlow (1911–1937). This B-25 served with the 22nd BG for about five months from September 1943 and at the end of that time (after a bomb log of 54 missions had been added) appeared in a variety of 408th squadron group photos taken at Nadzab, one of which appears on the cover.

Blondie, North American B-25, unidentified serial number, artist unknown, unit/s unidentified. This photo has been included on the basis that a similar view appears in the 5th AF's 61st Service Squadron souvenir history that was produced in the USA in 1945-46. The B-25 is believed to have been a 75mm cannon-armed G or H model but nothing further is presently known about the plane, her artwork or her identity.

NOSE ART OF THE 5TH AIR FORCE

BOOBY TRAP / Miss Jolly Roger, Consolidated B-24, 44-40193, artist identified only as "521," 321st BS, 90th BG. As will be seen in this chapter, nose art was often duplicated on both sides of the nose, but in this case there were two different artworks (BOOBY TRAP on the RHS, Miss Jolly Roger [q.v.] on the LHS), both separately named and completed, apparently, by different artists. The two photos here show the pin-up together with the 90th BG "Jolly Roger" grinning skull and crossed-bombs insignia (normally featured on the plane's vertical fins) as first completed (*at left*), and, *below*, after it was decided to scrub off the unit insignia. In the second photo, apart from the mark left on the B-24's skin where the black-painted unit insignia had been, note too the white background to the name, not so obvious against the shiny finish in the first photo. The same artist was also responsible for the stunning artwork on the 321st BS's "fat cat" A-20 LiTTLE CHiEF; see photos in chapter 5. This B-24 was salvaged in theater.

BOTTOM'S UP!, Consolidated B-24, 42-40834, artist unknown, unidentified BS, 90th BG. Despite the reasonably high number of missions flown by this B-24, surprisingly little is known of her. It seems likely to the author, however, that the artwork was a late addition, since the only photos seen of it all show thirty-three missions (the continuous line of bomb symbols seen in this photo was subsequently changed to three groups of ten and one group of three, all added using a vertical bomb stencil). Subsequently, BOTTOM'S UP! suffered extensive nose damage and was taken out of service at Nadzab and salvaged, and the shell of the bomber was left there. There were at least three examples of 5th AF B-24 nose art that featured a painting of a pin-up caught up in a barbed-wire fence, the others being "ON DE-FENSE" (q.v.) and the RIP SNORTER (q.v.), and while there was a pin-up by Gil Elvgren named 'On De-Fence' (note spelling) that may have inspired the first name, the young lady depicted was more modestly dressed and looking backward. What can be said with certainty is that this work and "ON DE-FENSE" were very similar in style, and one may have influenced the other, but details are lacking.

52

Butch, Douglas A-20, unidentified serial number, artist unknown, 90th BS, 3rd BG. The combat log of the 90th BS confirms that on December 3, 1943, "all of the Squadron's B-25s were turned in today and 15 A-20s received," which, it was optimistically hoped, could be made ready within a week. The 90th BS painted shark's mouths on their A-20s, as they had with their B-25s, but in this photo it can be seen that there has been a conscious attempt to paint out most of the mouth, leaving just a few teeth. This, together with the fact that a dark squadron color has been added to the tip of the fin and vertical stabilizer, would suggest that while this had been a 90th BS aircraft earlier (the squadron color was white), this A-20 had been subsequently transferred to another 3rd BG squadron, although which is still unclear. The location is suspected to be Nadzab, where the 3rd BG was based for three months from late January–February 1944. This may have been the same A-20 with tail letter "B" that appeared in a 3rd BG article in the "Down Under" edition of *Yank* magazine vol. 2, no. 7 (September 15, 1944).

BUZZZZ JOB, Consolidated B-24, 42-100290, artist unknown, 408th BS, 22nd BG. Note some repainted areas, the top one suggesting, perhaps, that an alteration to the illustration or name had occurred. This B-24 lasted only about four months in service, being lost without trace in bad weather on a courier flight between Owi Island and Nadzab on July 20, 1944. The fate of the seven men aboard remains unknown.

BUTCHER'S DAUGHTER, Consolidated B-24, 44-40190, artist "Short," 319th BS, 90th BG. Two views of this bomber, before and after her name was added. Interestingly, in the view at left the last three mission symbols have just been added, taking the total to twenty-two, but note also that while the photo at right still shows twenty-two missions, the number of aerial victory symbols has doubled from four to eight. A later photo shows more mission symbols added to the right of the pin-up. Later still, second and third rows of mission symbols were added prior to the *DAUGHTER*'s last mission on May 15, 1945. The artist's only other known work was *"HO HUM"* (q.v.) for the 400th BS.

Calamity Jane, Douglas A-20, 42-86612, artist unknown, 386th BS, 312th BG. This A-20 was assigned to Lt. (subsequently captain) Laurie W. Folmar in February 1944. He had married Elizabeth Jane Bean in August 1943, and this aircraft was named in honor of her. The inset photo here shows the artist at work, basing his illustration on an unidentified magazine cutting. Also note the background outline (probably in chalk at this early stage) of Texas (Folmar was born in Alabama but spent most of his life in the Lone Star State), which is not so obvious in the second view, ca. September 1944. It is suspected that this A-20 ended its days at Nadzab.

Cactus Kitten, North American B-25, 43-36041, artist George M. Blackwell, 501st BS, 345th BG. This was one of more than a dozen new B-25J-11 airplanes assigned to the 501st BS in October 1944, five of which received nose art soon after, all by Blackwell, with names painted by Cpl. Joseph Merenda. The others were *APACHE PRINCESS*, *LAZY DAISY MAE*, *Reina del PACIFICO*, and *WHITE WING*, photos of all of which can also be found in this chapter. This B-25 was lost over Saigon with her five-man crew on April 28, 1945; *Reina del PACIFICO* was lost during the same mission. *Via Neil Follett*

CALIFORNIA Sunshine, Douglas A-20, 42-86776, artist unknown, 388th BS, 312th BG. Although California is generally considered as a location with warm, dry summers, Maj. William H. Kemble Jr., 388th BS squadron commander, a Californian who completed his flight training in Texas, evidently disagreed. He was assigned this A-20 in February 1944, the artwork added to it being a very accurate copy of a pin-up by Gil Elvgren titled *Caught in the Draft*. At some point the bomb log was changed from vertical to slanted bomb symbols. The plane survived more than ninety missions and was subsequently salvaged after Kemble left the squadron to be rotated home.

Career Girl, Consolidated B-24, 42-41234, artist unknown, 528th BS and 530th BS, 380th BG. The name of this B-24, perhaps taken from advance publicity for a Hollywood musical of the same name released in January 1944, appeared on the LHS of the nose, while this pin-up appeared on the RHS. *Career Girl* was assigned to the 380th BG in November 1943 and flew three missions from northern Australia before being deployed to New Guinea in December. On December 14, however, while based at Dobodura, she was damaged when the LHS main undercarriage leg collapsed while being taxied, and never flew again. Some salvage of the bomber was carried out on-site, but the nose and wing center section were still in the Dobodura area as recently as 2018.

Caroline, Boeing B-17, 41-24420, artist unknown, 65th BS, 43rd BG. This B-17 had originally been named *SUPER SNOOPER* and had featured an unidentified cartoon character riding a bomb, artwork that extended over the rear window in the nose compartment. Following transfer to the 65th BS in April 1943, though, this early moniker and illustration were painted over and replaced by that shown here (note that where the earlier artwork had extended over the rear nose window, it was simply painted over, not removed). There were fewer than a dozen 65th BS B-17s that featured pin-up nose art, and it seems likely that there were only one or two artists responsible; certainly, the presentation of the names *Blonde Bomber* (q.v.) and *Caroline* would suggest that the same artist painted them both, and perhaps the pin-ups as well. The bomber later became an armed transport and changed her identity another two times, first as *"G.I." Jr.*, featuring a helmet-wearing youngster holding a spanner, which was subsequently replaced by another nude, this time unnamed. Photos of both artworks can be found toward the end of chapter 4.

CAROLYN MAE, Consolidated B-24, 44-40776, artist Enoch H. Wingert, 65th BS, 43rd BG. This B-24 was assigned to the 65th BS in July 1944, and the nose art seen here was subsequently added. Wingert signed off on all his known works, and in each case he added a personal logo comprising his own version of the squadron insignia, featuring two white dice on a dark background. The logo can be clearly seen in this photo to the lower right-hand corner of the blanket that the pin-up is sitting on. *CAROLYN MAE* was salvaged in 1945, but further details are not known. For Wingert's other known works, see *MAD RUSSIAN*, *PETTY GAL*, and *PUNJA KASI*, an unnamed B-24 (that later became *QUEEN OF THE CLOUDS*), and *WILLIE'S FOLLY* later in this chapter.

CARROT TOP, Consolidated B-24, 42-73114, artist Eugene F. Bucki, 528th BS, 380th BG. This B-24 was assigned to the 528th BS in November 1943 and named in honor of the wife of Lt. Sherwood H. Sheehan, who flew more missions in it than anyone else. Artist Bucki, one of the crew's gunners and formerly an outdoor-sign artist, based the artwork on the October pin-up in the 1944 *Esquire Varga Calendar*. One of the last 5th AF B-24s to be based in Australia, CARROT TOP flew seventy-seven missions before the 528th's move to the Philippines. It was during that transit flight to McGuire Field, Mindoro, on March 5, 1945, that she experienced fuel transfer problems, engine failure, and a subsequent crash landing. All the crew survived but one was badly burned, necessitating his return to the US for a full recovery. The B-24 was destroyed. *R. E. "Dusty" Hensel*

CHANGE O Luck, Consolidated B-24, 41-11868, artist unknown, 320th BS, 90th BG. This B-24, one of the first in the SWPA, had, it has been said, ongoing serviceability problems, so much so that its first name, reportedly, had been *Bucket of Bolts*. The new name and artwork, featuring a non-white-skinned pin-up, were supposed to have heralded a new beginning, but serviceability remained an issue. It is known that this nose art was still in place early in 1944, but the B-24 was subsequently converted to a transport airplane by the 479th Service Squadron and at that stage was apparently renamed WHITE CARGO before being passed on to the RAAF in March 1944. In RAAF service it was given a new serial number, A72-9, and in one late-war photo it can be seen that at some point it had been stripped of camouflage paint but was still wearing the WHITE CARGO name on the LHS; the RHS was probably blank. It was salvaged in 1945.

charmin' lady, North American B-25, 42-87444, artist unknown, 17th TRS, 71st TRG. The 17th TRS, or 17th Recco Squadron (B), as it seems to have been more commonly called, was the only B-25-equipped TRS in the SWPA. It served with the 5th AF from late 1943 until after war's end and prided itself on its ability to cope with any mission, whether it was reconnaissance, bombing, photography, leaflet dropping, searches, or anything else. Pin-up nose art seemed to have been restricted, perhaps, to only a handful of the squadron's aircraft; others included in this volume are *Filthy Filbert*, *Miss Exterminator*, *"MITCH" THE WITCH*, *Miss Charlene* (unconfirmed), *MONTANA MAID*, and *NAUGHTY MARIETTA* (unconfirmed). *Charmin' lady*, said to have completed more than a hundred missions, was lost in action in the Philippines on May 18, 1945; only one crew member survived. It has been suggested that her assigned pilot, Lt. Frederic E. Kluth, may have painted the nose art, which could be correct, but it should be noted that Kluth joined the "Fighting 17th" only in October 1944.

CHEROKEE STRIP, Consolidated F-7, 44-40198, artist Al G. Merkling, 20th CMS, 6th PRG. As will be seen, artwork names with double meanings were popular with pin-up art. While there is a real Cherokee Strip, a disputed section of land on the southern border of Kansas, clearly this *CHEROKEE STRIP* is something else. Paramount had released a film of the same name in 1940, described as a "historic romance of the west," and this would seem to have been why the name was used. This F-7 was one of only three from this squadron to fly one hundred missions or more; in fact, it flew the most missions of any 20th CMS camera ship, but photos of the artwork and mission symbols (which must have occupied most of the LHS) are few and far between. On the basis of the brightness of the aircraft's finish and the easily read constructor's number (4134) stencil forward of the antiglare panel, though, this photo was taken ca. August 1944, early in this F-7's service with the 20th CMS. *CHEROKEE STRIP* was salvaged in theater, location unknown.

Cherrie, Consolidated B-24, 44-42441, artist unknown, 320th BS, 90th BG. This photo was scanned from a strip of 35 mm contact prints of late-war B-24 nose art, possibly taken on Okinawa, some of the other airplanes on the strip being *Coming Home! SOON*, *Good Pickin's*, *MARY ANN*, and *the Red-headed Rebel*, photos of which follow. For other late-war "Moby Dick" squadron B-24s that combined the whale-look nose markings with a pin-up, see *AIR POCKET*, *DISPLAY OF ARMS*, *"GRRR"*, and *LIVE WIRE* in this chapter. *Cherrie* was returned to the United States postwar, and it would seem reasonable to expect that its artwork (incidentally, note the cherries on the bathing costume) was retained, but proof is currently lacking.

"CHICO", Boeing B-17, 41-2638, artist unknown, 65th and 63rd BSs, 43rd BG. This B-17 arrived in Australia on April 30, 1942, and served originally with the 19th BG. When the name and artwork were added is not known, but as of April 1943 (by which time the B-17 had been with the 65th BS for five months), only the name appeared. The pin-up was in place by September 1943, when *"CHICO"* was transferred to the 63rd BS, but the name was changed at that point to *I'm Willing*. Late in the year, this B-17 was returned to the US, but details of its later service are not known.

Classy Chassis, Douglas A-20, unidentified serial number, artist unknown, 90th BS, 3rd BG. Little is known about this A-20 apart from the fact that the name and artwork appeared on both sides of the nose. It's not an uncommon name for aircraft nose art (see chapter 4 for a C-47 with the same name), and the word "Chassis" is sometimes seen spelled Chassy. *Classy Chassy* was also the title of the first nose art book purchased by this author, way back in 1977. Since then, the study of the subject has reached heights probably unimaginable by that slim volume's authors.

COCKTAIL HOUR, Consolidated B-24, 44-40428, artist Sarkis E. Bartigian, 64th BS, 43rd BG. Another of Bartigian's elaborate paintings, this artwork was one of the most photographed on Ie Shima Island after the 43rd BG moved there in July 1945. Virtually nothing is known of the origins of Bartigian's works, but most seem to have been completed late in the war (an exception may have been *MICHIGAN*), and their size, complexity, and professional standard have certainly made them more famous than the aircraft they adorned. To the right of the artwork is the name of the crew chief, Sgt. Barnes. This B-24 was not returned to the USA postwar but was salvaged in theater, probably in the Philippines. For other Bartigian pin-up works in this chapter, see *THE DRAGON AND HIS TAIL*, *MABEL'S LABELS*, and *MICHIGAN*, the last named the next aircraft off the production line after *COCKTAIL HOUR*. Photos of two other Bartigian non-pin-up works, *IT AINT SO FUNNY* and *LAST HORIZON*, can be found in chapter 1. For other nightclub-themed nose art in this volume, see B-24M *DOUBLE TROUBLE* and A-20 *MIS-A-SIP*, which follow.

COME AND GET IT, Consolidated B-24, 42-40941, artist unknown, 64th BS, 43rd BG, later 19th BS, 22nd BG, later CRTC. With artwork copied from the 1943 *Esquire Varga Calender* and name taken from a 1941 swing record by Thomas "Fats" Waller (1904–43), with "more than vaguely sexual overtones," this B-24 saw limited 43rd BG service, becoming one of the 64th's B-24s made available in the first quarter of 1944 for use by the 19th BS as transition trainers while the 22nd BG changed to a heavy-bomber outfit. The name and artwork appeared on both sides of the nose, but the bomb log (a total of thirty-five missions, only the second row of which is visible in this photo) was painted on the LHS. The B-24 was subsequently on strength of the CRTC at Nadzab and, after being stripped of parts, was left there postwar; for a last mention and photo of this B-24, see appendix 3. *RAAF Museum*

BOMBER AND LONG-RANGE PHOTO RECON BEAUTIES

Coming Home! SOON, Consolidated B-24, unidentified serial number, artist unknown, unit(s) unidentified. This image is taken from a strip of 35 mm contact prints of late-war B-24 nose art, possibly taken on Okinawa, including *Cherrie*, seen earlier, and on that basis has been included as more than likely being a 5th AF aircraft (note the seldom-seen emphasis added; an indication that possibly the war was already over by the time this art was added). By chance, both this artwork and *COME AND GET IT*, seen opposite, were copied from the same pin-up picture, which originally appeared in the 1943 *Esquire Varga Calendar*.

"*Contented Lady*", Douglas A-20, unidentified serial number, artist unknown, 672nd BS, 417th BG. This A-20 was particularly noticeable due to the LHS dark rectangular background, which extended from just behind the nose cone to where the side cockpit window ended. The purpose of the background color seems to have been to accentuate any pin-up or mission log added to it, but after five rows of twenty missions added within the rectangle (in a light-colored paint), the bomb log (changed to a darker color) overflowed forward onto the nose. Assigned pilot was Lt. Walter H. Canter, while his crew chief was TSgt. Harry Friery. This photo was probably taken at Biak, where this and many other A-20s were left to be salvaged postwar.

Cookie, Douglas A-20, unidentified serial number, artist unknown, unit(s) unidentified. Despite the unknowns, this is still suspected to be a 5th AF airplane, but no further details are currently known.

59

"COOKIE", Consolidated B-24, 41-23839, artist unknown, 321st BS, 90th BG. It would appear from the two close-up photos at right that the artist originally intended to reproduce the same artwork on both sides of the nose but changed his mind as far as the rolling pin on the LHS was concerned, the inclusion of which would have partly defaced the stenciled airplane data panel (other artists were not so concerned; see, for example, C-47 *BISCUIT BOMBER* in chapter 4). The pilot originally assigned to *"COOKIE"* was Lt. Charles H. Cook, who served with the 321st BS from November 1942 to June 1943, after which he was rotated home. His old B-24, an early overall view of which is also included, was later also returned to the United States and survived most of World War II to be disposed of from Ontario Field, California. Note in the top right photo of the LHS of the nose that more than forty mission symbols can be seen, as well as, faintly, symbols for seven enemy fighters claimed shot down.

The CORAL QUEEN, Consolidated B-24, unidentified serial number, artist unknown, 400th BS, 90th BG. Despite the work put in by a lot of different researchers, all keen to identify the planes (particularly B-24s) on which nose art appeared, nothing more than the unit to which this B-24 was assigned is currently known about this example. It has been identified as a B-24D version, though, and that would suggest that the plane was an early loss or that the artwork was short lived and replaced by something else.

Crosby's Curse / CROSBYS CURSE, Consolidated B-24, 41-23836, artist unknown, 321st BS, 90th BG. It is suspected that this B-24 was best known by the name that appeared on its RHS rather than the small writing (*C.O.D.* [Cash on Delivery] *KNOT FOR TOJO*) seen here on the pin-up. The reason for the *Crosby's Curse* name (which was originally written in cursive script but sometime after the thirty-second mission was changed to capital letters) has not been determined, although it evidently related in some way to popular singer and film star of the day Bing Crosby (1903–77). Just when the pin-up was added is not known; originally the wording *Who-Shives-AGIT* appeared on the LHS, but this was painted over to make more room. The mission tally and claims for enemy fighters destroyed appeared on both sides of the cockpit. It has been reported that this B-24 was salvaged in December 1944.

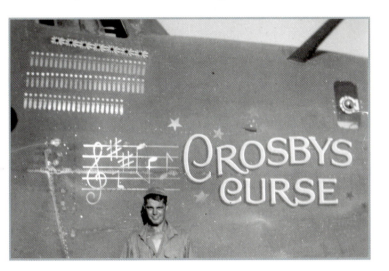

Cruisin Susan, Consolidated B-24, 42-73201, artist unknown, 531st BS, 380th BG. This B-24 had been assigned to the 531st BS late in 1943 and at that stage carried artwork of a gun-toting brown bear named *"TENN." SQUIRREL HUNTER* as shown at left. While based in Australia (until early 1945), it flew more than fifty missions, losing its camouflage paint and being renamed *Cruisin Susan* along the way, initially without a pin-up. Following transfer to the Philippines, it was destroyed in a crash landing that was caused by engine failure on return from a mission on April 7, 1945. All crew members, however, survived.

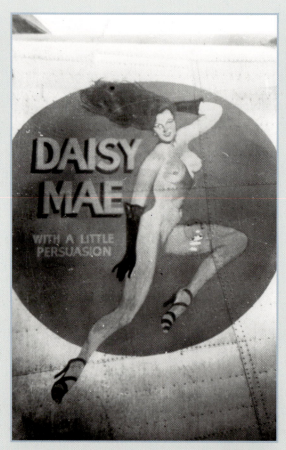

DAISY MAE, Consolidated B-24, 44-41845, artist James C. Nickloy, 2nd BS, 22nd BG. Various characters from Al Capp's extremely popular *Li'l Abner* cartoon series, particularly the beautiful, voluptuous Daisy Mae (full name Daisy Mae Scragg), became instant hits as nose art subjects, but Daisy was blonde and always dressed, albeit skimpily (see LAZY DAISY MAE in this chapter), and so there was no real similarity between this artwork and the cartoon character. In fact, it seems that the name and subtitle were simply added for their obvious sexual overtones if one was to substitute MAY for MAE. Just which version of the name (with or without the subtitle) appeared first is not known, but it seems likely that the pin-up was probably added at Clark Field, where the artist's unit, the 36th PRS, was based April–July 1945. DAISY MAE was flown back to the US postwar, where she was later scrapped. No photos of this B-24 have surfaced, confirming that the pin-up survived the long flight home, even if in altered form, and on that basis it seems most likely that it was removed while stopped over at Hickham Field, Hawaii.

DADDY'S GIRL, Consolidated B-24, 44-41852, artist Charles Chesnut, 33rd BS, 22nd BG. Details are scant on this B-24, but it is known to have been assigned to the 33rd BS in February 1945 and appears to have survived the war. Under the circumstances, this must have been one of Chesnut's last works; other known 1945 works by Chesnut were B-24s *th' Duchess* (q.v.) and two different versions of YANKEE GAL (q.v.), and B-25 *Fast Lady* (see photos in chapters 1 and 5).

DaLLy's DiLLy, Consolidated B-24, 42-73112, artist Glenn A. Miller, 528th BS, 380th BG. This B-24 was assigned to Lt. Joseph W. Dally early in 1944, and the artwork and name, a play on the word "dilly-dally," followed and apparently remained with the B-24 despite Dally leaving the 380th in August 1944. Artist SSgt. Miller, another of the 380th's talented artists, also completed *Puss & Boots* (q.v.) while serving with the 528th BS but lost his life on May 8, 1944, when Roy Parker's crew, of which he was a member, ditched after being shot up over Jefman Island off the northwestern tip of New Guinea and their B-24 broke up. *DaLLy's DiLLy* was luckier, flying more than a hundred missions (the last on May 11, 1945) before being left at Clark Field for salvage.

Dauntless "Dottie", Consolidated B-24, 42-40495, artist unknown, 528th and 530th BSs, 380th BG. "Dottie" began flying with the 528th BS at the end of May 1943, and, since it was often flown then by the crew of Lt. (later captain) William Shek, it was named in honor of Shek's wife, Dorothy, but there was no pin-up at that stage. According to website 380th.org, Shek's last mission in this B-24 occurred on October 17, 1943, and certainly by then the pin-up (*at right*) had been added. It would be easy to say that the artwork looks a little incomplete without something for the pin-up to lean on, but, in fact, the pin-up was copied from the July page in Earl MacPherson's *Artist's Sketch Pad Calendar* for 1943, and that is how the original illustration looked. When the camouflage paint was removed later, though, so was the nose art. Subsequently, however, a new *"Dottie"* based on the original was added (*above*), this time with a wagon wheel.

"DINKY", Consolidated B-24, 42-40325, artist unknown, 320th BS, 90th BG. "Dinky" was aircraft captain Lt. Lionel B. Potter's nickname for his wife, Winnie; they married in 1942. Potter had been a 320th Squadron original who flew at first as a second pilot but was later given his own command. This B-24 was badly damaged by enemy fighters on a Wewak raid on September 28, 1943, and was passed to a service squadron for repairs, after which a new nose turret was fitted. Potter was concerned that he may not see her again, but one of his last flights prior to returning to the US was to proudly return "DINKY" to the squadron on December 15 (the B-24's name originally lacked quotation marks, and the lettering was narrower in style). After that, the history of "DINKY" is not so easy to follow, and while reportedly she was not condemned until 1945, after Potter left, it seems likely that the nose art was changed. Potter's entertaining wartime diary entries from 1942–43 were transcribed by son Joshua some years ago and can be found online.

"Deanna's Dreamboat", Consolidated B-24, 44-42244, artist William B. McBroom, 530th BS, 380th BG. Although this photo has been published previously, its significance has been, for the most part, overlooked. The airplane's commander, Lt. Don Engen, seen in this photo (standing, far left), met popular wartime singer and actress Deanna Durbin (1921–2013) when she paid a visit to the Nevada base at which he and his crew were training in 1944, and Engen promised her that following their assignment to a frontline unit he would name his bomber after her. "Deanna's Dreamboat" was the result, the artwork copied from a studio portrait of Durbin. The B-24 was assigned to the 380th BG in April 1945, but it does not appear to have "become" Engen's plane until May, at some point subsequently the artwork being added. The date of the photo has not been recorded, but clearly it was seen as a PR opportunity for the 380th, with the group commander, Col. William Lee Brissey, standing next to Engen and everyone wearing crisp new uniforms especially for the occasion. A print of this photo appears to have been made available to all involved, with another going to Miss Durbin's agent, but it seems that the end of the war, soon after, took the edge off any promotional opportunities for either the 380th BG or Miss Durbin's film studio, Universal Pictures (who also had a copy of the photo made). To complete the story, "Deanna's Dreamboat", presumably with artwork still in place, was flown back to the US postwar but later scrapped at Kingman, Arizona, while Miss Durbin's film career lasted only marginally longer, until 1948. For another B-24 with Hollywood connections, see ROAD TO TOKYO later in this chapter, while for other pin-ups by McBroom in this volume, see "Dottie's Double", "FRISCO FRANNIE", Hell's Belle (unconfirmed), JUGGLIN' JOSIE (unconfirmed), LI'L D'-ICER, "ON DE-FENSE", and "PROP WASH", which follow.

DIRTY GERTY / G.I. JOE, Douglas A-20, unidentified serial number, artist unknown, 387th BG (unconfirmed), 312th BG. Since the invention of the camera, there has been a history of men behaving badly for a photo opportunity, such events being accentuated in an all-male environment. This wolf (G.I. JOE) and naked lady (DIRTY GERTY) depiction does not appear to have been documented elsewhere and was probably short lived. The name of the assigned pilot was Lt. Ammerman, and, as can be seen here, his crew chief was SSgt. H. Latham, but despite a thirty-five-mission bomb log, nothing further is currently known of this A-20's history.

DISPLAY OF ARMS, Consolidated B-24, 44-41478 (unconfirmed), artist unknown, 320th BS, 90th BG. This B-24, with nose art based on an Earl Moran pin-up, has been identified previously as 44-41274, but a second photo of what is believed to have been the same B-24 that appears in chapter 6 (both photos were from the same collection, and both aircraft lack an astrodome and feature a virtually nonexistent antiglare panel) shows the tail number to be 478, so unless it had been given a replacement vertical fin from 44-41478, then *DISPLAY OF ARMS* must have been that particular aircraft, not a B-24J model but a B-24L. For other late-war "Moby Dick" squadron B-24s that combined the whale-look nose markings with a pin-up, see *AIR POCKET*, *Cherrie*, *"GRRR"*, and *LIVE WIRE* in this chapter. 44-41478 was returned to the US postwar and subsequently scrapped.

The Dorothy Anne, Consolidated B-24, 42-41093, artist unknown, 64th BS, 43rd BG. Note where the last three digits of the serial number, 093, had been painted on the nose but subsequently painted out prior to squadron assignment. Reportedly the name appeared first and the artwork and *NOT IN STOCK* followed. This photo was probably taken towards the end of *The Dorothy Anne*'s service (it was lost on March 20, 1944, on a nonoperational flight), perhaps while undergoing major servicing, since not only has the dorsal turret been removed but so has the Perspex from the navigator's LHS side window.

"Dottie's Double" / *"DOTTIE'S DOUBLE"*, Consolidated B-24, 42-72964, artist William B. McBroom, 530th BS, 380th BG. This B-24 had been assigned to the 530th BS in December 1943, with Lt. Joe Cesario naming her after his then fiancé and taking her into action for the first time on December 13, 1943. He subsequently flew this B-24 often during the period December 1943 to July 1944, initially in New Guinea and later from Fenton Field. *"Dottie's Double"* later went on to become a "Century Girl," a one-hundred-mission-plus plane, but unlike *Dauntless "Dottie"* seen earlier, when *"Dottie's Double"*'s paintwork was removed, as shown in the second photo (with crew chief MSgt. Louis W. Pellegrini, *at right*), only the name was reapplied, not the pin-up. *Dottie* survived the war, after which, reportedly, she was flown to Biak for salvaging. *Photo at left from The History of the 380th Bomb Group (H) AAF, Affectionately Known as the Flying Circus (see bibliography)*

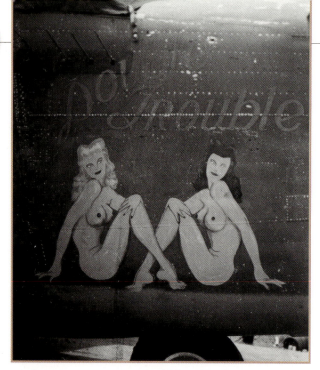

Double Trouble, Consolidated B-24, 42-41226, artist unknown, 64th BS (unconfirmed), 43rd BG, later 19th BS, 22nd BG. "Double trouble," most commonly two women, or one woman and alcohol, was—not surprisingly in a young man's world—very popular as a nose art theme (there were at least fourteen B-24s worldwide so named). Following service with the 43rd BG, which commenced in the last quarter of 1943, this B-24 was transferred to the 19th BS for conversion training, while the 19th, then at Charters Towers, northern Queensland, was reequipping with B-24s, but it was lost in an accident on January 26, 1944, resulting in one death. The artist responsible for this nose art (which featured a blonde and a redhead) may have also been responsible for *Mag the Hag* (q.v.).

THE DRAGON AND HIS TAIL, Consolidated B-24, 44-40973, artist Sarkis E. Bartigian, 64th BS, 43rd BG. Here is a closer view of the forward section of this incredible painting, which can be seen to better effect on the cover. Note the abbreviated "973" nose number, a late-war addition to 43rd BG B-24s. This B-24 survived the war and, according to its record card, was received by the agency responsible for assets disposal, the Reconstruction Finance Corp., at Kingman, Arizona, on November 2, 1945. While, as already noted, few examples of nude pin-up nose art seem to have made it back to the US, this was one exception, and the plane continued to be an object of curiosity until scrapped. Two later photos of this nose art appear in chapter 7.

DOUBLE TROUBLE, Consolidated B-24s, 42-40358, artist unknown, 320th BS, 90th BG (*above*) and 44-50602, artist unknown, 530th BS, 380th BG (*above right*). More double trouble, but the history of the 90th BG B-24 so named is little known, except that all the claims for enemy aircraft shot down occurred in one action, which was later used as the subject of a full-page magazine Army Air Forces recruiting advert. The artwork that accompanied the advert showed a B-24D stripped of camouflage paint named *Double Trouble* in action, but with no nose art. Photos of this nose art are uncommon, but whether it was subsequently deleted as suggested in the advert is not known. It could be, though, given that reportedly this B-24 lived on until condemned for salvage in 1945. The 380th BG's *DOUBLE TROUBLE* is more of an open book though. She flew her first mission in April 1945 and is seen here with twenty-four mission markers ca. June 1945. Postwar she was returned to the United States but did not escape the scrapper's torch. Note that this particular artwork was on both sides of the nose, but, perhaps because of the positioning of the fire extinguisher access panel, more photos seem to have been taken of the RHS artwork than that on the LHS. Note too that the cherry in the cocktail on the LHS was not colored in, but that on the RHS was.

BOMBER AND LONG-RANGE PHOTO RECON BEAUTIES

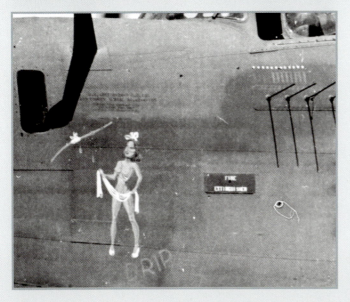

DRIP, Consolidated B-24, 42-41105, artist unknown, 321st BS, 90th BG. This B-24 was originally named *THE LEMON*, as seen here, but the lack of photos in this guise suggests that there was probably an early change to *DRIP* (the author has seen no evidence that it was ever called *The DRIP*). Where the old artwork was painted out shows well in the photo below left, while a close-up of the pin-up has been added for good measure. Similarities between this work and the 321st Squadron's *LIBERTY BELLE* (q.v.), even down to the pin-up's stance, would suggest that both were by the same artist. This B-24's history is little known, but the second photo confirms her involvement in at least twelve strikes. She was salvaged ca. December 1944, probably at the Townsville Air Depot.

"DREAM Gal", Consolidated B-24, 44-40919, artist unknown, 529th BS, 380th BG. Seen here with Flt. Lt. Col. Portway's RAAF crew (who flew this B-24 on December 7, 1944), *"DREAM Gal"* flew thirty-five missions from Australia between August 1944 and January 1945 and another forty-eight from the Philippines between March and July 1945, after which it was flown to Biak, where it was later salvaged. *Ian Parker*

NOSE ART OF THE 5TH AIR FORCE

DRUNKARD'S DREAM, Consolidated B-24, 42-110115, artist unknown, 531st BS, 380th BG. The pin-up used in this nose art was copied from Milt Caniff's *Miss Lace*, the much-loved star of the World War II cartoon strip *Male Call*, which was created just for military personnel (the 380th could even boast a B-24 named after the comic strip; see photos later in this chapter). The early photo (no mission symbols yet added) shows the artwork as first completed ca. May 1944 with the name to the RHS of the pin-up, while that below shows how it looked following alterations to the background (now red and larger in size) and name, now much bolder than before. Note also the name "*Lace*" at lower right. It is known that these changes were carried out after the thirty-sixth mission, its last from Australia (i.e., around February 1945). After flying more than seventy missions, this B-24 suffered a takeoff accident in the Philippines on June 18, 1945, which ended its career.

Duchess, th', Consolidated B-24, 44-49865, artist Charles R. Chesnut, 33rd BS, 22nd BG. One of Chesnut's last nose art paintings (see also *DADDY's GIRL*), this B-24 survived wartime service (it had been assigned to the 33rd BS only in February 1945) and was subsequently returned to the US afterward, the impressive artwork possibly being scraped off before arrival. In the end, though, this B-24 was just another of the thousands flown to Kingman, Arizona, all of which were eventually scrapped.

"*DUCHESS*", Consolidated B-24, 42-100262, artist unknown, 321st BS, 90th BG. Despite the history of the 90th BG being well recorded, the histories of individual airplanes assigned to it remain, in some cases, not well known. This is one such example.

The Duchess of Paducah, Consolidated B-24, 42-63991, artist unknown, 530th BS, 380th BG, later 63rd BS, 43rd BG. This nose art (based on the August page from the 1944 *Esquire Varga Calendar*) and name appeared on both sides of the nose of this B-24, but later, perhaps after it was assigned to the 63rd BS, an additional pin-up, loosely based on the April 1944 Varga Girl, was added below the cockpit on the LHS. This plane was one of the first two RCM B-24s assigned to the SWPA and arrived in Australia in January 1944 and, according to a depot status report, was at the Production Control Section at Archerfield, Queensland, at the end of April. It was subsequently assigned to the 530th BS, 380th BG, at Fenton, and website 380th.org records that the *Duchess* flew thirty missions with the 530th between May 19 and August 30, 1944, after which it served with the 63rd BS in New Guinea. This B-24 is known to have been salvaged ca. May 1945, but details are lacking.

"ELUSIVE-LIZZIE", North American B-25, 41-30118, artist unknown, 405th BS, 38th BG. This rare view of this B-25 following arrival in Australia in March 1943 and strafer conversion confirms the LHS name to be as shown. Another photo shows that the name and artwork were also applied to the RHS, but as of April 1943 the name on the LHS (and perhaps the RHS) had been painted over and, still later, the LHS name was changed to *"Miss America"*; perhaps the RHS name was also changed then too. The name (or names) and pin-ups were, however, short lived, since prior to the B-25's loss (shot down August 5, 1943), they had been replaced by the "Green Dragons" squadron markings (see chapter 6). The nickname CURLY was apparently also painted over when the B-25's name change occurred.

EMBARRASSED, Consolidated B-24, 44-40189, artist Harvey Levine, 531st BS, 380th BG. This nose art was painted for Lt. Stanley J. Buia's crew at a cost of $100; they flew *EMBARRASSED* on and off during the May–October 1944 period. Its last known flight was on August 28, 1945, and it was after that when this photo was taken. The text at bottom right of the photo (only partly visible here) states "*108 MISSIONS+,*" so the seventy-five-mission bomb log on the RHS had yet to be updated (some mission symbols did appear at top left of the pin-up, but they had been scrubbed off before this photo was taken; a fourth line of thirteen missions and a fifth line of twenty were subsequently added below the name). Surprising to this author was the fact that such a long-serving and rather tired B-24 (in squadron use for sixteen months) was chosen to be flown back to the US postwar for disposal, but it seems it was because of her distinguished service that it was hoped that she could be saved. Two postwar photos of the LHS of the nose of this century girl, showing how that side looked at the time, appear in chapter 7.

NOSE ART OF THE 5TH AIR FORCE

Emergency STRIP, North American B-25, 43-28136, artist unknown, 388th BS, 312th BG later 71st BS, 38th BG. A play on the wartime name that referred to a reserve military airdrome or airstrip suitable for airplane emergency landings, the pin-up—possibly inspired by the March pin-up from the 1944 *Esquire Varga Calendar*—was added while this B-25 was serving with the 388th BS in early 1945; the wolf's-head "Wolf Pack" squadron emblem came later, after this aircraft was transferred to the 71st BS toward the end of the war. Few other 71st BS B-25s carried pin-up nose art. For other examples of 71st BS fearsome nose art, though, see chapter 6.

ESQUIRE, Consolidated B-24, 42-73481, artist unknown, 531st BS, 380th BG. As can be seen, this B-24 paid homage to *Esquire* magazine, where Alberto Vargas's pin-ups were to be found, but it seems that the artwork only ever appeared on the RHS. *ESQUIRE* was received in Australia in December 1943 and flew mission number one on February 2, 1944. It was still in camouflage paint at that stage, and a drawing of just the head of the *Esquire* magazine mascot, "Esky," appeared above the name. A few months later, after the airplane's camouflage paint was removed, another version of the name and "Esky's" head appeared (*see below*), but at some later stage (while the squadron was still based in Australia), a new artwork comprising a pin-up holding a copy of *Esquire* magazine (with "Esky" on the cover) was added, initially with the pin-up's attention being drawn to the pages of the magazine as shown at bottom left. The final version, however, is as shown in the main photo, with the pin-up looking toward the "audience," with the addition of a wink for good measure. Despite the popularity of *Esquire* magazine during World War II (for classy pin-ups if nothing else), aircraft nose art artists rarely acknowledged the connection. Similarly, the Varga/Vargas name only ever rarely appeared as part of a wartime nose art name. This B-24 was written off following a crash landing in the Philippines in March 1945, so this artwork would seem to have been relatively short lived. *Main image, Eric Geddes; below right, Ken Crane via Bob Wiseman / Nigel Daw*

Fire Power, Consolidated B-24, 42-109986, artist Dick Ebbeson, 528th BS, 380th BG. This B-24 was originally named *Roberta and son* (named by B-24 captain Frank Raggio in honor of his family; son Robert F. Raggio was born in November 1943) and, at that stage, featured no pin-up (no fuselage national markings either; see inset photo). Raggio flew thirteen missions in *Roberta and son* between May and December 1944, but it seems that the 380th's move from northern Australia to the Philippines may have also been when Raggio transferred out and the nose art changed. As seen in the above photo, this B-24 went on to fly more than eighty missions altogether (this was to July 1945; the eventual bomb log comprised twenty bomb symbols in each of the top two rows, nineteen in the third row, sixteen in the fourth, eleven in the fifth, and at least two in the bottom row, which are not visible in this photo). *Fire Power* was salvaged postwar, location not recorded, but probably on Biak.

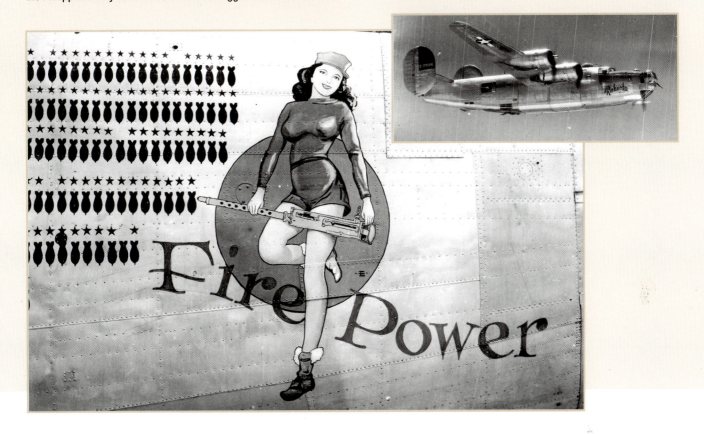

FEATHERMERCHANT'S FOLLY, Consolidated B-24, 42-100293 (unconfirmed), artist Eugene Grenvicz, 2nd BS, 22nd BG. A "feather merchant" (normally written as two words, not one) was wartime slang for a loafer or slacker, but just what the "folly" was is a little harder to be certain about. If the serial number quoted above for this B-24 is correct, then its first mission with the 2nd BS was on April 21, 1944, and its last, according to unit records, on December 14, 1944.

Filthy Filbert, North American B-25, unidentified serial number, artist unknown, 17th TRS, 71st TRG. Another 17th TRS pin-up example (this one based on *Esquire's* October 1943 Varga Girl); see also *charmin' lady*, *Miss Exterminator*, "MITCH" THE WITCH, and MONTANA MAID in this chapter for others. *Miss Charlene* (q.v.) and NAUGHTY MARIETTA (q.v.) may have also been from the 17th TRS. A check of the 17th's wartime tour book, *Strike*, reveals another photo of this nose art with the name *Filbert* higher on the side of the fuselage; concern over where the second row of mission markers would go evidently led to the name being repositioned lower as shown. The book does not, however, shed any light on whom "Filbert" was, but a cartoon included in it suggests that this B-25 was assigned to one of the squadron's four flight leaders.

"FIRIN' FANNIE", North American B-25, 41-30565, artist unknown, 408th BS, 22nd BG, later 823rd BS, 38th BG. Although operated from September 1943 by the 408th, initially without a name, as shown here that had been added to the LHS prior to the B-25's transfer out in January 1944. As to the pin-up, it was based on the August offering from the 1941 *Esquire Varga Calendar*, sans wide-brimmed hat (for an example of the pin-up wearing her hat, see C-47 *KEEP IT UNDER YOUR HAT* in chapter 4), and appeared on both sides of the nose facing rearward, with each pin-up's head being positioned directly below the cockpit area. A photo published in the 38th BG history *Sun Setters of the Southwest Pacific Area* confirms that there were no changes to the RHS artwork as of April 5, 1944, but this B-25 did not enjoy long service, being written off in 823rd BS hands following an accident on June 3, 1944.

FIRST NIGHTER, Consolidated B-24, 42-73340, artist unknown, 529th BS, 380th BG. This B-24 had a similar combat record to *Fire Power*, flying more than seventy missions between May 1944 and May 1945. What was different, however, was that she was salvaged after suffering antiaircraft (AA) fire over Taichu, Formosa, on May 18, 1945. The 529th was based at San Jose, Mindoro, at the time.

Firtil Myrtle, Consolidated B-24, 42-100042, artist unknown, 63rd BS, 43rd BG. Despite Col. Lindbergh's dislike of the "cheapness of the emblems and names painted on the bombers and fighters" and his specific mention of "Fertile Myrtle" (see introduction), this was the only 5th AF plane with such a name and nose art that the author is aware of (Col. Lindbergh's reference was probably to the 475th FG's "fat cat" B-25 *FERTILE MYRTLE*, but whether or not it featured nose art is not currently known). This B-24 was a replacement radar-equipped, anti-shipping, night attack bomber assigned to the 63rd Squadron in March 1944. She continued to serve with the 63rd until January 29, 1945, when, in a damaged condition from a raid on Takao and with wounded aboard, she ran off the airstrip at Lingayen and was subsequently salvaged. Her nose art had been added probably while the squadron was at Dobodura or Nadzab, and is seen here both in incomplete and completed forms after the bomb was added. Note also in these photos a chalked version of the name, evidently a preliminary version, above the finished work.

Flak Fled Flapper, Consolidated B-24, 44-40434, artist Dick Ebbeson, 528th BS, 380th BG. This B-24 was assigned to Lt. Joe J. Synar's crew in June 1944; they flew it on twenty missions from Australia and, later, another five from the Philippines. The inspiration for the nose art in this case was the central pin-up on a souvenir postcard from the Earl Carroll Theatre-Restaurant in Hollywood, which Synar and some of his crew had visited before their move overseas. The original artwork, in this case by pin-up artist K. O. Munson, was said to have been based on a photo of one of Carroll's popular showgirls, Helene Chilton. *Flapper* flew more than seventy missions in the SWPA altogether and survived the war but was subsequently flown to Biak, where it was later scrapped.

Flossie II, Douglas A-20, 43-9437, artist unknown, 386th BS, 312th BG. *Flossie II*, assigned to pilot Lt. Mack E. Austin, served with the 386th BS for around three months in 1944, until damaged in a flight line explosion on July 4, 1944. It is believed that she was later assigned to the CRTC at Nadzab, but whether nose repairs had been necessary, which may have affected the artwork, is not currently known.

FLAMIN' MAMIE, Consolidated B-24, 42-41062, artist unknown, 403rd BS, 43rd BG. Named after the popular 1920s jazz classic, MAMIE arrived in Australia with pin-up only, no name, as seen in this photo taken at the Townsville Air Depot. The name, it seems, was added after she was assigned to the 403rd BS, ca. September–October 1943. Over the next year she went on to fly one hundred missions, the last, reportedly, in October 1944. It has been thought that MAMIE was salvaged soon after, but her nose section, if nothing else, did last long enough to be seen and photographed in the Nadzab boneyard postwar; refer to appendix 3.

Flying Fannie, Consolidated B-24, 42-72780, artist unknown, 403rd BS, 43rd BG. This B-24 was received in Australia ca. October 1943 and was lost less than six months later, on March 22, 1944, as a result of engine failure after taking off from Nadzab with other 403rd planes on a bombing mission against AA positions near Boram airfield. She was fully loaded with fuel and bombs, and there was an explosion following the crash and all ten men aboard that day lost their lives. The streaks on the aircraft in this photo are rarely seen as clearly as this but are nothing more than condensation, the result of warm, moist air coming in contact with a cooler surface. The location is probably Dobodura or Nadzab.

NOSE ART OF THE 5TH AIR FORCE

"FLYING GINNY", North American B-25, 41-30017, artist unknown, 499th BS, 345th BG. This B-25 featured similar pin-ups on both sides of its nose, which were based on the August 1942 *Esquire Varga Calendar* artwork, but that on the RHS, named *Bette* (q.v), was clothed (as was the original calendar art). The differences in appearances and names were because the LHS artwork, seen here, was carried out under the directions of the plane's original pilot, Lt. Jack L. Broadhurst, while the RHS artwork was undertaken under the instructions of the copilot, Lt. Chandler S. Whipple (Whipple's girlfriend's name was Bette). Broadhurst left the squadron in September 1943, and Whipple took over as pilot (it seems likely that the squadron's new "Bats Outa Hell" nose insignia replaced any personal nose art by then), and this B-25 along with her five-man crew was lost on a mission not far from the northern coast of Papua New Guinea on October 5, 1943, in what were still early days for the 499th in action.

FOIL PROOF MARY, Consolidated B-24, 42-73126, artist unknown, 531st BS, 380th BG. This B-24 was in squadron service for only around two months, since it was lost returning from a reconnaissance flight on February 5, 1944, when both outboard motors failed. A crash landing was made on Croker Island, Northern Territory, but four of the crew, three gunners and the aircraft captain, lost their lives.

FORM 1-A, Consolidated B-24, 44-40229, artist unknown, 321st BS, 90th BG. During World War II, US military draftees were categorized into four groups: Forms I (available for service), II (deferred because of occupational status), III (deferred because of dependents), and IV (deferred specifically by law or because unfit for military service), with Form I-A men the top of "the heap" ("fit for general military service"), while IV-F "men were physically, mentally or morally unfit" was the bottom. The illustration was based on the cover pin-up from Earl MacPherson's 1944 *Artist's Sketch Pad Calendar* (for another example of this artwork see *OUR HONEY* in this chapter). This B-24 also carried the name (without artwork) *Peggy Lou* on the LHS, and following the death of Franklin D. Roosevelt and swearing-in of Harry S Truman as president, this was changed to *The HARRY S. TRUMAN* in the new president's honor. According to the B-24 Best Web website, the renaming coincided with the aircraft breaking the record for the number of missions flown by a B-24: 143. This bomber was another that was returned to the US postwar, presumably with the president's name still in place.

BOMBER AND LONG-RANGE PHOTO RECON BEAUTIES

FRANCIE II, Douglas A-20, 42-54117, artist unknown, 8th BS, 3rd BG. The history of this A-20 while with the 8th BS is little known, but what is known is that it was one of a number of that squadron's A-20s subsequently transferred to the 389th BS, 312th BG, in March 1944. It is not known whether the nose art remained in place or not, but, sadly, this and another two former 8th BS A-20s crashed into the Finisterre Mountain Range on return from a mission to Alexishafen on March 13, 1944; that is, within days of the planes' transfer in to the 389th BS. Wartime searches failed to find any of the three; it was not until 1982 that local tribesmen took a Westerner to the sites of the two of the crashes, and years later before the wreckage of *FRANCIE II* was subsequently found.

FREE FOR ALL!!!, Consolidated B-24, 44-42412, artist J. Oetienna (?), 531st BS, 380th BG. There was a big influx of replacement aircraft, new B-24Ms, into the 531st BS in June, July, and August 1945. Few of these had nose art added, but known examples, including *ATOMIC BLONDE*, *BACHELOR'S BROTHEL*, *FREE FOR ALL!!!*, and *POM POM EXPRESS*, all were completed by the same artist, a talented Mindoro local. *FREE FOR ALL!!!* flew only one mission before war's end; that was on July 24, 1945. Postwar this B-24 was returned to the US and subsequently scrapped, but whether the nose art was still in place by then is a moot point.

"*FRISCO FRANNIE*", Consolidated B-24, 42-73451, William B. McBroom, 530th BS, 380th BG. According to website 380th.org, this B-24 flew sixty-eight missions, fifty-one from northern Australia and another seventeen from the Philippines after transfer to the 531st BS. This artwork by McBroom (his sign-off appears below the pin-up's feet) was based on the Varga Girl from the December 1943 issue of *Esquire* magazine, which, as shown in this photo, included USAAF national markings and readily lent itself as a choice for airplane nose art, particularly on larger airplanes. *Gallant Lady / LADY LYNN*, which follows, was based on the same Varga Girl illustration, but the artist decided not to include the AAF "star and bar" insignia. For other versions of this Varga Girl, see *HEAVENLY BODY*, *Little Brat*, and *TITIAN TEMPTRESS* in this chapter; an unnamed P-47 in chapter 3; and two unnamed C-47s in chapter 4. No photos of this nose art after the bomber was stripped back to bare metal are known; perhaps it was removed altogether, but the second photo shows what the author believes to be the LHS of this bomber photographed at Clark Field ca. April 1945. The B-24 is still in 530th markings of the late 1944 period, and the bomb log shows fifty-five missions (according to the previously mentioned website, "*FRISCO FRANNIE*" flew her fifty-fifth mission in April 1945).

NOSE ART OF THE 5TH AIR FORCE

FRIVOLOUS SAL, Consolidated B-24, unidentified serial number, artist unknown, unidentified BS, 43rd BG. Note the positioning of the word *FRIVOLOUS*, with the V framing the pin-up's nether regions; as with the work of other artists who attempted to include such detail (see, for example, the 90th BG's *PISTOL PACKIN' MAMA* in this chapter), it is suspected that, similarly, this pin-up would have been required to be less revealing. Photos of *FRIVOLOUS SAL* do appear to be scarce, lending weight to the argument that the artwork or B-24 (or both) was or were not around for long, but without an airplane serial number, it is not possible to be conclusive. It is interesting to note, however, that the pin-up seems to have been added in theater, since the extended arm has been painted over the mounting plate for the radar aerials.

Gallant Lady / LADY LYNN, Consolidated B-24, 42-109991, artist unknown, 64th BS, 43rd BG. Here we see the same plane and artwork (a copy of the December 1943 Varga Girl) and its transition from *Gallant Lady* to *LADY LYNN*. *At top*, a slightly indistinct view of *Gallant Lady* following arrival at Townsville, Australia, ca. October 1943; *middle*, with old and new names after the decision by the assigned pilot, Lt. Joseph C. Cox, to rename the bomber in honor of his wife, Lynn, and, *bottom*, with one of two versions seen of Mrs Cox's name. This B-24 and another ten-man crew (not including Cox) failed to return to Nadzab from a mission on June 4, 1944.

"GEORGIA PEACH", Martin B-26, 40-1415, artist unknown, 33rd BS, 22nd BG. The B-26s of the 5th AF were in action against the Japanese from April 1942 onward, and on that basis, this must have been one of the first pin-up nose art paintings to have been added to any 5th AF bomber. Unfortunately, just when that happened is not known with certainty, but it may have been as early as May 1942 (for another early 5th AF B-26 with pin-up nose art, see *Ou'r Gal*). The plane was flown by a number of different crews, but just who it was who had the Georgia connection has not been established. After limited service with the 33rd BS, this B-26 was sent back to Australia for a complete overhaul and paint removal, after which it was assigned to the 19th BS and was renamed *FURY* (see photo in chapter 7).

Gladys, Consolidated B-24, 44-40364, artist Jack Eipper, 319th BS, 90th BG. She was formerly *Jini* (q.v.), and this photo was taken at Garbutt, Townsville, Queensland, in the immediate postwar period (note that the aircraft armament has already been removed). The record card for this B-24 indicates that it was received by the 5th AF in May 1944 and salvaged in theater postwar, but just where this occurred is not known. For other late-war nonnude 319th BS nose art examples, see *Lovely Louise*, *Miss Kiwanis*, *Phyllis J. of WORCESTER*, and *THE PUGNOSE PRINCESS* in this chapter.

Gloria C II, Douglas A-20, 43-9114, artist unknown, 386th BS, 312th BG. Research for *Rampage of the Roarin' '20s* established that while this A-20 had originally served with the 3rd BG, it was received by the 386th BS in March 1944 and assigned to Lt. Paul F. Teague, who requested that the unidentified artist add a likeness of the August pin-up from the 1944 *Esquire Varga Calendar* to the LHS. After that, the name was added; Gloria Ceely was Teague's then girlfriend (later they married). Teague flew many missions in this aircraft before returning stateside in October 1944, after which the A-20 was renamed *O'Riley's Daughter II* (q.v.).

NOSE ART OF THE 5TH AIR FORCE

GOLDEN LADY, Consolidated B-24, 42-40914 (unconfirmed), artist Joseph C. DiMauro, 321st BS, 90th BG, later CRTC. DiMauro, nose gunner in M. L. "Shad" Shaddox's B-24 crew, painted this pin-up on both sides of the nose of this B-24 following the aircraft's acceptance tests at Herington Army Airfield, Kansas. Shaddox's crew were responsible for ferrying the bomber to Australia and expected that they would stay with her when their posting came through, but following their arrival at Townsville in July 1943, they were assigned to the 64th BS, 43rd BG, while *GOLDEN LADY* went to the 90th BG. The golden nude went without a name for at least four missions, as seen in the first photo, after which the moniker by which it had become known was added. *GOLDEN LADY* saw long service with the 90th BG before being pensioned off to the CRTC at Nadzab. The two other views used here show the RHS of *GOLDEN LADY* in her heyday with the 90th, and a LHS close-up taken later, while with the CRTC, displaying more than a hundred mission symbols (the abbreviation AP in the CRTC stencil may be for Airplane Pool). See also *HEAVENLY BODY*.

GONE WITH THE WIND, Consolidated B-24, 41-24286, artist unknown, 400th BS, 90th BG. This B-24 started out with the name *"San Jose Special"* on both sides of the nose, but the name on the LHS was subsequently changed to *GONE WITH THE WIND* and the artwork shown here added. The new name obviously had been taken from the award-winning 1939 film of the same name, but, clearly, that is where the connection ends. The photo below shows the LHS after 110 missions had been flown (the hundredth being that specially marked eleventh from right in the bottom row), while the wider shot was taken later, after another ten mission symbols have been added to the middle row and the gusty conditions of the wind have been given a greater emphasis. Also note the damage to the radar aerials in the intervening time, and the change in the style of enemy aircraft victory symbols, from miniature plan-view aircraft to Rising Sun flags. The pilot's name, just visible in both photos, is Lt. G. Kubiskie. The name of the copilot, Lt. G. L. Richey, appeared under the cockpit window on the RHS, where another bomb log was maintained and the *"San Jose Special"* name (Kubiskie hailed from there) was retained. The color variations that are evident in the two images are due to the use of different film types.

Good Pickin's, Consolidated B-24, unidentified serial number, artist unknown, unit(s) unidentified. This photo is taken from a strip of 35 mm contact prints of late-war B-24 nose art, possibly taken on Okinawa, including *Cherrie, seen earlier*, and, on that basis has been included as more than likely being a 5th AF aircraft. The pin-up was copied from the illustration on the 1940s pin-up card shown at left. These cards were available to the general public through vending machines that could be found in amusement arcades. An earlier 5th AF B-24 with nose art based on the same illustration was the 22nd BG's *TEMPTATION* (q.v.).

"GRRR", Consolidated B-24, unidentified serial number, artist unknown, 320th BS, 90th BG. A growl more than a name, this was another late-war "Moby Dick" squadron B-24 that combined the whale-look nose markings as well as a pin-up; for others, see *AIR POCKET*, *Cherrie*, *DISPLAY OF ARMS*, and *LIVE WIRE* in this chapter. Note the playful, stylized, twin-tailed "whale" in 320th BS markings included in the painting, an unusual but nice touch.

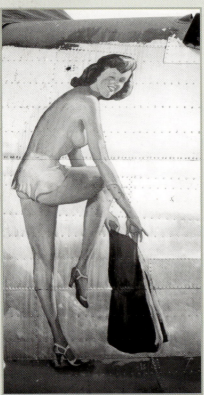

gunmoll 2nd, Consolidated B-24, 42-40970, artist unknown, 319th BS, 90th BG. Close examination of the stenciled data panel in the photo above (*left of the pin-up's head*) confirms the aircraft serial number as quoted here to be correct. Other researchers have suggested that another 319th B-24, *THE STRIP POLKA* (q.v.), was 42-40970, but this author has not been able to confirm that, although it can be said that it appears that both aircraft were of the same subtype (B-24D-CO-120). Certainly, both B-24s carried different artworks. The RHS artwork was an accurate copy of Gil Elvgren's 1939 pin-up titled *French Dressing*, and while the color of the dress the pin-up is holding was lost a little on the olive-drab background, as seen at far right the camouflage paint was later removed, presenting a better opportunity for the artwork to stand out. For a later, perhaps last, photo of the RHS artwork, see chapter 7.

Gypsy and *GYPSY*, Consolidated B-24, 42-41133, artist Dick Ebbeson, various BSs, 380th BG and Consolidated B-24, 44-40366, artist unknown, 33rd BS, 22nd BG. Both these pin-ups were based on the unnamed April pin-up that appeared in the 1943 *Esquire Varga Calendar*, yet both aircraft carried the same name. The 380th *Gypsy* (*below*) was in squadron service by November 1943, and its nose art was probably added the following month or January 1944, it being during that time that it was flown by the group commander, Col. William Miller, who named it such because he felt that he was leading a band of gypsies who had no permanent home. That *Gypsy* was lost in March 1944, but the other *GYPSY* was not received by the 33rd BS until almost three months later (becoming the first natural-metal-finish [NMF] B-24 in that squadron), so there appears to have been no obvious connection between the two. The 33rd BS work was later scraped off and replaced by a new pin-up named *Slightly DANGEROUS* (q.v.).

Gypsy Rose, Boeing B-17, 41-9193, artist unknown, 65th BS, 43rd BG. This was a former 435th BS, 19th BG B-17 subsequently passed to the 43rd BG in November 1942. Early service was with the 403rd BS, after which, in January 1943, it was transferred to the 65th BS, where the artwork and name were added in tribute to America's well-known Queen of Burlesque, Gypsy Rose Lee (1911–70), although, reportedly, Lee never showed as much bare skin as the artwork suggested. This photo was taken on May 18, 1943, only six days before *Gypsy Rose* was lost when ditched off the northern coast of New Guinea after running low on fuel while returning from a raid on Rabaul. All the crew survived the ditching and were able to be safely returned to duty, but the copilot, Lt. William J. Sarsfield, was lost as captain of *naughty but nice* (q.v.) a little more than a month later.

HEAVEN CAN WAIT, Consolidated B-24, 42-41216, artist unknown, 320th BS, 90th BG. The name given to this angelic pin-up was undoubtedly a spin-off from a 1943 film of the same name that was nominated for three Academy Awards. So popular was the name, in fact, that at least another nine B-24s, most with accompanying pin-up artwork, are known to have existed. This was the only one to serve with the 5th AF, though, and it was lost following a six-plane attack on Wewak on March 11, 1944, all eleven crew members losing their lives. It was not until October 2017 that it was possible to confirm that wreckage from the bomber had been found in Hansa Bay.

Heavenly Body, Consolidated B-24, 42-73116, artist Dick Ebbeson, 528th BS, 380th BG. In this photo and the next, we see two examples of another popular World War II bomber name. This one was based on an undated work by pin-up artist Al Buell (1910–96), titled *Lovely to Look At*. *Heavenly Body* flew with the 528th BS from January 1944 until lost on a weather reconnaissance mission on March 14, 1945. All aboard escaped the doomed airplane, but only six men, from what was a newly assigned crew, were subsequently rescued from the South China Sea. This chapter's heading photo is also of this B-24.

HEAVENLY BODY, Consolidated B-24, 42-73484, artist Joseph C. DiMauro, 64th BS, 43rd BG. Mention has already been made of artist DiMauro in association with his *GOLDEN LADY* pin-up seen earlier. The full-figured *HEAVENLY BODY*, based on the December 1943 *Esquire* Varga Girl pin-up, was another of his popular works and, unlike *GOLDEN LADY*, was signed off by him. He died in 2001, his son-in-law, Hugh "Skip" Gibson, subsequently commenting that following training as an illustrator, "he honed his talent on the sides of warplanes." Currently, however, *GOLDEN LADY* and *HEAVENLY BODY* are the only two examples of aircraft nose art that have positively been identified as DiMauro works. Research for the *Ken's Men against the Empire* 43rd BG history concluded that this B-24 flew her last combat mission on May 28, 1944.

HARD TO GET, Douglas A-20, 43-9427, artist Al G. Merkling, 8th BS, 3rd BG. There were, indeed, very few white women in the SWPA during World War II, and so this was a name to which servicemen would have quickly related. Whether Merkling had already decided on the name prior to the completion of the artwork is unknown, but the two views afford readers the opportunity to spot the differences made prior to the work being considered completed. This was Merkling's only artwork on an A-20, and while it is not known when the work was done, it seems that it was short lived, since this airplane was lost in action on June 12, 1944.

Hell's Belle, Consolidated B-24, 42-41222, first artwork artist unknown, second artwork artist William B. McBroom (unconfirmed), 530th BS, 380th BG. This B-24 arrived in Australia with the stretched-out pin-up in place on both sides of the nose, as shown at top right and bottom left. After the nose "greenhouse" was replaced by a turret at the Townsville Air Depot and the bomber was assigned to the 380th BG, it seems that someone there, a chaplain perhaps, did not like the existing artwork (was the pose considered too provocative?). As a result, it was subsequently painted over and replaced by a copy of Elvgren's popular artwork *French Dressing*, as seen at bottom right, probably by 530th BS artist Bill McBroom (that is suspected to be his sign-off below the pin-up's raised foot). According to website 380th.org, this B-24 participated in a total of eighty missions between November 21, 1943, and January 7, 1945, based primarily in Australia's Northern Territory except for a stint in New Guinea between December 1943 and January 1944, when twenty-one missions were flown in a twenty-one-day period. *Hell's Belle* was damaged in an air-to-air battle with enemy fighters while on a reconnaissance mission on May 9, 1944, but it was back at Fenton from the Townsville Air Depot two months later. By then, if not earlier, the camouflage paint had probably been stripped away and the nose art removed, since no photos showing the pin-up girl on other than a camouflaged background are known to exist. A subsequent survey of the airplane's condition before the 380th's move to the Philippines evidently considered that this B-24 was past its prime, and, accordingly, she was salvaged, probably at Darwin.

"HELL'S BELLE", Consolidated B-24, 41-24290, artist unknown, 400th BS, 90th BG. This glasshouse-nosed B-24 was, perhaps, one of the first 5th AF heavy bombers with nose art involving a topless female to be featured in newspapers, when an official photo of it "after scoring a direct hit on a 5,000-ton Jap transport off Kairiru Island on the north coast of New Guinea" was released for general publication. The photo, however, was taken from a distance, and the detail of the nose art was not readily apparent. Over the February–May 1944 period, *"HELL'S BELLE"* was one of nine 5th AF B-24s passed to the RAAF for use as crew trainers, and a last photo of it, minus nose art, can be found in chapter 7.

HERE'S HOWE, North American B-25, unidentified serial number, 90th BS, 3rd BG. This B-25 was assigned to Lt. (later captain) "Chuck" Howe, and it is seen here in two photos, the first (*left*) at Townsville soon after its arrival from the US with just the pin-up in place, and the second in what is suspected to have been a late 1943 photo taken by SSgt. Joseph E. Hartman, 5th AF Combat Camera Unit, with the CO of the 90th from July 1943, Maj. John "Jock" P. Henebry, in the cockpit talking to crew chief Sgt. Richard C. Gentry. One of Henebry's first decisions as CO was that his planes would carry shark's-teeth nose markings, more examples of which can be found in chapter 6. Note how the protective antiblast panel added (at Townsville) forward of the side guns has necessitated some alterations to the original look of the pin-up. Henebry left the squadron in October and became CO of the 3rd BG in November. A last photo of this nose art can be found in chapter 7.

HIP PARADE, Consolidated B-24, 44-40430, artist unknown, 64th BS, 43rd BG. A much-photographed late-war B-24M, the nose art is seen here up close and at a distance in flight (the B-24 in the background is 44-40428, *COCKTAIL HOUR* [q.v.]). The diagonal fin stripe clearly visible in the latter photo was the 64th BS squadron marking. Note too the late-war reintroduction of prewar-style red-and-white rudder stripes; this decoration was proving popular on many 5th AF NMF planes by this time. *HIP PARADE* survived the war and is believed to have ended her days on Biak.

HiT PARADER and *HIT PARADER II*, Consolidated B-24s, 42-41087 and unidentified serial number, both artists unknown, both 319th BS, 90th BG. Reportedly, *HiT PARADER* had originally been named *The MILK RUN* on the LHS, but both the name and an accompanying small illustration of a diaper-wearing baby holding a bottle were done away with in favor of this new name and pin-up art on both sides. The photo at the top shows *HiT PARADER*'s RHS artwork (on the LHS appeared a marching drum majorette complete with bass drum), while below is *HIT PARADER II*'s RHS artwork, inspired, perhaps, by an Earl Moran pin-up. *HiT PARADER* and crew were lost without trace in the course of a six-ship strike against Hollandia on the night of February 28, 1944. Wiley O. Woods Jr., in his detailed history of the 90th BG, records that two of the six B-24s involved were lost that night, and notes that none of the six crews had ever flown a night mission before. As to *HIT PARADER II*, apart from the fact that she flew at least twenty-one missions, without a serial number to check, no further details are currently known.

"*HITT AND MISS*", North American B-25, 41-30040, artist unknown, 498th BS, 345th BG. An early example of a pin-up riding a bomb (for other examples in this chapter, see B-25 *BLONDE BOMBER*, A-20 *Classy Chassis*, B-24 *Firtil Myrtle*, B-24 *JUNE BRIDE*, B-26 *"MARGIE"*, and B-25s *MONTANA MAID* and *NEAR MISS*), this B-25 was assigned to the 498th BS in March 1943 and is seen here at the Townsville Air Depot prior to conversion as a strafer. Given that the pilot assigned to this ship was Lt. Earl J. Hitt, the name and artwork followed soon after, but after the strafer conversions the 498th started repainting the noses of their B-25s in what became a falcon-head squadron marking, as a result of which the bomb-riding pin-up did not last long. The name, however, was subsequently reapplied. This B-25, in the hands of another crew, was lost in action over New Guinea on March 29, 1944.

"HO HUM", Consolidated B-24, 42-109983, artist "Short," 400th BS, 90th BG. This beautiful, larger-than-life artwork was based on the Alberto Vargas gatefold pin-up from the April 1944 edition of *Esquire* magazine. The nose art was not initially signed off; this came only sometime after the first row of twenty mission symbols was added, perhaps as a result of inquiries received as to who the talented artist was. This was certainly a classy work; in the view above, note how the mission symbols at the right-hand end of the top two rows have been given the impression of being partly covered by the pin-up's right-side arm. The second photo is a rare view of an unidentified squadron member adding one or more mission symbols to the top row; just how many missions she completed prior to her loss on April 8, 1945, is not known, but at least sixty-five, as seen above. The air-to-air photo shows not only the mixture of official and unofficial markings in use late war (note the 90th's version of the "Jolly Roger" on the vertical fin, with a grinning skull above crossed bombs, high visibility tail number, and, in common with the just-seen *HIP PARADE*, the reintroduction of pre-Pacific war rudder stripes), but the ventral gun position and the adjacent open section of bomb bay. While this photo was probably not taken en route to or from a bombing mission, the calm surroundings belie the fact that wartime flying, even at the best of times, was fraught with danger; *"HO HUM"* was lost due to an onboard fuel explosion from which only four of the crew survived. As for the artist, nothing further is known about him except that he was also responsible for the artwork for the 319th BS's *BUTCHER'S DAUGHTER* (q.v.).

HOBO QUEEN II, Consolidated B-32, 42-108532, artist unknown, 386th BS, 312th BG. This B-32 was one of the first three of this new very heavy bomber type to see action against the Japanese. That was at the end of May 1945, as part of the original four-week test program under the command of Col. Frank R. Cook. Cook named this particular B-32 after a globetrotting B-29 trials airplane he had taken to Europe and, later, India in 1944. Another five B-32s were received by the 386th BS in August, but by then the two atomic bombs had been dropped and the war was almost over. One of the other original three B-32s also received pin-up nose art; that was *The Lady is Fresh* (q.v.). The original artworks on both these aircraft were painted under the LHS cockpit window, but following the delivery of these planes to the 312th BG, the old artworks were removed, and new, larger works (using the same names) were added behind the cockpit area, centered between the two forward fuselage side windows. It would seem likely that this was done simply to keep up with the size of other bomber nose art encountered in these last days of World War II, particularly given that these B-32s were new kids on the block. These two photos show *HOBO QUEEN*'s original and revised artworks. For details of the fate of this bomber and two more photos of her, see chapter 7.

HOT BUDDY, Consolidated B-24, unidentified serial number, artist unknown, unidentified BS, 90th BG (unconfirmed). One of the photos of new B-24 nose art purchased by the author for this project; despite the impressive bomb log, nothing is currently known of this bomber or its fate (the name, at least, seems to have been only recently added, going by the freshly drawn chalk lines above and below it). Bomb group identification is also tentative but is based on the fact that this and some other 90th BG nose art photos in this volume (e.g., *"COOKIE"* [RHS view], *gunmoll 2nd* [LHS view], *MARGIE*, and *PATCHES*), purchased, it should be pointed out, at different times from different sellers, all feature the same stamp on the reverse: "PASSED BY EXAMINER 16354."

NOSE ART OF THE 5TH AIR FORCE

HOT ROCKS, Consolidated B-24, 42-73489, artist unknown, 531st BS, 380th BG. Reportedly named by the squadron commander, Capt. Francis M. Seale, this artwork was copied from the 1944 *Esquire Varga Calendar* and applied to this B-24 probably early that year, prior to its camouflage being stripped back to bare metal. After the paint was removed, the plane was given new artwork and name, *THE SULTAN'S DAUGHTER* (q.v.). Altogether this B-24 flew sixty missions from Australia / New Guinea prior to the 380th BG's transfer to the Philippines, but just how many of these were flown as *HOT ROCKS* is not currently known.

HOTSEE!, North American B-25, unidentified serial number, artist unknown, unit(s) unidentified. There must have been a story about this artwork, but what was it? The dress of the swordsman suggests that its origins lie in a seventeenth-century story, perhaps the popular novel relating to that era, *The Three Musketeers*. Given that this is the only photo seen by the author of this artwork, it may be that it was short lived, but details are lacking. One suggestion has been that this B-25 may been used by a 22nd BG squadron, but there is no reference to it in the bomb group's 2006 authoritative history, *Revenge of the Red Raiders*. Via Malcolm Long

HOW'M-I-DOIN', Consolidated B-24, 42-41223, artist unknown, 319th BS, 90th BG, later CRTC. Seen here both early on and toward the end of its active service; the size of the bomb stencil used for the mission log on this B-24 was a particularly prominent feature. It is interesting to note that when ordered to be stripped of its olive-drab camouflage paint, the entire nose (i.e., the section forward of the main plane) was left as was, presumably due to concerns over losing the originality of the unofficial markings added. For a last look at the nose art and mission symbols (still showing, it appears, seventy-one missions) while this B-24 awaited her fate at Nadzab postwar, see chapter 7.

HOW'S YOUR OLE' TOMATO, North American B-25, 41-30664, artist unknown, 2nd BS, 22nd BG, later 500th BS, 345th BG. Again, what a pity the who, where, and when of this photo are not known. Given the lack of a bomb log, though, then it would seem that this photo was taken early on, around August 1943. This B-25 remained with the 2nd BS as squadron number 14 (a little difficult to make out in this photo, but just behind the nose cupola) until January 1944 and was later transferred to the 500th BS, 345th BG, but was lost on a training flight near Nadzab on March 13, 1944, all six men aboard losing their lives. Whether the pin-up and name were retained while the B-25 was in 345th BG hands is not currently known.

"I'LL BE AROUND", Consolidated B-24, 42-100037, artist unknown, 63rd BS, 43rd BG. Another of the many artworks based on Vargas's January offering from the 1944 *Esquire Calendar* (see introduction), according to research by Glenn R. Horton Jr., this one was painted at Fairfield-Suisun Army Air Base (now known as Travis Air Force Base), California, prior to the flight across the Pacific. The same artist was also responsible for *"MISS LIBERTY"* (q.v.), *"SWEET SIXTEEN"* (q.v.), and at least one other pin-up on a B-24 that subsequently flew with the 13th AF. *"I'LL BE AROUND"* was not around for long, only a few months, as a result of a takeoff accident on Owi Island on July 26, 1944. In this accident, one crew member, the bombardier, lost his life.

IMPATIENT VIRGIN, North American B-25, 41-30046, artist unknown, 498th BS, 345th BG. These two photos show this B-25 prior to and after the strafer modification and falcon squadron insignia were added, although only the "neck ruffle" component of the latter can be seen. Note a possible change in lettering color and the addition of the name "Hallum" in the second photo; "Lyn" Hallum designed the squadron insignia and evidently signed off some of his work (for more information on him, also see *NEAR MISS* in this chapter). This B-25 flew with the 498th BS from March 1943 until it was damaged over Boram, New Guinea, on November 27, 1943, and had to be ditched at sea. It is considered that all crew members survived that ditching, but with no chance of rescue, they were captured. Their fate remains unknown.

"*Je Reviens*", Consolidated B-24, 42-72808, artist unknown, 529th BS, 380th BG. Translated as meaning "I'll be back" (a 312th BG Douglas A-20 carried the same name), the name of a popular French perfume line of the day by the House of Worth, the nose art painting in this case was based on the *Esquire* September 1943 Varga Girl and was probably added at Fairfield-Suisun Army Air Base, California (by the end of the war, the largest such base on the US West Coast), just after that issue of the magazine "hit" the newsstands (this B-24 left Fairfield-Suisun, with the destination Townsville, Australia, on September 16, 1943). These photos show the nose area of this B-24 prior to and after her original nose glasshouse was exchanged for a turret, work that was carried out at the Townsville Air Depot. Note in the photo below the notation added to the nose, and the recently added and as-yet-unpainted turret strengthener. She was subsequently assigned to the 529th BS in October 1943 and flew a total of fifty-seven missions between November 1943 and August 1944. "*Je Reviens*" was reportedly struck off charge in October 1944 after being salvaged back at Townsville.

ISLAND QUEEN, Consolidated B-24, 42-100230, artist Harold H. Heighton, 408th BS, 22nd BG. Heighton was granted permission to paint the name and artwork on this B-24 as a member of the ferry crew responsible in early 1944 for delivering her to the SWPA (he was copilot), the inspiration for the work coming from that year's *Esquire Varga Calendar*. There was some hope, or expectation even, that these B-24s and ferry crews would stay together once assigned to a squadron, but given that both generally parted ways on arrival in Australia, it was unlikely that that would ever happen. In this case, though, both did wind up in the 22nd BG, but the crew went to the 2nd BS while the B-24 went to the 408th. *ISLAND QUEEN* remained in frontline service until October 1944, later becoming a source of spare parts, and was subsequently written off before war's end.

In The Mood, Douglas A-20, 43-9669 (unconfirmed), artist unknown, 672nd BS, 417th BG. "In the Mood" was a very popular Glenn Miller hit from 1939–40, so popular, in fact, that in 2004 it was inducted into the Library of Congress National Recording Registry, but the tune's lyrics were somewhat sedate when compared with this artwork. The assigned pilot was Lt. "Art" R. Gresens, and his crew chief (whose name is partly visible in this photo) was TSgt. Doug Dallafior. 43-9669 was one of four 417th BG A-20s lost on "Black Sunday," April 16, 1944, while returning to their base at Saidor in very bad weather and poor visibility. Gresens actually made it back to Saidor, but two crashed planes on the runway were difficult to avoid and his A-20 struck one, a B-25, causing an undercarriage leg to collapse and *In the Mood* to veer off to the right and hit an embankment. Fortunately, there were no injuries. Note in the photo the large background to the pin-up, which covered over not only the airplane data panel but also the bomb log; perhaps the latter was reapplied later.

JACK POT, Consolidated B-24, 42-40280, artist unknown, 321st BS, 90th BG. This was probably the only wartime aircraft nose art that combined a pin-up with some part (in this case, the coin hopper) of a "one-armed bandit" (slot machine), but the prize was much more than the coins! The three bell symbols in a row at the top of the artwork (in fact, three Liberty Bell symbols) confirmed for the player that the maximum amount possible had been won. This B-24 crashed in the Port Moresby area after a midair collision with another 321st BS ship, *JOLTIN' JANIE II*, on the return flight from a mission that had to be aborted due to bad weather. None of her crew survived.

"*Jezebelle*" / *Jezebelle*, Consolidated B-24, 42-72953, artist(s) unknown, 529th BS, 380th BG. Jezebel (note spelling; reportedly also spelled Jezabel) was "the bad girl of the Bible," and her name became a readily recognizable bad-girl reference. Assigned to the 529th BS in November 1943, she is seen here both in early and later life; note in the earlier photo the well-painted 5th AF insignia on the nosewheel cover, possibly short lived given the official view that displaying identifiable unit insignia on USAAF aircraft during wartime was not permitted. The second view is suspected to have been taken at Biak at the end of this B-24's service and shows how the same B-24 looked long after the camouflage paint and original pin-up were scrubbed off. Replacing that earlier pin-up was an unhappy newlywed thumbing a ride from Niagara Falls to Reno, Nevada, where liberal divorce laws could provide a quick end to a marriage. The new nose art, based on Gil Elvgren's calendar art picture *The High Sign*, may have been based on someone's personal experience, given the precise mileage quoted! For other examples of nose art with a bad-girl theme, see *SATAN'S BABY*, *Satan's Secretary*, and '*SATANS SISTER*', which follow.

Jini, Consolidated B-24, 44-40364, artist Jack Eipper, 319th BS, 90th BG. It seems that "Jini" was the nickname of the artist's girlfriend (later his wife), Geneva, but just how long her name remained on the B-24 is not known. What is known is that other photos show the same artwork named *Gladys* (q.v.) in much-smaller writing. On the basis of the fact that one of these photos was taken in the immediate postwar period, it does seem most likely that *Jini*, rather than *Gladys*, was this B-24's original name.

"Juarez Whistle", Consolidated B-24, 42-40496, artist unknown, 530th BS, 380th BG. With artwork copied from *Esquire* magazine's Varga Girl for June 1943, this, on the face of it, unusually named B-24 was a reminder of happy days for 380th BG personnel in training, whistling at the pretty young ladies of Ciudad Juárez, Mexico, while on their time off from Biggs Field, El Paso, Texas, across the other side of the Rio Grande. The B-24 was one of the first assigned to the 530th and flew at least twenty-seven missions with the squadron, the last in December 1943. Although reportedly damaged in February 1944 and then salvaged, this B-24 must have been repaired since it went on to survive wartime service to be left at Biak, with original nose art and camouflage still in place. All photos of the RHS nose art seen by the author show an officer's name under the copilot's window, but it is too indistinct to make out in this photo, and its significance is currently unknown. As with the photo of *Flying Fannie*, seen earlier, note the condensation of moisture on the bomber's upper surfaces, which has subsequently run down the sides.

JUGGLIN' JOSIE, Consolidated B-24, 42-41237, artist William B. McBroom (unconfirmed), 530th BS, 380th BG. This B-24 was delivered to Townsville in October 1943 and assigned to the 530th BS, flying its first mission on November 17. *JOSIE* was deployed to New Guinea during December 1943 and early January 1944 and returned to Fenton, Northern Territory of Australia, from where she participated in a massed 380th strike against Ambon on the nineteenth. After that, for reasons unknown, *JOSIE* was rarely used operationally, perhaps seeing more use in a training role. On July 25, 1944, while being used to check out a new 529th BS copilot, she was involved in a crash landing at Darwin and was subsequently salvaged. A last photo of her can be found in chapter 7. The similarities between the *LI'L D'-ICER* artwork (q.v.) and this one have led to the author's suspicion that both were by McBroom, although neither appear to have been signed off by him.

JUNGLE QUEEN II / JUNGLE QUEEN, Consolidated B-24, 42-40510, artist unknown, 529th BS, 380th BG, later 65th BS, 43rd BG. The *JUNGLE QUEEN II* artwork was, it seems, added in the US and named after an earlier forced landing in Central America by the crew that subsequently delivered her to Australia. She was one of the first B-24s assigned to the 529th BS, and her 380th BG days ended in December 1943, when it was flown to Townsville for the installation of a nose turret. Subsequently transferred to the 43rd BG, her original name was overpainted, and she simply became *JUNGLE QUEEN*, as shown in the photo below. Note also in this photo that while the original 380th bomb log showing twenty-one missions was retained, it has been affected by the need to fit a replacement panel. Similarly, replacement panels visible at the middle bottom of the photo can be seen to have affected the pin-up. The two symbols for enemy fighters shot down were claimed on the *QUEEN*'s first mission from Australia, to Koepang, Timor, on June 11, 1943. The aircraft was eventually pensioned off at Nadzab and is mentioned in a 1946 article reproduced in appendix 3.

JUNGLE QUEEN, North American B-25, 41-30066, artist unknown, 408th BS, 22nd BG, later 71st BS, 38th BG and 388th BS, 312th BG. Transferred from the 500th BS, 345th BG, under the name *Mary "F"* (q.v.), to the 408th Squadron in September 1943, soon after she was renamed *JUNGLE QUEEN* and the RHS pin-up given a decorative circular background (*above*). *JUNGLE QUEEN* was transferred out of the 408th in January 1944 and subsequently moved on to the 71st BS, 38th BG, until around August. According to the 312th BG history, *Rampage of the Roarin' '20s*, *JUNGLE QUEEN* was later received by that group's 388th BS but her days were numbered, and she was salvaged at Nadzab (see photo in chapter 7).

JUNE BRIDE, Consolidated B-24, unidentified serial number, artist unknown, 403rd BS, 43rd BG, later CRTC (unconfirmed). Despite the lengthy and multifaceted research carried out for the *Ken's Men against the Empire* volumes, nothing more than the suggestion that this B-24 survived 403rd service to be passed to the CRTC has so far been established. Another photo of this nose art shows fourteen mission symbols in place below the cockpit window.

The K.O. KID, Consolidated B-24, 44-40342, artist unknown, 528th BS, 380th BG. For all intents and purposes, the name of this B-24 referred to delivering a knockout blow against the Japanese, but it was also a reference to assigned pilot Lt. Kenneth O. Hunt. This B-24 flew the first of more than thirty missions from Australia on June 6, 1944, the last on February 2, 1945 (Hunt flew only five of these), and she subsequently flew more than fifty more from the Philippines and one from Okinawa. She was known to have been flown back to the Philippines on July 25, 1945, where it has been reported that *The KID* was subsequently salvaged postwar; it is possible that her last flight was actually to Biak, which is where the majority of the 380th BG's unwanted B-24s ended their days.

KANSAS-CITY KITTY, Consolidated B-24, 44-41255, artist Charles R. Chesnut, 33rd BS, 22nd BG. Although it has been suggested that Chesnut, like so many other nose art artists, based his works on Alberto Vargas's beautiful pin-ups, it has not been possible for this author to tie any of them back to Vargas, so clearly his inspirations lay elsewhere. In the case of *KANSAS-CITY KITTY*, which was named in honor of crew chief TSgt. Charles F. Donnelly, who hailed from Kansas City, it was copied from a photo going around at the time of a nude model outstretched on a sofa, over which had been draped a leopard skin rug, a background, however, that Chesnut decided not to include. The two photos here show the artwork before and after the name was added. *KITTY* survived the war and at least forty-seven missions but was subsequently scrapped, due, perhaps, to minor postwar damage.

KAY-18, Consolidated F-7, 44-40656, artist unknown, 4th Reconnaissance Squadron (Long Range, Photographic). She was attached to the 5th AF only from May 3, 1945, "for administration, supply and flight control," but nevertheless a number of the squadron's NMF F-7Bs (there were eight on strength as of the beginning of June, twelve by the end of August) featured pin-ups; other examples included in this chapter are PHOTO JEANNE, THIS ABOVE ALL, and WELL DEVELOPED, as well as OVER EXPOSED, a 4th Squadron F-7A. The name *KAY-18* was derived from the Fairchild Aerial Camera Corp.'s K-18 medium/high-altitude reconnaissance camera, one of the camera types used by the squadron (that is a representation of a K-18 camera in the illustration). Note squadron identification 4-J.

"Kentucky Virgin", Consolidated B-24, 42-41073, artist B. Balliet, 65th BS, 90th BG. This was the B-24 assigned to Kentucky native Maj. Joshua H. Barnes Jr., commanding officer of the 65th BS, ca. October 1943, but the image and name with its subtext *"but not for long"!* together with the "going off like a firecracker" suggestion (below the pin-up is a cherry bomb firecracker with its fuse lit) seems to have led to complaints from concerned chaplains. By way of a compromise, the subtext was painted over and the B-24's name changed to read *V. . .– SURE POP* (q.v.). Little is known of the artist, and this was perhaps the only bomber artwork he completed, but more of his works (all on C-47s) can be found in chapter 5.

Lady from Leyte, Consolidated B-24, 44-40807, artist Ernest W. Bako, 64th BS, 43rd BG. Bako completed two nose art paintings incorporating Philippine Islands place-names, with both this one and *Manila Calling* (q.v.) being very similar in style since they were based on a popular pin-up photo of actress Carole Landis. During World War II, Bako served in the US Navy in the 60th NCB (this painting was signed off "E. W. BAKO 60th CB"), and postwar he received his master of arts degree from Kansas State University and became an art teacher. Art remained an important part of his life until his death at the age of eighty-two, in 2004. This B-24 was most likely in service from around mid-1944 but, reportedly, was salvaged in January 1945.

The Lady is Fresh, Consolidated B-32, 42-108529, artist unknown, 386th BS, 312th BG. Another of the first three B-32s to see action against the Japanese, like *HOBO QUEEN II* (q.v.) it featured a pin-up on the LHS of the nose from the outset. And as with *HOBO QUEEN II*, the original work was removed and a new one, seen here, larger than the original, was added just behind the cockpit area, centered between the first two side windows. Postwar this was one of four B-32s returned to the US from the Pacific, but, as with the B-24s, it was no longer required and later scrapped.

LADY LIL, North American B-25, 44-29577, artist unknown, 498th BS, 345th BG. Seen in an aircraft park (probably at or near Clark Field) is this late-war B-25 described in the detailed and comprehensive 345th BG history, *Warpath across the Pacific*, as "the most colorfully-marked 498th aircraft flown by the Squadron in 1945." Interested readers will find a ca. June 1945 photo of *LADY LIL* in that volume, but this shot was taken later (perhaps just after war's end, although note that the machine guns in the dorsal turret have yet to be removed) and shows that some other, previously undocumented, changes had occurred in the intervening few months. First, while the name had originally appeared across the area separated by the black-and-white zigzag "neck ruffle," the area to the left of the zigzag (representing a falcon's head feathers) was subsequently repainted in a much-darker green, as shown, and it seems that those parts of the name in the "head" area were painted over (as was the formerly extended right leg of the Vargaesque pin-up). The name *LIL* does seem to have been retained though; if the author's eyesight is correct, it can be found between the renewed zigzag and the pin-up's RHS forearm. The pin-up looks as though she is missing some hair now too. Finally, note that while it has been suggested that this B-25 was stripped of her original factory finish, clearly this work had not been completed when this photo was taken. Once the war ended, it may never have been.

"Lady Luck", Consolidated B-24, 42-110116, artist Sgt. Wheatley, 528th BS, 380th BG. One of the most important roles for aircraft nose art was that of a good-luck charm, and, not surprisingly, the name *Lady Luck* was popular for that reason. As Glenn R. Horton Jr. comments in his comprehensive 380th Bomb Group history, *The Best in the Southwest*, this particular *"Lady Luck"* lived up to her name, surviving the war and at least ninety missions. Wheatley was also responsible for at least one other 380th BG pin-up, *Battle Weary* (q.v.).

"LADY LUCK", Consolidated B-24, 44-50795, artist unknown, 33rd BS, 22nd BG. This artwork was based on a popular character created by Chicago-based artist Paul Benson that was included in a portfolio of prints published by him in 1941, but despite the B-24's assignment to the 33rd BS late in the war, it failed to make it through to the end, crashing on takeoff from Lipa airfield near Manila on August 12, 1945. While the B-24 was totally destroyed and the crew's luck held out, eleven out of twenty paratroop passengers being carried in the bomb bay lost their lives.

The LAST STRAW, Boeing B-17, 41-2432, artist Ernie Vandal, 63rd BS, 43rd BG, later 69th TCS, 433rd TCG. This was another B-17 that had originally served with the 19th BG and was transferred to the 43rd BG (64th BS) in November 1942. Due to damage received on the ground during an enemy bombing raid on January 25, 1943, the necessary repairs took months, and the airplane was not flown again until June 17, 1943. In July it was transferred to the 63rd BS, and it was here that this almost three-dimensional pin-up, somewhat unusually painted over the rear nose compartment window, was added. *The LAST STRAW* served with the 63rd BS only until October 1943, and during that time the B-17F-style side gun window seen in the photo was also added. Subsequent service was with the 54th Troop Carrier Wing (TCW), and it seems most likely that the pin-up and name remained in existence during this time. In addition, the nose armament was further modified from two separate forward-firing machine guns to a twin mount.

Lak-a-Nuki, Douglas A-20, 43-9404, artist unknown, 389th BS, 312th BG. A photo of the LHS of this A-20 can be found in chapter 1. Apparently there was no name on the RHS, just this artwork, but all the nose armament appears to be named, and the .50 cal. machine gun visible in this photo has the stenciled name JUMPING JOE above it. As mentioned in chapter 1, this A-20 was on the 389th BS's books only from March to June 1944. After that, it was transferred to the 417th BG, but without, perhaps, both the name and artwork.

LAZY DAISY MAE, North American B-25, 43-36012, artist George M. Blackwell, 501st BS, 345th BG. Shown here both in unfinished and finished forms; see the photo caption for B-24 *DAISY MAE* in this chapter for brief background on this well-known and extremely popular cartoon character. This aircraft was one of more than a dozen new B-25J-11s assigned to the 501st BS in October 1944, five of which received nose art soon after, all by Blackwell, with names painted by Cpl. Joseph Merenda. The others were *APACHE PRINCESS*, *Cactus Kitten*, *Reina del PACIFICO*, and *WHITE WING*, photos of all of which can also be found in this chapter. This B-25 dropped out of a group formation en route to the Luzon invasion front on the morning of January 9, 1945, for reasons unknown, and was lost without trace. No remains of the aircraft or those aboard have ever been found.

Lewd Lady, North American B-25, 41-30521, artist unknown, 408th BS, 22nd BG, later 823rd BS, 38th BG. Its nose art was based on the September page from the 1943 *Esquire Varga Calendar*, and these two views show the nose of this B-25 before and after the name was done away with, a situation not previously reported. After only six months service with the 408th, this B-25 was passed to the 823rd BS, 38th BG, with, it is suspected, the pin-up in place, but not the name, it seems. It remained with the 823rd until September 1944, but the fate of this particular *Lady* is not currently known. Note in the RHS background of the photo below a B-25 with white tail markings; this was the squadron insignia for the 2nd BS, 22nd BG, while equipped with B-25s, but the fact that the white panels were both outward and inward facing has not been pointed out previously.

LI'L D'-ICER, Consolidated B-24, 42-72795, artist William B. McBroom, 530th BS, 380th BG. Applying a pin-up to an aircraft was one thing, but to name it required constant originality. US cartoonist Zack Mosley in his *Smilin' Jack* newspaper comic strips would appear to have been the inspiration in this case and that of similar-named bombers that follow. Mosley referred to the various women with whom aviator Jack became romantically involved as "de-icers," and this term obviously caught on. Thanks to the research carried out for the 380th.org website, it is now known that this B-24 completed a lot more missions than previously thought: seventeen in New Guinea (December 1943–January 1944) and then eleven from northern Australia, back to New Guinea for another five, and then another thirty-two from Fenton (March–September 1944) and ten from Darwin (October 1944–January 1945). LI'L D'-ICER was subsequently salvaged in Australia. *Ken Crane via Bob Wiseman/Nigel Daw*

LIBERTY BELLE, Consolidated B-24, 41-23902, artist unknown, 321st BS, 90th BG. This take on probably the best-known symbol of American independence, the Liberty Bell, became another popular nose art name for US bomber aircraft during World War II. In addition, though, this is a good example of early B-24 pin-up nose art with both small artwork and mission symbols, each relatively inconspicuous; the 90th BG wartime souvenir book, *The Jolly Rogers: Southwest Pacific, 1942–1944*, comments that this piece of unofficial artwork was among the first for them. It was added, apparently, ca. late 1942 (see also *BOMBS TO NIP ON* in the introduction), and similarities between this artwork and the 321st Squadron's *DRIP* (q.v.), even down to the pin-up's stance, would suggest that both were by the same artist. The only known large nose art painting of a pin-up (and not a particularly good example, at that) on an early B-24 was *SADIE* (q.v.), which, however, enjoyed only a brief appearance. This LIBERTY BELLE survived service in New Guinea to be returned to the US, where it was scrapped postwar.

LIBERTY BELLE, Consolidated B-24, 42-100206, artist unknown, 33rd BS, 22nd BG. This B-24 flew missions with the 33rd BS for seven months but failed to return from a massed attack on the oil refineries at Balikpapan on October 10, 1944. She was able to reach the target area despite interception by enemy fighters but afterward was singled out for attention as the aircraft's captain, Lt. Joseph C. Tafaro, tried to limp home on three engines. Fortune favored Tafaro's crew, though, and after another forty minutes of further attacks, the Japanese gave up and flew back to their bases. Tafaro subsequently crash-landed the heavily damaged B-24 at Batoedaka Island (now Palau Batudaka) in the Celebes, without apparent serious injury to any of the crew, and after two days the men were found and rescued. Tafaro, who had, in fact, been injured in the landing, was later awarded the Silver Star for his gallantry in action. Notice that some early crew nicknames had been painted out by the time this photo was taken; the one below the cockpit was *"HERKY."*

LIBERTY BELLE, Consolidated B-24, 42-40686, artist unknown, 63rd BS, 43rd BG. Research for the *Ken's Men against the Empire* 43rd BG history determined that this B-24 was one of at least two assigned to the 63rd BS in the second quarter of 1944 that had already served in an antisubmarine role elsewhere prior to 5th AF service. It is suspected that the nose art probably was also added in the course of those earlier days but retained subsequently. Received by the 63rd ca. June 1944, it remained in service until the end of October 1944, when she was extensively damaged by enemy action. Lt. Laurence F. Grimm, aircraft captain, nursed the B-24 back to Tacloban, but the nosewheel collapsed on landing and the damage sustained was too great to warrant repair. Fortunately, there were no serious injuries to the crew.

LIBERTY Belle Consolidated B-24, 44-50894, artist Raymond A. Hafner, 529th BS, 380th BG. This example was the last of five 5th AF B-24s so named. It entered service in June 1945 and flew only seven strikes before the war ended. The record card for this B-24 notes that it had a short-lived history, being salvaged by the end of 1945, but no further details are known.

LIBERTY BELLE II, Consolidated B-24, 44-41234, artist Charles R. Chesnut, 33rd BS, 22nd BG. This B-24 replaced *LIBERTY BELLE*, seen at the top of the previous page, and flew with the 33rd BS until just after war's end. The two views here show *BELLE* both in "as new" condition and probably at the end of her service, with a bomb log of ninety-eight missions, a higher number than previously reported likely.

"Lil" De Icer, North American B-25, 41-30075, artist unknown, 500th BS, 345th BG. Assigned to the 500th BS in March 1943, this B-25 had a relatively short service life, ditching at sea due to engine failure following the massed B-25 attack on Rabaul of October 24, 1943. The close-up view, above, of the LHS of this artwork, apart from suffering wartime film development problems, reveals that the name had originally been added in capital letters, but that the words *DE ICER* were subsequently painted over to make way for the pin-up, but note that the original *"LIL"* name was retained. This also happened on the RHS. The original name, but no longer in capitals, however, was reapplied to both sides of the nose, but farther forward, as seen in the second view. Adjacent to the word *"Lil"* in that view is *NORMY*, the nickname of navigator Lt. Norman Shubert.

LiL' DEiCER II, Martin B-26, 41-17601, artist unknown, 408th BS, 22nd BG. The first 408th B-26 with this name crashed on May 15, 1942, with the deaths of all eight men aboard. This replacement plane was reportedly not assigned to the squadron until months later; the enlarged Roman number "II" can be seen in the photo below, taken at Port Moresby in 1943, which also reveals just how small the pin-up was. Research for the 22nd BG history *Revenge of the Red Raiders* concluded that this was something of a mystery ship, with only a small number of combat missions to her name, and that she was transferred out around the second quarter of 1943. Later stripped of camouflage and with new nose art added at the Townsville Air Depot (see photo in chapter 7), this B-26 may have subsequently returned to the 22nd BG, but only for second-line duties, it seems.

Lilas Marie and *Lilas Marie The 2nd.*, Consolidated B-24s, unidentified serial number (*Lilas Marie*) and 44-40720 (*Lilas Marie The 2nd*), artist(s) unknown, 400th BS (*Lilas Marie*) and 319th BS (*Lilas Marie The 2nd.*), 90th BG. Whether the same crew flew these two aircraft or there was some other reason for using the same name (despite the different squadrons involved) is not currently known. The above right photo shows the then very shiny 44-40720 prior to the name (and smile) being added. As *Lilas Marie The 2nd.*, this bomber was salvaged in theater due to an accident, but more-precise details are not known to this author.

LiL "DAISY" CUTTER, Consolidated B-24, 42-40666, artist Orville R. Fritsch, 403rd and 65th BSs, 43rd BG, later 2nd BS, 22nd BG. This artwork was based on *Esquire* magazine's September 1941 Varga Girl and was probably added soon after receipt by the 403rd BS by Fritsch (note his name adjacent to the pin-up's high heels), who was also responsible for the *Miss McCook* artwork (q.v.). While Daisy is a girl's name, Daisy Cutter was a nickname for a bomb with an extended fuse assembly that caused it to explode just above ground level, around the height of a daisy. After service with the 43rd BG, this B-24 became one of the transition trainers used by the 22nd BG and, according to the *Revenge of the Red Raiders* group history, later went to the 5th Bomber Command Replacement Pool.

Little Audry, Martin B-26, 401432, artist unknown, 19th BS, 22nd BG. The name of this aircraft (note the spelling) is known to have been applied during the time that it was camouflaged and had been assigned to the 2nd BS, but the artwork, which was probably applied to the LHS only, would appear to have been added only after the paint was removed (this work, carried out at Townsville, occurred progressively from around April 1943), and in the two close-up photos can be seen here in its original and altered forms. The inspiration for the pin-up was the June pin-up from the 1943 *Esquire Varga Calendar*. The photo above, taken at Cairns, provides a particularly good overall view of this aircraft while with the 19th BS, the so-called Silver Fleet, which paid homage to an earlier "Silver Fleet," Eastern Air Lines' Douglas commercial airliners of the 1930s, promoted then (and again postwar) as "the Great Silver Fleet." *Cairns photo, A. A. "Bill" Penglase*

"*Little Butch*", Douglas A-20, 42-54162 (unconfirmed), artist unknown, 673rd BS, 417th BG. This artwork had originally been applied when the A-20 was assigned to Lt. Tom Waddell of the 89th BS, 3rd BG, and was named by him *"Sweet Marie" Number Three*. Following transfer to the 673rd BS, 417th BG, though, it was assigned to Lt. (later captain) George E. Worsham Jr., seen here, who renamed it *"Little Butch"*. The crew chief's name also shows in this photo but is in smaller lettering and cannot be determined with certainty. After the 673rd BS, this A-20 was pensioned off to the CRTC and presumably ended the war in the Nadzab boneyard.

LITTLE JODY, Consolidated B-24, unidentified serial number, artist unknown, unidentified BS, 90th BG. Another example of 5th AF late-war heavy-bomber nose art; nothing further is currently known about the plane (a B-24M model) or the well-executed artwork.

"*Little DOC*", Douglas A-20, 43-9413, artist unknown, 388th BS, 312th BG. This A-20, assigned to Capt. Edward T. Cassidy, carried just the name LITTLE DOC for some time before that was painted out and the pin-up and the new version of the name as shown here were added. While being ferried by another pilot from Hollandia to the 312th's new base at Tanauan, Leyte, on January 5, 1945, *"Little DOC"* experienced engine trouble and had to be ditched, and while an ASR Catalina later searched the area, no survivors were found. The crew chief, SSgt. Les Franz, whose name also appears in this photo, was one of the three crew members that day who lost their lives.

Little Brat, Douglas A-20, 43-9041, artist unknown, 386th BS, 312th BG. This A-20's pin-up was another fine work inspired by *Esquire* magazine's Varga Girl for December 1943, although with the earlier style of Air Corps national insignia showing. It had originally been assigned to the 3rd BG but was transferred to the 312th in February 1944, the original pilot assigned to this A-20 (as shown in this photo) being Lt. R. A. Wilson (after promotion to captain, Wilson commanded the 385th BS from October 1944 to May 1945). The A-20 was transferred out at the end of the year and probably ended its days at Nadzab.

"*Little Lulu*", Consolidated B-24, 42-109999, artist unknown, 529th BS, 380th BG. This B-24 flew her first mission on May 13, 1944, but the artwork (loosely based on the June offering from the 1943 *Esquire Varga Calendar*) and name, known to have been added later and presumably borrowed from the *Saturday Evening Post*'s popular cartoon character of the same name, are unlikely to have stayed in place long, since they were removed with the camouflage paint when the bomber was stripped back to NMF soon after (as a result, photos of this nose art are not common). At some point, apparently after the 529th was transferred to the Philippines, a new artwork and new name, *Madame Queen* (q.v.), were added.

Little Joe, Consolidated F-7, 42-64054, artist Al G. Merkling, 20th CMS, 6th PRG. A number of USAAF World War II aircraft, including a 380th BG B-24, were given this name; it is the term used when playing the dice game called craps and a pair of twos are rolled, as depicted in the photo below. In this case, though, the name was also a tribute to the squadron commander, Maj. Joe Davis, who, unofficially at least, was apparently known as such. The photo showing the incomplete work is interesting in that it seems likely that Merkling was still deliberating over how he would finish it off. Note also Merkling's rough indication of mountain ranges in his work; he really went to a lot of trouble. Of nineteen missions flown when the second photo was taken, five can be seen to have been unsuccessful due to weather-related problems. *Little Joe* served longer than any other F-7 in the 20th Squadron, from April 1944 to May 1945, racking up seventy-one missions in the process, but just how many more mission symbols were made to fit on the nose of this aircraft is not known.

LIVE WIRE, Consolidated B-24, 44-41235, artist unknown, 320th BS, 90th BG. The name and artwork on this B-24 were taken from a Gil Elvgren pin-up originally published in 1937. The aircraft was lost on July 15, 1945, when the crew was ordered to bail out by the aircraft's captain, Lt. Samuel J. Bowers, following engine problems the bomber was experiencing. This incident, however, occurred well out into the South China Sea, and only half the crew survived to be rescued. John S. Alcorn in his "Jolly Rogers" history volume notes that *OLD IRON SIDES* was the B-24 the Bowers crew usually flew; a photo of the latter B-24 can be found in chapter 6. For other late-war "Moby Dick" squadron B-24s that combined the whale-look nose markings with a pin-up, see *AIR POCKET*, *Cherrie*, *DISPLAY OF ARMS*, and *"GRRR"* in this chapter. *LIVE WIRE* was the last 90th BG B-24 lost in action during World War II.

LOUISIANA LULLABY, Consolidated B-24, 42-63986, artist unknown, 319th BS, 90th BG. With artwork said to have been copied from a photo of a New Orleans beauty queen and featuring a different pin-up on the RHS (added much later), this B-24 and her crew were lost on June 11, 1944, in the course of a massed attack on Peleliu in the Palau island group. The airplane was able to ditch, but no rescue of survivors (at least two were seen) proved possible that day, and no trace of any of them could be found a day later. This photo reveals that prior to her loss, *LOUISIANA LULLABY* flew at least sixty-seven missions.

Lovely Louise, Consolidated B-24, 44-41332, artist unknown, 319th BS, 90th BG. This B-24 was named in honor of the wife of navigator Calvin Harrison and, as suggested by the detail in the artwork, was copied from a photo of her. The two married in 1945 and remained together for forty-five years, until Mrs. Harrison's death in 1990. The bomb log is partly cropped in this photo but is known to have been fifty-two (forty-two at top, ten below) ca. May 1945. *Lovely Louise*, whose name was intricately painted to resemble rope, was destroyed in a landing accident at McGuire Field, Philippines, on May 10, 1945, but had been another of the squadron's late-war nonnude nose art paintings based on real women; see also *Jini, Miss Kiwanis, Phyllis J. of WORCESTER*, and, most likely, *THE PUGNOSE PRINCESS* in this chapter.

LUCKY [legs], Consolidated B-24, 42-40514, artist unknown, 528th and 529th BSs, 380th BG. This name and artwork (note the four-leaf clovers and pair of dice showing "lucky" number 7), both of which were taken directly from the cover of a paperback edition of Erle Stanley Gardner's Perry Mason story *The Case of the Lucky Legs*, appeared on both sides of the nose of this B-24. The bomber served with the 528th BS from April to August 1943 and the 529th BS from August to October 1943. From there, *LUCKY* was eventually passed to the RAAF for use as a crew trainer, but that was only after substantial repair work was carried out following its last flight with the 380th BG on October 18, 1943, when its brakes failed on landing at Darwin. Renumbered A72-11 by the RAAF and with nose art removed (probably during its refurbishment), this B-24 survived the war but was scrapped soon after; see photo in chapter 7.

LUCKY LUCILLE, Consolidated B-24, 42-41224, artist unknown, 64th BS, 43rd BG. This B-24 left the USA for frontline service in October 1943, the pin-up having been copied from the Varga Girl in the October 1943 copy of *Esquire* magazine. The name, on the other hand, was added much later, after she had proved herself to be a lucky ship. Total missions flown would probably have exceeded seventy prior to *LUCILLE* being salvaged ca. July 1944. For other examples of versions of this pin-up, see B-24 *PATCHES* in this chapter, P-38 *Thoughts of Midnite* in chapter 3, and C-47s *BYE, BYE, BLUES, Pretty Baby*, and *SPEEDY STEEDE* in chapter 4.

'Lucky Strike', Consolidated B-24, 44-41876, artist James C. Nickloy, 528th and 530th BSs, 380th BG. Given the popularity of the Lucky Strike cigarette brand in the 1930s and 1940s (promoted ca. 1944 as "THE *Cigarette* THATS [sic] *Winning* THE WAR"), there is little wonder that someone thought it would make a good name to accompany a pin-up on a plane. This B-24 flew more than fifty missions from February 28 to August 28, 1945 (only the first two with the 528th BS), but it seems that the nose art was probably added quite late in the piece, since the only time when the artist's unit, the 36th PRS, and the 380th BG operated together was on Okinawa, beginning in August 1945. Postwar, 'Lucky Strike' was returned to the US but was subsequently scrapped.

'Luvablass', Consolidated B-24, 44-42263, artist Raymond A. Hafner, 529th BS, 380th BG. This nose art combined a made-up name with a pin-up based on a wartime Brown & Bigelow calendar topper by Earl Moran (1893–1984). Such names were an attempt at toning down what otherwise may be considered a lewd comment (in this case, "lovable ass"). No changes are known to have been ordered during this B-24's three months of frontline service, so there appears to have been no objections to the name, but see *MYAKIN-BACK*, which follows, for an example of another that was not so lucky. This B-24 was returned to US following the end of the war but was subsequently scrapped. Close examination of this photo shows the artist's sign-off was "HAF-CLIFF," but the significance of the "CLIFF" part is not currently known.

LUGER LUGGIN LASSIE, North American B-25, unidentified serial number, artist unknown, 498th BS, 345th BG. One of the 75 mm cannon-armed G- or H-model B-25s sent to the 5th AF that saw short-lived service due to their unpopularity; this photo was taken at the Townsville Air Depot following the plane's delivery from the US. It was subsequently assigned to the 498th BS, 345th BG, where the original name was retained and a new one, CANNON "PACK-IN" MAMA, was added to the right of the pin-up. Most of these cannon-armed B-25s seem to have been returned to Townsville, where they were condemned, and this, presumably, was the fate of this one, which had been named after the famous German Luger pistol.

MABEL'S LABELS, Consolidated B-24, 44-49854, artist Sarkis E. Bartigian, 64th BS, 43rd BG. This large and beautiful portrait of the artist's wife, Mabel, was added sometime in 1945 (this B-24 did not leave the US for overseas until January 13, 1945), and, as mentioned in the introduction, such artworks were seen as acceptable ways of spending spare time ("diversions," the original reference called them, a "way to lick the deadly monotony of waiting out that 90 per cent of the war that isn't action"). The war ended in August 1945, earlier than most ever expected, and by November 1945 this B-24 was returned to the US and received at Kingman, Arizona, for open-air storage and subsequent disposal. These two clear views of the plane and its artwork were taken in the immediate postwar period, before and after the dorsal turret was removed for the long flight home.

MAD RUSSIAN, Consolidated B-24, 44-41846, artist Enoch H. Wingert, 65th BS, 43rd BG. Wingert worked on at least six pin-up paintings for the 65th BS: *CAROLYN MAE*, *MAD RUSSIAN*, *PETTY GAL*, *PUNJA KASI*, *QUEEN OF THE CLOUDS*, and *WILLIE'S FOLLY*. Research for volume 2 of *Ken's Men against the Empire* concluded that in this case, though, while Wingert painted the work, which referred to the assigned pilot, Lt. Andrew Burochonock, it was based on a design by Sarkis E. Bartigian. Below the name of this B-24 can be seen the nickname "Bud," which was, perhaps, the way that Bartigian was generally known in the squadron. Bartigian did not sign off his own works, but Wingert did; his personal logo appears to have been his own version of the squadron insignia, featuring two white dice on a dark background. Another late-war artwork; while this B-24 survived the war and was returned to the US, whether that was with or without the nose art is not currently known.

Madame Queen, Consolidated B-24, 42-109999, artist unknown, 529th BS, 380th BG. Formerly *"Little Lulu"* (q.v.), the *Madame Queen* name and artwork were added to the RHS of the B-24 at some stage subsequently. She flew thirty-three missions from Australia and thirty-five from the Philippines but was abandoned off the coast of the Philippines on June 25, 1945, due to the impracticability of a safe landing. The plane had been on a noncombat flight at the time and there were only five men aboard, all of whom were able to safely bail out without further incident.

Mag the Hag, Consolidated B-24, 42-41084, artist unknown, 64th BS, 43rd BG, later 19th BS and 2nd BS, 22nd BG. This B-24 had an early history similar to *Double Trouble* (q.v.), and, in fact, both artworks may have been by the same artist. In this case, though, the bomber survived its time as a conversion trainer with the 22nd BG (January–April 1944) to be transferred to the 5th Bomber Command Replacement Pool at Nadzab. It does appear, however, that she was salvaged before war's end.

Male Call / MALE CALL, Consolidated B-24, 42-72799, second artwork artist Harvey Levine, 531st BS, 380th BG. This B-24 took up the name of Milt Caniff's popular wartime cartoon strip series mentioned earlier (see *Drunkard's Dream / DRUNKARD'S DREAM*), initially without any pin-up. It had been assigned to the 531st BS in November 1943, and the pin-up seen here (*at left*) was subsequently added and the style of the name and lettering was changed from "MALE CALL" to *Male Call*, but that artist remains unidentified, and just when this occurred is not known. Around December 1944 (after the plane had done more than eighty missions), however, the artwork was changed and the lettering reverted to capitals. Seen here below after ninety-two missions, *MALE CALL* went on to notch its one hundredth mission on March 16, 1945, and added at least another fifteen before being flown to Biak, ca. July 1945, to be salvaged.

MAID in the USA, Consolidated B-24, 44-40341, artist unknown, 319th BS, 90th BG. The B-24 was, of course, made in the United States (becoming the most produced bomber plane ever), but here is a play on those words and a very classy, beautiful artwork with a completely different meaning. The pin-up may also have been the squadron's last featuring a nude (see also *QUEEN MAE*). This B-24 survived the war to be flown back to the US, but probably minus the artwork.

Manila Calling, Consolidated B-24, 44-40800, artist Ernest W. Bako, 65th BS, 43rd BG. Another of Bako's artworks (see also *Lady from Leyte* in this chapter); this artist seems to have been the only one to have connected nose art with the Philippine Islands, where, at the time, the 43rd BG was based. As mentioned earlier, Bako's two known nose art examples were based on the same pin-up photo of actress Carole Landis. It is interesting to note that Landis had starred in a 1942 movie of this same name, so not only would it seem that Bako was a fan, but one could see that the name of the film could still work for a bomber nose art painting two years later, although he did initially misspell Manila (*"Manilla"*), which he subsequently corrected. Reportedly, *Manila Calling* served with the 65th only around four months and was subsequently salvaged, reason unknown.

MARGIE, Consolidated B-24, 41-24018, artist unknown, 320th BS, 90th BG. What is clever about this artwork is how the artist has given the impression that the unraveling of the material in which the pin-up is dressed is being controlled from within the cockpit. After 5th AF service, this B-24 was among the first war-weary B-24s made available to the RAAF, and it became an instructional airframe at the heavy-bomber operational training unit, No. 7 OTU, at Tocumwal, New South Wales, following its arrival there in February 1944. In RAAF service the B-24 carried RAAF serial number A72-3, but it seems likely that the nose art was done away with, since no photos have yet surfaced to suggest that it was retained.

"MARGIE", Martin B-26, 40-1516, artist unknown, 33rd BS, 22nd BG. This B-26 started out with the name *CALAMITY JANE* prior to or following arrival in Australia at the end of March 1942. Subsequently it was renamed *EL VALIENTE* and featured a small caricature of Dopey, as depicted by Walt Disney in his 1937 animated film *Snow White*, later becoming *"MARGIE"*, named, perhaps, after the jazz standard of the day. According to the authors of detailed 22nd BG history *Revenge of the Red Raiders*, the transition to the bomb-riding pin-up is suspected to have occurred ca. January 1943. A few months later, when the remaining B-26s were transferred to the 19th BS and camouflage was removed, this aircraft was reportedly renamed again!

MARIE, Consolidated B-24, 42-40922, artist unknown, 64th BS, 43rd BG, later 22nd BG and CRTC. Early and late views of the nose art, with the close-up, in fact, photographed before the name was added. The second view (right), with MARIE now showing a bomb log of forty-five missions, as well as four Purple Hearts (indicating that there had been four crew members wounded during those missions) and two Rising Suns for enemy aircraft claimed shot down, is likely to have been taken following 43rd BG service, when MARIE was being used either by the 22nd BG for B-24 conversion training, or, after that, when she was left at Nadzab for CRTC use. The CRTC came into existence in June 1944, but MARIE did not see long service with that unit, since she was salvaged in early 1945.

Marie, Douglas A-20, 43-9472, artist unknown, 386th BS, 312th BG. This A-20, with nose art based on the September page from the 1944 Esquire Varga Calendar, served with the 386th BS for around four months until transferred to the 90th BS, 3rd BG, in June 1944. This unit probably did away with the pin-up and replaced it with its shark's-teeth squadron marking, but, in any event, Marie's time with the 90th was short lived due to an accident. This is an early photo, since the original print shows that mission symbols have yet to be added.

MARY ANN, Consolidated B-24, unidentified serial number, artist unknown, unit(s) unidentified. This image is taken from a strip of 35 mm contact prints of late-war B-24 nose art, possibly taken on Okinawa, including Cherrie, seen earlier, and, on that basis has been included as more than likely being a 5th AF aircraft, possibly also from the 90th BG. It was returned to the US postwar and subsequently scrapped at Kingman.

Mary Annette, North American B-25, unidentified serial number, artist unknown, unidentified BS, 3rd BG (unconfirmed). Photographed at the Townsville Air Depot, this hitherto unknown artwork with Texan connections was signed off by the artist, and while his signature cannot be read, below that it is stated that he belonged to a Long Beach–based subdepot (the 58th?). Although the artwork is more about the horse than the rider, given the name and the fact that both artwork and name appear to have both been short lived, the photo was still considered worthy of inclusion.

Mary "F", North American B-25, 41-30066, artist unknown, 500th BS, 345th BG. This pin-up was based on the September 1943 offering from the *Esquire Varga Calendar* (although with some significant changes) and, together with the name, was added either prior to or during the B-25's service with the 500th BS, 345th BG. Following transfer to the 408th BS, 22nd BG (also in September 1943), she was renamed *JUNGLE QUEEN* (q.v.). Lt Delosse Poe was the original pilot assigned to this ship.

Mary Joyce & Ruby, Consolidated B-24, 42-41077, artist unknown, 400th BS, 90th BG. This B-24 was named first, then the stunning painting was added, this being the only photo seen by the author proving that, for a while at least, the original name and artwork coexisted (it is possible, of course, that this photo was taken immediately prior to the name being changed). It was subsequently renamed *NOT IN STOCK* (q.v.) and, as such, was well photographed.

The MARY JO / Mary Jo, North American B-25, 41-30048, artist unknown, 500th BS, 345th BG. This B-25 was taken overseas and flown for much of the time until October 1943 by Capt. Lyle E. "Rip" Anacker, but for all that time it wore the MARY JO name only, no pin-up (*see top photo*). Anacker, "D"-flight leader, was killed flying another aircraft with a different crew on an attack on Japanese supplies and shipping on October 18, 1943, but after that, his original copilot, Lt. Dale Speicher, was given command of *MARY JO* (note that both his and Anacker's names appear below the cockpit window). Evidently no nose art had been added to this B-25 as late as May 1944, but sometime between then and October the Vargas-inspired work seen below appeared. By the latter date, when *Mary Jo* was transferred out as war weary, this old strafer had flown more than one hundred missions.

The MAYFLOWER, Consolidated B-24, 42-40853, artist unknown, 64th BS, 43rd BG. The original *Mayflower* was an English sailing ship that in 1620 brought the first Pilgrims, then called Puritans, to North America. A subtext on the nose reads ALL THE PURITANS COME ACROSS ON THIS, but it seems unlikely to this author that this comment actually relates to the ship's famous voyage. The photo below shows the pin-up, added stateside, in its original naked form, while in the photo at right, taken from a similar vantage point to the first, skimpy clothing has been added, but there is little change to the overall look. Note too the slightly altered form of name in the second photo: the painter involved took the opportunity to dress that up too. This B-24 was salvaged in theater during 1944 following 43rd BG service.

"Mary M", Consolidated B-24, 44-40370, artist unknown, 530th BS, 380th BG. Glenn R. Horton Jr.'s extensive research into the 380th BG established that the name of this aircraft was derived from the fact that the men who worked on her (by chance, all of whom had surnames beginning with M) had a wife or sweetheart named Mary, so *"Mary M"* she became. According to the 380th.org website, *"Mary M"* flew thirty-three missions from Australia and another fifty-three from the Philippines, where she also ended her days.

MEXICAN SPITFIRE, North American B-25, 41-30592, artist unknown, 500th BS, 345th BG. Named after the central character in a series of *Mexican Spitfire* films (played by beautiful Mexican actress Lupe Vélez) that were released between 1940 and 1943, this B-25 is believed to have originally served with the 3rd BG. A depot status report from late April 1944, however, indicates that at that stage, 41-30592 had been with the 49th Service Squadron but was then en route to the 500th BS. *MEXICAN SPITFIRE*'s service with the 500th BS was, however, only brief. On September 2, 1944, in the course of a three-squadron mission against targets in the Celebes, she was hit by ship-based AA and forced to ditch at sea. At least five of the six-man crew were seen to escape the sinking B-25, but it was not possible for the other crews to provide top cover for long (in the process, another 500th plane, *HELL'S FIRE* [see photo in chapter 6], was shot down by enemy fighters), and the fate of her crew remains unknown.

"MILADY", Consolidated B-24, 42-73134, artist unknown, 531st BS, 380th BG. Both sides of the nose of this B-24 are seen in these two photos, the first taken ca. March 1944 after twelve missions and a twin-engine "Nick" fighter was claimed as destroyed over Ambon, and the second taken probably nine months later, well after the original camouflage had been removed. While the pin-up was retained on both sides after that time, the mission symbols appeared only on the LHS.

Flt. Lt. Martin Law's RAAF crew, below, was the last to fly "MILADY" prior to her loss at the hands of a newly arrived US crew undertaking a training flight out of Darwin on January 17, 1945. The RAAF crew, in fact, flew this B-24 on five of its last six missions (three strikes and two searches), on December 2, 19, and 30, 1944, and January 5 and 7, 1945. For a local perspective on the plane and particularly on its loss, see "History of Wagait Beach" at www.wagait.nt.gov.au. *Crew photo, Mrs. Margot Law*

MICHIGAN, Consolidated B-24, 44-40429, artist Sarkis E. Bartigian, 64th BS, 43rd BG. The soldier in this photo gives some perspective as to how impressive this artwork that centered on a larger-than-life "sweater girl" (a young lady who wore a tight sweater to accentuate her bustline) was. Only eight mission markers can be seen at this stage, but MICHIGAN went on to clock up at least seventy-five by the end of the war, the markers subsequently being repositioned in three rows of twenty-five directly under the cockpit window. By chance, it was Bartigian who also painted the nose art on the preceding aircraft off the production line, 44-40428, which was also assigned to the 64th BS and became better known as COCKTAIL HOUR (q.v.). The B-24 off the production line after MICHIGAN, 44-40430, was also assigned to the 64th BS and became HIP PARADE (q.v.). MICHIGAN was not returned to the US postwar but was salvaged in theater, probably in the Philippines.

MICKIE'S MENACE, Consolidated B-24, 44-41128, artist unknown, 64th BS, 43rd BG. This B-24 was assigned to the 64th BS in November 1944 and survived wartime service to be returned to the US, but just who completed the artwork and what the significance of the bowling pins is remain currently unknown.

million$Baby and *MILLION$BABY*, Consolidated B-24s 44-40335 and 44-50768, artist for 44-40335 A. Praver, both 64th BS, 43rd BG. The artwork at left (on 44-40335) has been signed off A. PRAVER, 460th AAFBU [Army Air Forces Base Unit] Sq. "B." The B-24, *at right*, a B-24M, replaced that at left, a B-24J, which was salvaged in theater, and took up the same name as well as a new version of the same nose art (the basis for both had been the September pin-up from the 1944 *Esquire Varga Calendar*). There has been a suggestion that a short story written by author Jerry Boyd (1930–2002; pen name F. X. Toole) titled *Million $$$ Baby* was named after either one of these planes or a third B-24 with the same name operated by the 8th AF. This particular story and two others written by Boyd formed the basis of the story portrayed in the 2004 Academy Award–winning film that was also called *Million Dollar Baby*. The source of both the 2004 film title and the three B-24 names may, however, have simply been an earlier film of the same name, a romantic comedy released in 1941. The second B-24 survived the war and was returned to the US, but the huge artwork was probably scrubbed off en route.

Mischievous MARY II, Douglas A-20, 43-21374, artist unknown, 388th BS, 312th BG. As can be seen in this photo, the assigned pilot was Capt. Lowell H. Morrow, and, perhaps unsurprisingly, Mary was Mary E. Braid, his then girlfriend or fiancée. This A-20, which had begun 5th AF service with the 13th BS, 3rd BG, was assigned to the 388th in June 1944 and reportedly flew 149 missions to December 1944, when its frontline service ended. Along the way, after Morrow returned to the US, this A-20 was assigned to a new pilot, Lt. R. J. Dicker, but the original name and artwork were retained. Morrow later married Mary, but, sadly, the two died together in a motor vehicle accident in 1968.

MIS-A-SIP, Douglas A-20, 43-21429, artist unknown, 387th BS, 312th BG. Note the very neatly applied extensive bomb log, which comprised seven rows (only six of which are visible in this photo), each one acknowledging twenty missions. This A-20 originally served with the 417th BG, and it seems likely that some of these missions were from that earlier time, but the nose art was added only after the plane was transferred to the 312th BG, ca. February 1945, its assigned pilot being Lt. Jesse G. Hughes Jr., from Mississippi. This photo is suspected to have been taken at Biak, where *MIS-A-SIP* was left postwar to be salvaged.

BOMBER AND LONG-RANGE PHOTO RECON BEAUTIES

MISS B HAVIN, North American B-25, 43-36176, artist unknown, 498th BS, 345th BG. This B-25 was assigned to the 498th BS in October 1944, and the bold artwork was added prior to the end of the year. The nose art proved to be short lived, however, since the B-25 was lost on March 30, 1945, while loaned to the 499th BS, a victim of the combination of low flying and the detonation of one of her own bombs. The plane was forced to ditch not far from its attack point off the coast of Hainan Island, and while three of the crew were able to be rescued by submarine the next morning, the remaining two men, who had been positioned in the turret and tail gun positions, were lost.

Miss BeHaven, Douglas A-20, 44-062, artist unknown, 388th BS, 312th BG. This A-20 was assigned initially to Lt. Harry Zditosky in March 1945, and it is suspected that the name and artwork were added soon after. There is a black name panel at top left of the artwork, but it cannot be read in this photo since the sun is reflecting from it. After Zditosky left the squadron in June, *Miss BeHaven* was assigned to Lt. Eugene A. Johnson, a former 380th BG B-24 copilot, and it is understood that the bomb log shown here (sixty-six missions) was Johnson's end-of-war tally of missions he flew both in the 530th (of the 380th BG) and 388th Squadrons. For other late-war 388th A-20s that featured nose art added to the squadron's heart-shaped insignia to accentuate squadron identity, see *OOOOOH! LADY*, *Perk's Pet*, *Queen o' Hearts*, *RIDIN' HIGH*, and one of the unnamed A-20s in this chapter.

Miss Charlene, North American B-25, unidentified serial number, artist unknown, unit(s) unidentified. From a 5th AF photo collection that also included the photo of *"MISS PAT"*, which follows, this B-25 appears to be a J-11 version, presumably received in the SWPA around September or October 1944. The artwork was based on the May pin-up in the 1944 *Esquire Varga Calendar*, but further details are not currently known.

"Miss Deed", Consolidated B-24, 41-24070, artist unknown, 321st BS, 90th BG. This artwork was based on a prewar photo by famed photographer Alfred Cheney Johnston (1885–1971) and drew a lot of attention given the risqué subject matter; at this stage, probably 1943, totally nude pin-ups in 5th AF units were still rare. This B-24 (which had earlier been responsible for discovering the Japanese fleet subsequently annihilated in the Battle of the Bismarck Sea) was another one of the nine passed to the RAAF in the February–May 1944 period. It saw out the rest of the war as an instructional airframe and was scrapped soon after.

Miss Exterminator, North American B-25, 42-87450, artist unknown, 71st TRS, 17th TRG. This wonderfully clear LHS view of the entire aircraft shows off its pre-June 1944 white unit tail markings across the bottom of the vertical stabilizer, and rudder plus vertical line up the vertical stabilizer adjacent to the hinges, which (going by the inside of the RHS vertical stabilizer) meets up with another white line along the inside top edge. In keeping with the exterminator theme, the pin-up, based on a pin-up by Zoë Mozert (1907–93) titled *Incendiary Blonde*, is operating a so-called Flit gun (a hand-pump style of sprayer "gun" that dispensed insecticide, becoming so well known that it became a generic term for all such pre-aerosol bug killers), but against much-bigger prey, a cartoon rat with a Japanese face.

MISS GIVING, Consolidated B-24, 42-40489, artist Dick Ebbeson, 528th BS, 380th BG. This B-24 flew one or more missions with the 319th BS, 90th BG, prior to use by the 528th BS. With the latter unit, though, it flew twenty-four missions between June 11, 1943, and December 3, 1943, in the process Ebbeson adding this, his first nose art painting. The style of lettering was altered along the way, but this is how it looked for most of its 380th service. Subsequently, *MISS GIVING* was flown to the Townsville Air Depot, from where she did not return, instead becoming part of the group of nine B-24s gifted to the RAAF for training purposes in February–March 1944. In RAAF hands, *MISS GIVING* was given a new serial number, A72-4, and the nose art was probably painted over. She was written off following a hangar fire in October 1944.

The MISS HAP, Consolidated B-24, 42-100221, artist Raymond A. Hafner, 529th BS, 380th BG. This B-24 flew fifty missions from Australia and twenty-five from the Philippines prior to being removed from the 529th BS's books in June 1945. Over that time she featured a copy of the popular October 1943 Varga Girl, but in an altered position, not horizontal as originally painted by Vargas. This was another of Hafner's earliest works (it had been added by May 1944; also see *ADELAIDE FEVER* and *"Six Bitts"*), and although he did not sign it off to begin with, he added his moniker—HAfNER (see close-up)—after the camouflage finish was removed. The B-24's mission markers had originally appeared directly below the cockpit window in white on the OD background, but they were relocated in black, as shown after the camouflage paint was removed. A second row was later added, but it seems likely that the total number of bomb stencils added never exceeded sixty-four before the ship was flown to Biak for salvaging.

Miss Jolly Roger / BOOBY TRAP, Consolidated B-24, 44-40193, artist unknown, 321st BS, 90th BG. This artwork appeared on the LHS of *BOOBY TRAP*, seen earlier in this chapter. As mentioned earlier, this is a rare case where different artworks with different names (completed, apparently, by different artists) appeared on different sides of the same aircraft. When this photo was taken, *Miss Jolly Roger* had flown fifty-three missions; she was salvaged in theater, details unknown, after flying more than a hundred missions.

Miss Kiwanis, Consolidated B-24, 44-40431, artist Jack Eipper, 319th BS, 90th BG. This artwork was copied from a photo of crew member Sgt. Harry L. Dow's then fiancée, Laura Charewicz, who had won a Miss Kiwanis contest in Lawrence, Massachusetts, in 1943 and was another example of the 319th's late-war nonnude nose art. According to the record card for this B-24, it was returned to the US postwar but did not go to open-air storage (that is, not initially, at least), being transferred to Air Transport Command for use as an executive transport instead. No other details are available, but it seems unlikely that the artwork was retained.

Miss LIBERTY BELLE, Consolidated B-24, unidentified serial number, artist unknown, unidentified BS, unidentified BG. One of two photos of this B-24 that the author has, both taken at Garbutt, Townsville, it is most likely that this B-24 was en route to a 5th AF unit (perhaps the artwork was changed at Garbutt), but further details are presently unknown. The three objects surrounding the pin-up in this particular work are expected to be anti-aircraft bursts.

"MISS LIBERTY", Consolidated B-24, 42-40479, artist unknown, 63rd BS, 43rd BG. This B-24, with its nose art based primarily on the August pin-up from the 1944 *Esquire Varga Calendar*, but with the idea of the flowing hair and cape-like object complete with USAAF insignia billowing behind taken from *Esquire*'s December 1943 Varga Girl, was written off following major damage caused to the aircraft when a Japanese night fighter with jammed guns rammed the B-24 over Davao, Philippines, in the early hours of September 5, 1944. Amazingly, despite injuries on both sides, both crews lived to tell the tale (the B-24 pilot, Lt. Roland T. Fisher, was awarded a DFC for his handling of this very difficult situation), and later, after a record of the encounter from the Japanese perspective appeared in an early account of the history of the kamikaze fliers, Fisher, with the assistance of the book's authors, tracked down the Japanese pilot, which culminated in the two men meeting in 1972.

"MISS PAT", North American B-25, unidentified serial number, artist unknown, unit(s) unidentified. This photo and that of *Miss Charlene*, seen earlier, were from the same 5th AF photo collection, and on that basis, both have been included. Another photo in the same collection was of the 345th BG's *MISS B HAVIN* (q.v.), which tends to date the three as having been taken in late 1944, but nothing else is currently known.

MISS POSSUM MY TEXAS GAL, Douglas A-20, unidentified serial number, artist Joseph A. DiLorenzo, 8th BS, 3rd BG. Good pin-up artists were in demand and sometimes provided artworks for other units if the price, presumably, was right. DiLorenzo was a member of the 389th BS, 312th BG, but he produced this work for the 8th BS, 3rd BG. Both squadrons were based at Hollandia between July and November 1944, and this must have been when this work was produced. By this time, DiLorenzo was adding black spade-shaped backgrounds to his 389th BS artworks, so, to differentiate this work from his others, he added the black heart-shaped background. Another of the 312th BG squadrons, the 388th, later added for the most part red heart-shaped backgrounds to their nose art, and this has led to some confusion over identifying the unit to which *MISS POSSUM* belonged, but the author is confident that he has the identification correct.

Miss McCook, Consolidated B-24, 42-41070, artist Orville R. Fritsch, 403rd BS, 43rd BG. This B-24 was received in Australia in August 1943 and was subsequently assigned to the 403rd BS. The name (based on various connections with McCook, Nebraska; Fritsch, who was the crew chief, subsequently moved there following his discharge from the Army and continued to reside there until his death at the age of ninety-four in 2011), which appeared on both sides of the nose, and nose art are suspected to have been added soon after, the artwork being based on Vargas's August 1943 *Esquire* magazine gatefold. In this photo, mission markers for forty-seven (twenty-five in yellow, nearest the camera, followed by another twenty-two in what may be gray) are visible; *Miss McCook* went on to complete at least eighty missions prior to being declared war weary ca. August 1944. Fritsch completed at least one other B-24 nose artwork, *LiL "DAISY" CUTTER* (q.v.).

BOMBER AND LONG-RANGE PHOTO RECON BEAUTIES

"*Mission Belle*" / *Mission Belle*, Consolidated B-24, 42-40389, artist unknown, 400th BS, 90th BG. This pin-up was accurately copied from the June pin-up out of the 1943 *Esquire Varga Calendar*, minus the scant clothing originally offered by Vargas. As seen in the photo at right, the original elaborate style of name (*below*) was overpainted in favor of a simpler version soon after receipt by the 400th BS. In the last photo, the original painting can be seen to have been preserved following the removal of the camouflage paint, but another version of the name has been added, while the bomb log and symbols for enemy fighters claimed as shot down have now been removed from the LHS. *Mission Belle* finished the war at Nadzab, and she is mentioned in a 1946 article reproduced in appendix 3.

"*MISSLEADING*", Consolidated B-24, 42-100204, artist unknown, 19th BS, 22nd BG. Although this B-24 was a 19th BS original and in frontline service from March 1944, the pin-up was based on the *Esquire* magazine Varga Girl of October 1944 and therefore must date from after that date (the name is suspected to have had its origins in the fact that the 22nd BG motto, approved in 1941 along with the group insignia, was *Ducemus—We Lead*). The B-24, which was one of a number of examples from the Pacific war to retain its camouflage paint into 1945, went on to take part in ninety-nine missions, the last on May 31, 1945, when she was severely damaged by antiaircraft fire over Formosa. Despite injuries among the crew (particularly badly wounded was the pilot, Lt. Charles E. Critchfield), an emergency landing on two engines without brakes was successfully made at Laoag, Luzon, without loss of life, but the bomber was beyond repair.

'*Missouri Miss*', Consolidated B-24, 44-41811, artist unknown, 528th BS, 380th BG. This B-24, with the pin-up based on the January page from the 1945 *Esquire Varga Calender*, flew the first of more than fifty missions on February 27, 1945. She survived the war and was subsequently returned to the US but sat at Kingman, Arizona, along with thousands of other B-24s, until scrapped.

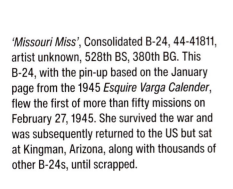

"MITCH" THE WITCH, North American B-25, 42-87293, artist unknown, 17th TRS, 71st TRG. This B-25 (or Mitchell; hence the nose art name, it seems) was something of a celebrity by the end of the war since it had flown at least 172 missions, probably a 5th AF record. Along the way it had also claimed two enemy planes (the first a well-documented "Sally" medium bomber over the Bismarck Sea on February 25, 1944) and, subsequently, a number of enemy vessels as well. A two-page partial plan view of this famous squadron identity can be found in the "Fighting 17th's" 1943–44 souvenir tour book, *Strike*. With the war over, the B-25 was condemned and salvaged, probably in the Philippines.

MODEST MAIDEN, Consolidated B-24, 42-109994, artist unknown, 403rd BS, 43rd BG. This B-24 arrived in Australia at the end of March 1944 and survived at least seventy-five wartime missions to subsequently be salvaged, probably at Biak, in 1945. Note that the style of lettering used on this B-24 and *OUTA' THIS WORLD* (q.v.) are very similar, suggesting that that work was carried out by the same person, but whether he also painted the pin-ups is not known.

MONTANA MAID, North American B-25, 42-87296, artist unknown, 17th TRS, 71st TRG. Suspected to have been delivered to the 17th TRS around the same time as *"MITCH" THE WITCH*, above, just who named this B-25 is not presently known, but a check of the squadron's 1943-1944 souvenir book, *Strike*, did confirm that there were two officers from Montana serving with the squadron at that time. The globetrotting *MONTANA MAID* (the backdrop can be seen to be a globe of Earth, the artist having added symbols to suggest that it is in motion) was lost on December 26, 1944, after running out of fuel and crashing into a mountain on the island of Panay, Philippines, resulting in the deaths of all seven men aboard.

MY JOY, Douglas A-20, 43-22156, artist unknown, 674th BS, 417th BG. This A-20, with what must have been one of the shortest names but that was created using the largest lettering ever to be seen on an A-20, appears in a number of photos in the 1946 tour book *The Sky Lancer*. No further details are currently available, except that it is known that it ended its days in the scrap heap on Biak. *Via Malcolm Long*

The MUSTANG, Boeing B-17, 41-24554, artist Ernie Vandal, 63rd BS, 43rd BG. This B-17 served very briefly with the 403rd BS before being transferred to the 63rd BS by the end of December 1942. Artist Ernie Vandal was the airplane's crew chief, and, under the circumstances, this may have been the first artwork he completed. But that artwork, a horse's head, and name possibly graced only the LHS of the nose to begin with (see photo below). At some point, a horse's head was also painted on the RHS of the nose, and a cowgirl pin-up was added immediately behind (again, covering the rear window of the nose compartment, as Vandal had also done with *The LAST STRAW*, seen earlier), but the photo at lower left shows the incomplete work with a light-colored surround to the cowgirl, the whole thing, despite its complexity, looking like just one painting. Most photos of the RHS of the nose of this B-17, however, show the light-colored background having been overpainted in black, which has led to suggestions that the black paint covered something else prior to the cowgirl being added, but that can now be seen to be incorrect. This B-17 was returned to the US in November 1943, and, as shown in the last photo, by then the modified horse's head had been done away with completely, and this impressive, though exaggerated, bomb log plus victory symbols for nine ships sunk, seventeen enemy aircraft shot down, and seven Purple Hearts (one for each time a crew member had been wounded in action) was added. The name of the well-dressed artist working on the victory symbols is not known, but the location is the Townsville Air Depot, Queensland. The purple hearts and victory symbols were also added to the LHS nose, and *The MUSTANG* survived the war with that and the LHS artwork in place (see photo in chapter 7), but the cowgirl pin-up may not have been so lucky, since nose art with images of undressed women on aircraft in training units stateside was frowned upon.

naughty but nice, Boeing B-17, 41-2430, artist James H. Mayman (unconfirmed), 65th BS, 43rd BG. Transferred into the 65th from the 19th BG in November 1942 (while it is not known when the nose art was added), the bomber was shot down by a Japanese night fighter pre-dawn on June 26, 1943, so it is likely that the pin-up was not in place long beforehand. All except one crew member, the navigator, Lt. José L. Holquin, were lost with the bomber, and remarkably, despite being wounded and contemplating suicide at one point, Holquin lived on his wits for three weeks before New Guinea natives came to his aid. These men were forced to hand him on to the enemy, however, due to the impossibility of Holquin being rescued and the men's fear of reprisals when he was found. Holquin survived Rabaul imprisonment, one of only a handful of prisoners of war to do so. A recent photo of the nose art appears in chapter 7. *From Down Under* (see bibliography)

MYAKIN-BACK, Douglas A-20, 42-86738, artist unknown, 388th BS, 312th BG. Former 389th BS pilot Joseph W. Rutter recorded in his book *Wreaking Havoc: A Year in an A-20* that his unit's Catholic chaplain was totally against risqué subject matter used as airplane nose art. This probably explains why the original *MYAKIN-BACK* nose art seen here was required to be changed. The situation was even captured in a wartime cartoon (uncredited, but probably drawn by Cpl. Frank G. Farina, taken from the 3rd BG's souvenir book, *The Reaper's Harvest*—both the 3rd and 312th BGs were at Hollandia together), adding weight to just how unusual a circumstance this was. The photo below right shows what changes were made to the original artwork: the name was painted out, the light-colored background was painted over, and the pin-up was no longer topless. The altered work, in fact, now more closely resembled the May pin-up from the 1944 *Esquire Varga Calendar*, on which the nose art had originally been based! While this may seem to have been a rather extreme case of making an example, if nothing else it demonstrated that chaplains still exerted some influence! This A-20, whose original assigned pilot had been Lt. Walter J. Bartlett, reportedly ended the war at Nadzab, where it was subsequently scrapped.

Nancy Jane, Consolidated B-24, 42-73480, artist unknown, 403rd BS, 43rd BG. As seen in the photo above this B-24 had the pin-up added first, while the name came later, after at least thirteen missions (the dark smear may have been oil subsequently wiped off). She served with the 403rd from the beginning of 1944 until just before the end of World War II and is seen here in the second photo with her eventual total bomb log, thirty-nine missions altogether.

NAUGHTY MARIETTA, North American B-25, unidentified serial number, artist "frederic," 17th TRS (unconfirmed), 71st TRG (unconfirmed). Few photos of this strafer are known, but another late 1944 image seen by the author confirms that the cutback of camouflage paint around the cockpit area is similar to that on *charmin' lady* (q.v.), it being on this basis that seems most likely that the two B-25s were from the same squadron. The name of this B-25 was taken from the title of a popular 1935 MGM musical, based on a much-earlier operetta of the same name. A 5th AF P-40 of the 8th FS, 49th FG, carried the same name without nose art.

NEAR MISS, North American B-25, 41-30026, artist Allen L. ("Lyn") Hallum, 498th BS, 345th BG. As many readers will by now have noticed, bomb-riding pin-ups were popular representations for bomber nose art. As to the name, this was a somewhat uncommon but clever choice (a near miss in air force terminology would normally refer to a bomb that narrowly failed to hit its target, but in this case the near miss is just that, a young woman close at hand, even if only by way of illustration). Artist Hallum, who hailed from Hereford, Texas, and had been employed as a commercial artist before enlistment, was a member of this crew, the navigator/bombardier; in this photo he is standing directly below the artwork. To his left is Sgt. Mark W. Murphy, engineer, and to his right, the copilot, Lt. Anthony Buchwald, and the pilot, Lt. Garvice D. McCall. *NEAR MISS* survived 498th BS service to be left behind at Nadzab and was probably scrapped there. Her crew also survived 498th service, but Hallum, who has also been credited as instigator of the "Falcons" squadron insignia (see chapter 6), was a Korean War casualty, missing in action on October 3, 1950. He was then serving with the 13th BS, 3rd Bomb Wing.

the Nervous Virgin, Douglas A-20, 43-21320, artist unknown, 387th BS, 312th BG. The inspiration for this artwork was shapely cartoon character Moonbeam McSwine from Al Capp's very popular *Li'l Abner* series (Moonbeam also featured in the nose art on 5th AF C-47 *OLE MAN MOE*; see photo in chapter 4), but in this case the name had a double meaning since it also referred to the nervousness and lack of battle experience of the assigned pilot, Lt. Edgar R. Bistika. This A-20 was with the 387th from March 1944 until it was destroyed in a takeoff accident on February 14, 1945.

Nobody's Baby, Consolidated B-24, 42-40346, artist unknown, 319th BS, 90th BG. This B-24 was probably named after a popular song of the day, "I'm Nobody's Baby," originally recorded in the 1920s but given new prominence when sung by Judy Garland in the 1940 film *Andy Hardy Meets Debutante*. The plane was lost in a Japanese bombing raid on Fenton airfield, Northern Territory, on June 30, 1943, becoming the only 90th BG loss to enemy action in Australia during World War II.

Net Results, Consolidated B-24s, 42-109976, artist unknown, 19th BS, 22nd BG, and 44-41875, artist Dick Ebbeson, 528th BS, 380th BG. Based on a popular Gil Elvgren calendar pin-up of the same name, while we have seen the widespread copying of pin-up illustrations, this was a rare case where two different 5th AF squadrons decided to retain the original name as well as the artwork. The earlier B-24, top, was the first to feature it, presumably from April 1944, when it is known to have joined the 19th BS. Ebbeson's beautiful artwork, below, was not added until 1945 (44-41875 did not join the 528th until February 1945) and may have been influenced by the earlier work, but details are lacking. Both *Net Results* survived the war (in the latter stages of the earlier B-24's service, the abbreviated number 9976 was added, presumably, to both sides of the nose, the number on the RHS appearing directly below the pin-up's feet), but only 44-41875 was returned to the US (where it was later scrapped). Whether Ebbeson's painting had already been removed beforehand is not currently known.

NOCTURNAL 'MISSION, Consolidated B-24, 44-42250 (unconfirmed), artist unknown, 529th BS (unconfirmed), 380th BG. The apostrophe may seem odd but is presumably a stand-in for a missing letter, in this case "E." This B-24 was a late addition to the 380th BG, flying just one strike and an armed patrol before war's end, after which the plane was returned to the US and eventually scrapped. Perhaps surprisingly, the nose art remained intact until the end.

NOT IN STOCK, Consolidated B-24, 42-41077, artist unknown, 400th BS, 90th BG. This plane was formerly called *Mary Joyce & Ruby* (q.v.), and the change of name and well-executed artwork has made this a well-known 400th BS B-24, but its subsequent squadron service appears little known. Note that the pin-up's pose in this photo, and that of *"NORMA"* below, suggest that both artists, although different in style, based their works on the same original source material.

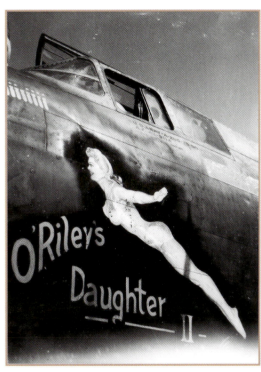

O'Riley's Daughter II, Douglas A-20, 43-9114, artist unknown, 386th BS, 312th BG. Formerly named *Gloria C II* (q.v.), the name change to *O'Riley's Daughter II* (after a bawdy traditional Irish song that was popular with soldiers as a drinking song for a century or more) occurred in October 1944 after her original pilot, Paul Teague, left the squadron (Teague's first A-20 had been named *O'RILEY'S DAUGHTER*). Note how the bomb log has also been changed, reflecting, perhaps, just the missions flown in new hands. According to the research for the 312th's history volume, *Rampage of the Roarin' '20s*, though, the A-20 remained in the 386th's hands only until February 1945, after which it was salvaged.

"NORMA", Consolidated B-24, 42-72948, artist unknown, 400th BS, 90th BG. This B-24 featured two versions of *"NORMA"*, both painted on the RHS. The first was probably that seen in the photo above of what appears to be a gun-toting kangaroo, the other the more photogenic yet somewhat unhappy-looking nude perched on an armchair. The Army Air Forces Aid Society's 1944 pocketbook, *AAF: The Official Guide to the Army Air Forces*, notes that "names on planes are . . . often meaningful only to the crew," as, undoubtedly, some of the artwork was too, and that being the case, *"NORMA"* would be a case in point. Nothing further is known about this B-24 except that it was salvaged ca. March 1944.

Ole' TOMATO, Consolidated B-24, 42-100291, artist Charles R. Chesnut, 33rd BS, 22nd BG. Another "Ole' Tomato" nose art name (for an earlier one, see *HOW'S YOUR OLE' TOMATO*); just what it referred to is not known to the author, although it does seem that the pin-up is squeezing an old tomato in her right hand. An early Chesnut nose art painting; after little more than six months with the 33rd BS, this B-24 was shot down by AA over Matina airstrip, Mindanao, on September 1, 1944, in the opening round of major 5th AF daylight raids on airfields near Davao. All eleven crew (an extra gunner had been given permission to fly with them that day) were lost. Another 33rd BS B-24, *TEMPTATION* (q.v.), was also lost on this same occasion. For other Chesnut artworks on camouflaged B-24s, see *Our Gal III*, *Redhot Ridinhood*, *Round Trip Ticket*, *SWEET RACKET*, the first *Tail Wind*, and the first *YANKEE GAL* in this chapter. *Via Charles Schaedel*

"*ON DE-FENSE*", Consolidated B-24, 42-109995, artist Bill McBroom, 530th BS, 380th BG. There were at least three examples of 5th AF B-24 nose art that featured a painting of a pin-up caught up in a barbed-wire fence, the others being *BOTTOM'S UP* (q.v.) and the *RIP SNORTER* (q.v.). There was a pin-up by famous artist Gil Elvgren named *On De-Fence* (note spelling) that probably inspired this name and artwork, but the young lady depicted was more modestly dressed and looking backward. What can be said with certainty is that this work and *BOTTOM'S UP!* were very similar in style, and one may have influenced the other, but substantiation is lacking. This B-24 flew the first of around eighty missions with the 530th BS on May 6, 1944, and the last on June 21, 1945. On the following day, on takeoff for another mission from Murtha Field, Mindoro, as lead aircraft, a series of mishaps, starting with a propeller governor failure on no. 2 engine, left the pilot, Lt. Bob Riehle, little option but to return to base. It proved possible to drop the bombload safely, but at the expense of the bomb bay doors. With limited maneuverability and space available, Riehle brought the bomber down, miraculously jumping over other 380th machines waiting to take off, but the no. 4 propeller on one B-24, *Toddy* (q.v.), struck the RHS main plane of "*ON DE-FENSE*", setting the fuel wing tanks on fire. The stricken ship ended up north of the runway in a low-lying area, with six of the crew dead or dying.

OOOOOH! LADY, Douglas A-20, 43-22175, artist unknown, 388th BS, 312th BG. This A-20 had originally been assigned to the 386th BS but was later transferred to the 388th after repairs became necessary following a takeoff accident. It is not known what, if any, nose art was in place while the A-20 was with the 386th, but given that the artwork seen here (based on the June 1943 Varga Girl pin-up) is astride the late-war red heart-shaped insignia of the 388th BS, then it is suspected that it was a 388th artist who created it. By the end of the war, this A-20 had flown at least sixty missions.

"*Our Baby*", North American B-25, 41-30522 (unconfirmed), artist unknown, 500th BS (unconfirmed), 345th BG (unconfirmed). If the tie-in between name and airplane serial number is correct, then this is, indeed, a little-seen 500th BS pin-up, another example of nose art based on the June 1943 Varga Girl, but this time sans the close-fitting clothing. The original artwork was of the complete figure, but after gun packs were added, the necessity for blast panels cut off the lower section of the artwork, as shown. B-25 41-30522 was on the 500th BS's books for only around four months and was ditched after AA damage during a raid on the Hansa Bay area on November 20, 1943. Of the six-man crew, it seems likely that one did not survive the ditching, while the other five made it ashore, where they were subsequently captured. Within days, however, those men were executed by their captors.

Ou'r Gal, Martin B-26, 40-1407, artist unknown, 33rd BS, 22nd BG. The origins of this artwork have not been traced, but chances are that it was an early example of bomber nose art added in the US prior to an overseas delivery flight. The pin-up and name (complete with unnecessary apostrophe) also appeared on the RHS of this B-26. *Ou'r Gal* arrived in Australia on March 30, 1942, and went into action in New Guinea soon after but appears to have seen only limited frontline service, often being flown by Lt. John H. Disbro, who had graduated from copilot to pilot during this time. After the 33rd BS lost its B-26s (at which stage the camouflage was removed, as was, presumably, the nose art) and converted to B-25s, Disbro named his next aircraft "*Our Gal*" II, a photo of which follows. The first line of the text on the pin-up's thigh reads "BOY OH BOY."

"*Our Gal*" II, North American B-25, 41-30666, artist George McGowan, 33rd BS, 22nd BG, later to 345th and 312th BGs. This nose art began as seen in the RHS photo with a single pin-up girl, modeled on a cheerleader, a copy of which was also added to the LHS nose. Later, somewhat unusually, five much-smaller pin-ups were added to the LHS, while at least three others were added to the RHS and another was painted on the inside of the underside crew entry hatch (bottom right of LHS photo). Most of these smaller works, it seems, were based on pin-ups by Alberto Vargas. The two names just visible on the nose in the LHS photo are Capt. Oswalt and Lt. Horan; Oswalt was the crew's bombardier, while Horan was the Australian Army Air liaison officer attached to the 33rd BS and often a passenger aboard this B-25, which was semiregularly flown by the commanding officer, Capt. John H. Disbro (the name "CAPT. DISBRO" appears under the cockpit window ledge on the LHS, while the name under the window ledge on the RHS is "LT. EDGEMON"). It has been said that there was a pin-up for every member of the crew, but clearly, even adding in one extra for Horan, there were extras. This B-25 stayed with the 33rd BS for about four months prior to transfer to the 500th BS, 345th BG, in February 1944 (but only for a few days), thence to the 498th BS, 345th BG (for around a month). Transferred to 5th Bomber Command Replacement Pool in early April 1944, it was subsequently passed to the 389th BS, 312th BG, and used by that squadron, presumably, in a transport role until a taxiing accident ended her career on August 28, 1944. For all this time it is thought that all the pin-up artworks that had been added were retained.

Our Gal III, Consolidated B-24, 42-100313, artist Charles R. Chesnut, 33rd BS, 22nd BG. This aircraft arrived at Nadzab for the 33rd BS in February 1944 already carrying the name *"SPECIAL DELIVERY"* and the cartoon character artwork as seen in the inset photo (on March 10, 1944, the 22nd BG commanding officer, Lt. Col. Richard W. Robinson, led the group's very first B-24 mission in *"SPECIAL DELIVERY"*, and perhaps it was chosen for him to fly that day because of its name; the writing on the cartoon character's cap is "B-24"). The nose art remained like that (on both sides of the nose) for at least a month but was later changed to *Our Gal III*, presumably at the request of the then Maj. Disbro (see previous page). Clearly, olive-drab paint was in short supply at the time, since the old artwork was painted over in a darker color that did not match. The new artwork is believed to have been one of Chesnut's earliest works (for others, see *Ole' TOMATO*, *Redhot Ridinhood*, *Round Trip Ticket*, *SWEET RACKET*, the first *Tail Wind*, and the first *YANKEE GAL* in this chapter). Disbro was not around long to enjoy *Our Gal III*, though, since his term as commanding officer of 33rd BS came to an end on May 1, 1944.

"OUR HONEY", Consolidated B-24, 44-40860, artist unknown, 19th BS, 22nd BG. This nose art was based on the cover pin-up from Earl MacPherson's 1944 *Artist's Sketch Pad* calendar (for another example of this artwork, see *FORM 1-A* in this chapter), but, sadly, *HONEY* had a brief existence. Assigned to the 19th BS in September 1944, it served with this unit roughly only four months before it was destroyed in a take-off accident from its Samar Island base on January 21, 1945. None of the twelve men aboard, including 22nd BG commander Col. Robinson, mentioned earlier, survived.

OVER EXPOSED, Consolidated F-7, 42-64241, artist unknown, 4th Photo Charting Squadron / 4th Reconnaissance Squadron (Long Range, Photographic). Western representations of native beauties as aircraft nose art subjects were uncommon, but here we have such an example (for two others in this chapter, see F-7 *PHOTO JEANNE* and B-25 *"Tail Wind"*). Such an artwork, however, was most likely added before crewmen saw any active service or native inhabitants, and was simply another figment of male imagination. Unit records indicate that when the 4th Reconnaissance Squadron (previously 4th PCS) began its attachment to the 5th AF, it still had four F-7As, such as *OVER EXPOSED* (photo included on that basis), on hand, but these were in the process of being exchanged for F-7Bs.

OUTA' THIS WORLD and OUTA THIS WORLD, Consolidated B-24s, 42-110001 and 44-41257, artists unknown, CRTC (001) and 65th BS, 43rd BG (257). Lt. Hugh J. Ryan's crew ferried 42-110001 to Australia ca. March 1944 and, like other crews, paid for nose art to be added beforehand. When the men were assigned to the 65th BS without their original charge, though, they transferred their affections to 44-41257, on which a copy of the original LHS artwork was added ca. October 1944. The first OUTA' THIS WORLD, meanwhile, had been assigned directly to the CRTC at Nadzab and is seen in the photo below in CRTC markings (the wording that has been painted out on the nose read "SCHOOL AP"; later the last three digits of the plane's serial number were added) with Flt. Lt. Ray Kelly's RAAF crew ca. September 1944. The view at top right shows the RHS of the same plane earlier at Townsville, but the artwork, a mirror image of the September pin-up from the 1944 *Esquire Varga Calendar*, is incomplete and may have been short lived, since this is the only photo this author has seen of it. The last view is of the artwork on 44-41257, which, it is understood, flew her last combat mission on August 8, 1945, and soon after was flown to Biak for open-air storage. *CRTC photo, Mrs. Barbara Prime*

PANAMA HATTIE, Boeing B-17, 41-24381, artist Ernie Vandal, 63rd BS, 43rd BG. While this B-17 served briefly in the Panama Canal Zone with the 6th BG prior to being assigned to the 43rd BG, it seems unlikely that it carried nose art until Vandal added this tribute to its earlier service. The name was taken from the Cole Porter Broadway smash hit, subsequently a very popular 1942 MGM musical, but the origins of the artwork have yet to be traced. After completing active service as a bomber during 1942–43, HATTIE was converted to an armed transport for the 54th TCW and given new nose artwork featuring a quizzical baby, with one arm supporting its chin and the other outstretched in front of him/her, and a new name, WELL GODDAM, a photo of which can be found in chapter 7. *Boeing Aircraft Co.*

PANNELL JOB, North American B-25, 41-30024, artist unknown, 500th BS, 345th BG. This was the second nose art painting to grace this B-25 strafer, which had originally been assigned to the 498th BS and featured a detailed artwork of a very angry Native American chief named *"RED WRATH"* on the RHS (see photo in chapter 6). Later, the 498th's falcon-head unit insignia was also added to the nose (again, see chapter 6). In April 1944 this B-25 was transferred to the 500th BS, the earlier name and artwork were painted over, and this pin-up and name were added (the assigned pilot at the time was Lt. Ray Pannell), but the B-25 served with the 500th for only just over two months before being lost on a training flight on June 11. This photo of *PANNELL JOB* showing eighty-three mission symbols in place was taken at Nadzab, ca. May 1944.

Paper Doll, Consolidated B-24, unidentified serial number, artist unknown, unit(s) unidentified. The popularity of pin-ups in magazines during World War II led to them becoming known in some quarters as "paper dolls" (the original paper doll was just that, a paper or thin card representation of a person—man, women, or child—which, dressed in different outfits also made of paper or thin card and held on by tabs, tended to be a child's plaything). This, in turn, probably led to the popularity of the song of the same name recorded by the Mills Brothers in 1943, which went to number one in the Billboard singles chart for twelve weeks from late in the year until early 1944 (the lyrics even appeared in *Yank* magazine at the time). The fact that little is known about this B-24 does suggest that it was either an early loss or that the artwork (a nude version of the July pin-up from the 1943 *Esquire Varga Calendar*) and name were replaced.

PAPPY'S PASSION and *PAPPY'S PASSION II*, Consolidated B-24, 42-100222, artist unknown, 319th BS, 90th BG and Consolidated B-24, 42-73121, artist unknown, 531st BS and 380th BG, respectively. The similarities of these two works, particularly the fact that no other 5th AF artists are known to have come up with the "babe"-carrying stork idea elsewhere, the virtually identical lettering and positioning of the artwork (*PAPPY's PASSION* name and artwork had originally been applied to a camouflaged background but was carefully retained when the camouflage was removed) would suggest that the same artist was responsible for both, but details are lacking. *PAPPY'S PASSION II* had originally been named *ROYAL FLUSH II* (q.v.) and had been repainted and renamed only following the stripping back of her coat of camouflage paint. Comparing the two, in the second work there is a smaller stork, now wearing shoes and sporting a different hat style, whose wings are in the up position, while the pin-up has a different hairstyle and is no longer fully reclining and looking up, but saluting onlookers with a raised glass. Note too that while the *ROYAL FLUSH II* / *PAPPY'S PASSION II* bomb log (fifty-four missions shown; the documented total was sixty-one, but seventy-four bomb stencils were eventually added) was also on the RHS, but that for *PAPPY'S PASSION* (which eventually was to feature a bomb log of 138 missions) was on the LHS. *PAPPY'S PASSION II* photo Eric Geddes

PATCHED UP PIECE, Consolidated F-7, 42-64047, artist Al G. Merkling, 20th CMS, 6th PRG. A photograph of Merkling working on this nose art is included at the beginning of the previous chapter, but here are two later shots, the first taken when the aircraft was being stripped of camouflage paint. Note the care being taken to preserve all the original artwork, but as seen in the second photo, the first name added was done away with and reapplied in new form, and a circular background was added to the pin-up. Not only did the new background make it easier to retain the original outline of the pin-up, but it would have helped emphasis the work, given that it was now on a bare-metal fuselage. This F-7, although well photographed (the last photo seen of her by the author shows the mission symbols, without a star, to have had cloud symbols added), had but a short service life, with her first mission on April 5, 1944, and the last on September 2 of that year. What became of her subsequently is not currently known.

PATCHES, Consolidated B-24, 41-23673, artist unknown, 320th BS, 90th BG. There is no name visible in this photo, since it appeared only on the LHS of the aircraft. The bomb log and enemy aircraft claims, however, appeared on both sides. The pin-up must have been a late addition to the B-24, since this was another one of the 90th BG's early ships, but the artwork was based on the Varga Girl that appeared as the gatefold in *Esquire*'s October 1943 issue; hence it could have been added only after that. Internet source pacificwrecks.com states that this B-24 was salvaged in April 1945. For other examples of copies of this pin-up, see B-24 *LUCKY LUCILLE* and B-25 *The WAC-A-TEER OFF DUTY* in this chapter, P-38 *Thoughts of Midnite* in chapter 3, and C-47s *BYE, BYE, BLUES*, *Pretty Baby I*, and *SPEEDY STEEDE* in chapter 4.

"PATChES", Consolidated B-24, 42-73474, artist unknown, 531st BS, 380th BG. Although this was another popular bomber nose art name, there were only the two B-24s so named in the 5th AF. This one was in 531st BS service throughout 1944 and right up until April 20, 1945, when she failed to return to base after developing engine trouble en route to Saigon, a target that the 380th BG was bombing for the first time. Since this entailed a long overwater crossing, it is presumed that *"PATChES"* was forced to ditch, but no trace of the bomber or her crew has ever been found. *Graham Turner via Geoff Turner*

PATIENT KITTEN, Consolidated B-24, 44-41031, artist Charles R. Chesnut, 33rd BS, 22nd BG. Although much photographed, sadly this B-24 was in the hands of the 33rd BS for only little more than six months before it was lost with all crew members after a direct hit by Japanese AA over Formosa on April 15, 1945.

'PATTY'S PIG', Consolidated B-24, 44-40398, artist unknown, 531st BS, 380th BG. Assigned to the 531st in May 1944, on October 9, 1944, in the course of a five-plane bombing mission against Koepang, Timor, while on her nineteenth mission, 'PATTY'S PIG' was shot down by AA and crashed into Koepang Bay. Five of the crew, who included a RAAF RCM operator, were seen to bail out, but postwar inquiries found that there was no record of any of the crew having been taken prisoner of war.

PEACE OFFERING, Consolidated B-24, 44-50811, artist Raymond A. Hafner, 529th BS, 380th BG. This pin-up, which bears a striking resemblance to the June 1945 Varga Girl, is suspected to have been the second to last of the nine that Hafner created for the 529th BS. This B-24 was in action by early June 1945 and flew nineteen strikes before the war ended. It was later returned to the US and, like the vast majority of B-24s that came back, whether from late-war production or not, was subsequently salvaged and the remains cut up and melted down.

THE PETER HEATER / THE HEATER, Consolidated B-24, 42-40917, artist unknown, 320th BS, 90th BG. With artwork based on George Petty's *Esquire* magazine's gatefold of November 1941 (minus white telephone and negligee), it would appear that it did not take long for the combination of the nude pin-up and the name THE PETER HEATER to strike discord, as a result of which, apparently, the word PETER was ordered to be removed. As seen here, the offending word was painted out, but the fact that it had been censored was noted. The alterations made, however (note that the painted-out section was in a much-lighter color), drew only more attention to the name. Note also that this B-24 seems to have started out with another artwork, subsequently deleted. Ending the war at Nadzab; see appendix 3 for a suggestion that the original name was later reinstated.

PETTY GAL, Consolidated B-24, 44-40373, artist Enoch H. Wingert, 65th BS, 43rd BG. Although many readers may have considered that this artwork paid homage to the work of the original *Esquire* magazine pin-up artist George Petty (who was later replaced by Alberto Vargas), in fact Lt. Morris E. Petty was the aircraft captain and his copilot was Horace V. Petty (no relation). This B-24 flew at least thirty-eight missions prior to her last on May 18, 1945. On that occasion, she was badly damaged after being hit by antiaircraft gunfire near Formosa and had to be nursed back to Lingayen airfield, where she was left. A last photo of the artwork, the setting for which is very similar in style to that featured in another of the artist's works, *PUNJA KASI* (q.v.), appears in chapter 7.

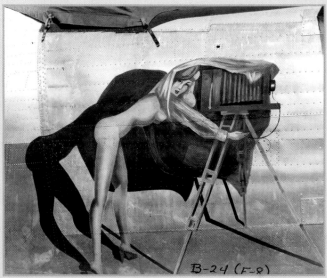

PHOTO QUEEN!, Consolidated F-7, 42-73049, artist Al G. Merkling, 20th CMS, 6th PRG. Here are another group of photos, all from different sources, of different stages of a Merkling artwork; the first shows the complete pin-up together with her view-style camera, tripod, and dark focusing cover, the second with shading added, the third with incomplete lettering, and the last in its completed form, displaying a mission log comprising fourteen camera symbols, although only seven have had stars added, signifying successfully completed. Note in this last image above how the aircraft's name is formed from tens of make-believe photo images (some of them pin-ups!); forty-one in the word *QUEEN* alone. This F-7 apparently flew no further missions after August 1944 and ended the war on Biak Island, where it was later scrapped.

PHOTO JEANNE, Consolidated F-7, unidentified serial number, artist unknown, 4th Reconnaissance Squadron (Long Range, Photographic). There was an earlier 4th Squadron F-7 (an F-7A) with native-themed nose art named *OVER EXPOSED* (q.v.), and here is another, this time with some of her crew. Note the addition of a camera in this case, though, an artist's impression, it seems, of how a female native spy working undercover in the Pacific may have looked! *PHOTO JEANNE* carried squadron identity 4-K. For nose art on other NMF F-7Bs of this squadron, see *KAY-18*, *THIS ABOVE ALL*, and *WELL DEVELOPED* in this chapter.

Phyllis J. of WORCESTER, Consolidated B-24, 44-40228, artist unknown, 319th BS, 90th BG. This B-24 was named by the squadron CO, Capt. Charles D. Briggs Jr., in honor of his wife, Phyllis Jane, from Worcester, Massachusetts; the couple had married in 1942. The plane flew at least ten missions before the artwork, probably based on a photo of Mrs. Briggs but dressed in pirate-era nautical attire, was added and was another example of the 319th's late-war nonnude nose art based on real women. In fact, it may have been Capt. Briggs who instigated this practice that promoted more-wholesome nose art on his bombers. Mrs. Briggs's outfit in the artwork was in keeping with the 90th BG's "Jolly Roger" pirate-inspired nickname and insignia (with crossed bombs replacing the original bones this normally appeared on the vertical fins of 90th BG B-24s). A later photo of *Phyllis J. of WORCESTER* with an ominous-looking "X" on the nose can be found in chapter 7.

PICKLED PEACH, Consolidated B-24, 42-73483, artist unknown, 403rd BS, 43rd BG. The name is a slang term, perhaps one that originated in California ca. 1930s–1940s, referring to an attractive but intoxicated young lady. The name and illustration were copied from a postcard of the day (*at right*), illustrated by "Justmet" from the "California Dish" series. This was the second rendition of the artwork; the first featured what appears to have been the same pin-up but with the name written as per the postcard, with *Pickled* to the left of the leg to the floor and *Peach* to the right. It seems that the crew wanted the artwork to stand out more, though, so the cloudlike backdrop was added (which also covered the original printing) and the much-larger name was painted in block text, as shown. This B-24 was lost in an aircraft accident northwest of Townsville, Queensland, on a flight from Dobodura to Townsville on March 28, 1944, which claimed the lives of all seven men aboard.

PISTOL PACKIN MAMA, Douglas A-20, 43-9391, artist unknown, 387th BS, 312th BG. This was a former 417th BG plane received by the 387th BS on March 20, 1944, after which it was assigned to Lt. John C. Alsup and the pin-up and name, both of which were taken from *Esquire* magazine's March 1944 Vargas gatefold, were added (the photo at right shows how the original artwork looked). This example of the most popular bomber nose art name of World War II (which originally, with apostrophe, came from the tremendously popular 1943 film and song of the same name) had but short service with the 312th, since the A-20 was destroyed due to fire and explosion while being serviced at Nadzab on July 4, 1944. Fortunately, there were no injuries, but ten A-20s of the 386th and 387th Squadrons were damaged, one beyond repair.

PISTOL PACKIN' MAMA, Consolidated B-24, 42-40594, artist unknown, 321st BS, 90th BG. This example of *PISTOL PACKIN' MAMA* was based on the August pin-up from Earl MacPherson's 1943 *Artist's Sketch Pad Calendar* (for another example of the same artwork, see *Dauntless "Dottie"* in this chapter), but with the pin-up essentially completely nude apart from a belt, vest, and hat! The view at right shows the RHS following the B-24's arrival at the Townsville Air Depot, where it appears to have been the sixteenth B-24D received there to have its existing glasshouse nose earmarked for replacement by a hydraulic turret. The nose art is still quite new at this stage (ca. July 1943), the artist having followed the look of MacPherson's cowgirl very closely. The view below left shows the LHS after the turret was fitted, while it seems that a rough attempt has been made to add detail to the pin-up's formally blank nether regions. This appears to have drawn complaints, though, since the offending area was later covered up by the addition of shorts; see last photo. This B-24 and its ten-man crew were lost in action on October 12, 1943. For another example of "cleaned-up" artwork, see A-20 *MYAKIN-BACK* in this chapter.

"*PISTOL PACKIN' MAMA*", Consolidated B-24, 42-41209, artist unknown, 319th BS, 90th BG. It may have been just a coincidence that two 90th BG B-24s carried this same name around the same time; as mentioned above, the first one was lost in October 1943, while this one was ditched at sea as a result of suffering AA damage on December 1, 1943. Four of the crew failed to escape the sinking aircraft, but the balance was able to be rescued late the following day after another 319th crew found the survivors on rafts and orbited their location for four and a half hours, saving a rescue PBY a lot of search work. As a postscript it is interesting to note that, perhaps intentionally, no other 90th BG B-24 is known to have carried the *PISTOL PACKIN' MAMA* name after 42-41209 was lost.

PISTOL PACKIN' MAMA, Martin B-26, 40-1388, artist unknown, 19th BS, 22nd BG. This B-26 was an early arrival in Australia where it was subsequently given the name "*Lil Rebel*". At some stage in the first half of 1943 the camouflage on most of the 22nd BG's remaining B-26s was stripped off and soon after this plane returned to frontline service in New Guinea as *PISTOL PACKIN' MAMA*. This photo shows her overall look around the end of 1943 not long before these last 5th AF B-26s were returned to Australia, mostly for scrapping although 40-1388 did survive a little longer thanks to subsequent usage at the Townsville Air Depot. In this photo *PISTOL PACKIN' MAMA* displays a four-lined bomb log of 80 missions, making it a high scorer for the Pacific, but not all of these seem to have been documented in unit records.

"*Pistol Packin' Mama*", North American B-25, 41-30764, artist unknown, 33rd and 2nd BSs, 22nd BG, later 501st BS, 345th BG and 17th TRS, 71st TRG. This B-25 was assigned to the 33rd BS in September 1943 and moved to the 2nd BS in January 1944, to the 501st BS by the end of that same month, and then on to the 17th TRS in June. Note in this photo the painted-out area to the left of the pin-up, evidence of a change of plan for the nose art along the way. This photo was taken at Nadzab while the B-25 was in 501st BS hands; she went on to amass more than a hundred missions.

PLEASURE BENT, Consolidated B-24, 42-100157, artist Harold H. Heighton, 2nd BS, 22nd BG. Contact with the artist's family soon after his death in 2016 established that this was one of his works. His first work, completed stateside, was *ISLAND QUEEN* (q.v.), and his only known other work was *BAYBEE* (q.v.). *PLEASURE BENT* remained with the 2nd BS for more than a year, until April 18, 1945, when it forced-landed at Laoag airstrip, Luzon, after a mission to Formosa (the squadron was then based at Clark Field) and was subsequently salvaged. Her bomb log at the time showed eighteen missions.

POISON IVEY, Consolidated B-24, 42-41249, artist unknown, 529th BS, 380th BG. This photo was taken at Garbutt, Queensland, prior to the B-24's assignment. It has been documented that *IVEY* did subsequently serve with the 529th BS from November 1943 until August 1944, but the lack of photos of her do suggest that in squadron use the nose art may have been short lived.

POM POM EXPRESS, Consolidated B-24, 44-50396 (unconfirmed), artist J. Oetienna (?), 531st BS, 380th BG. "Pom pom" was a euphemism for sexual intercourse, and while the source of the term is not currently known, it seems to have been in limited use from around the time that US forces occupied the Philippines; the cartoon below is from the "Philippine Edition," June 2, 1945, of the newspaper published by the Liberty ship–based 3rd Aircraft Repair Unit (Floating). As mentioned earlier, the artist who completed the work, a Mindoro local, was also responsible for three other nose art paintings for the 531st—*ATOMIC BLONDE*, *BACHELOR'S BROTHEL*, and *FREE FOR ALL!!!*, but *POM POM EXPRESS* flew more missions than any of the others, more than thirty, since it was in service earlier, from April 1945. Just how soon after that the artwork was added is not known, but the early photo seen here is a rare view of the artwork, based on an original by K. O. Munson, still with a long way to go. Within a matter of months, this B-24 was returned to the US and left at Kingman, Arizona; the fact that it does not seem to have been photographed there suggests that, most likely, the pin-up had been removed beforehand. Also see *Texas Pom Pom* in this chapter.

"PROP WASH", Consolidated B-24, 42-73475, artist William B. McBroom, 530th BS, 380th BG. With artwork based on Gil Elvgren's pin-up in a work titled *Caught in the Draft* (see also A-20 *CALIFORNIA Sunshine*), but minus the umbrella and now with a small dog in tow, this B-24 was another one of the 380th BG "Century Girls" (there were twelve altogether) that completed more than one hundred missions. That occurred over the January 1944–June 1945 period, after which it seems that *"PROP WASH"* (according to one 530th veteran, *Prop* and *Wash* were also the names bestowed on two squadron dogs) was taken off operational flying and subsequently flown to Biak for salvaging. While not all the names can be seen in this photo, note that the lettering did have white edging to begin with, a minor detail that is not apparent in most photos. For other nose art by McBroom, see *"Deanna's Dreamboat"*, *"Dottie's Double"*, *"FRISCO FRANNIE"*, *Hell's Belle* (unconfirmed), *JUGGLIN' JOSIE* (unconfirmed), *LI'L D'-ICER*, *"ON DE-FENSE"*, and *ROUGH KNIGHT*, and *She' Asta* (unconfirmed), *"SLEEPY TIME GAL"*, and *Sandra Kay* in this chapter.

PRETTY BABY, Consolidated B-24, 42-109987, artist unknown, 319th BS, 90th BG. These four photos chart different stages of this artwork. In the first photo, above, it looks fresh and may well have been newly applied. In the second photo, below, most of her camouflage paint has been removed, but it can be seen that the nose art area has yet to be touched. As shown in the third photo, the pin-up was retained but the original name was removed. Note that *PRETTY BABY*'s mission log shows sixty-nine missions flown at this stage. The last photo at bottom right confirms that the name was reinstated (in enlarged form) prior to her seventieth mission, but just when this was is not currently known. *PRETTY BABY* ended the war on Biak.

"PUDGY", Consolidated B-24, 41-23830, artist unknown, 320th BS, 90th BG. Another early 90th BG nude pin-up, this time featuring a copy of one of George Petty's last pin-ups from *Esquire* magazine (in this case, the September 1941 issue) on both sides of the nose. The bomb log appeared only on the LHS, but note that the most-recent missions are represented by stars only. The wartime "Jolly Rogers" souvenir book stated that *"PUDGY"* ran up more than ninety missions, but only around half that number show in this photo, and photos of either side of the nose at any stage of her frontline service seem hard to find. *"PUDGY"* was declared war weary in 1944 and salvaged in the Philippines late that year.

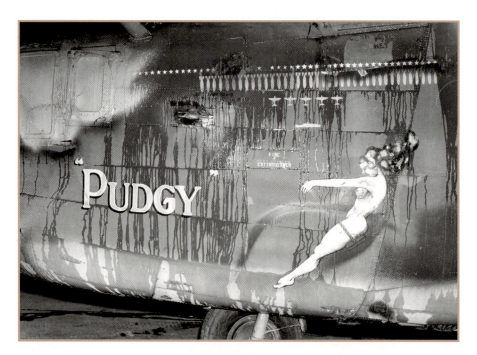

THE PUGNOSE PRINCESS, Consolidated B-24, 44-42229, artist unknown, 319th BS, 90th BG. Unlike *"PUDGY"*, above, this was a very late-war 90th BG nose art example added apparently during the last weeks of the war, since the name of the squadron's last wartime base, Ie Shima, features on the suitcase. This was another example of the 319th's late-war nonnude nose art and is a rare example of a 5th AF nose art (in this case, a "sweater girl") featuring a pin-up with other than a white complexion. Below the suitcase (*at left*) is the name of the artist, but it is too difficult to make out in this photo. For photos of an early 90th BG B-24 named *PUG NOSE*, probably in reference to the shape of the bomber's nose, see chapter 5.

Right: PUNJA KASI, Consolidated B-24, 44-40806, artist Enoch H. Wingert, 65th BS, 43rd BG. It would seem that the name of this B-24, which is in Malay language and can be loosely translated as "please give," was probably learned by the artist from locals on Owi Island, Dutch New Guinea, where the 43rd BG was based for most of the second half of 1944 (owing to its relative simplicity, the Malay language was, at that time, in widespread use throughout the then Dutch East Indies, including the western part of New Guinea). The abbreviated nose number 806 appeared on both sides of the bomber's nose along with the name *KEN'S MEN* in large letters on the LHS. This B-24 was subsequently salvaged, location unknown. Note the similarities in settings of this painting and that featured on another of Wingert's works, *PETTY GAL* (q.v.).

Queen Ann, Consolidated B-24, 42-110119, artist unknown, 33rd BS, 22nd BG. Despite this B-24 serving for more than a year with the 33rd BS and achieving more than a hundred combat missions, photos of her are not common, and details of her origins are lacking: rather a pity for such a beautiful pin-up. The bomb log is a little difficult to make out in this photo but began to the right of the word *Ann* in rows of fifteen divided into three groups of five. When she was last seen, probably on Biak Island, there appears to have been seven such rows to her credit.

Puss & Boots, Consolidated B-24 42-72942, artist Glenn A. Miller, 528th BS, 380th BG. Originally featuring a prancing horse and named *Prince Valiant* after a popular comic strip hero of the day, this B-24 was assigned to the 528th in November 1943. The glasshouse nose seen in the inset photo was exchanged for a hydraulic turret at Townsville in early 1944, and the *Puss & Boots* nose art was added later, after the olive-drab paint had been scraped off. The wide-ranging missions flown by 380th BG crews are well represented by this B-24: the first five from Fenton, Northern Territory, in December 1943; then to New Guinea for around a week, when it flew another four in the hands of a 530th BS crew; then back to Fenton by January 8, 1944; but by the end of February, back to New Guinea again on another deployment. After flying another three strikes, their *Puss & Boots* returned to Fenton, from where another fourteen missions were flown in March–August 1944. Following a move to Darwin, Northern Territory, she flew another seventeen missions between October 1944 and January 1945, on one occasion landing at Morotai Island. Subsequently the 380th BG relocated again, this time to the Philippines, from where her last eighteen missions were flown, the last on June 1, 1945. The bomber was subsequently assessed as war weary and, like the B-24 with Miller's other nose art, *DaLLy's DiLLy* (q.v.), was probably left at Clark Field for salvaging.

"*Queen Hi*", Consolidated B-24, 44-40432, artist Raymond A. Hafner, 529th BS, 380th BG. This stunning and complicated artwork, which, in emphasized form, brought a courtesan card to life, is seen here in early and later stages. Although website 380th.org lists forty-seven missions from northern Australia between June 27, 1944, and January 12, 1945, and forty-eight (four of them transit flights) from the Philippines between March 7 and August 14–15, 1945, for this B-24, the late-war photo at right (note the fading in the lettering, numbers and heart symbols by this time) suggests that this was another case where the full extent of her missions (symbols for only seventy-six have been added) was never properly kept up to date. Postwar, this B-24 remained with FEAF for a time before being salvaged, details of which are not available.

QUEEN MAE, Consolidated B-24, 44-40314, artist Al G. Merkling, 319th BS, 90th BG. This complicated and impressive artwork, which features one of the 319th's last nude works, is seen here in three views: a close-up of the finished work, facial detail from the unfinished painting, and from a distance after ten missions. The close-up of the pin-up's face, taken from the incomplete work, surely ranks as one of the most beautiful faces to appear on any bomber in World War II. Note the 90th BG skull-and-crossed-bombs insignia on the robe and rod in the other photos (for another example of 90th BG publicity, see also *ROAD TO TOKYO* in this chapter). This nose art was probably added at either Nadzab or Mokmer on Biak Island, bases shared by the 20th CMS and the 319th BS during 1944. *QUEEN MAE* went on to notch at least seventy completed missions but did not survive the war, since she was salvaged ca. June 1945.

Queen o' Hearts, Douglas A-20, 44-232, artist unknown, 388th BS, 312th BG. At first glance, not only is this photo a little burned out but the name above the Vargas-inspired artwork (based on *Esquire* magazine's April 1945 pin-up) makes no sense at all. This is because that lettering is simply the shadow effect of the *Queen o' Hearts* name, yet to be added. This A-20 was assigned to Capt. Wayne R. Brodine, who took command of the 388th BS in May 1945. The crew chief's name, also visible here, is TSgt. J. S. Figuerido. Although the 388th BS heart insignias were reportedly red, this photo may have been taken using orthochromatic film, which would turn a red tone much darker. Note too that the squadron insignia is not presented in the usual upright position (see also *OOOOOH! LADY* for a smaller but similarly positioned heart that is clearly in red).

QUEEN of HEARTS, Consolidated B-24, 42-40904, artist unknown, 63rd BS, 43rd BG. This was another of the original twelve 63rd BS B-24s that arrived in New Guinea in October 1943 for radar-equipped antishipping night missions. It seems that not all these planes carried pin-up nose art, but three others that did were *ART'S CART*, *LIBERTY BELLE*, and *Who's Next?*, photos of which appear in this chapter.

QUEEN OF HEARTS, Consolidated B-24, 44-40185, artist unknown, 320th BS, 90th BG. Although a slightly indistinct image, this nose art pin-up was based on the December 1943 Varga Girl, but with hearts substituted for the USAAF national markings as incorporated in the painting by Vargas. Originally described in the magazine's accompanying poem by Phil Stack as a "Heavenly Body," "winging her way through the sky," this pin-up was another popular inspiration for nose art artists.

The Queen Of Spades, Douglas A-20, 43-21309, artist Joseph A. DiLorenzo, 389th BS, 312th BG. This A-20, originally operated by 674th BS, 417th BG (whether with or without nose art is not currently known), was in 389th BS service from around March 1944 until January 28, 1945, when it crashed at Los Negros Island, in the Admiralty Islands group, resulting in the deaths of both men aboard and fourteen soldiers on the ground.

Queen Of The CLouds / Queen of the Clouds, Consolidated B-24, unidentified serial number(s), artist(s) unknown, 403rd BS (unconfirmed), 43rd BG. At least one source has suggested that these two artworks appeared on different B-24s, but given their similarity, particularly the top edge of the background cloud and how it cuts across the bottom corner of the nose window, it seems more likely that the work at left was an early version, while that at right was an improved later version on the same plane (the faded antiglare panel suggests that some time had elapsed before the early version was replaced; perhaps it too had noticeably faded). A close examination of the improved work reveals that it was signed off (see within the cloud at far right), but the detail is too small to pick up in this particular photo. There was another B-24, also from the 43rd BG, named QUEEN OF THE CLOUDS (in capital letters) a photo of which, prior to the name being added, can be found in the section on unnamed nose art toward the end of this chapter.

QUITCH, North American B-25, 41-30518, artist Charles L. Itt (unconfirmed), 501st BS, 345th BG. Part queen and part witch, there were three versions of the QUITCH pin-up. The first, named "QUITCH" (note the added quotation marks), was a nude female lying on her stomach on a broomstick, legs up in the air, her hands supporting her raised head, to which a witch's hat had been added. Accordingly, it has been said that due to complaints about the nudity, briefs and a bra top were added, and this became the second version of the artwork. "QUITCH" had been with the 501st since August 1943, and the second version artwork is said to have been still in place as of February 1944. However, it was subsequently painted over and replaced, as shown in this photo. Also note the bomb log, eighty-one missions, which dates the photo as late June 1944, when the original pilot assigned to this B-25, Lt. Symens, left the squadron. QUITCH stayed with the squadron until August 15, 1944, when it had to be ditched off Noemfoor following a midair collision, one crew member being injured in the process.

"QUEEN OF THE STRIP", Consolidated B-24, 44-42214, artist Raymond A. Hafner, 529th BS, 380th BG. This was probably Hafner's last pin-up artwork; he had come a long way since his early efforts such as *ADELAIDE FEVER* (q.v.). This late-war addition to the 529th BS flew only one mission prior to war's end, a patrol off southern Japan on August 28, 1945. Later it was returned to the US, but the absence of photos of her in open-air storage at Kingman, Arizona, postwar would suggest that the artwork was short lived, probably having been removed prior to her return.

QUEER DEAR / Queerdeer, Consolidated B-24, 42-40935, *Queerdeer* artist Dick Ebbeson, 528th BS, 380th BG. This B-24, with its early artwork featuring a nude holding a bottle of Four Roses Kentucky Straight Bourbon, was received by the 380th BG around late-August/early September 1943 and after only two missions was loaned to the 43rd BG in New Guinea. The bottom photo on this page is from a New Guinea-related collection and confirms that this artwork was already in place then. The plane returned to Australia in October 1943 and, whilst it is unknown when Ebbeson added the RHS artwork seen in the top photo (the parallel lines across the are shadows from the radar aerials) it is understood that it was one of his earliest works and it obviously occurred prior to the removal of the plane's camouflage paint in 1944. The artwork, as with the 529th BS's "Je Reviens" (q.v.), is based on the *Esquire* September 1943 Varga Girl but given a Native American look (note the feather). Apart from the two missions with the 43rd BG, this B-24 completed 63 missions with the 528th BS and is seen in the middle photo with members of Arch Dunne's RAAF crew in September 1944 (note the B-24's absence of fuselage national insignia). The last mission for *Queerdeer* came on January 12, 1945, from Darwin, after which it was transferred to the 531st BS and salvaged. *Middle photo, R. E. "Dusty" Hensel*

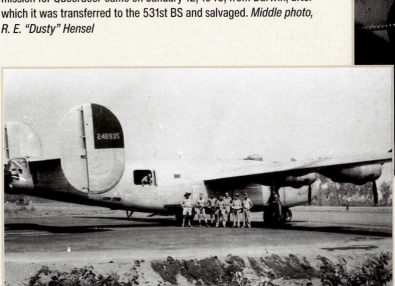

Ready Betty 'Gone Forever', Boeing B-17, 41-2637, artist unknown, 65th BS and 63rd BS, 43rd BG. This is another B-17 with early SWPA service that was subsequently transferred to the 65th BS, in this case in June 1943, where the pin-up nose art (based on the September offering in the 1943 *Esquire Varga Calendar*) was added (for other examples of 65th BS B-17 nose art, see *Blonde Bomber, Caroline, Chico, naughty but nice*, and *YANKEE DIDD'LER* in this chapter). It has been suggested that the original name of this B-17 was *'Gone Forever'* and that the *Ready Betty* was added later, but there appears to be no proof of this. After about three months' service with the 65th BS, *Betty* was passed to the 63rd BS, where the artwork was retained, but in November 1943 the bomber was returned to the US, and it is suspected that at that point the pin-up was either dressed up or painted out. Interestingly, this was another B-17 returned to the States with a much-exaggerated mission log (207 bomb symbols, seventeen "Jap Zeros," and seven Purple Hearts! Another was 41-2649, which does not seem to have had a name or nose art in 43rd BG service, but both were added later; see photo of *MY "Oklahoma" GAL* in chapter 7). For another nose art example that expressed the 'Gone Forever' sentiment (complete with winged cherry), see the C-46 of that name in chapter 4.

Rangy Lil, Consolidated B-24, 44-41867, artist Dick Ebbeson, 528th BS, 380th BG. *Lil* was assigned to the 380th in February 1945 and flew her first mission on March 6, 1945; her last (of more than fifty) was probably on July 24, 1945. She was subsequently returned to the US with nose art (copied from the January page of the 1945 *Esquire Varga Calendar*) intact, but after a time in open-air storage at Kingman, Arizona, the B-24 was cut up and subsequently melted down.

"READY WILLING AND ABLE", Consolidated B-24, 42-41078, artist unknown, 319th BS, 90th BG. This pin-up was based on a color photo of model and actress Leslie Brooks (1922–2011) that had appeared in *Esquire* magazine's October 1943 issue, but the oft-photographed nose art was only short lived, since the airplane and her ten-man crew all were lost without a trace on March 5, 1944.

BOMBER AND LONG-RANGE PHOTO RECON BEAUTIES

RED HEADED GAL, North American B-25, 41-12797, artist Ernie Vandal, Headquarters V Bomber Command. It has been reported that this B-25 was assigned to Brig. Gen. Kenneth N. Walker following his appointment to command V Bomber Command. He took over that role in September 1942 but lost his life while participating in a bombing raid against Rabaul in a B-17 just four months later. The B-25 was still with V Bomber Command on August 20, 1943, when this photo was taken, but reportedly it later served with the 3rd BG. After that, it was stripped of its original camouflage and markings and became another odd-job "fat cat" airplane, retaining the same name but with the addition of a new pin-up. A photo of the new nose art can be found in chapter 7.

Right: the *Red-headed Rebel*, Consolidated B-24, unidentified serial number, artist unknown, unit(s) unidentified. This image is taken from a strip of 35 mm contact prints of late-war B-24 nose art, many of which are of 90th BG planes and, on that basis, has been included as more than likely another 5th AF airplane. Other examples from the same strip of prints included in this chapter are *Cherrie*, *Coming Home! SOON*, *Good Pickin's*, and *MARY ANN*.

Redhot Ridinhood, Consolidated B-24, 42-100202, artist Charles R. Chesnut, 33rd BS, 22nd BG. Named after popular 1943 MGM Technicolor cartoon "Red Hot Riding Hood" directed by Tex Avery (1908-1980), this B-24 was assigned to the 33rd BS in February 1944, and the artwork is expected to have been another early Chesnut work (for other early Chesnut nose on camouflaged B-24s see *Ole' TOMATO*, *Our Gal III*, *Round Trip Ticket*, *SWEET RACKET*, the first *Tail Wind* and the first *YANKEE GAL*). "Red" was salvaged following a landing accident at Biak on November 2, 1944, but the name (together with a new Chesnut nose art painting) lived-on (*see below*).

RED-HOT RIDEN-HOOD II, Consolidated B-24, 44-40402, artist Charles R. Chesnut, 33rd BS, 22nd BG. This B-24 was initially assigned to the 2nd BS in June 1944 and following its transfer to the 33rd Squadron and the loss of the above B-24 became her replacement. Turn the page for another photo and more information.

RED-HOT RIDEN-HOOD II, seen on the previous page, subsequently became RED-HOT RIDEN-HOOD III, but why this occurred remains unexplained. After flying at least 40 missions she was left at Clark Field circa July 1945, and a last photo of her can be found in chapter 7.

Reina del PACIFICO, North American B-25, 43-36020, artist George M. Blackwell, 501st BS, 345th BG. Note the translation below the artwork, "QUEEN OF THE PACIFIC." This was one of more than a dozen new B-25J-11 airplanes assigned to the 501st BS in October 1944, five of which received nose art soon after, all by Blackwell, with names painted by Cpl. Joseph Merenda. The others were APACHE PRINCESS, Cactus Kitten, LAZY DAISY MAE, and WHITE WING, photos of all of which can be found in this chapter. This B-25 was lost on the same mission as Cactus Kitten on April 28, 1945.

RIDIN' HIGH, Douglas A-20, 42-22166, artist unknown, 388th BS, 312th BG. Formerly Maj. Joseph B. Bilitzke's *Baby Blitz II*, when he left the squadron to return to the US in May 1945 this A-20 was assigned to Lt. Michael Pisani, who had the original artwork and name changed as shown (the new name was that of a popular song of the day, written by Cole Porter and first performed by Ethel Merman). The same artist was probably responsible for other late-war 388th BS nose art, including *Miss BeHaven*. RIDIN' HIGH was subsequently reassigned to Flight Officer J. W. Hill, and it is his name, together with crew chief TSgt. F. E. Carr, that was in place when this photo, on Biak Island, was taken. This A-20 had run up a substantial bomb log by this time, 150 missions, expressed in thirty groups of five bomb symbols, a few of which are faintly visible at top left.

Rio Rita, Consolidated B-24, 41-24127, artist Talbot Garner, 404th BS, 43rd BG, later No. 7 Operational Training Unit (OTU) RAAF. This B-24, which had previously carried the name VALHALLA on the RHS, was renamed *Rio Rita* after the popular MGM 1942 adventure and musical-comedy film of the same name. *Rita*'s artwork included a hint of pubic hair, something of a taboo for that time, but given that its airing was limited (it was believed that it was added ca. July 1943, but the B-24 was taken out of service after heavy damage sustained in a mission to Wewak on August 29), there was little time for complaint. That was not the end of the aircraft or its nose art, though, since *Rita* was subsequently repaired and transferred to the RAAF. Received at the Australian heavy-bomber training base at Tocumwal, New South Wales, in May 1944 under new identity, A72-10, but with nose art in place and name reapplied in capital letters a little farther forward from where it had originally appeared, it is suspected that RAAF hierarchy soon required, however, that these unofficial markings be painted over. From *Down Under*.

the RIP SNORTER, Consolidated F-7, 42-73047, artist Al G. Merkling, 20th CMS, 6th PRG. This well-photographed F-7 flew only twelve missions with the 20th CMS between April and July 1944, after which its history has gone unrecorded until May 25, 1945, when 20th CMS researcher Chuck Varney notes that it was destroyed while landing at Biak. It is seen here in three views, the first up close with Merkling while he was working on the pin-up; the second, a little indistinct and from a distance (probably at Nadzab), shows the completed work still on a camouflaged background but with the camouflage paint in the process of being removed; and, in the last photo, a later close-up view that shows well the final look (the representation of the bull was based on the animal that appeared in many "Bull" Durham Tobacco advertisements). Many photos of this plane's nose art show no mission symbols in place at all, but, as the last image confirms, at least eleven were eventually added (note the stars, indicating that only six were successful). For another example of artwork featuring the somewhat odd theme of a young woman caught up in fencing wire (this time without the bull), see *BOTTOM'S UP!* earlier in this chapter; perhaps one artwork influenced the other.

THE ROARING TWENTIES, Douglas A-20, unidentified serial number, artist unknown, 673rd BS, 417th BG. The "Roaring Twenties," the popular name for the 1920–29 decade and already firmly embedded in popular culture before World War II began, was given a new lease of life in 1944 in New Guinea, of all places. This was because of the success achieved by 5th AF Douglas A-20s in low-level raids against Japanese-held areas there. As a result of this success, by August 1944 the 312th BG had decided to call itself the "ROARIN' 20s," and a new group insignia was designed featuring that name, which appeared on at least one A-20. This 673rd BS A-20 (the crew chief's name identifies it as a 673rd BS plane) adopted the same name; depending on when it was added it may have been the first A-20 to be so-named. Interestingly, the pin-up, while based on the June offering from the 1944 *Esquire Varga Calendar*, was a lot smaller that generally seen on 5th AF bombers by 1944.

ROAD TO TOKYO, Consolidated B-24, 44-40400, artist unknown, 319th BS, 90th BG. This artwork (*below*) was hastily applied at Biak on a recently received aircraft, not only to make Bob Hope's USO troupe feel at home prior to their show on August 25, 1944 (it will be remembered by many readers that Hope had starred with Bing Crosby and Dorothy Lamour in a number of "Road" movies for Paramount), but also to provide good publicity for the 90th BG, best known as "the Jolly Rogers" or "the Jolly Roger" BG (note the sign at left of the artwork on the aircraft). The artist appears to have attempted to include all the main members of Hope's troupe in the illustration, and the young lady at right certainly bears a resemblance to actress Frances Langford (1913–2005), who was one of them. In 1946, Langford starred in an RKO movie called *The Bamboo Blonde*, being the story of a 20th AF bomber pilot, played by Ralph Edwards, who falls in love with a nightclub singer (Langford) and whose crew subsequently arrange for a bathing-suit-clad likeness of her, named *THE BAMBOO BLONDE*, to be painted on their B-29. The photo at left, with costar Edwards (1913–2005), shows the end result.

ROARIN' ROSIE, Consolidated B-24, 41-23698, artist unknown, 319th BS, 90th BG. While this B-24 was among the first assigned to the 90th BG, just when the nose art was added is a moot point. The fact that both pin-ups can be seen to be using telephones suggests that they may have been based on George Petty artworks (whose pin-ups were often "on the phone"), that on the RHS (*above*) looking similar to the October 1941 *Esquire* Petty Gal. The gunners of this B-24's crew were officially credited with shooting down seventeen enemy fighters, "more than any other USAAF bomber in the Pacific" at that (undated) stage. While that number would, undoubtedly, be difficult to substantiate now, the bomber was subsequently flown back to the US, where its SWPA service would have further enhanced the reputation of the 5th AF.

"ROBBIE 'L", Consolidated B-24, 42-40979, artist unknown, 531st BS, 380th BG. The original *"ROBBIE 'L"* was written off in a takeoff accident at Fenton in June 1943 and sometime later this B-24 took on the same name and a new pin-up was added. There are twenty-nine mission symbols showing in this photo, and if that is the actual total at the time (a top row of eighteen does, however, seem to be an odd number), then the photo was taken around February 1944. The camouflage paint was later stripped off and a new painting based on Vargas's *Pistol Packin' Mama* pin-up added to the LHS, and, as such, *"ROBBIE 'L"* continued to see action until August 1944, after which, apparently, it was salvaged.

ROUGH KNIGHT / *Rough Night!* / *Rough Knight*, Consolidated B-24, 42-100209, artist William B. McBroom, 530th BS, 380th BG. Yet another pin-up copied from "Miss January" in the 1944 *Esquire Varga Calendar*, these three views show how the original artwork looked on paint, the revised artwork on bare-metal finish, and the final change in the name from *Rough Night!* back to *Rough Knight*. Note in the final photo, too, that the artist had by then added his surname to just below the pin-up's circular background. This was one of the 380th BG "Century Girls," which flew more than one hundred missions and was fortunate enough not only to survive the war but to be earmarked for return to the US for disposal (the French-language text, added postwar perhaps, seems to reflect both the end of the war and the flight home and can be translated as "I'm going" (*Je monté*) and "I fly" (*Je volé*). She was flown back to Washington by a crew captained by the 380th BG CO, Col. Forrest L. Brissey, leaving Okinawa on August 30, 1945. Back in the US, though, despite early talk of a war bond tour this never eventuated, and *Rough Knight* was just one more war-weary B-24 at Kingman, Arizona, with no prospect of a future and was eventually scrapped. *Rough Night!* photo, Eric Geddes

Rough Stuff!, Douglas A-20, 43-9038, artist unknown, 388th BS, 312th BG. This A-20 was assigned to the 388th BS in February 1944 and, at some point over the next couple of months, was named *My True Love* without accompanying artwork. That was subsequently removed and replaced by this artwork, based on a photo of English-born actress Betty Bryant (1920–2005) that had appeared in the "Down Under" edition of *Yank* magazine of March 31, 1944 (Bryant had starred in the popular wartime Australian movie *40,000 Horsemen*). Below the pin-up can be seen the name *Esther*, the then girlfriend or fiancée of assigned pilot Capt. Bertram N. Heyman (they married in 1946). *Rough Stuff!* remained with the 388th BS until October 1944, participating in at least fifty-five missions, and was subsequently passed on to the CRTC. For a nose-on view of this A-20 that shows an early version of the original skull-and-crossbones unofficial 312th BG insignia, see chapter 6.

Round Trip Ticket, Consolidated B-24, 42-100193, artist Charles R. Chesnut, 33rd BS, 22nd BG. Featuring an early Chesnut artwork that was probably influenced by Gil Elvgren's popular hitchhiker pin-up titled *Kneeding a Lift*, this B-24 was assigned to the 33rd BS in February 1944 and remained in service until October 25, 1944, when its rear fuselage and tail control surfaces were damaged by AA fire. It was able to make the return flight to base but was subsequently condemned for salvage. The photo above left suggests that the word "Ticket" has yet to be added, so perhaps it was an afterthought. That at above right is a good overall view showing all the name whilst the enlarged view at right shows the sign added by the pin-up's feet, which is not visible in the other two photos due to shadow. For other Chesnut works on camouflaged B-24s, see *Ole' TOMATO, Our Gal III, Redhot Ridinhood, SWEET RACKET*, the first *Tail Wind*, and the first *YANKEE GAL*.

ROUND TRIP Ticket, Consolidated B-24, 44-41538, artist Charles R. Chesnut, 33rd BS, 22nd BG. The second 33rd BS B-24 using this name was assigned to the squadron in December 1944 and survived the war but was wrecked due to a tire blowout on landing at Okinawa on August 26, 1945. One passenger aboard the B-24 died, the last of more than four hundred 22nd BG casualties between 1942 and 1945. Note the boldness of Chesnut's new work when compared with the original *Round Trip Ticket*, photos of which appear on the previous page. The sign he included is also much more prominent and has the USA at the top this time.

RUBY'S RICKSHA, Consolidated B-24, 44-40426, artist unknown, 320th BS, 90th BG. With the war dragging on and the Japanese Empire rapidly shrinking, Lew Evans's crew seem to have been thinking ahead about what life in occupied Japan might be like (a rickshaw—note correct spelling—is a small Japanese, man-powered, two-wheeled, passenger-carrying vehicle). Ruby was the name of Lew Evans's wife.

ROYAL FLUSH and ROYAL FLUSH II, Consolidated B-24, 42-73131 (*ROYAL FLUSH*) and 42-73121 (*ROYAL FLUSH II*), artists unknown, 320th BS, 90th BG (*ROYAL FLUSH*) and 531st BS, 380th BG (*ROYAL FLUSH II*). It is suspected that these artworks were completed prior to these B-24s leaving the States, the fact that both planes were off the production line so closely together suggesting that the artist of *ROYAL FLUSH II* had been suitably impressed enough to use the name of an existing artwork that he had seen for his more time-consuming work, which clearly featured greater detail. While *ROYAL FLUSH II* was based primarily in Australia's Northern Territory, both planes operated in New Guinea in early 1944, and the photo used here of *ROYAL FLUSH II* was taken after a New Guinea mission on March 8, when a third enemy fighter was claimed destroyed by one of this B-24's gunners. Later in the year, when the time came to strip away the camouflage paint of *ROYAL FLUSH II*, both the name and pin-up seen here were removed and replaced by a new artwork and name, *PAPPY'S PASSION II* (q.v.), which, coincidentally, was based on an earlier 90th BG B-24 nose art design.

NOSE ART OF THE 5TH AIR FORCE

RUM AND COKE, Consolidated B-24, 44-49827, artist unknown, 65th BS, 43rd BG. We have already seen the popularity of pin-ups combined with alcohol as nose art subject matter (e.g., *COCKTAIL HOUR*, *DOUBLE TROUBLE*, and *MIS-A-SIP*). Coming up with a catchy name for the artwork, however, was not always easy (see, for example, *QUEER DEAR*), but popular culture sometimes helped. In this case, we see the unidentified artist at work on this B-24 (what a pity he has yet to be identified; one suggestion has been that it was another work by Bartigian, but this does not appear to be a photo of him), while the second photo shows the finished product, named after, in abbreviated form, the very popular hit song of the day "Rum and Coca-Cola," which was recorded by the Andrews Sisters in late 1944. While the fame of both the song and drink live on, this B-24's military service was short lived; as a result of a landing accident on Ie Shima on September 7, 1945, it was condemned and salvaged.

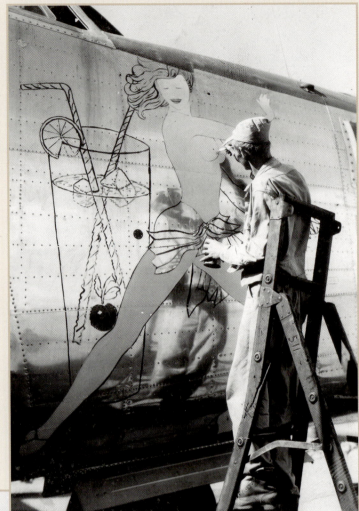

The "SACK", North American B-25, 41-12909, artist unknown, 405th BS, 38th BG. This B-25 began frontline service in September 1942 as *BLACK BARNEY "The WHITE RUSSIAN"*, a nickname that appeared on both sides of the nose (without other artwork) and referred to its pilot, Lt. Barney L. Johnson Jr. After only a handful of missions had been flown, though, the plane's original name was changed—due, it seems, to a change of crew—to *The "SAD SACK"*, in admiration of Sgt. George Baker's popular cartoon character. The pin-up was a later addition and was probably based on one of a number of now-famous publicity photos of actress Jane Russell (1921–2011) for Howard Hughes's film *The Outlaw*, but minus her skimpy clothing! Since the name appeared on both sides of the nose, the pin-up was added to both sides too, the word *SAD* being intentionally crossed out in both places. Under the cockpit window ledge on the RHS, the name DON was added. This photo was taken at the Townsville Air Depot, and with one source stating that this B-25 was condemned on March 10, 1943, then it seems likely that this photo may have been one of the last taken of her. A bomb log was added to the nose on the RHS, but how many missions were shown is not currently known.

SACK BOUND, Consolidated B-24, 42-73471, artist unknown, 63rd BS (unconfirmed), 43rd BG. Given the presence of the basic, US-marked, military-style camp bed, this would appear to have been the artist's impression of how he imagined the sleeping quarters in a Women's Army Corps (WAC) compound might look. Members of the WAC were the first women, other than nurses, to serve with the US Army, but an online history of the corps by Judith A. Bellafaire notes that "WACs in the SWPA had a highly restricted lifestyle. Fearing incidents between the women and the large number of male troops in the area, some of whom had not seen an American woman for 18 months, the theater headquarters directed that WACs (as well as Army nurses) be locked within barbed-wire compounds at all times, except when escorted by armed guards to work or to some approved recreation. No leaves or passes were allowed." See history.army.mil/brochures/WAC/WAC.HTM.

"Sack Time", Consolidated B-24, 42-41219, artist unknown, 531st BS, 380th BG. *"Sack Time"* flew twenty-three missions with the 531st BS but suffered extensive nose damage while parked at Long Strip, Northern Territory, on January 17, 1944, when struck by another B-24 landing with engine trouble. The incoming bomber effectively bounced off the nose of *"Sack Time"* before veering off course into another parked 531st B-24 (42-41248 *BEBE*) and "careening down the runway in a fireball." Eleven men died, and later *"Sack Time"* was provided with a "false nose" by the 30th Material Squadron to enable it to be flown back to Townsville. This photo shows that after the temporary repairs had been carried out, the artwork remained in place, but most of the name had gone. According to the plane's "Individual Aircraft Record Card," it was returned to the US in August 1944.

NOSE ART OF THE 5TH AIR FORCE

Sadie, Consolidated B-24, 41-24289, artist unknown, 400th BS, 90th BG. This B-24 was apparently assigned to the 90th BG in March 1943, its somewhat unattractive pin-up being notable for its size at a time when such artworks on bombers were generally much smaller. Given that the artwork was subsequently painted over, and the aircraft renamed *CONNELL'S SPECIAL The 2nd*, though, perhaps this original pin-up art was short lived. This B-24 survived its many SWPA missions and was subsequently flown back to the US, where it is noted as being condemned for salvage in December 1945.

SAN SUSAN, Douglas A-20, 43-9110, artist unknown, 386th BS, 312th BG. This A-20, with a pin-up based on a Zoë Mozert artwork titled *Naval Maneuvers*, served with the 386th BS from February to July 1944, her assigned pilot being Lt. William C. Wallace. Although the quality of the image is not the best (it was scanned from a very small original print), forty-six mission symbols can be seen, suggesting it was probably taken toward the end of the plane's 312th BG service. It later served with the 3rd BG and was lost in a crash on February 24, 1945, but whether or not it still had this nose art in place at the time is not known.

SANDY, Consolidated B-24, 42-100324, artist unknown, 408th BS, 22nd BG. This B-24 served initially with the 2nd BS of the 22nd BG, but only for a short time, and it is not thought that the name and artwork were added until the aircraft was transferred to the 408th. Serving with this squadron for only about seven months, *SANDY* and her ten-man crew were lost without a trace on October 14, 1944.

Satan's Secretary, Consolidated B-24, 42-63989, artist unknown, 528th BS, 380th BG. This B-24 began flying with the 528th BS in November 1943. The artwork is based on the September pin-up from the 1944 *Esquire Varga Calendar*, but just when it was added is not known—presumably not until the camouflage paint was removed, since no photos of her before that are known. This B-24 flew more than seventy missions, including eleven in New Guinea, but she was salvaged in Australia following her last mission from Darwin on February 2, 1945.

BOMBER AND LONG-RANGE PHOTO RECON BEAUTIES

SATAN'S BABY, Consolidated B-24, 44-40186, artist unknown, 63rd BS (unconfirmed), 43rd BG (unconfirmed). The first known example of 5th AF nose art to include a impression of Satan would seem to be one named "*Satan's Angel*", added to an original B-25, serial number 41-30037, from 498th BS, 345th BG. That artwork, shown in the photo below, was probably considered quite extreme in 1943, but it pales into insignificance when compared with that seen here (probably photographed in 1945), which combined Satan and nudity together. Surprisingly, this example of "bad girl" nose art does not seem to have been ordered to be removed or altered in any way, and the bomber is believed to have survived limited wartime service to be flown to Biak for open-air storage prior to being salvaged. Despite numerous sources identifying the unit to which this bomber was assigned as the 63rd BS, this B-24 is not mentioned anywhere in the second volume of the detailed 43rd BG history, *Ken's Men against the Empire*.

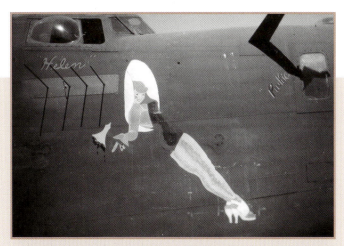

'*SATANS SISTER*', Consolidated B-24, 42-40680, LHS artist Thomas A. Moody, 403rd BS, 43rd BG, later 2nd BS, 22nd BG. According to the research for the 43rd BG history volumes *Ken's Men against the Empire*, this B-24 featured the two artworks shown, but only that on the LHS, which was based on the June 1943 *Esquire* magazine Varga Girl, was named. It has previously been mentioned that ferry crews rarely ended up with the planes that they delivered, but this was one exception, the pin-up artist being a member of that crew (the tail gunner), which was under the captaincy of Lt. John E. Bond. After service with the 43rd BG commencing in mid-1943, this was another B-24 used for crew conversion training by the 22nd BG in early 1944, subsequently (ca. April 1944) being left at Nadzab, where she was withdrawn from service. A last photo of the LHS nose art, which shows that in the second row of the bomb log all but the first two mission symbols had visibly faded, can be found in appendix 3.

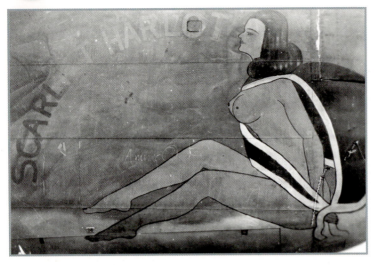

SCARLET HARLOT, North American B-25, unidentified serial number, artist unknown, unit(s) unidentified. Photographed at Garbutt prior to strafer conversion, this is the only photo of this nose art seen by the author. Chances are that it was short lived and replaced, perhaps, by unit markings.

SEAFOOD MAMA, Consolidated B-24, 41-24219, artist unknown, 321st BS, 90th BG. The name of this bomber would appear to have been taken from one of the numerous versions of the popular song "Hold Tight (Want Some Seafood Mama)," first released in 1938, the mermaid artwork suggesting some additional connection, but details are lacking. This B-24 and her ten-man crew were lost in action on July 12, 1943, shot down in the course of a bombing raid against Rabaul.

Above: Shag-on, Douglas A-20, 43-9134, artist unknown, 386th BS, 312th BG. Another example of artwork copied from the Vargas January 1944 *Esquire* pin-up, and the name that went with it was surprisingly bold by wartime standards; "shag" was (and is) a slang term of British origin for sexual intercourse, so to "shag-on" would seem to refer to wishful thinking in the pursuit of that. The term may have been learned by 5th AF personnel from Australian sources and used in the hope that a "foreign" word would not attract undue attention. The A-20, which had also carried the name *Passionate Peggy* (painted over by the time this photo had been taken; see lower left of photo), was originally assigned to Lt. M. D. Gentry, whose name can be seen, and was with the 386th BS from around February to October 1944. After transfer to the CRTC (at Nadzab), it was lost on a bombing mission east of Muschu Island on February 9, 1945.

Below: SEVEN DAY LEAVE, North American B-25, 41-30611, artist unknown, 408th BS, 22nd BG. This B-25 served with the 408th BS between October 1943 and January 1944. Unfortunately, the names of the men in the photo are not known, but it is suspected that they are 408th BS personnel, the occasion possibly being the end of their time with this aircraft (all of the 408th's B-25s were transferred out ca. January 1944). This B-25 was subsequently assigned to the 71st BS, 38th BG (known as the "Wolf Pack"), and received that squadron's fearsome wolf's-head markings and a new name, *SOUTHERN BELLE*, but its service was cut short when, on "Black Sunday," April 16, 1944, it was badly damaged in an emergency landing at Saidor. Fortunately, there were no casualties.

She 'Asta, Consolidated B-24, 42-40512, artist William B. McBroom (unconfirmed), 530th and 531st BSs, 380th BG. The name of this B-24, on the basis of comments by her crew that "she [the plane] 'asta" [has to] go and "'asta' come back," was added to both sides of the nose, but the pin-up, based on the September offering from the 1943 *Esquire Varga Calendar*, appeared only on the RHS. *She 'Asta* flew her first mission with the 530th BS in June 1943, after a familiarization flight with the 319th BS, 90th BG, but little more than a month later was transferred, along with her crew, to the 531st. Transferred back to the 530th in September, her 380th BG service ended in December after a total of only twenty-eight missions (during which eight enemy fighters were claimed by the crew's gunners). After refurbishment, this B-24 became another of the D models gifted to the RAAF as crew trainers, arriving at the heavy-bomber training base at Tocumwal, New South Wales, on April 13, 1944, as A72-5. Former RAAF "Lib" instructor Ed Crabtree, who had flown this B-24 while serving with the 530th BS, recalled that in RAAF service, *She 'Asta*'s nose art was removed. *Mrs. Joan Barlow*

Shamrock Sherry, Consolidated B-24, unidentified serial number, artist unknown, 321st BS (unconfirmed), 90th BG. This is another example of a late-war nose artwork about which little is known, but another photo of this B-24, used in the introduction, was identified as coming from an officer of the 321st BS; hence the tentative squadron identification.

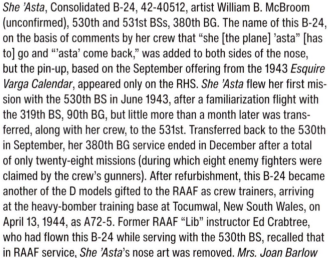

SHIRLEY ANN, Consolidated B-24, 42-73163, artist unknown, 63rd BS and 65th BS, 43rd BG. This B-24 arrived in the SWPA in October 1943 with artwork (based on the September page from the 1942 *Esquire Varga Calendar*) and name probably in place. She served with the 63rd BS until around February 1944, when she was transferred to the 65th. The authors of the second volume of the 43rd BG history *Ken's Men against the Empire* have noted that *SHIRLEY ANN* left the 43rd BG by the end of July 1944, but she was photographed by a member of the 6th ARU(F) in 1945 (probably in the Philippines), so some questions remain. Her official record card indicates that she remained on the books until salvaged overseas in October 1945.

NOSE ART OF THE 5TH AIR FORCE

"SHOO-SHOO BABY", Consolidated B-24, 42-109984, artist unknown, 408th BS, 22nd BG. This artwork (a nude version of a scantily clad Earl MacPherson pin-up) and name (taken from a popular Andrews Sisters' hit song of the day; see below) were added, as shown in the first photo, prior to this B-24's ferry flight to Australia ca. March 1944. "SHOO-SHOO BABY" was assigned to the 408th BS in April 1944, serving with that unit until a forced landing due to engine failure on May 6, 1945. In the second photo, the pin-up can be seen to have been joined by the "Red Raiders" group insignia, which was the way the 22nd BG became to be known following the appointment of a new commander, Col. Richard W. Robinson, in March 1944 (a B-26 that Robinson had flown in 1942 had been known unofficially as "Red Raider," since Robinson and two of his crew were redheads). Note also in that photo the addition of repair patches to the B-24's nose following frontline service. *Sheet music, Leeds Music Corp.*

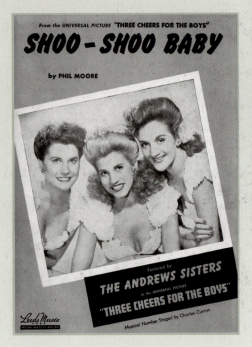

Shy-Chi Baby, Consolidated B-24, 44-40920, artist Robert Wenzel, 531st BS, 380th BG. This B-24, named after a Chicago-based romantic interest, was another 380th BG ship that saw around twelve months of service: August 1944–August 1945. She went on to fly ninety-seven missions, according to squadron records at the time, although website 380th.org can account for only ninety-two (thirty-seven in Australia, fifty-three from the Philippines, and two transit flights). Interestingly, it appears that only fifty-nine mission symbols ever appeared on the fuselage, fifty in the top row, four at the LHS of the second row (not visible here), and five at the RHS of the second row. This B-24 was subsequently returned to the US and left at Kingman, where it was later scrapped. A last photo of her can be found in chapter 7.

"Silver Lady", Consolidated B-24, 44-40371, artist unknown, 530th BS, 380th BG. This B-24 put in around seventy missions between June 1944 and August 1945, after which it was apparently flown back to the Philippines (or, perhaps, Biak) to be salvaged. The artwork, based on an Earl Moran pin-up titled *High Blond Pressure*, is seen here in an early form, in close-up after such refinements as folds to the clothing, shine to the hair and shoes, shadows, whites to the eyes, and a lovely smile were added, and, in the last photo, after the addition of a background shadow and wider white edging to the name and quotation marks. *Top photo, Eric Geddes; bottom right photo, Gerald Reynolds via Ken Merrick*

SITTING PRETTY, Consolidated B-24, 42-100034, artist unknown, 63rd BS, 43rd BG. Despite the fact that this B-24 was in 63rd Squadron service for a little over twelve months from March 1944, photos of the nose art are uncommon. In this photo, the name has evidently only recently been added, since preparatory chalk lines are still plainly visible. Note the similarity of the pose of this pin-up with that of *"Silver Lady"* above; perhaps both artists took their inspiration from the same original pin-up art. A last view of this B-24, taken while being salvaged at Clark Field, can be found in chapter 7.

"Six Bitts", Consolidated B-24, 42-100214, artist Raymond A. Hafner, 529th BS, 380th BG. Named after a comment by the pilot (and later 529th CO), Herbert L. Woodward, about his own perceived worth ("a couple of bucks and six bits"), artist Hafner no doubt added the nude to the six "bits" (the three twenty-five-cent coins visible in this photo were the equivalent of six "bits") for effect. This B-24 had been assigned to the 529th BS around February 1944 and went on to complete more than one hundred missions, about half from Australian bases and the rest from the Philippines, but the nose art (which appeared on both sides of the nose) was added only after the bomber was stripped back to NMF (see photo in chapter 1). Research by 380th BG researcher Glenn R. Horton Jr. established that Woodward flew the ship's one hundredth mission; that was on May 3, 1945, while he was the group operations officer. "Six Bitts" survived the war but was subsequently flown to Biak for salvaging. By then, 111 bomb symbols had been added to the LHS of her nose.

SKY LADY, Consolidated B-24, 41-24043, artist unknown, 320th BS and 400th BS, 90th BG. This B-24, which featured a copy of the November 1942 Varga Girl pin-up, failed to return from a massed attack planned for Rabaul on October 18, 1943 (due to poor weather over the target, an alternative target was attacked). On the return flight, the formation was broken up over the Owen Stanley Mountain range, but SKY LADY was already in difficulty with engine trouble, and the crew were ordered to bail out. All lived to tell the tale of their New Guinea jungle escape north of Mt Yule and subsequent rescue, but one crew member landed in a tree and received a severe back injury after cutting himself free and falling to ground. All men were found by friendly natives and taken to the Catholic mission outstation at Kerau, an incredible journey that took eight days. At Kerau the crew were able to rest and eat well for more than a week before moving to Tapini, where there was an emergency landing ground and radio contact with Port Moresby was possible. RAAF Tiger Moths successfully undertook the retrieval work in a series of flights from Tapini back to Rogers Field, about 30 miles out from Port Moresby (because of its location, it was also called the 30 Mile Strip). From here the crew of SKY LADY was returned to their home base aboard a C-47 named "FLAMINGO", later renamed Pel (see photo in chapter 4). Via Malcolm Long

"SKY LADY", Consolidated B-24, unidentified serial number, artist unknown, 400th BS, 90th BG. It seems likely that this B-24 replaced the one above, the pin-up in this case being based on the August 1943 Varga Girl. It is known that this B-24 subsequently flew more than twenty missions, but her fate is currently unknown.

"SKY WITCH", Consolidated B-24, 42-72815, artist unknown, 400th BS, 90th BG. While 5th AF B-24s were maintained for frontline usage as long as possible, this seems to have rarely stretched for more than a year, particularly in New Guinea. "SKY WITCH" was one such example, though, retained longer than other B-24s, perhaps, because of its usefulness in the long-range reconnaissance role after being fitted with additional fuel tanks for that purpose. Few photos of this B-24 or its nose art seem to have been taken, but it is likely that the name and pin-up were limited to the RHS only. This aircraft's last mission occurred on November 7, 1944, and a photo taken after that can be found in chapter 7.

SLEEPY TIME / SLEEPY TIME GAL, Douglas A-20, unidentified serial number, artist Joseph A. DiLorenzo, 389th BS, 312th BG. Accurately copied by DiLorenzo from a Gil Elvgren pin-up titled *Sleepy-Time Girl*; note in these photos that in one, the name is incomplete but the object on which the pin-up girl is sitting, a patchwork ottoman, is present in its entirety (as it was in the original Elvgren illustration), while in the other photo the name is in place in full, but only the top of the ottoman is visible. Clearly some changes were made along the way; was the addition of the word *GAL*, in larger letters than *SLEEPY TIME*, an afterthought perhaps? Certainly, "Sleepy Time Gal" (the name came from a much-copied 1920s hit tune), or versions thereof, became another popular nose art name during World War II. Researchers have come up with two serial number possibilities for this A-20, as a result of which there is a difference of opinion over whether it survived 389th BS service or not.

"SLEEPY TIME GAL", Consolidated B-24, 42-110120, artist William B. McBroom, 530th BS, 380th BG. This artwork was painted in the Northern Territory of Australia by squadron artist McBroom on the basis of the Vargas gatefold he found in what was probably the most recent issue of *Esquire* magazine on hand, that of April 1944 (the B-24's first mission was flown on May 11, 1944, at which stage, perhaps, the artwork had not been added). As shown in this photo, the bomber was originally in overall olive-drab finish, but soon after it had been assigned, it was ordered to be stripped of its camouflage. This was done, but the nose art and name were able to be encircled and retained without any alteration. On October 29, 1944, while she was on her thirty-sixth mission, *"SLEEPY TIME GAL"* was lost while being flown by a RAAF crew with an Australian army officer as passenger. Postwar inquiries determined that a Japanese AA unit hit a low-flying Allied bomber that may have been *"SLEEPY TIME GAL"*. The last message received from the crew was that they were preparing to ditch. No trace of the aircraft or those aboard has ever been found. For other examples of nose art in this volume that are based on the *Esquire* April 1944 gatefold, see A-20 *SNIPER*, which follows in this chapter, C-47 *MORNIN AFTER* in chapter 4, and B-25 *LET'S FACE IT* in chapter 7.

SLEEPY-TIME GAL, Consolidated B-24, 44-41311, artist Charles R. Chesnut, 33rd BS, 22nd BG. As mentioned above, this was another popular name to accompany nose art, but the name already existed in popular culture thanks to a hit song from the 1920s. It became well known again in World War II thanks to a Republic Pictures film of the same name, a comedy, which was released in 1942. According to the research for the 22nd BG history *Revenge of the Red Raiders*, this B-24 flew at least seventy-two missions over a period of around eight months and, postwar, was flown back to the US, where it was subsequently scrapped.

Slightly DANGEROUS, Consolidated B-24, 44-40366, artist Charles R. Chesnut, 33rd BS, 22nd BG. This B-24, which became another "Century Girl" for the 22nd BG, had earlier featured a different pin-up and been named *GYPSY* (q.v.) but was renamed, and this beautiful new artwork was added in tribute, perhaps, to the popular 1943 MGM romantic comedy of the same name, which featured another beautiful blonde, Lana Turner, one of the best-known and most popular pin-up girls of World War II. The film did well at the box office, while the B-24 survived the war to be flown back to the US, where, unfortunately, it was just one more B-24 at Kingman, Arizona, in, as aviation enthusiast and photographer William T. Larkins, who visited the base, called it, "a sea of B-24s," left in open-air storage, all destined to be scrapped.

SLIGHTLY DANGEROUS, Consolidated B-24, 42-73333, artist unknown, 531st BS, 380th BG. Another "Century Girl," this time from the 380th BG, this B-24 had been assigned to the 531st BS in February 1944 and for some months flew under the name of *UNDECIDED*, with a large question mark added between the letters "C" and "I." Although it has been reported that the changeover to the new name and artwork occurred around October 1944, it seems to have been after the thirty-first mission was flown; that is, ca. July 1944 (see photos on website 380th.org). As with *"Toddy"* (q.v.), the bomb log seen here was a little behind by the time the one-hundred-mission mark had been reached (ninety-six missions show in this photo); the enthusiasm required to maintain long-running bomb logs on aircraft sides by this stage of the war was probably waning! Website 380th.org lists the one hundredth (and last) mission of the war for *SLIGHTLY DANGEROUS* as occurring on July 12, 1945, sometime after which she was subsequently flown to Biak to be salvaged.

SLOW MOTION, Consolidated B-24, 42-109992, artist unknown, 403rd BS, 43rd BG. The author is indebted to the B-24 Best Web website for late identification (2024) of this B-24. She was transferred to the 408th BS, 22nd BG, in April 1944, where the original name and nose art were replaced by a beautiful pin-up named LOST ANGEL but the bomber and her 10 man crew were lost at Balikpapan on October 14, 1944.

SMOKEY, Douglas A-20, 43-22212 (unconfirmed), artist unknown, 673rd BS (unconfirmed), 417th BG (unconfirmed). Despite the lovely pin-up (but why the miniature Donald Duck in his sailor suit?) and a considerable bomb log, little is known about this A-20. The assigned pilot's name, however, is known to have been Patterson and it is on that basis that the unit identification has been made.

SNAFU NO. II, Consolidated B-24, 42-41120, artist unknown, 529th BS, 380th BG. A popular World War II expression taken from the phrase "Situation normal, all fouled up," or, in more-popular vernacular, "Situation normal, all fuxxed up," surprisingly SNAFU does not rank a mention in early postwar abbreviation summaries (in *Encyclopaedia Britannica*'s *10 Eventful Years*, published in 1947, for example) but has since become well known through popular culture. The first *SNAFU*, one of the 529th BS's original B-24s, was written off after only twenty missions as a result of being damaged beyond repair in a takeoff accident at Fenton, Northern Territory, on September 15, 1943 (see photo in chapter 7). She was replaced by *SNAFU NO. II*, with almost identical nose art but with the notable addition of a curly-haired youngster. The artwork appeared on both sides of the nose, as shown here. This B-24 went on to survive sixty-two missions, nineteen of them in New Guinea, the balance flown from Fenton and later Darwin, Northern Territory, until she too was sent off to be salvaged (that was in February 1945). These two B-24s were uncommon examples of USAAF bombers featuring pregnant pin-ups as nose art, but in each case the art was cartoonish in appearance and probably seen more as a lighthearted way of illustrating the name rather than anything else (a late-war eyebrow-raiser was a B-25 named *WHODUNIT? The 2nd*, photos of which can be found in appendix 2).

Smoky, North American B-25, unidentified serial number, artist unknown, unit(s) unidentified. This photo was part of a small 5th AF photo collection purchased by the author in 2015, the only other B-25 photo included being that of the 22nd BG's *Bashful* (q.v.).

SNIPER, Douglas A-20, 44-424, artist unknown, 675th BS, 417th BG. The names Wilson and Cardoza, visible at top left of this photo, are those of the pilot, Lt. Leland E. Wilson, and his crew chief, TSgt. Frank Cardoza, while the artwork is another copy of the Vargas gatefold from the April 1944 issue of *Esquire* magazine. No other details are currently known about this plane or its crew.

"SOOPER DROOPER", Consolidated B-24, 42-40515, artist unknown, 64th BS, 43rd BG. This B-24 originally served with the 380th BG in 1943 without the advantage of a power-operated nose turret. At that stage, the name was carried on both sides of the nose but without additional artwork. Flown back to the Townsville Air Depot for the installation of a nose turret in December 1943, this B-24 was subsequently assigned to the 43rd BG upon completion of the work and received with a new version of the name, now in quotation marks, on the LHS, together with, it seems, this pin-up (and unexplained "friend") on the RHS. Other researchers have not made this connection earlier, but it is suspected that the photo was taken at Nadzab, and it is known that *"SOOPER DROOPER"* was left behind there by the 64th BS by mid-1944. She was still there in 1945, though, when the pin-up was described by one observer as a "beautiful dame in deshabille" (see appendix 3); hence the author's considered opinion that this photo is of that artwork.

"SQUAW PEAK", Consolidated B-24, 44-40801, artist Raymond A. Hafner, 529th BS, 380th BG. Assigned to Lt. Robert L. Chandler from Arizona, who is said to have named this B-24 after one of the high points of the Phoenix Mountains; the fact that Chandler had a Native American, MSgt. Gilbert N. Murdock, as crew chief may have also been a contributing factor in the name (and artwork). Murdock, from Oklahoma and formerly crew chief for *ADELAIDE FEVER*, is seen here, *at left*, with his assistant, Sgt. Vernon S. Brown. The artwork seems to have been added around August 1944, and this photo must have been taken soon after, since no mission markers have yet been added (they appeared directly above the artwork). *"SQUAW PEAK"* survived just over five months of missions from Australia and then operated from the Philippines in March and April 1945 but, over Formosa on April 15, was accidentally struck by bombs from another 380th BG B-24 above. Of the eleven men aboard, four died, but the remaining seven, all of whom were taken prisoner, amazingly, survived the war. As to the real Squaw Peak, it was renamed Piestewa Peak in 2003 in honor of Lori Ann Piestewa, the first Native American woman to die in combat while serving in the US military; that occurred earlier that year during the Iraq War.

BOMBER AND LONG-RANGE PHOTO RECON BEAUTIES

STAR DUSTER, Consolidated B-24, 41-23869, artist unknown, 321st BS, 90th BG. It appears that this B-24 was received by the 321st BS early in 1943, and, according to the 90th BG's wartime souvenir book, *The Jolly Rogers: Southwest Pacific, 1942–1944*, she survived sixty-seven missions before being returned to the US. Whether or not the nose art was retained following her return is not known, but she ended her days at Bush Field, Georgia, in 1945. She is seen in this very marked photo toward the end of her SWPA service, artwork wiped over with, perhaps, an oily cloth just for the photo, while the sixty mission symbols and, above them, nine symbols representing enemy fighters claimed destroyed look decidedly faded.

Star Eyes, Consolidated B-24, 44-40397, artist unknown, 408th BS, 22nd BG. The history of *Star Eyes* paralleled that of the 33rd BS's *Slightly DANGEROUS* (q.v.); both were built by Consolidated at San Diego as part of the same production batch, and both were assigned to the 5th AF and received at Townsville around the same time. Both survived the war after flying more than a hundred missions, each as part of the same bomb group, and then both of them were flown back to the US postwar, where they ended up at Kingman, Arizona, and were later scrapped. According to the extensive research that went into the 22nd's history, *Revenge of the Red Raiders*, B-24s flying back to the US via Hawaii for disposal, such as these two aircraft, were ordered to have clothes added to undressed pin-up nose art prior to departing Hickam Army Air Field, and given that no photos of either *Star Eyes* or *Slightly DANGEROUS* at Kingman have surfaced, it is likely that these two paintings were removed completely rather than altered as suggested.

THE STRIP POLKA, Consolidated B-24, 42-40970 (unconfirmed), artist unknown, 319th BS, 90th BG. Named after an Andrews Sisters' hit song from 1942, these two photos show how the artwork differed on both sides. A little difficult to make out in the LHS photo, above, is the fact the pin-up has been partly painted over the aircraft's serial number; only the 42- prefix remains, and while it has been suggested that the serial number of this B-24 was 42-40970 and that plane was assigned to the 5th AF, the only confirmed unofficial name it was given was *gunmoll 2nd* (q.v.).

THE SULTAN'S DAUGHTER, Consolidated B-24, 42-73489, artist unknown, 531st BS, 380th BG. This was yet another of the 380th BG "Century Girls" that flew more than one hundred missions, fifty-nine from Australia, one in New Guinea, and the balance while based in the Philippines. She had been assigned to the 531st BS around February 1944 and had originally been named HOT ROCKS (q.v.) and featured a different artwork, but this new name and artwork were added following the stripping back of camouflage paint later that year (date unknown). This photo was taken ca. November–December 1944, following forty-seven missions. THE SULTAN'S DAUGHTER survived the war but was subsequently flown to Biak for salvaging. *Don Tietzel via Deane Tietzel*

"SWAMP ANGEL", Consolidated B-24, unidentified serial number, artist unknown, 64th BS, 43rd BG. For a variety of reasons, some examples of nose art are less common than others, this being one such case. In all the years of collecting material for this project, this was the only photograph of "SWAMP ANGEL" to come to the author's attention. While the artwork is based on the October pin-up in the 1944 *Esquire Varga Calendar*, the paucity of photos of her would suggest that her service was limited, and apart from the fact that it seems likely that her original crew was captained by Lt. Thomas P. Russell (hence the squadron identification above), no further information is currently available.

SWEET RACKET, Consolidated B-24, 42-100188, artist Charles R. Chesnut, 33rd BS, 22nd BG. This is expected to have been another of Chesnut's early artworks; most were on NMF B-24s, the only works identified as his on camouflaged B-24s being *Ole' TOMATO*, *Our Gal III*, *Redhot Ridinhood*, *Round Trip Ticket*, the first *Tail Wind*, and the first *YANKEE GAL*. SWEET RACKET was assigned to the 33rd BS in February 1944 but after nine months was condemned for salvage, reason unknown.

"SWEET SIXTEEN", Consolidated B-24, 42-73394, artist unknown, 63rd BS, 43rd BG. This was one of three artworks added to SWPA-bound B-24s at Fairfield-Suisun Army Air Base, California, by the same artist. All three (the other two were "I'LL BE AROUND" and "MISS LIBERTY") were subsequently assigned to the 63rd BS. The connection between the name and artwork (which was based on the March pin-up from the 1944 *Esquire Varga Calendar*) seems obvious, the age of consent in certain US states, but should that not sit well with any inquisitive parties, 16 was also the sum of the last three digits of this B-24's serial number, the abbreviated tail number being a common way of differentiating between these bombers as the war progressed. "SWEET SIXTEEN" survived wartime service to be salvaged in theater, probably in the Philippines.

SWEET TAKE-OFF, Consolidated B-24, 42-100220, artist unknown, 2nd BS, 22nd BG, later CRTC. The authors of the 22nd BG history *Revenge of the Red Raiders* note that this B-24 served with the 2nd BS from April until September 1944, when it was "transferred out for unknown reason." The reason may have been a shortage of B-24s at the CRTC (then at Nadzab) at that time; the second photo here was taken at Nadzab probably on December 1, 1944, when this B-24 was being used for the advanced training of RAAF Liberator crews by CRTC personnel, with RAAF records noting that there were ten CRTC B-24s in use ca. October–November 1944. While in 2nd BS hands, this B-24 carried a squadron letter on a red color patch on the inside and outside of the vertical fins, but, as can be seen in the lower photo, these identification markings were subsequently painted out. This B-24 went with the CRTC to the Philippines, and a last photo of her can be found in chapter 7. *CRTC photo, Brian Featherstone*

Sweet WILLUMS II, Douglas A-20, 42-86721, artist unknown, 386th BS, 312th BG. "Sweet Willums" was the nickname of the assigned pilot, Lt. Claud C. Haisley, for his then girlfriend or fiancée, Margaret Williams (the two married in 1945), while the artwork was based on an Earl MacPherson pin-up (the same pin-up that inspired the artwork on *"SHOO-SHOO BABY"*). The 312th BG had originally used P-40s for a short time, and it was one of them that carried the original *Sweet Willums* name. The close-up photo is from early in the A-20's service, since no crew names or mission symbols have yet been added. According to research for the 312th history volume, *Rampage of the Roarin' '20s*, Haisley flew fifty-six missions in this A-20 between February 1944 and January 1945. His plane's last flight, reportedly, was on January 31, 1945, after Haisley had left the squadron, when she had to be ditched at sea off San Jose, Philippines, due to engine failure. In the poor-quality lower photo, though, *Sweet WILLUMS II* was photographed on Biak after 312th BG service, with nose art still in place but bomb log and any ownership particulars neatly painted out, so her actual fate may be different from that recorded.

NOSE ART OF THE 5TH AIR FORCE

Tail Wind / TAIL WIND, Consolidated B-24s, 42-100210 and 44-41652, artist Charles R. Chesnut, 33rd BS, 22nd BG. That the artistic standard of pin-ups on planes could be improved upon if more time was available to the artist is illustrated in more ways than one by these two photos. The early work (on the camouflaged B-24) was probably one of Chesnut's earliest nose art paintings (for others on camouflaged B-24s, see *Ole' TOMATO*, *Our Gal III*, *Redhot Ridinhood*, *Round Trip Ticket*, *SWEET RACKET*, and the first *YANKEE GAL*). This B-24 remained in squadron service from February 1944 until November 1944, when it was attacked by a Japanese fighter while it was orbiting Tacloban waiting to land. There were no casualties, but the aircraft was badly damaged and was not considered repairable. A new B-24 replaced *Tail Wind* in December, and it was given the same name (although in capital letters this time) with the beautiful pin-up seen at lower left. This TAIL WIND served with the 33rd BS for little more than three months before being shot down over Formosa on March 23, 1945. On this occasion, though, there were no survivors. Note at lower right on the second photo the IV ASAC arrowhead stencil.

"*Tail Wind*", North American B-25, 41-30230, artist unknown, 2nd BS, 22nd BG, later 501st BS, 345th BG. This B-25, with another artist's impression of an SWPA native beauty as a pin-up (along similar lines are C-47s *Belle of the Isles* and *The Coral Princess* in chapter 4), served with the 2nd BS from around July 1943 until transferred to the 501st BS, 345th BG, in February 1944. The nose number was an abbreviated 2nd BS squadron identification (squadron number 14 was *HOW'S YOUR OLE' TOMATO*, seen earlier). After little more than two months with the 501st, however, "*Tail Wind*" was stripped of armor and armament and converted for fast-transport duties and then passed on to the 388th BS, 312th BG, by which time it seems that the pin-up, which had appeared on both sides of the nose, and original name had gone. It remained with the 388th BS until early 1945. *Via Malcolm Long*

TABU, Consolidated B-24, 42-109993, artist unknown, 408th BS, 22nd BG. As with "*Tail Wind*" (*right*), this was another US artist's impression of how a Pacific Island beauty may look, but with a name that clearly implied a "look but don't touch" warning. This B-24 was assigned to the 408th BS in April 1944 and remained with the squadron until a takeoff accident on September 3, 1944, after which it was salvaged.

"TEMPERMENTAL LADY", Consolidated B-24, 42-100174, artist unknown, 408th BS, 22nd BG. This B-24, with a pin-up based on the September page from the 1944 *Esquire Varga Calendar*, was assigned to the 408th BS in March 1944 and flew with that squadron until April 14, 1945, when she was damaged by AA over China, ran off a Clark Field runway following a landing made without brakes, and was badly twisted while being moved. The authors of *Revenge of the Red Raiders* note that tail number 174 was then the oldest B-24 serving with the 408th, and that she had flown in excess of seventy missions. The two bottom lines of the stencil under the cockpit window read *SEMPER PIZZDOFF / LOCAL 459*, suggesting to the author that one or more of the crew had earlier been connected in some way with another 5th AF B-24 named *SEMPER PIZZDOFF*, the identify of which remains currently unknown.

TEMPTATION, Consolidated B-24, 42-100196, artist unknown, 33rd BS, 22nd BG. Another example of artwork based on the Mutoscope Company's card titled *Good Pickin's* (a later example was the B-24 of that name seen earlier in this chapter), this B-24 flew its first mission with the 33rd BS in March 1944 but was lost with her entire crew on September 1, 1944, in the opening round of major 5th AF daylight raids on airfields near Davao. Another 33rd BS B-24, *Ole' TOMATO* (q.v.), was also lost on this occasion.

TARGET FOR TONIGHT, Consolidated B-24, 42-41060, artist unknown, 65th BS, 43rd BG. While this B-24 took its name from a well-known 1941 British documentary that promoted the then largely unknown role of RAF Bomber Command, clearly the addition of the pin-up (this one based on the September 1943 *Esquire* Varga Girl) implied a much more earthy meaning. This B-24 was assigned to the 65th BS ca. September 1943, and it was reportedly taken off operational flying in May 1944 after flying forty-seven missions (according to her bomb log) and was later salvaged in the Philippines. These two photos show early and later versions of the name and nose art; in the photo at left, the outlining of the pin-up, added at Fairfield-Suisun Army Air Base, is incomplete, while the name, added in New Guinea, seems to be a preliminary version that also lacks the dot over the letter "I," seen in the photo above.

NOSE ART OF THE 5TH AIR FORCE

TEN KNIGHTS in a BAR ROOM, Consolidated B-24, 42-72806, artist unknown, 321st BS, 90th BG. Although the redheaded female rider was very much an accessory to the impressive white stallion with the golden wings, not to include this photo in this chapter may have led to criticism, so here it is. Named after the then-well-known temperance novel *Ten Nights in a Bar Room*, later turned into two films (the most recent of which had been released in 1931), the ten knights in this case referred to the B-24's crew, all of whom were reported missing after their plane was shot down by a Japanese fighter following a twenty-four-ship mission against Wewak on December 1, 1943 (also lost on that occasion were *"PISTOL PACKIN' MAMA"* and *"PUDGY"*). Remains of the plane and its crew were found in 1970, but by then, positive identification of the "knights" was possible only in one instance.

THIS ABOVE ALL, Consolidated F-7, 44-40376, artist unknown, 4th Reconnaissance Squadron (Long Range, Photographic). Good overall view of this plane with nose art, which was based on the January offering in the 1945 *Esquire Varga Calendar*. This squadron had earlier been designated the 4th Photo Charting Squadron, and that unit's insignia, which comprised a leather-clad laughing airman riding a winged camera, appears forward of the pin-up and can be seen well in this photo. The words "This above all" had originally appeared in a quotation by Polonius in Shakespeare's *Hamlet* but had come to some prominence again in 1942 as the title of a romance film starring Tyrone Power and Joan Fontaine. For other 4th Squadron F-7 nose art, see *KAY-18*, *OVER EXPOSED*, *PHOTO JEANNE*, and *WELL DEVELOPED* in this chapter.

Texas Pom Pom, Douglas A-20, 43-9478, artist "Howell," 674th BS (unconfirmed), 417th BG (unconfirmed), later 389th BS, 312th BG. This A-20 had originally been assigned to the 417th BG, and it could be that it was there that the pin-up, which was approximately three-quarters life-size and copied from the untraced wartime source shown was added (there was a Cpl. Leonard H. Howell, perhaps the artist, serving with the 674th BS, 417th BG). The *Texas Pom Pom* name was added to the LHS of the nose in very neat cursive script, which was the hallmark of the 389th BS's talented sign writer Joseph A. DiLorenzo (see chapter 1), but her squadron service was short lived due to a landing-gear failure at Gusap, New Guinea, on June 5, 1944, after which she was salvaged. There were many instances of DiLorenzo adding a name to the LHS of a 389th Squadron A-20 (never to the RHS?), and this seems to have been an early example of this practice.

172

BOMBER AND LONG-RANGE PHOTO RECON BEAUTIES

THREE POINT LANDING, Consolidated B-24, unidentified serial number, artist unknown, unidentified BS, 43rd BG (unconfirmed). With both pin-up and name taken from an artwork by Art Frahm (1907–81), probably a calendar topper, few photos of this nose art are known to exist, and the 43rd BG identification is speculative, but as the photo below confirms, this was one painting that was added in the field, probably at Nadzab. As in the case of *RUM AND COKE*, seen earlier, here is another photo of a nose art artist at work whose name has gone unrecorded. What can be said, though, is that such photos (of artists other than Al Merkling working on heavy-bomber nose art in the SWPA) are quite uncommon; most onlookers waited for the artwork to be completed before they photographed them. Unfortunately, the absence of more photos of this B-24 suggests that her service history after the artwork was added was short lived.

"TIGER LADY", North American B-25, 41-30016, artist unknown, 499th BS, 345th BG. This B-25 was among the first to serve with this squadron, joining the unit around March 1943. Just when this rather unusual pin-up was added is not known (just the name was repeated on the LHS), but the "Bats Outa Hell" unit insignia replaced it toward the end of the year, along with a new name, *The Wilda Marie*. As such, the B-25 remained in 499th hands until August 1944 and even appeared on a surrender leaflet dropped on enemy forces; see photos in chapter 6.

'TINKIE', North American B-25, 41-30315, artist unknown, 498th and 500th BSs, 345th BG. Originally assigned to the 3rd BG, this B-25 was received by the 498th BS in January 1944, and it is believed that this is when the pet name and artwork were added. She was lost with her six-man crew in extremely bad weather on "Black Sunday," April 16, 1944, shortly after the plane had been transferred to the 500th BS, and it is thought that it probably plunged into the Bismarck Sea, more specifically Astrolabe Bay. No wreckage of the plane has ever been found.

TITIAN TEMPTRESS, Consolidated B-24, 42-100318, artist unknown, 2nd BS, 22nd BG. Note that this B-24 had carried other, unidentified, nose art initially, the replacement being added following receipt of the ship by the 2nd BS at Nadzab. Titian was the English name for famed sixteenth-century painter Tiziano Vecelli, so it seems likely that whoever suggested the new name for the B-24 was either an art lover or someone who was simply aware of Titian's nudes, one of which, *Venus of Urbino*, was given prominence by Mark Twain (1835–1910) in his lengthy 1880 travelogue, *A Tramp Abroad*, as "the foulest, the vilest, the obscenest picture the world possesses." The *Venus of Urbino* lives on, permanently on display in the Uffizi Gallery Museum, Florence, but, sadly, this tribute to its artist with its modern twist, a wartime pin-up (a copy, in fact, of the December 1943 Varga Girl but, initially, as seen in the inset image, more revealing), existed just from ca. March 1944 until the *TEMPTRESS* was salvaged ca. August 1945.

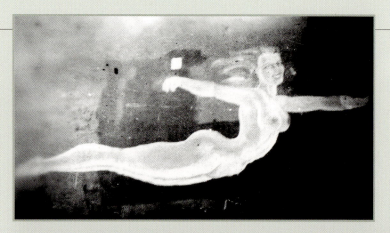

"TODDY" / "Toddy", Consolidated B-24, 42-100226, artist William "Pat" Greeson, 531st BS, 380th BG. Another of the 380th BG "Century Girls" which completed one hundred or more missions, this B-24 had flown its first mission in February 1944, but apparently without a pin-up at that stage, since it was still in camouflage. Following the removal of the camouflage paint, ca. April or May, though, the pin-up and name *"TODDY"* above the pin-up were added. Not long after, though, the original name was scrubbed off and repainted below the pin-up in larger print, as shown in the second photo. Note that in both photos, no bomb log has yet been started; this happened later and appeared on the LHS as well as the RHS along with the name and the squadron badge, which featured an irate Donald Duck cartoon character. Despite flying one-hundred-plus missions, only ninety-one bomb symbols were ever painted on the nose. On the RHS, this was made up of three rows of twenty-five missions and one of sixteen, but on the LHS it was one row of twenty-five, two of twenty-six, and one of fourteen! This B-24, seen below in flight over northern Australia circa June-August 1944 with its small, almost indistinguishable tail number and a rarely-seen (on NMF B-24s of this squadron) painted rudder, was salvaged in theater, reportedly at Clark Field, postwar.

TONDELAYO, North American B-25, 41-30669, artist unknown, 500th BS, 345th BG. One of a number of World War II US bombers named after the central character—"the exciting tropical temptress"—of the 1942 MGM film *White Cargo*, but with artwork based on the June pin-up from the 1943 *Esquire Varga Calendar*, this seems to have been the only "Tondelayo" to have seen service in the SWPA. She was assigned to the 500th BS in August 1943 and less than two months later, on October 18, was one of six 500th BS B-25s that attacked Japanese supplies and shipping near Rabaul, subsequently claiming two merchant vessels as sunk. The attack, which also led to the bow of a submarine chaser being blown off, drew an angry response from defending Japanese naval fighter pilots, who set upon the two flights of three planes, and while the first flight was able to return to base, two of the second flight were shot down, and *TONDELAYO* was badly damaged during attacks that lasted for more than an hour. All crew members aboard the three B-25s were subsequently awarded Silver Star decorations, but for the majority this came posthumously. After lengthy repairs, *TONDELAYO* returned to 500th BS service in May 1944, the LHS view reproduced here showing a close-up of the nose after claims for her last mission the previous October (one merchant vessel and nine of the ten enemy aircraft symbols shown) had been added. Her assigned pilot then was Lt. Frederick W. "Boppo" Dick. The RHS view shows the nose prior to its repaint, at which time the artwork was masked out and thus able to be retained. As to *TONDELAYO*'s fate, she was eventually pensioned off, stripped of armament and all camouflage and markings, and returned to the 345th BG for second-line duties named *CHOW HOUND*, featuring a very professional nose art painting of cartoon character "Pluto" clenching a food basket in his teeth. For more on *TONDELAYO*, see chapter 7.

TRAMP, Consolidated B-24, 42-72790, artist unknown, 530th BS, 380th BG. An early and a later view of this shortlived nose art. The *TRAMP* name (not readily visible in the photo at right as the rounded lettering is hidden within the rounded shape of the clouds at the base of the painting) and artwork only existed for a short time because once a nose turret was fitted to this B-24 and it was returned to the 380th BG, this look was subsequently painted over and changed to a caricature of an angelic young child named *Sandra Kay* (see photo in chapter 7).

TWO BOB TiLLiE, Consolidated B-24, 42-72952, artist unknown, 65th BS, 43rd BG. There was a prominent brothel madam operating in Sydney, Australia, well known as "Tilly" or "Tillie" (her real name was Matilda) Devine (1900–70), and it seems quite likely that the term *TWO BOB TILLIE* was a nickname that American servicemen bestowed upon her after hearing stories of cheap sex that may have been said to be on offer. Until the introduction of decimal currency in 1966, "two bob" was an Aussie slang term meaning two shillings, the equivalent, at the time, of about thirty-two cents in the US: not a lot of money. This B-24 served in the SWPA for around a year, until AA damage to the LHS main undercarriage caused it to collapse on landing at Pitoe Strip, Morotai Island, in October 1944. From there it was bulldozed off and moved to the scrap heap.

TWIN NIFTIES / TWIN NIFTY'S, Consolidated B-24, 42-40348, artist Edward Dehler (unconfirmed), 400th BS, 90th BG. Both this B-24 and its successor (*see next page*) featured two different spellings of "Nifties," due, perhaps, to confusion as to whether or not the word was a possessive noun (it is not; hence no apostrophe is necessary). She was lost southwest of Wewak following a night raid in the early hours of August 17, 1943; there were no survivors.

TWIN NIFTIES II/TWIN NIFTYS II, Consolidated B-24, 42-40928, artist unknown, 400th BS, 90th BG. This B-24 was originally assigned to the 319th BS, where it was named *DIRTY GERTIE* in tribute to the squadron's original *"DIRTY GERTIE",* which was lost in a midair explosion with all her crew on March 16, 1943. Following transfer to the 400th BS, though, it was decided to rename her after the recently lost *TWIN NIFTIES/TWIN NIFTY'S* (*see previous page*). The four photos here show two of the LHS, one a close-up and the other taken after the names of visiting celebrities actor Gary Cooper, actresses Phyllis Brooks and Una Merkel, and concert accordionist Andy Arcari had been added (their visit was in December 1943; this B-24 had completed only seventeen missions at that time), while the remaining views are of two different stages of the artwork on the RHS with changes to the artwork evident from the shoulders up. *TWIN NIFTIES II/NIFTYS II* ended the war at Nadzab with a bomb log of more than fifty missions and is mentioned in a 1946 article reproduced in appendix 3. *Early RHS view below via Kevin Gogler*

NOSE ART OF THE 5TH AIR FORCE

UNDECIDED/Undecided, Consolidated B-24, 42-109990, artist unknown, 530th BS, 380th BG. This B-24 flew about sixty missions between May 1944 and May 1945, half from Australian bases, the rest from the Philippines, but, interestingly, became, it seems, the only 5th AF B-24 to feature two different Varga pin-ups at different times. Those pin-ups are seen here at four different stages; the original work, based on the May 1944 *Esquire* magazine Varga Girl, and an early photo of the new art-work on NMF with pin-up (based on Vargas's rear cover offering taken from the October 1944 overseas edition of *Esquire*) on a flying carpet-like base, while the two other photos show how the base was subsequently altered to represent, perhaps, a leather-look cushion (note the addition of four round objects to the side of the base; press studs?); the last image, although not as sharp as the others, is of what is believed to be the final look. *Undecided* was returned to the US in 1945 and, following open-air storage at Kingman, was subsequently scrapped.

UNDER EXPOSED!, Consolidated F-7, 42-73052, artist Al G. Merkling, 20th CMS, 6th PRG. While Merkling's ideas for his artworks were generally his own, this was one exception: a copy of the January 1944 Varga Girl, but turned around and given the appearance of standing up rather than sitting down. Few photos are available of this F-7, since it was in service in New Guinea for only about seven weeks before crashing into the island's highest mountain, Mount Wilhelm, in predawn darkness on May 22, 1944; there were no survivors from her eleven-man crew. The three photos show, first, an early version with a dark-haired pin-up and dark lettering, then a close-up of the completed work, with the pin-up now golden-haired and the lettering white, while the third photo shows that work had already begun to strip back the aircraft to a bare-metal finish prior to its loss (whether or not that had been completed prior to that last flight is not known).

Unidentified Douglas A-20, unidentified serial number, artist unknown, 388th BS, 312th BG. The late-war use of playing-card symbols as tactical markings for 312th BG A-20s (clubs for the 386th BS, diamonds for the 387th, hearts for the 388th, and spades for the 389th) also provided a convenient background for squadron nose art (for a previous example in this volume, see the 388th BS's *RIDIN' HIGH*). Unfortunately, though, there is no information currently available to further identify this aircraft (which may have been named) or her crew. The pin-up is based on the March pin-up from the 1942 *Esquire Varga Calendar*.

Unidentified Douglas A-20, unidentified serial number, artist unknown, 389th BS, 312th BG. For most 389th A-20s with nose art, though, names given to them appeared only on the LHS, so on which plane this pin-up appeared is not currently known. Examples of named 389th A-20s with currently unknown RHS nose art are *Emily Jane*, *Ginnie*, *Libby*, *Little Joe*, *Ludy*, *Marie*, and *'Olga' the II*. This pin-up was based on the September pin-up from Earl MacPherson's 1943 *Artist's Sketch Pad Calendar*, but facing right rather than left.

Unidentified North American B-25, unidentified serial number, artist unknown, unit(s) unidentified. It is suspected that this photo was taken at the Townsville Air Depot, and while the pin-up was based on the September 1942 Varga Girl, perhaps dating the photo as from late 1942 or early 1943, no other details are known. It is possible that a name had been added to the LHS of the nose, but it has yet to be identified.

Unidentified North American B-25, unidentified serial number, artist unknown, unit(s) unidentified. Although this photo came from a SWPA collection, all that can be said about it is that the plane is definitely a B-25. Clearly the painting was roughly executed and may have been short lived, but it was named, although the only part of that name that can be seen in this photo is "*The*."

Unnamed Consolidated B-24, 44-41540, artist Enoch H. Wingert, 65th BS, 43rd BG. While the location and date of this photo are not known, what is known is that this pin-up was later named *QUEEN OF THE CLOUDS* (photos of two other artworks named *Queen of the Clouds* appear earlier in this chapter). This was another B-24 that survived the war, was returned to the US but never flew again, and was subsequently scrapped.

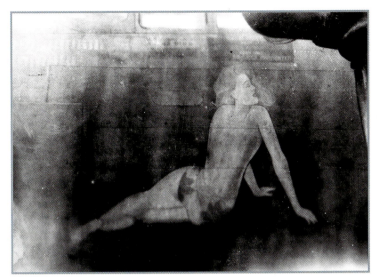

Unnamed Douglas A-20, unidentified serial number, artist unknown, unidentified BS, 417th BG (unconfirmed). On the basis that this plane was reportedly photographed at Saidor in April 1944, it may be from the 417th BG, but further details, apart from the name of the soldier in the photo, Ernie Strancar, are not known. The artwork has been copied from the well-known 1939 Elvgren pin-up titled *French Dressing*.

Unnamed Douglas A-20, 43-9109, artist unknown, 386th BS, 312th BG. With nose art based on the October pin-up from the 1944 *Esquire Varga Calendar*, this A-20 was assigned to the 386th BS in February 1944 and left the unit after being damaged in a flight line explosion at Nadzab on July 4, 1944, but another photo reproduced in chapter 7 (q.v.) confirms that the plane was not scrapped as quickly as previously reported and, in fact, probably survived the war. The crew chief's surname, part of which is visible in this photo, was Parmenter.

Unnamed Douglas A-20, 43-9624, artist unknown, 389th BS, 312th BG. With a pin-up, the origin of which was the *Esquire* April 1943 Varga Girl, but minus trumpet and with a change of clothing, this A-20, squadron identifying letter D, had been assigned to the 389th BS in March 1944 but was lost to AA fire during an attack on the Boela oil field on Ceram Island on July 14, 1944. Neither crew member survived.

Unnamed Douglas A-20, 43-21489, artist Joseph A. DiLorenzo, 389th BS, 312th BG. An apparently newly completed artwork (note the shine of the black spade background), this pin-up was subsequently named *Slightly dangerous* (for other nose art by DiLorenzo, see *The Queen Of Spades*, MISS POSSUM MY TEXAS GAL, and SLEEPY TIME / SLEEPY TIME GAL). This A-20 was in 389th BS hands from mid-1944 until it collided with another A-20 soon after takeoff from Floridablanca airfield on May 19, 1945. Both A-20s crashed, and three of the four crew aboard the two aircraft lost their lives.

Unnamed Martin B-26, 40-1446, artist Pershing A. Arbogast or Anthony J. Chunis, 2nd BS, 22nd BG. One of the 22nd BG's earliest B-26s, 40-1446 was flown to Australia in April 1942. Repairs were necessary due to damage caused by enemy action over Lae in May, and it was probably during this time on the ground that the artwork was started, although it was never fully completed; it was the artist's original intention that there would be a fluttering American flag behind the pin-up, held aloft in the fingers of her outstretched hands, but this was never added. Similarly, no name was added, although "Miss Mercury" had been reserved for that purpose, a name by which she became commonly known. This B-26 was damaged due to undercarriage failure in the course of an emergency landing at Milne Bay on December 18, 1942, and never flew again. At least eight mission markers show in this photo, as well as, forward of the pin-up adjacent to the nose cone, a claim for an enemy aircraft destroyed.

Unnamed Martin B-26, unidentified serial number, artist unknown, 19th BS, 22nd BG. While the 22nd BG had begun its 5th AF service equipped with B-26s, commencing in May 1943 three of its four squadrons began converting to B-25s, leaving those B-26s that were left to soldier on with the 19th BS. As part of their refurbishment, these planes were stripped of camouflage and as the "Silver Fleet" returned to operations in New Guinea in July 1943. Most of these medium bombers featured nose art of some kind on the LHS, but pin-up art was scarce, one exception already seen being PISTOL PACKIN' MAMA (q.v.). While the quality of this photo is poor, the fact that it has not been seen in print before is some compensation, but, unfortunately, the identity of the plane is currently unknown.

V..._ SURE POP, Consolidated B-24, 42-41073, artist B. Balliet, 65th BS, 90th BG. Formerly *"Kentucky Virgin"* (q.v.), it would seem that complaints may have led to this particular change of name, but the significance of the abbreviation *V* (or is it double *V*?; three dots and a dash represent the letter V in Morse code) and the name is currently unknown. A close examination of the photo shows that Balliet assigned this work as job #22, the highest number seen for any of the artist's works and perhaps his last. This B-24 soldiered on until at least July 1944.

The VIGOROUS VIRGIN, North American B-25, 41-30161, artist unknown, 71st BS, 38th BG, later 90th BS, 3rd BG. This name and pin-up originally appeared on both sides of this B-25, with the extra note on the LHS, *My Love*. The name that appeared at top right, is that of the one-time second pilot, Lt. Joseph F. Meyers, who went missing aboard another B-25 with eleven others on January 21, 1944. By then, the plane had been converted to a strafer and transferred to the 3rd BG, the artwork from the knees up being retained (at least on the LHS), but the name and the rest of the painting were lost. The same changes probably occurred on the RHS too, and in 90th BS service the squadron's well-known shark's-teeth markings were added. In fact, they remained in place on the B-25 during the course of its later service with the 345th BG. By then, though, the pin-up had gone completely, and new nose art and name, *The AVOCA AVENGER* (see photo in chapter 6), had been added.

"VIRGIN ABROAD", Consolidated B-24, 44-50941, artist Raymond A. Hafner, 529th BS, 380th BG. Based on a beautiful painting by talented magazine cover and calendar artist Victor Tchetchet (1891–1974), in common with *Luvablass*, a photo of which appears earlier, close examination of this photo also reveals the sign-off HAF-CLIFF, but who "CLIFF" was has not yet been established. This was one of the last two pin-ups completed by Hafner for his squadron; the two B-24s involved (the other was *PEACE OFFERING*) were on squadron strength for only around two months before the war ended. A last photo of this B-24 (with *PEACE OFFERING* in the background) can be found in chapter 7. Returned to the US postwar, like all the other B-24s that were returned, this one was subsequently salvaged and scrapped.

the ViVACiOUS ViRGiN!, Consolidated B-24, unidentified serial number, artist unknown, unit(s) unidentified. The camera that took this photo also took the shots of P-38s *MY PET* and *Polly*, in the following chapter and, on that basis, it has been included as a B-24 possibly belonging to a 5th AF squadron, photographed in the northern Pacific, Ie Shima, perhaps, ca. August 1945. Of the four 5th AF bomb groups equipped with B-24s in 1945, only those of the 90th BG have yet to be afforded a detailed listing; hence it may be that this is a previously unidentified 90th BG example.

The WAC-A-TEER, North American B-25, 41-30601, artist unknown, 33rd and 2nd BSs, 22nd BG. The LHS illustration of a young lady in WAC (Women's Army Corps) uniform, probably based on a photo received, was the first to be added to this B-25. Later, the RHS pin-up was added, based on the Varga Girl that had appeared in the October 1943 issue of *Esquire* magazine. As seen at left, the RHS pin-up was subtitled *OFF DUTY*, and this, in turn, prompted the LHS subtitle *ON DUTY*. Note that the bomb log appears on both sides. *WAC-A-TEER* is, of course, a made-up word, just as, more than ten years later, Mouseketeer referred to a member of the Mickey Mouse Club. This B-25 served mainly with the 33rd BS (September 1943–January 1944), spending only weeks with the 2nd BS prior to being transferred to the 500th BS, 345th BG. For a last photo of what may be this B-25 at Nadzab postwar, see appendix 3.

WHITE WING, North American B-25, 43-36172, artist George M. Blackwell, 501st BS, 345th BG. This was one of more than a dozen new B-25J-11 aircraft assigned to the 501st BS in October 1944, five of which received nose art soon after, all by Blackwell, with names painted by Cpl. Joseph Merenda. The others were *APACHE PRINCESS*, *Cactus Kitten*, *LAZY DAISY MAE*, and *Reina del PACIFICO*, photos of all of which can also be found in this chapter. Of these, *WHITE WING* was the only one to survive the war. Just where and when this photo was taken is not known (possibly San Marcelino in the February–May 1945 period), but it is a little different from most other photos in this volume since it is not a close-up or a posed view.

WELL DEVELOPED, Consolidated F-7, 44-40209, artist M. von Mulldorfer, 4th Reconnaissance Squadron (Long Range, Photographic). It would be no surprise to readers to learn that photographic squadrons often used photographic terms as airplane names; here is a good example. This F-7 carried squadron identification 4-I farther forward on the nose and subsequently flew thirty-five missions, each marked by a camera symbol, of which only eighteen featured stars added above to show that they had been completed successfully. Artist von Mulldorfer is suspected to be Menrad von Mulldorfer (1910–91), who achieved some fame in the 1950s for his work as associate production designer on the movie *Unknown World* and later as one of the special-effects designers and creators on Regal Films' *Kronos*.

Who's Next?, Consolidated B-24, 42-41049, artist unknown, 63rd BS, 43rd BG. This B-24 was another of 63rd BS's twelve original so-called Scott Project planes that arrived in New Guinea ca. October 1943. After lengthy service, however, it went missing in the course of a night attack in poor weather conditions on December 7, 1944. It was later established that the bomber had struck Mount Malasimbo on Mindoro; there were no survivors among the twelve-man crew. For an illustrated account of an arduous 2013 hike to the plane's crash site, see thephilippinesinWorldWarII.wordpress.com. As with *ART'S CART*, *Career Girl*, and *LIBERTY BELLE*, seen earlier, note the altered chin shape following the installation of an A6A gun turret (built originally as a B-24 tail turret) in the nose. *Via Kevin Gogler*

WILLIE'S FOLLY, Consolidated B-24, 44-41547, artist Enoch H. Wingert, 65th BS, 43rd BG. Wingert worked on at least five other pin-up paintings: *CAROLYN MAE*, *MAD RUSSIAN*, *PETTY GAL*, and *PUNJA KASI*, as well as an unnamed B-24, photos of all of which can be found earlier in these pages. This photo is a little indistinct, but clearly the pin-up is based on the June artwork in the 1944 *Esquire Varga Calendar*. *WILLIE'S FOLLY* survived the war and was returned to the US but was one of the thousands of B-17s and B-24s flown to Kingman, Arizona, that sat there until scrapped.

WINDY CITY KITTY, Consolidated B-24, 44-42362, artist unknown, 64th BS, 43rd BG. Despite "Windy City" being a well-known nickname for Chicago, the "Windy City Kitty" name for pin-ups appears to have been limited to those units that had access to Jack Crowe's wartime comic strip of the same name that appeared in the "Down Under" edition of *Yank* magazine (the last issue of which was dated November 17, 1944). The *Kitty*, seen here, however, was no cartoon character but a nick name given to a local prostitute (or group of prostitutes) who accessed the 43rd BG encampment at Clark Field to provide their services. The 43rd were based there from March to July 1945, the second volume of the Group history noting that despite a guarded perimeter fence, "the guards had an arrangement to look the other way" when it came to these activities. While the pin-up (a dusky-skinned nude version of the June 1943 Varga Girl) and tents can be clearly seen, note the soldier in the closest tent is whistling and holding paper money above his head. The artist's motives in his depiction of what happened are unknown, but it is interesting to note that this B-24 survived the war and was returned to the US and, when last seen at Kingman, Arizona, ca. 1947, the artwork was still intact!

WINDY CITY KITTY, Consolidated B-24, unidentified serial number, artist unknown, unidentified BS, 90th BG. As seen in the inset image, the artwork on this B-24 was copied from a black-and-white nude pin-up photo probably purchased through mail order as part of a numbered set. Note, though, that she has been given a change of hair color. After the pin-up was added, it took some time for the name to appear, taken from Sgt. Jack Crowe's comic strip character of the same name, which appeared in the "Down Under" edition of *Yank* magazine, which was not added until at least thirteen missions had been flown. This B-24's history is little known despite participation in more than thirty missions claims for a Japanese warship sunk, and three enemy aircraft shot down.

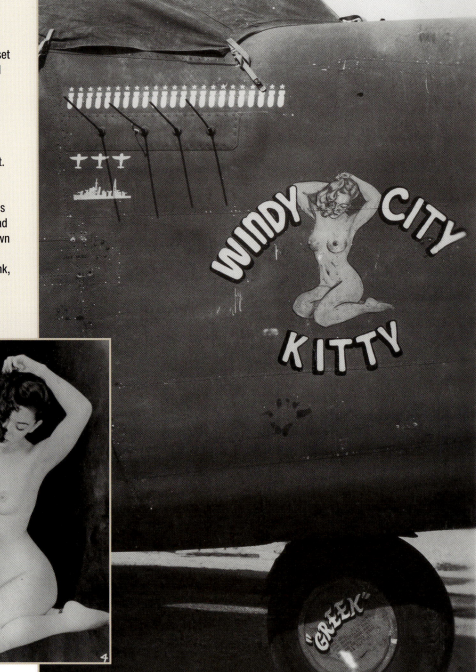

YANKEE GAL, Consolidated B-24, 44-49656, artist Charles R. Chesnut, 33rd BS, 22nd BG. In November 1944, a new B-24, serial number 44-40916, was assigned to the 33rd and given the name *YANKEE GAL II*, but she disappeared on a return flight to Samar in bad weather on January 23, 1945. Instead of naming the replacement aircraft *YANKEE GAL III*, the original name was used again. This new *YANKEE GAL*, much more sedate than the first (*see page 188*) and one of Chesnut's last nose art paintings, served for only less than two months before being salvaged, reason unknown.

"*50 CAL GAL*", Consolidated B-24, 41-23759, artist unknown, 321st BS, 90th BG. Named only on the LHS, the RHS of this B-24 featured this pin-up (unfortunately indistinct in this image), to which the gent in the photo, famous US actor and comedian Joe E. Brown (1891–1973), added his autograph, some crosses, and the word *Unlimited*. This occurred during a visit to the squadron at Port Moresby in April 1943. A later photo of this side of the nose shows Brown's signature and message present but no artwork; perhaps it was ordered to be removed in case of complaints from folks at home over what they may have thought of as Brown's endorsement of the pin-up. The hugely popular Brown did great work entertaining the troops all over the world, earning him a Bronze Star, one of only two awarded to civilians in World War II.

the WOLF and *WOLF PACK*, Consolidated B-24s, 42-73472 and 42-73476, neither artist known, both 403rd BS, 43rd BG. These B-24s were received by the 403rd BS in January 1944 with, it is thought, their nose art paintings already added. It is known that the pin-up on *WOLF* was added to both sides of that aircraft, but it appears that the *WOLF PACK* artwork was only on that B-24's RHS. Some comic has chalked names adjacent to the "wolves" on the latter B-24; this is suspected to have occurred at the Townsville Air Depot. *WOLF* was salvaged by the end of 1944, but *WOLF PACK* lasted longer, until June 1945, by which time it had flown a thousand combat hours and at least ninety-six missions. The air-to-air view of *WOLF* was taken near Nadzab ca. mid-1944 and shows well the 403rd's white tail identification markings. Note, though, that the positioning of the airplane serial number toward the top of the vertical stabilizer has reduced the height of the squadron marking there.

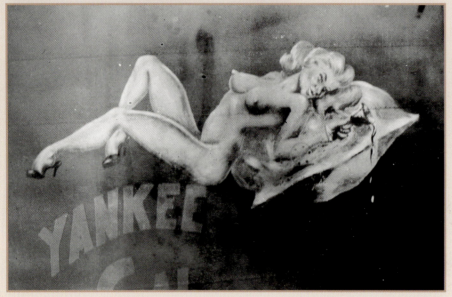

YANKEE DIDDL'ER, Boeing B-17, 41-2458, artist unknown, 65th BS, 43rd BG, later 39th TCS, 317th TCG; *YANKEE GAL*, Consolidated B-24, 42-100173, artist Charles R. Chesnut, 33rd BS, 22nd BG. As readers near the end of this chapter, the author hopes that they will agree with him that overtly sexual poses as bomber nose art were limited. By chance, here are two examples of that style that follow one another alphabetically, but the first is from 1943, the other from around a year later. The look of both artworks is the same, but what a difference a year made (due, it seems, to the influx of many new talented artists such as Chesnut) to the finished look. The extensive research into 43rd BG B-17 combat missions by the authors of *Ken's Men against the Empire*, volume 1, concluded that this B-17's first mission with the 65th BS occurred on February 25, 1943, its last on August 8, 1943. *YANKEE GAL*'s service was limited to a similar time frame, but in 1944, after which she was salvaged due to unspecified damage. As to *DIDDL'ER*'s fate, she was among those B-17s chosen for conversion to the armed transport role (work that was carried out at the Townsville Air Depot), and it has been reported that both the nose art and bomb log were painted out at this point, but a late-war photo of the shell of, by then, an apparently stripped *DIDDL'ER* revealed that the artwork was still in place, accompanied by a large "25," the B-17's 39th TCS field number. Note in the photo here the darker background to the first three letters of the name, suggesting, perhaps, an alteration along the way.

CHAPTER 3
Fighter and Photo Recon Fillies

After the 5th AF's early reliance on the Bell P-39 and Curtiss P-40s fighters both in defensive and offensive roles in the SWPA, by early 1944 it was Lockheed P-38s and Republic P-47s that saw the most combat. Only one nose art example on Bell's early fighter is included in this chapter (rather than on a P-39, it is on a P400, the export version of the P-39 officially regarded as "an earlier inferior variant"), since pin-up nose art on this type was limited (there were, it seems, more pin-ups on the automobile-style cockpit doors of Bell's pursuit ship, and photos of some of these can be found in appendix 1). As to the P-40, it was early examples operated by the 49th FG in northern Australia that featured a variety of the flamboyant unofficial markings seen on 5th AF planes, but probable concern over whether pin-ups would be allowed seems to have led to only a few examples being completed. Noteworthy too is that most early 49th FG artwork was not featured on the nose but was added to the sides of the fuselage, just above the plane's wing root. Nevertheless, seventeen different examples of pin-up nose art on P-40s have been collected by the author, mostly the work of Johnnie Dunn of the 7th FS, 49th FG, probably added mainly to the planes ca. mid-1944 (as of June 1944, there were still sixty-two P-40s in tactical units in New Guinea, all P-40Ns).

By comparison, though, the same summary of 5th AF airplane numbers in New Guinea indicates that there were 214 P-38s (plus thirty-four of the F-5 photoreconnaissance model), and a massive 413 P-47Ds as well. Little wonder, then, that this chapter features mainly P-38/F-5 and P-47 nose art, and it would be reasonably safe to say that most of the photos included are from that 1944–45 period. The other aircraft types included in this chapter are night fighters: the Douglas P-70 and the Northrop P-61, again mostly from the 1944–45 period, but only five examples of pin-ups on these planes could be found to be included. As with the bombers, the idea of decorating fighters with nose art developed rapidly, to quote one unit history, the late-war P-38s of the 8th FG, while based on Ie Shima Island, becoming particularly famous for its bold nudes.

Unlike the 5th AF's bombers, none of these planes were decorated with other than factory-applied markings until their arrival in forward areas. Thus, all the nose art that follows in this chapter must have been applied in the numerous squadrons to which these planes were assigned.

Overall views of 5th AF Republic P-47s with pin-up nose art are not as common as close-ups of the artworks, but here is an unnamed example, serial number 43-35634, artist unknown, of the 311th FS, 58th FG, featuring what would now be termed an exotic dancer (a close-up of the pin-up follows toward the end of this chapter). P-47s of the 58th FG, specialists in ground attack, featured a wide range of nose art, including, as will be seen, some of the best copies of *Esquire* magazine's Varga Girls. The black panel forward of the cockpit area identified the pilot (Lt. A. A. Marston), crew chief (SSgt. B. C. Bridgers), and assistant crew chief (SSgt. Roy Glaspie).

AIR A CUTIE, Bell P400, unidentified serial number, artist unknown, 36th FS, 8th FG. This early example of 5th AF fighter pin-up nose art is a great start to this chapter because the Airacobra (this name was applied both to P-39 and export P-400 models) was the first USAAF fighter type to see action in New Guinea, plus this larger-than-life painting made the aircraft well known. In fact, there were two versions of the LHS painting, this being the second with the pin-up's right arm down; the first had her arm stretching up and over the nose band. The aircraft's name is a little difficult to make out in this photo but begins at the top of the cockpit door and runs from there to the right in a straight line. On the RHS, the name was on a slight angle and ran toward the nose from the cockpit door, while the artwork was changed, with the pin-up as if in a flying position without goggles this time, but with arms fully extended. It must have looked very impressive to onlookers as the plane took off and landed.

'BAMA BELLE, Republic P-47, unidentified serial number, artist Jack B. Wallace (unconfirmed), 310th FS, 58th FG. This P-47, suspected to have had a red cowling, may have been that assigned to Lt. Glenn W. Evans, who was the only 310th pilot who hailed from Alabama listed in the group's 1945 souvenir book, *Memoirs of the 58th Fighter Group*. For the most part, artists worked only within their own squadron, but Jack B. Wallace, a 310th FS armorer, completed works for the 69th FS (another 58th FG squadron) as well; see *Bashful Barbs*, *LANA*, *Passionate Patsy*, *PIONEER PEGGY*, and one of three in the section on unnamed P-47 nose art.

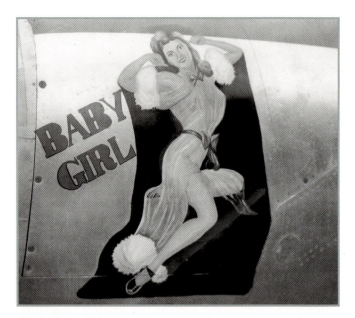

BABY GIRL, Lockheed P-38, 44-26216 (unconfirmed), artist unknown, 36th FS, 8th FG. Research more than thirty years ago by early nose art photo collectors John M. and Donna Campbell established that the name on this P-38 was later dropped when she was assigned to Capt. Robert L. Maynard; however, the artwork was retained. Victory symbols subsequently added to the nose related to two kills achieved by Maynard in November and December 1944.

Bare-ly Yours, Lockheed P-38, unidentified serial number, artist unknown, 35th FS, 8th FG. As with many of the other late-war 8th FG P-38s included in this chapter, little is known about this aircraft, except that it carried squadron letter "Q" on its engine cowlings at one time. Perhaps noteworthy is that, in this case, the artwork is on the RHS of the nose rather than the LHS, but some other examples of RHS nose art on P-38s do follow.

Left: *Betty Lou*, Republic P-47, unidentified serial number, artist unknown, 341st FS, 348th FG. The 348th FG and its P-47s joined the 5th AF mid-1943, subsequently becoming the most successful P-47-equipped fighter group in the war against Japan. This pin-up, applied originally on the fighter when carrying squadron number 48 and still in OD camouflage finish, was based on the *Esquire* May 1944 Varga Girl illustration. No sooner, it seems, had the nose art been added, though, that the process of removing the OD paint began; in the process, the blonde hair color was changed to brunette, and the slip-on sandals went from a dark to a light color. Photo taken probably after the squadron gave up its P-47s for P-51s early in 1945.

Bashful Barbs, Republic P-47, unidentified serial number, Jack B. Wallace (unconfirmed), 310th FS, 58th FG. Given that this and the photo of 'BAMA BELLE, seen earlier, came from the same collection, this is suspected to be another example of Wallace's stunning pin-up work. *Barbs* was based on the November pin-up from the 1943 *Esquire Varga Calendar*, but minus the tiger cub and with both of the pin-up's arms lowered.

Black Market Babe, Lockheed P-38, 42-67147, artist Peter Lasho, 432nd FS, 475th FG. The P-38 seen in these two photos was assigned to Lt. Billy M. Gresham, who scored six enemy aircraft destroyed and one probable over the period from August 1943 to March 1944. Artist Lasho, like Gresham, joined the 432nd FS in New Guinea, but unlike Gresham (who died in October 1944 when his parachute failed to open after a test flight went wrong), went on to the Philippines and later Ie Shima with the squadron. He seems to have been the main, if not only, squadron artist and as such would have been responsible for most, if not all, of the squadron's nose art. The only other 432nd FS nose art example definitely bearing his name, as seen by this author, however, is *Strictly Sex* (q.v.). Lasho's obituary (he died in 2006) also mentions that he was responsible for decorating PUTT PUTT MARU, the P-38 of the group commander, Col. Charles H. MacDonald, which, however, did not feature a pin-up.

BLACK WIDOW NF, Douglas P-70, unidentified serial number, artist unknown, Detachment "A" NFS and 418th NFS. A detachment of the 6th NFS was active in New Guinea from April 1943 until it was absorbed into the 418th NFS in November 1943, having, in the meantime, been redesignated the Detachment "A" NFS in September. The detachment commanding officer from September was Capt. Robert W. McLeod, and this was his airplane. When McLeod was the commanding officer, there were only five P-70s on hand; along the way, two P-38Gs were converted for night fighter work, but they were still being trialed when the 418th NFS took over. Readers wanting to learn more about these units are referred to Garry Pape's *Queen of the Midnight Skies: The Story of America's Air Force Night Fighters*.

CRO. BAIT, Lockheed P-38, unidentified serial number, artist "Whitt." (Lt. William Whittington), 8th FS, 49th FG. While there was no squadron number on the nose of CRO. BAIT at the time this photo was taken, a photo in Ernest R. McDowell's 49th FG history shows this P-38 carrying squadron number 64 when assigned to Lt. Fred C. Beach, and the above unit identification has been made on that basis. Note that the pilot when this photo was taken, though, was also the artist, Whittington (in fact, perhaps he had been the plane's original pilot). This P-38 was later passed on to the 35th FS, 8th FG, where the artwork was retained but renamed *The SOONER The Better* (q.v.). Whittington was also responsible for at least one other P-38 nose art: *"Honey ChiLe"* (q.v.).

Camera Shy / Piggy Back, Lockheed F-5, unidentified serial number, artist unknown, 26th and 25th PRSs, 6th PRG. The F-5 photo recon model of the P-38 gradually replaced the earlier F-4 version, and, as of June 18, 1944, there were no F-4s in New Guinea but more than thirty F-5s, mainly of the F-5B type. On the basis that at one stage this plane carried squadron number 561, then it had a different artwork on the LHS, named *Piggy Back*, a photo of which can be found later in this chapter. The basis of the *Camera Shy* artwork was Gil Elvgren's well-known mirror image pin-up from 1940 titled *Double Exposure* (an A-20 included in the unnamed section toward the end of chapter 2 carried similar artwork). For other photo recon P-38 nose art (all examples are suspected to be on F-5 models), see *"Harriett"*, *Little Lorraine*, *LOUISE!*, *Naughty Dotty*, *Paper Doll*, and two others in the unnamed section of this chapter.

Daddy Please and *Dawn Patrol*, Curtiss P-40s, unidentified serial numbers, artist Johnnie Dunn, both 7th FS, 49th FG. Johnnie Dunn would appear to be the most prolific of nose art artists serving in 5th AF fighter squadrons, with artworks on more than ten P-40s and one P-38 known. Unfortunately, though, no information about him has been found. See *"Milk Wagon Express"* for the artwork Dunn painted on RHS of *Daddy Please*; there was no artwork on the LHS of *Dawn Patrol*, just the name *BETS* (Ernest R. McDowell, in his previously mentioned 49th FG history, explained that as a rule, "Group practice" in the 49th FG was for the pilot's choice of name or artwork, or both, to appear on the RHS of the aircraft, while the crew chief's choice appeared on the LHS). The *Dawn Patrol* name was taken from one of two popular films of the same name produced in the 1930s about a dangerous World War I aerial mission, but clearly the name has a different meaning here. For other Dunn nose art, see *Empty Saddle*, *Grade A*, *Island Dream*, *LAP DOG!* (the P-38 mentioned), *"Milk Wagon Express"*, *My Anxious Mama!*, *O'Riley's Daughter*, *Pop's Blue Ribbon*, and *SCARLET NIGHT*.

DEAR RITA II, Lockheed P-38, unidentified serial number, artist unknown, 36th FS, 8th FG. This P-38 was assigned to Lt. Francis M. Collins, and the artwork was based on the *Esquire* June 1943 Varga Girl illustration, with some costume changes and the addition of a background star. Note the very small victory symbol below the names of Collins and his crew chief, "Moe" Howard; this was one of a number of aerial victories achieved on November 6, 1944, by 35th FS and 36th FS pilots in the course of a sweep over Fabrica airfield on the island of Negros. Behind *DEAR RITA II* in this photo can be seen Lt. Ken B. Lloyd's P-38, which was later named *Dark Eyes* (for a closer look at this nose art, see the unnamed P-38 photo section later in this chapter).

Dorothy Mae, Curtiss P-40, unidentified serial number, artist unknown, 8th FS, 49th FG. Although seen before, this image, a late addition but scanned from an original print, was a welcome addition to the author's collection. According to the 49th FG history *Protect and Avenge*, this particular P-40 was assigned to 8th FS old hand Andy Reynolds in the third week of December 1943 and originally carried squadron number 58. The pin-up, added a little later perhaps, was based on a pin-up found in the 1944 *Esquire Varga Calendar*. Unnamed originally, the P-40 was later assigned to a new pilot who, it is suspected, arranged to have the name added. Also note the change of squadron number to "44."

Empty Saddle, Curtiss P-40, 42-105513, artist Johnnie Dunn, 7th FS, 49th FG. This is another of Dunn's works that carries a date, in this case July 5, 1944 (*see close-up*); it is likely that most of his P-40 artwork was from around the same time (*Milk Wagon Express* and *My Anxious Mama!*, which follow, were two others that are known to have been completed in July 1944). Widely remembered as 7th FS CO Maj. Arland Stanton's favorite P-40, *Empty Saddle* was also known as *KEYSTONE KATHLENE*, a name it carried on the LHS of the nose. It was abandoned at Finschafen, New Guinea, and the remains were recovered from there by Australian World War II aircraft restorer Ian Whitney in 1987.

Fun WASN'T IT!, Republic P-47, unidentified serial number, artist unknown, unit(s) unidentified. This photo and that of P-47 *Who ME?* (q.v.) were purchased together as part of a 5th AF photo collection, and while details are lacking, it would be a safe bet to suggest that the two artworks not only were by the same artist but appeared early on (second half of 1943) and were most likely short lived due to their suggestive nature, particularly given the implication in this case.

G.I. Miss U, Lockheed P-38, unidentified serial number, artist unknown, 35th FS, 8th FG. This artwork, which seems to have been painted on the RHS only, was copied from the September pin-up in K. O. Munson's *Artist's Sketch Pad Calendar* for 1945. Bill Hankey used the same inspiration for his painting of *LOUISE!* (q.v.). Note the aircraft letter "U" (the countershading of which was a 35th FS hallmark); perhaps the name was inspired by this identification letter.

G.I. Virgin, Lockheed P-38, unidentified serial number, artist unknown, unidentified FS, 8th FG. This P-38, with a faded antiglare panel, carried squadron letter "D," and while no other details are known, it is another example of a late-war 8th FG plane with nose art on the RHS rather than the LHS.

GERRI, Republic P-47, unidentified serial number, artist unknown, unidentified FS, 58th FG. The accompanying name for this beautiful artwork, based on the December pin-up from the 1944 *Esquire Varga Calendar*, is difficult to see in this photo but appears immediately below the painting at lower left. This P-47 may have featured another name as well, since what may be part of the first letter of another name could be seen at far right on the original print.

Glamour-Puss II, Lockheed P-38, unidentified serial number, artist unknown, 80th FS, 8th FG. Here are two views of this P-38, both probably taken on Ie Shima in 1945. *At left*, the artwork can be seen to be incomplete, with just the first word in place (all in black paint; some color was added later to the unfilled section of the letter "G") and pin-up shadow absent, while, *at right*, is the completed work. The pilot assigned to this P-38 (which carried squadron letter "L") was Lt. Chester L. Schachterle.

NOSE ART OF THE 5TH AIR FORCE

GLORIA, Republic P-47, unidentified serial number, artist unknown, 341st FS, 348th FG. Little is currently known about this detailed and beautifully executed artwork or the P-47 on which it appeared, but another photo shows that the aircraft carried squadron number 32 at one stage. Why the artwork looks as though it has been defaced is not known.

"Harriett", Lockheed F-5, unidentified serial number, artist Bill Hankey, 6th PRG. Hankey produced this artwork for the former executive officer of the 6th PRG, later (from January 1945) commanding officer, Lt. Col. Ben K. Armstrong, in honor of his sweetheart, apparently using a photo stuck down to the fuselage, just as Maj. Richard Bong had done with his P-38 named *Marge* (q.v.). Armstrong flew 112 combat missions with the 6th Group; his F-5 was probably assigned to Group Headquarters.

HELL ON THE DOUBLE, Lockheed P-38, unidentified serial number, artist unknown, 36th FS, 8th FG. With a name that would seem to reflect one pilot's thoughts as to the speed of his P-38, this very clear photo picks up the fact that the pilot's name was Lt. B. P. Morgan. Morgan, from Florida, lost his life on February 8, 1945, after his P-38—probably this aircraft—was hit by enemy antiaircraft fire and his parachute failed to open after he bailed out. This photo was taken prior to the change in positioning of 8th FG squadron identification numbers from both sides of the nose of the aircraft to the outer side of both engine cowlings in September 1944. The black objects that appear fanned out below the names of the pilot and crew chief are rarely seen (on 8th FG P-38s) bombing-mission symbols.

Grade A, Curtiss P-40, unidentified serial number, artist Johnnie Dunn, 7th FS, 49th FG. This P-40 carried the name *RUSTY LOAD* (but no pin-up) on the RHS. No other details are known at present.

196

"Honey ChiLe", Lockheed P-38, unidentified serial number, artist "Whitt." (Lt. William Whittington), 8th FS (unconfirmed), 49th FG. There had been an earlier 8th FS P-38 with the same name, and this *"Honey ChiLe"* seems to have been her successor. She survived the war and was part of the initial USAAF presence in occupied Japan. For another of this artist's work, see CRO. BAIT earlier in the chapter.

HUT-SUT, Republic P-47, unidentified serial number, artist G. (?) V. (?) Wilson, unidentified FS, 58th FG. It has already been mentioned in chapter 2 that the wartime publication *The Official Guide to the Army Air Forces*, published in 1944, notes in a photo caption that "names on planes are . . . often meaningful only to the crew." This seems to be another case in point. While the artist signed off this work, a check of the volume *Memoirs of the 58th Fighter Group* (which was compiled as of April 1, 1945, and includes all names and addresses of 58th FG personnel at that time) failed to identify him.

Island Dream, Curtiss P-40, 42-105304 (unconfirmed), artist Johnnie Dunn, 7th FS, 49th FG. This P-40 also carried squadron number 15 at one time. Alterations to the nose panel have caused most of the word *Island* to be painted out, as well as part of the background for Dunn's pin-up.

JAIL BAIT, Republic P-47, unidentified serial number, artist unknown, 340th FS (unconfirmed), 348th FG. A slang term dating from the 1920s, if not earlier, referring to the likelihood of ending up in jail for having sex with a minor (a young woman who website Wikipedia notes "usually appears older"), this was not a common wartime nose art name, and this P-47, in fact, was probably the only 5th AF plane to be so named. This P-47 is believed to have carried squadron number "11," and it is on that basis that the identification of the squadron has been made.

Kit II, Republic P-47, 42-75294, artist unknown, 40th FS, 35th FG. Two views of this artwork, another example based on the December 1943 Varga Girl, before and after the name was added. The overall view of this P-47 (personal snaps like this of 5th AF P-47s are not common) provided the aircraft's serial number, enabled squadron identification, and confirmed group identification (the 40th FS used plane numbers from 40 to 69), while the red lightning bolt at the tip of the tail was a group identifier. Also note the cowling adornment, another group identifier.

Jean Creamer, Lockheed P-38, unidentified serial number, artist unknown, 36th FS, 8th FG. This P-38, which carried squadron letter "E," had originally been assigned to Capt. Robert J. Mullenberg, but his name (which had appeared along with that of the crew chief, SSgt. C. Willits, to the right of the word *Creamer*) had been removed by the time this photo was taken. This, together with the repainting of the black antiglare panel and the addition of decorative white edging, though, suggests that this photo was taken after the end of the war, prior to the unit's move to Japan. The artwork was based on the July pin-up in K. O. Munson's *Artist's Sketch Pad Calendar* for 1945, sans sunglasses.

Lady GODiVA, Republic P-47, unidentified serial number, artist unknown, 310th or 311th FS, 58th FG. There have been many artists' impressions of how the legendary eleventh-century English noblewoman, who is said to have ridden on horseback through the streets of Coventry covered only by her long, flowing hair, may have looked, but none of them looked like this. It would seem that in this case (and that of a 388th BS, 312th BG Douglas A-20), some difficulty in coming up with a punchy original name led to this choice, which was well known from schoolboy history books. Apart from the fact that this *Lady GODiVA* was gun-toting, virtually lost in this image is the fact that she was also riding a bomb in the nose art painting.

FIGHTER AND PHOTO RECON FILLIES

LADY ORCHID or ORCHID LADY, Republic P-47, unidentified serial number, artist unknown, unidentified FS, 348th FG (unconfirmed). The positioning of the word LADY suggested to this author that the name of this P-47 was LADY ORCHID, but there was a famous American film actress from the 1920s, Corinne Griffith (1894–1979), who was known as "the Orchid Lady of the Screen," so perhaps this plane was named after her. No further information is known.

LANA, Republic P-47, unidentified serial number, artist Jack B. Wallace (unconfirmed), 69th FS, 58th FG. A good example of the impact of popular culture on airplane nose art ca. mid-1944 was the name and pin-up on this P-47, the former a tribute to popular actress and wartime sex symbol Lana Turner (1921–95), the latter an almost exact likeness of the Varga Girl from the May 1944 issue of *Esquire* magazine (for another example of this artwork on a P-47, see *Betty Lou* earlier in the chapter). Close examination of this photo suggests that the sign-off below the letter "N" is that of 310th FS armorer Jack B. Wallace; see 'BAMA BELLE for further comment.

LAP DOG!, Lockheed P-38, unidentified serial number, artist Johnnie Dunn, 7th FS, 49th FG. Dunn's 7th FS P-40 artworks are well known (see *Daddy Please*, *Dawn Patrol*, *Empty Saddle*, *Grade A*, *Island Dream*, "Milk Wagon Express", *My Anxious Mama!*, *O'Riley's Daughter*, *Pop's Blue Ribbon*, and SCARLET NIGHT in this chapter for other examples), and it would almost seem that he went "out of business" after that, but he was evidently coaxed back at least once, this being his only painting seen thus far on a P-38. This work, perhaps his most beautiful pin-up, is not signed off as the earlier works were, but is noted as having been DONE by DUNN just above the dark section at lower left and is dated August 1945 on the far right. A later photo, most likely taken in Japan, shows that this P-38 carried squadron number 14 at that stage.

Lazy Lady, Lockheed P-38, unidentified serial number, artist unknown, 35th FS, 8th FG. Here, two RAAF pilots have been photographed with this P-38 on Noemfoor Island, September 1944. It was assigned to Lt. Glen C. Holder, who had, prior to the squadron's transition to P-38s in early 1944, flown a P-40 that also carried aircraft letter "L," but no pin-up. *Via Bob Piper*

Little Lorraine and *LOUISE!*, Lockheed F-5s, unidentified serial numbers, artist Bill Hankey, both 8th PRS, 6th PRG. Here are two examples of Bill Hankey's pin-up artistry. *Little Lorraine* (based on the October pin-up that appeared in the 1944 *Esquire Varga Calendar*) is seen here showing its squadron number and colored spinners (she was assigned to at least two pilots, Capt J. T. Carmen and Lt. G. B. Frankforter). Note in this case that Hankey added only one of his trademark stars in place of dots on the "i's." By 1945, pin-up artist K. O. Munson's *Artist's Sketch Pad Calendar* was reaching new heights of popularity because his models were mostly nude. One of the most popular pages was that of September 1945, from which Hankey based the lovely illustration of *LOUISE!* A photo of Hankey working on this nose art can be found in chapter 1.

Marge, Lockheed P-38, 42-103993, 9th FS, 49th FG. While most young unattached men serving in the armed forces saw no problem with the painted pin-ups added to military aircraft, clearly for others the love for a girlfriend, fiancée, or wife outweighed any real interest in risqué nose art. One famous flier who saw it this way was Capt. (later major) Richard Bong, seen in the second photo here, who had met the love of his life, Marjorie Vattendahll (1923–2003), in November 1943 while he was home on leave after more than a year's service in the SWPA and achieving twenty-one aerial victories against enemy aircraft. After returning to the SWPA (to V Fighter Command headquarters as an instructor) in February 1944, when he did fly with his old unit, the 9th FS, he often flew this aircraft, his ownership made clear by the addition of the enlargement of a beautiful photo of Marge stuck to the nose (and protected by a coating of varnish) and victory symbols as shown. By late March–early April 1944, Bong was hot on the heels of the leading US ace from World War I, Eddie Rickenbacker, as the new ace of aces, leading to a lot of publicity back home regarding him and his P-38, with Bong commenting in a letter to his mother that "I hope I haven't gotten Marge into too much trouble . . . but it sure is a hell of a lot better than a lot of these naked women we see on the planes here!" Bong went on to beat Rickenbacker's score, became engaged to Marge, receive the Congressional Medal of Honor, and subsequently marry Marge, but he died testing a Lockheed P-80 jet fighter on August 6, 1945. He was just twenty-four years old but in the last two years of his life had achieved legendary status and, in so doing, had become a poster boy for the 5th AF. These photos were taken ca. March 1944 after stencils for twenty-five enemy aircraft had been added, but one claim was subsequently downgraded to a probable. The photo of Bong with his P-38, perhaps intentionally, did not include any portion of the plane's name or the photo of Marge. *Bong photo, US Official from Victory magazine, vol. 2, no. 6 (1945)*

Marie Elena, Lockheed P-38, unidentified serial number, artist unknown, 432nd FS, 475th FG. Another of the many copies of the January pin-up from Alberto Vargas's 1944 *Esquire Varga Calendar* (for other examples, see the introduction); whether this nose art was another of Peter Lasho's works (see *Black Market Babe* and *Strictly Sex* in this chapter) is not currently known. The surname of the pilot (just visible in the photo) is Lundy; Lt. Noel R. Lundy, a 432nd FS pilot, was lost in action on September 13, 1943, in a P-38 identified as 42-66734, but whether or not this photo is of that airplane is not currently known.

LIL BOOTSIE "ADA", Republic P-47, unidentified serial number, artist unknown, 310th or 311th FS, 58th FG. Early on in its history, while its aircraft were still in camouflage, the 58th FG adopted a policy of painting the sides of their engine cowlings in different colors to aid squadron identification: white for the 69th FS, yellow for the 310th, and blue for the 311th. Once NMF P-47s were received, however (or camouflage removed), the squadron color was limited to a horizontal band, as shown here, but the author will leave assumptions as to the band's color to others more qualified to comment.

Mary Liz, Republic P-47, unidentified serial number, artist unknown, 69th FS, 58th FG. This P-47 was assigned to Lt. Sam McFarland and is shown here at two different stages; above in a 69th FS lineup with the nose art on an all-white cowling (the combination of an "A" prefix to the squadron number as visible on the second P-47 in the lineup, together with the white cowling sides, identified a 69th FS P-47) and at left, after NMF P-47s were received, or, in this case, camouflage was removed, a horizontal band featuring the squadron color was added to the cowling. As with *Marie Elena* seen earlier, this is another example of a pin-up copied from the January offering in the 1944 *Esquire Varga Calendar*. The wartime souvenir book *Memoirs of the 58th Fighter Group* includes a photo of McFarland's perhaps last P-47 that shows it carried the name *Mary Liz III 3rd*, but it featured no pin-up.

'MARY LOU', Curtiss P-40, unidentified serial number, artist unknown, 8th FS and 7th FS, 49th FG. This P-40, with a pin-up based in part on the September page from the 1944 *Esquire Varga Calendar*, started out as shown with squadron number 47 in the 8th FS but, reportedly, was later transferred to the 7th FS, where it became squadron number 19. 8th FS pin-up nose art on its P-40s was limited, and this is the only example that is featured in this volume.

MIDNIGHT MAMA, Northrop P-61, unidentified serial number, artist unknown, 421st NFS. This squadron was the first 5th AF P-61-equipped unit to see action in the SWPA; that was in June 1944 (note that the nose radomes were painted white at first, but later this was changed to black). As a night fighter aircraft, there were lots of references to night-time "activity" in the names thought up for them, but 421st NFS pin-up nose art was not widespread (two other 421st pin-ups featured in this chapter are NOCTURNAL NEMESIS and *Nocturnal Nuisance*). The name appeared on both sides of this aircraft, but the artwork, appropriately a Sydney "lady of the night," appeared only on the RHS. (For comments on Sydney's Kings Cross area, see C-47 *Kings Cross SHUTTLE* in the following chapter.)

"Milk Wagon Express", Curtiss P-40, unidentified serial number, artist Johnnie Dunn, 7th FS, 49th FG. This artwork, another completed in July 1944, as, perhaps, all of Dunn's P-40 artworks were, appeared on the RHS of *Daddy Please* (q.v.). Note that this P-40 carried two different squadron numbers at different times: 00 and 10. It was lost in the process of buzzing Cyclops field at Hollandia on July 17, 1944, just sixteen days after Dunn finished the nose art. There was no escape for the twenty-two-year-old pilot; he died instantly.

Miss Bea, Republic P-47, unidentified serial number, artist unknown, 310th FS, 58th FG. One of the last P-47 pin-up nose art photos collected for this project; the pilot with the airplane is Lt. Ross N. Mathis. The artwork is another copy of the December 1943 *Esquire* magazine Varga Girl pin-up, as seen on P-47 *Kit II* earlier in this chapter and widely reproduced elsewhere (three examples follow on C-47s in chapter 4).

Miss Cheri, Lockheed P-38, unidentified serial number, artist unknown, 80th FS (unconfirmed), 8th FG (unconfirmed). This photo and the early views of *Glamour Puss II* and *Obscene Corrine* (before the name was added) that appear in this chapter all were part of the same collection. It is suspected that this is also an early photo, since it is known that *Miss Cheri* was subsequently renamed *Miss Mecca II* and, as such, was seen on Ie Shima in 1945, but who was responsible for the name change and just when it occurred is not known.

MISS GINNY, Lockheed P-38, 44-26337, artist unknown, 80th FS (unconfirmed), 8th FG. On the basis that the same artist responsible for the *Pilot* and *Crew* names on this P-38 was also responsible for the same information on *PEGGY's PEGASUS* (q.v.), then this P-38 was probably also from the 80th FS. No other details are currently known.

Mr. Period, Republic P-47, unidentified serial number, artist unknown, 341st FS, 348th FG. While only part of the second word in the name can be seen here, another photo seen by the author confirms the existence of "*Mr.*" at some stage. The full name would seem to be an abbreviated form of "missed her period," but whether this was supposed to be a warning against unprotected sex or was a real-life experience is not known (a 9th AF B-26 was named *Mister Period Twice*). The pin-up is a nice copy of the Varga Girl from the August 1943 issue of *Esquire*. Note a small two-digit squadron number, "45," at the lower right of the engine cowling.

"*MUGGSIE*", Republic P-47, unidentified serial number, artist unknown, 341st FS, 348th FG. Like *Mr. Period*, at left, this P-47 also has a two-digit number on the bottom of the cowling, probably "33"; this number was a smaller version of what appeared on camouflaged 348th FG P-47s on the fin, above the stenciled aircraft serial number. Initial squadron numbers used by the 341st FS were in the range 26–50.

MY BET III / MY PET / MY PET Dorothy Marie, Lockheed P-38, 44-25923 (unconfirmed), artist unknown, 36th FS, 8th FG. As noted earlier, replacement bomber aircraft often stuck with the same name as used before, but numbers (usually Roman numerals) were added to differentiate them. While this practice was not so common in 5th AF fighter squadrons, here is an example, but it appears to have been short lived, since the word *BET* was subsequently changed to *PET*, as shown here. This change was probably due to a change in pilots assigned to the aircraft; when the first photo (*above left*) was taken, the pilot was still Lt. Charles H. Finnell, but, reportedly, it was later a Lt. Dixon. As seen here, a new name, *Dorothy Marie*, was added above *MY PET*, but whether this combination or simply *MY PET* was the final version (note that in both cases, white edging has been added to the antiglare panel) is not currently known. The *Dorothy Marie* photo also confirms that the nose panel on which most of the artwork had been painted was removed from an earlier P-38, but which one is not known.

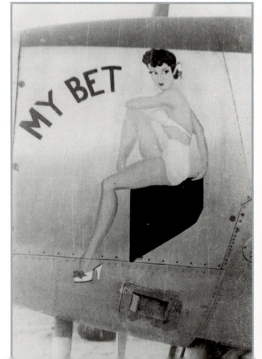

MY BET, Lockheed P-38, unidentified serial number, artist unknown, 36th FS, 8th FG. On the basis that *MY BET III*, above, had been Lt. Charles H. Finnell's aircraft, then probably *MY BET* was the first of his P-38s. He claimed one enemy aircraft destroyed, perhaps while flying this aircraft, on December 20, 1944.

My Anxious Mama!, Curtiss P-40, unidentified serial number, artist Johnnie Dunn, 7th FS, 49th FG. If, as is likely, this P-40 always carried the same squadron number, then the LHS featured the name *IKEY III* (this name can be seen in the background of the photo of *SCARLET NIGHT* that appears later in this chapter). Note that the artwork has been dated July 1944, suggesting that this (and, perhaps, other Dunn P-40 artwork) was not around for long, since all the squadron P-40s were gone within two months.

MY GAL Jeannie, Lockheed P-38, unidentified serial number, artist unknown, unidentified FS, 8th FG. Although it has nose art based on the January pin-up from the 1945 *Esquire Varga Calendar*, little more is known of the P-38 involved except that it survived the war to become part of the 8th FG's force sent to Japan in November 1945. Since the 8th converted to P-51s soon after, it seems likely that the group's remaining P-38s, such as *Jeannie*, saw only limited use in Japan and were subsequently salvaged there.

"NICE PIECE", Lockheed P-38, unidentified serial number, artist unknown, 80th FS, 8th FG. The first of three 8th FG P-38s in this chapter with the same nose number (see also *Pam* and *WINDY CITY RUTHIE*), this may have been another fighter flown by Lt Kenneth G. Ladd, since a ten-victory "scoreboard" can just be made out in the photo. Also note the altered armament, six machine guns instead of the usual four. Little else is known about *"NICE PIECE"*. John C. Stanaway and Lawrence J. Hickey noted in their 8th FG history, *Attack & Conquer*, that the altered armament "apparently was dropped for some reason."

Naughty Dotty, Lockheed F-5, unidentified serial number, artist unknown, 8th PRS (unconfirmed), 6th PRG. This F-5's nose art was copied from the pin-up of *Willful Winnie of New Guinea* shown here, taken from the 91st Reconnaissance Wing's *The Wing-ding* four-page newspaper of May 13, 1944, but no other information on the plane is known. The spinner colors used by the 8th PRS were red/white/blue, but another photo of this F-5 shows that the tip of the spinner had earlier been white. The artwork and *Willful Winnie* name were also used on an 80th FS P-38; see photo later in this chapter.

NOSE ART OF THE 5TH AIR FORCE

NOCTURNAL NEMESIS and Nocturnal Nuisance, Northrop P-61s, 42-5502 (NEMESIS) and 42-5494 (Nuisance, but unconfirmed) artist(s) unknown, both 421st NFS. NOCTURNAL NEMESIS featured the nickname "Skippy" on the LHS as well as "Pilot Lt. DAVE T. CORTS" below the LHS cockpit window. For a closer view of the pin-up, see chapter 6. As to Nocturnal Nuisance, while this is, unfortunately, a slightly blurred image of this aircraft, it has been included here not only because it is a previously unpublished view of an aircraft that had (if the serial number quoted is correct) only a brief service existence (May–July 1944), but because it also gives an idea of its massive size. Note the addition of the silver drop tanks under the wings of Nocturnal Nuisance as well.

O'Riley's Daughter, Curtiss P-40, 42-105405 (unconfirmed), artist Johnnie Dunn, 7th FS, 49th FG. As already mentioned in chapter 2 in relation to Douglas A-20 O'Riley's Daughter II, this name was taken from a bawdy popular traditional Irish song. Unfortunately, though, the history of the plane is virtually unknown. Dates noted on Dunn's other P-40 nose art in this chapter, however, suggest that all the works were done ca. July 1944, toward the end of the line for these fighters, which were subsequently replaced with P-38s.

Obscene Corrine, Lockheed P-38, unidentified serial number, artist unknown, 36th FS, 8th FG. These two photos show this P-38 before and after the name was added. In the earlier view, the name of the pilot assigned to the aircraft was a Lt. Locke, but by the time the second photo was taken, the pilot's name (not visible in the photo) is believed to be Lt. R. A. Ward. Certainly, it was Ward who flew this P-38 as part of the extensive 5th AF escort for the flight of the two Japanese bombers bringing the Japanese surrender legation from Japan to Ie Shima on August 19, 1945.

FIGHTER AND PHOTO RECON FILLIES

Pam, Lockheed P-38, unidentified serial number, artist unknown, 36th FS, 8th FG. At least two views of this particular nose art that featured an accurate copy of the October pin-up from the 1944 *Esquire Varga Calendar* have been published prior to this, the best in Robert J. Stava's *Combat Recon* volume (see bibliography), which also reveals that the squadron identification was not simply "3," as suggested by this photo, but "3d." The image seen here does, however, confirm that there was only one victory symbol at the time, and that the assigned pilot's name was of only a few letters in length, ending in "ff." It is considered most likely, therefore, that this was then Lt. Thomas R. Huff's P-38; his first claim for an enemy fighter shot down occurred on November 9, 1943. Following his promotion to captain, Huff commanded the 36th FS in October–November 1944, when he also claimed the destruction of a second enemy aircraft.

Passionate Patsy, Republic P-47, 42-23190, artist Jack B. Wallace (unconfirmed), 310th FS, 58th FG. Perhaps the best-known nose art on a 5th AF P-47, but *Patsy*'s early history is not known. Two photos of different 310th pilots, Lt. Ralph Barnes Jr. and Lt. Ross N. Mathis, next to the nose of this P-47 appear in the group's wartime souvenir book, *Memoirs of the 58th Fighter Group*, but there is no comment as to whether either had any real connection with this plane. Barnes's name comes up in other sources as her assigned pilot, but given that he was married and his wife's name was Harriet, this seems unlikely. This photo came from my father's small collection of 5th and 13th AF nose art that was assembled by him in 1945.

Paper Doll, Lockheed F-5, 4267357 (unconfirmed), artist unknown, 25th PRS, 6th PRG. Another reference to wartime pin-up pictures (also see the B-24 of the same name in chapter 2); while the author has not been able to identify the origins of this artwork, it is interesting to note that a B-24 with similar artwork and the same name (but in capital letters) was operating from Italy for a time in 1944, suggesting that there was, indeed, a pin-up named *Paper Doll* that had appeared in print beforehand.

PAY OFF, Lockheed P-38, unidentified serial number, artist unknown, 36th FS, 8th FG. The first of three late-war 8th FG P-38 nose art examples that follow by virtue of being in alphabetical order, this image was taken from an original wartime negative. From the same source also came other close-ups of nose art taken from original negatives published in this chapter, all of which are suspected to have been 8th FG planes (see *MY GAL Jeannie* and *So Inviting*, plus the last unnamed example). Note in the background another 36th FS P-38 and its under-wing squadron markings.

NOSE ART OF THE 5TH AIR FORCE

Pecks Bad Girl, Lockheed P-38, 44-25133 (unconfirmed), artist unknown, 36th FS, 8th FG. This P-38, squadron identification letter "V," was named after the pilot assigned to it, Capt. Charles I. Peck. When the name was added, no apostrophe was included, but as already noted, not everyone "gets" apostrophe usage (for another example where an apostrophe was not included, see *SATANS SISTER* in chapter 2). Peck claimed an enemy fighter, an "Oscar," in this P-38 on December 21, 1944.

Piggy Back / Camera Shy, Lockheed F-5, unidentified serial number, artist unknown, 26th and 25th PRSs, 6th PRG. The author suspects that this artwork of a Native American piggy-backing her baby appeared on the LHS of an F-5 named *Camera Shy* (q.v.) on the RHS. Another photo of *Piggy Back* has been seen with a different squadron number, 075, but which squadron used each squadron number is not currently known.

PEGGY'S PEGASUS, Lockheed P-38, unidentified serial number, artist unknown, 80th FS, 8th FG. This was assigned to a Lt. Kirkpatrick and known to have carried squadron letter "S," but the only other information this author can add is that this is another example, like *Jean Creamer* (q.v.), of an artwork based on the July pin-up in K. O. Munson's *Artist's Sketch Pad Calendar* for 1945, but in this case the sunglasses being worn by the pin-up in the calendar have not been included. The artwork is seen here before and after the name was added; note that in the "after" photo, the style of sign writing of the *Pilot* and *Crew* names is the same as that on *MISS GINNY* (q.v.).

Pop's Blue Ribbon and *Rosy Cheeks*, Curtiss P-40s, unidentified serial number, artist of *Pop's Blue Ribbon*, Johnnie Dunn, artist of *Rosy Cheeks* unknown, 7th FS, 49th FG. Another two well-known 7th FS P-40 artworks (*Rosy Cheeks*, assigned to the squadron's commanding officer, Maj. Edward A. Peck, carried the name RHODE ISLAND RED on the LHS; Peck hailed from Providence, Rhode Island), but little more can be added at this stage except that the squadron numbers seen here confirm the squadron identification.

PIONEER PEGGY, Republic P-47, unidentified serial number, artist Jack B. Wallace, 310th FS, 58th FG. Assigned to Lt. Herman F. Guffey; the explanation for his choice of name has been found in the book *Memoirs of the 58th Fighter Group*: "While in training as a cadet, he [Guffey] married; and as a result of the devoted way his wife trekked around the country with him during those hectic days, he has named his plane 'Pioneer Peggy.'"

POLLY, Lockheed P-38, unidentified serial number, artist unknown, 36th FS (unconfirmed), 8th FG. Seen here before and after the name was added, note also in the after photo the repainted antiglare panel now with white edging added, apparently an artistic refinement after hostilities ended; for photos of two other P-38s so marked, see *Jean Creamer* and MY BET III / MY PET / MY PET *Dorothy Marie* in this chapter.

"SAN ANTONIO ROSE", Lockheed P-38, 42-103984, artist PFC. C. Cornelius, 80th FS, 8th FG. This P-38 was assigned to Lt. Charles B. Ray from Tilden, Texas (not far from San Antonio), in the late 1943–early 1944 period, and it was in it that Ray claimed three (out of five) enemy aircraft shot down. Not visible in this photo is the aircraft's nose "Y" identification letter forward of the artwork. The inset photo is of the artist's salute to the pilot; it reads *GOOD HUNTING! HAPPY LANDINGS! PFC. C. CORNELIUS BKLYN N.Y.*

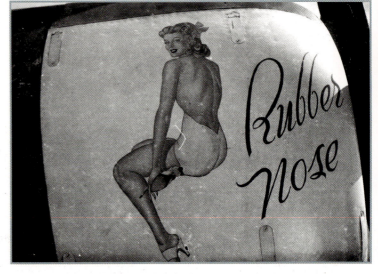

SACK-TIME SAL, Republic P-47, unidentified serial number, artist unknown, unit(s) unidentified. Despite one victory being claimed by the pilot, neither he nor the aircraft has yet been identified. Note the difference between the victory marking seen here when compared to others in this chapter. This may eventually help identify the unit that this P-47 belonged to, since other aircraft from the same unit are suspected to have used the same stencil.

Rubber Nose, Republic P-47, 42-22xxx, artist unknown, 69th FS, 58th FG. Here is another great copy of a Vargas pin-up on a 69th FS P-47, which is virtually a duplicate of the July 1944 Varga Girl, but wearing a white rather than floral bathing suit. For others, see *LANA*, *Mary Liz*, and another on an unnamed P-47 toward the end of this chapter.

SCARLET NIGHT, Curtiss P-40, 42-105xxx, artist Johnnie Dunn, 7th FS, 49th FG. This is the only one of Dunn's artworks known to have appeared on a P-40 that had been stripped of paint. That work began ca. June 1944, and given that all the 7th Squadron's P-40s had been transferred out in September, this photo probably dates from the third quarter of 1944.

FIGHTER AND PHOTO RECON FILLIES

Shady's Lady, Lockheed P-38, 44-26412, artist unknown, 80th FS, 8th FG. This view shows the aircraft, which carried squadron letter "P," following the end of hostilities and with its impressive score of bombing and reconnaissance missions still in place. The artwork is based on an Alberto Vargas Varga Girl from 1941. Her assigned pilot, William R. Pruner, continued flying for the next twenty years but lost his life in the Vietnam War after his Air America C-47 was shot down and he was captured by the Vietcong.

The Sixty-niner, Republic P-47, unidentified serial number, artist unknown, unit(s) unidentified. All that can definitely be said about this photo is that it was taken in New Guinea and is one of only two seen by the author of this artwork. The origin of the name was probably simply the fact that 69 was its squadron number, and while the term *Sixty-niner* may have, perhaps, been lesser known in the 1940s than more recently, all the unknowns about the plane do seem to add up to the fact that the artwork was short lived.

'SLEEPY TIME GAL', Republic P-47, 42-23224, artist unknown, 69th FS, 58th FG. This is one of the better known of the 69th FS's P-47s as nice side views of her have appeared elsewhere. See, in particular, Ernest R. McDowell's *Thunderbolt: The Republic P-47 Thunderbolt in the Pacific Theater*. Originally, while the P-47 wore camouflage (like *Mary Liz* above), the pin-up appeared on a white background, but after the camouflage was removed, dark banding, seen here, was added. Interestingly, another photo to be found later in this chapter suggests that the 69th FS marking for NMF P-47s was a white band on a bare-metal cowling; was this perhaps changed, though, after the 69th FS color went from white to red? This is another photo from my father's small wartime nose art photo collection.

Slick CHICK, Republic P-47, 42-27617 (unconfirmed), artist unknown, 311th FS, 58th FG. This may have been the aircraft assigned to Lt. David C. Batey, who joined the 311th in October 1944. No further details are known.

NOSE ART OF THE 5TH AIR FORCE

Slightly Dangerous, Lockheed P-38, 42-66750 (unconfirmed), artist unknown, 432nd FS, 475th FG. While this image is slightly blurred, the nose art appears to comprise a naked pin-up with a cactus plant—a somewhat unusual combination, but in keeping with the "Slightly Dangerous" theme (a moniker popular at the time thanks to MGM's 1943 romantic comedy of the same name). The artist may have been Peter Lasho, but confirmation is currently lacking. This photo and a view from a similar angle of *Black Market Babe* that appears earlier in this chapter were from the same collection, but apart from the fact that this P-38 was assigned to Capt. Arthur L. Peregoy, little else is known about it. Peregoy did survive his SWPA service, though, and it is possible that this was the aircraft that he later claimed was the best in the squadron, and in which he flew many of his 150 missions.

SNATCHER, Lockheed P-38, unidentified serial number, artist unknown, 36th FS, 8th FG. Other photos of this aircraft show that it carried squadron letter "O" and that the pilot assigned to it at one time was Lt. Raymond W. Loh, but Loh and other 8th FG personnel lost their lives aboard a C-47 on a travel flight somewhere between Finschafen and Noemfoor in December 1944, so this aircraft is suspected to have subsequently been used by another pilot.

So Inviting, Lockheed P-38, unidentified serial number, artist unknown, unidentified FS, 8th FG. From the same Ie Shima collection as *MY GAL Jeannie*, *PAY OFF*, and one other unnamed P-38, photos of which follow, nothing further is currently known about this P-38, but given that most 8th FG nose art appeared on the LHS of the nose, perhaps this fighter did feature another artwork and name on the LHS side, by which it is better known. The pin-up was based on a wartime Brown & Bigelow calendar topper by Earl Moran, for another version of which see 'Luvablass' in chapter 2.

The SOONER The Better, Lockheed P-38, unidentified serial number, artist "Whitt." (Lt. William Whittington), 35th FS, 8th FG. Here is the former *CRO. BAIT* (q.v.) after transfer from the 8th FS, 49th FG, and renaming. Apparently, this P-38 was flown without a name for a while (the squadron letter worn at this time was "I"), but her assigned pilot, Capt. R. Gladson Turnbull, had the name added (perhaps after the war had ended?). It reflected the thoughts of most servicemen at the time. A late-war B-24 named *Coming Home! SOON* (see chapter 2) expressed a similar sentiment.

SPINDLE SHANKS, Curtiss P-40, unidentified serial number, artist unknown, 7th FS, 49th FG. This artwork would appear to have been based on a mirror image of the "spindle shanks" (a nickname for long, slender legs) of the November pin-up from the 1944 *Esquire Varga Calendar*. Leg-only airplane nose art was uncommon during World War II, but for another example, see B-24 *LUCKY* in chapter 2. This photo was taken in New Guinea, probably at Gusap, ca. the first quarter of 1944.

Strictly Sex, Lockheed P-38, 42-67140, artist Peter Lasho, 432nd FS, 475th FG. A P-38 said to have been assigned to pilot Lt. Noel Lundy (see also *Marie Elena* in this chapter); there was no beating around the bush with this name, but it may have been subject to complaint and thus short lived. For another example of Lasho's work and other information about him, see *Black Market Babe* in this chapter.

Thoughts of Midnite, Lockheed P-38, 42-66825, artist unknown, 431st FS, 475th FG. This impressive artwork was based on the October 1943 *Esquire* magazine Varga Girl pin-up, which was accompanied by a Phil Stack verse titled "Torches at Midnight," which became the basis for the name that accompanied the nose art. The assigned pilot's name at the time was Lt. R. L. Herman, and the Japanese flag below his name was for a Japanese fighter he shot down in the Rabaul area on November 7, 1943. Prior to this, the P-38 was assigned to Capt. Verl E. Jett, and he had it decorated with four Japanese flags representing victories claimed in December 1942 and August 1943.

Unnamed Curtiss P-40, unidentified serial number, artist unknown, 8th FS, 49th FG. The combination of airplane type and finish (definitely a camouflaged P-40) and an identifiable squadron airplane number (the 8th FS used numbers in the 40–69 block) has led to this unit identification, but no other details are known.

NOSE ART OF THE 5TH AIR FORCE

Unnamed Curtiss P-40s, unidentified serial numbers, artist unknown, 82nd or 110th TRS, 71st TRG. The last of the 49th FG's P-40s were grounded and left at Mokmer strip, Biak, "as of the morning of September 11th [1944]," and the best of these were used to equip the 82nd and 110th Squadrons, which had previously been equipped with P-39Qs (see appendix 1). Reportedly, these two squadrons used a range of squadron numbers similar to those used by the 49th FG's 7th FS and 8th FS, so squadron numbers alone are not particularly helpful for unit identification. The officer in the photo at right, said to have been taken in 1945, is a Lt. Costello, but it is not known which unit he served with.

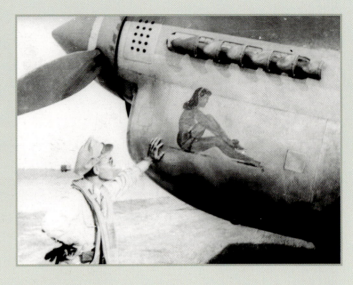

Unnamed Lockheed F-5, unidentified serial number, artist unknown, 8th PRS, 6th PRG. This F-5 is suspected to have been that assigned to Lt. Wallace M. Danvers and later named *BAYOU BABY*. Danvers appears to have joined the 8th PRS in late 1943, and it was probably around this time at Nadzab when this photo was taken (following promotion, he later flew with the 25th PRS). The nose art in this case was copied from *Esquire* magazine's June 1943 Varga Girl, but further information concerning the plane has not been found.

Unnamed Lockheed P-38, 43-2384 (unconfirmed), artist Yale L. Saffro, 80th FS, 8th FG. This beautiful pin-up of Yale Saffro's wife, Ruth, appeared on the RHS of this aircraft, while the upper torso and head of an imaginary angel, complete with wings and a halo, probably also painted by Saffro, appeared on the other side of the nose. Forward of both artworks was squadron identification letter "I." Saffro is best known as Lt. Kenneth G. Ladd's crew chief (see photos of *VIRGIN* [crossed through] and *"WINDY CITY RUTHIE"*, which follow), but this P-38 was, perhaps, the first in the squadron that he was responsible for. Reportedly, it was damaged beyond repair in a takeoff accident on October 15, 1943.

Unnamed Lockheed F-5, unidentified serial number, artist unknown, unit(s) unidentified. Another view of this nose art confirms that it is on a photoreconnaissance Lockheed F-5, and apart from the fact that it is known that F-5s replaced earlier F-4s in New Guinea by June 1944, nothing further is currently known about the plane or the unit to which it belonged.

Unnamed Lockheed P-38, unidentified serial number, artist unknown, 80th FS, 8th FG. Lt. Ken B. Lloyd with his P-38 that was later named *Dark Eyes*. The artwork was based on a photo of his fiancée, Evelyn Brugge, whom he married within a week of his return to the US in June 1945. The photo is not dated but was taken after Lloyd's victory over a Japanese fighter on August 17, 1944. Although Lloyd died in 2006, a memoir of his wartime service can be found online at 80fsheadhunters.org, in which he notes that the P-38 he flew when he achieved the victory had been fitted with additional machine guns; this was probably *"NICE PIECE"* (q.v.). *Ken B. Lloyd Jr.*

Unnamed Lockheed P-38, unidentified serial number, artist unknown, 35th FS, 8th FG. Squadron letter "M"; later photos show that the squadron's black-panther insignia was subsequently added to the nose cone forward of the pin-up.

Unnamed Lockheed P-38, unidentified serial number, artist unknown, 36th FS, 8th FG. Two photos, from different sources but apparently of the same airplane, since the style of the squadron number is identical in both. Names and pin-ups on engine cowlings of P-38s were not uncommon.

Unnamed Lockheed P-38, 44-27132 (unconfirmed), artist unknown, 36th FS, 8th FG. This P-38, assigned to Capt. Phil McLain, was subsequently named *Ready Maid*. The artwork adjacent to the aircraft letter is the 36th FS squadron "Flying Fiends" insignia, approved in 1931, this being the late World War II version as seen on the squadron sign at Ie Shima, shown in the photo below. (N.B.: The name CAPE GLOUSTER on the sign should read CAPE GLOUCESTER.)

Unnamed Lockheed P-38, unidentified serial number, artist unknown, 36th FS, 8th FG. This P-38, known as "the Sultan's Daughter" (in tribute, perhaps, to the nose art seen on a 380th BG B-24 of the same name?), was assigned to Lt. S. L. King and carried squadron letter "Y," but, again, apart from being another example of a late-war 8th FG aircraft, little more is known about it.

Unnamed Lockheed P-38, unidentified serial numbers, artist unknown, unidentified FS, 8th FG. This photo was from the same Ie Shima collection as *MY GAL Jeannie*, *PAY OFF*, *Polly* (prior to the name being added), and *So Inviting* seen earlier. Unfortunately, nothing further is known about this example.

Unnamed Lockheed P-38, unidentified serial numbers, artist unknown, unit(s) unidentified. This photo was reportedly taken on Biak Island in 1944 and is, therefore, likely to be of a 5th AF P-38, but further details, apart from the fact that the soldier in the photo is believed to be the assistant crew chief, Cpl. Frank N. Brooks, are currently unknown.

Unnamed Republic P-47, unidentified serial number, artist unknown, 341st FS, 348th FG. This long-legged beauty has been identified as that added to Lt. Francis D. Fredenburgh Jr.'s P-47. The location is stated to be Port Moresby; the 341st FS was based at Jackson's Field at Moresby from late June 1943 until around the middle of December.

Unnamed Northrop P-61, 42-5592, artist unknown, 418th NFS. The 418th NFS was the first night fighter squadron to be sent to the Pacific theater but was not equipped with P-61s until September 1944. Some nose art paintings on the squadron's P-61s have been identified, but this is the first seen by the author that features a pin-up (the origin of the pin-up has not been traced but appears to be the same as the original pin-up painted on the 380th BG's *Male Call*, a photo of which can be found in chapter 2). This particular plane, in the squadron markings of a crescent, star, and dividing band, crashed in the Philippines due to engine failure on March 16, 1945. The pilot lost his life in this accident, while his crewman was taken prisoner of war.

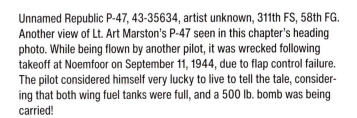

Unnamed Republic P-47, 43-35634, artist unknown, 311th FS, 58th FG. Another view of Lt. Art Marston's P-47 seen in this chapter's heading photo. While being flown by another pilot, it was wrecked following takeoff at Noemfoor on September 11, 1944, due to flap control failure. The pilot considered himself very lucky to live to tell the tale, considering that both wing fuel tanks were full, and a 500 lb. bomb was being carried!

Unnamed Republic P-47, unidentified serial number, artist Jack B. Wallace (unconfirmed), 69th FS, 58th FG. Here is the last of three great copies of Vargas's pin-ups on 69th FS P-47s (for the other two, see *LANA* and *Rubber Nose*), but whether the 310th FS's Jack B. Wallace painted them remains unknown. Note the new-style 69th FS cowling markings, a simple white horizontal band on NMF. It has been reported that when cowling banding was introduced to the 58th FG, the 69th FS color changed from white to red, but this photo confirms that white was used, even if only, perhaps, briefly. For photos of 69th FS P-47s with what may be a red horizontal band but still on a white cowling background, see *Mary Liz* and *SLEEPY TIME GAL*.

U.S. ANGEL, Republic P-47, unidentified serial number, artist unknown, unit(s) unidentified. Despite the lack of identification of this aircraft, it is suspected that it was assigned to a 5th AF unit, with the striped vertical stabilizer of the B-24 behind (more commonly applied to planes in 5th AF units than, say, 13th AF units) adding weight to that argument. The location may be Biak.

Vagrant Virgin, Lockheed P-38, 44-26976, artist unknown, 36th FS, 8th FG. Although it is identified elsewhere as 44-26176, a close examination of this photo shows the serial number to be as quoted above. Note in this photo how faded the olive-drab antiglare panel is on the top of the fuselage, the scalloped top edge of the artwork extending over the bottom edge of the top panel. Later, the antiglare panel was repainted in gloss black and extended down and under the nose, with photos suggesting that the earlier scalloped top edge was probably overpainted. White edging was also added at this later stage while the unit was still on Ie Shima, prior to the move to Japan, but the artwork was not affected. This P-38, which was initially assigned to Lt. Louis V. Bellusci and later to Lt. Peter Macgowan, is known to have carried squadron letter "A" at one time.

VIRGIN [crossed through], Lockheed P-38, unidentified serial number, artist Yale Saffro, 80th FS, 8th FG. Although a little difficult to see in this photo, the name has a large X over it, centered on the letter "r"; hence the reference to the name being crossed through. This pin-up was another copy of Gil Elvgren's 1939 illustration *French Dressing* (for another example, see the unnamed C-47 section in chapter 4). The plane was assigned to Lt. Kenneth G. Ladd and may well have been what replaced the unnamed OD P-38 with artwork also by Saffro, seen on page 214. It was probably replaced by *"WINDY CITY RUTHIE"* (q.v.), which carried the same squadron number followed by a small Roman numeral "II."

VIRGINIA MARIE, Lockheed P-38, 42-104508, artist unknown, 433rd FS, 475th FG. This P-38, assigned to Lt. Carroll R. "Andy" Anderson, was named after Anderson's wife and was probably photographed on Biak in late 1944. The pin-up appeared only on the LHS, but on the RHS was the name *Margaret*, in tribute to the pilot's mother. Family records show that Anderson flew eighty-nine missions with the 475th FG, but how many of these were flown in this aircraft, squadron number 194, is not known. *Via Craig Fuller*

Who ME?, Republic P-47, unidentified serial number, artist unknown, unit(s) unidentified. This photo and that of P-47 *Fun WASN'T IT!* (q.v.) were purchased together as part of a 5th AF photo collection, and while details are lacking, it would be a safe bet to suggest that the two artworks not only were by the same artist but appeared early on (second half of 1943). They were, however, probably short lived due to their suggestive nature.

Wilful Winnie, Lockheed P-38, serial number unidentified, artist unknown, 80th FS, 8th FG. Lt. Allen E. Hill's P-38 ca. mid-1944 was this aircraft named *Hill's Angels* on the LHS and *Wilful Winnie* on the right (a different pin-up was painted on each side of the nose). As mentioned earlier, this artwork and name were taken from a pin-up drawing that appeared in the 91st Photo Reconnaissance Wing's *The Wing-ding* newspaper issue of May 13, 1944 (see F-5 nose art *Naughty Dotty* earlier in this chapter for another example of this artwork). The aircraft started out with squadron letter "H" on the nose, but in the later close-up shot it was "T," and the illustration of Disney cartoon character Dopey to the left of the pin-up has been replaced by an unidentified circular object.

"WINDY CITY RUTHIE", Lockheed P-38, unidentified serial number, artist Yale L. Saffro, 80th FS, 8th FG. While the author is apologetic that a better image of the nose art of this P-38 flown by Lt. Kenneth G. Ladd could not be found, the nose markings involved are largely unaffected by the obvious print damage. Ladd had achieved ten victories at the time that the photo was taken, thus dating it as after April 3, 1944. Note that the nose number "3" is followed by a Roman numeral "II"; therefore it seems that this P-38 replaced *VIRGIN* [crossed through] (q.v.). Note also that the artwork is very similar in style to that displayed on the first of the unnamed P-38 nose art photos included on a previous page. That is because both were representations of Saffro's wife, Ruth; hence, too, the name used. Ladd, subsequently promoted to captain, became commanding officer of the 36th FS but failed to return from a mission on October 14, 1944.

X-L-ENT NITA, Republic P-47, unidentified serial number, artist unknown, unit(s) unidentified. Although the top word here is obviously an abbreviated form of "excellent," it has been only since the advent of cell-phone texting that the term (with no hyphens) really became popular, but here it is on an unidentified P-47 ca. 1945 (the origin of this photo suggests that it was a 5th AF aircraft, probably photographed on Biak). The accompanying artwork was based on the September pin-up from the 1944 *Esquire Varga Calendar*. Note that the name *NITA* is known to have been a later addition to the cowling, perhaps due to a change of assigned pilot.

CHAPTER 4
Cargo Cuties

The main cargo-carrying airplane used by the 5th AF, was, certainly until late 1944, the Douglas C-47, the famous military derivative of the prewar DC-3 airliner. Despite small beginnings in the 5th's air transport capability during 1942 and into early 1943, Gen. Kenney could proudly tell readers of the official *Air Force* magazine in 1944 that with the Japanese pushed back in New Guinea north of the Owen Stanley mountains, and thanks to "complete air control[,] we ferried a division of Americans across the [Owen Stanley] mountains and for the next two months, until Papua was regained, supplied them and the Australians by air. Troops, food, ammunition, artillery, jeeps, in fact, everything that would go into the door of a C-47 went over the 'hump' [the Himalayas] and the sick and wounded came back." As of September 30, 1944, the 5th AF could boast 324 C-47s and four C-46s and four B-17 "troop carriers" in service or tactical units in New Guinea, while there were another twenty-two C-47s with the FEAF CRTC.

The low number of Curtiss C-46s represented in the foregoing statistics is because these planes, which could carry greater weights longer distances, were just then entering SWPA service; by the end of the war, though, they equipped many squadrons. Not all these planes had nose art—some had names only and no artwork, but this chapter provides the widest-yet range of photos of 5th AF "cargo cuties"; mostly C-47s but the reader will find more than twenty photos of nose art on C-46s plus two of nose art on B-17 "troop carriers."

Heading photo. 5th AF C-47s at rest, probably at Townsville's Stockroute Airfield (notice the cattle, *at left*, seeking shade). Of the six aircraft visible, five have nose art.

More "cargo cutie" nose art, on former 5th and 13th AF C-47s transferred to Far East Air Service Command following its creation in 1944, can be found in appendix 2.

ACE of [hearts], Douglas C-47, unidentified serial number, artist B. Balliet, 57th TCS (unconfirmed), 375th TCG (unconfirmed). Appropriately, this chapter's first photo, other than that used in the heading, is of one of this artist's many works on C-47s. It would seem that Balliet, whose name is known only because he signed off each of his works—there were at least twenty-two (he numbered each one; this was his second work)—may have served in a troop carrier squadron, but confirmation is currently lacking. As to his other works, though, see *BETTS the BEAUT / Pink Stuff, DEFENSELESS VIRGIN, JOANNE, MISS BEHAVIOR, OLE MAN MOE, STEPPIN' OUT!, "SUCKA", SURE SKIN, TEXAS HELLCAT*, one of the unnamed C-47s, *WHOOO! The "GRAY GHOST"*, and *YOUR'S* in this chapter, and *"Kentucky Virgin"* and its later incarnation, *V..._ SURE POP*, in chapter 2. *ACE's* field number, while not visible in this photo, is believed to have been 161, the unit identification above being dependent on that premise.

THE ALBUQUERQUE QUEEN, Douglas C-47, 43-30756 (unconfirmed), artist unknown, 70th TCS, 433rd TCG. The first of three C-47s in this chapter with nose art based on the *Esquire* magazine Varga Girl for December 1943 (the other two were unnamed and appear toward the end of the chapter); at the time the close-up photo was purchased, all that was known about it was that it was taken in New Guinea in October 1944. Fortunately, though, it is now known that her field number was 379, thus allowing the unit identification above (C-47s of the 70th TCS bore field numbers in the range 376–399). Hidden from view in this photo are the initials "N.M." painted on the garment fluttering behind the pin-up. This C-47 later served with the 46th TCS, 317th TCG as field number X77 but minus the name.

THE AMAZON, Douglas C-47, 42-23659, artist unknown, 46th TCS, 317th TCG. One of the new C-47s received by the 46th in June 1943, *THE AMAZON* was among the mass of planes sent to Port Moresby in connection with the first paratroop drop in New Guinea at Nadzab, which occurred on September 5, 1943. For ease of identification, three-digit field (or squadron) numbers were given to all planes involved (seventy-nine C-47s and five B-17s), *THE AMAZON*'s being 438, partly visible in this photo. Despite the success of the Nadzab operations, though, this C-47's military service was short lived due to a forced landing on December 1, 1943. By that time the field number had been changed to 85.

AMPLE LASS, Douglas C-47, 43-16242 (unconfirmed), artist unknown, 55th TCS, 375th TCG. A close look of the artwork reveals that the pin-up is dressed, but from a distance she appears to be totally nude. The name is similarly thinly veiled; clearly *AMPLE ASS* was meant. Perhaps both the artwork and name were short lived, since this photo has been the only one depicting this artwork that this author has seen. If the serial number quoted is correct, this C-47 was condemned and salvaged in 1947.

BAD LANDING, Douglas C-47, 43-16296, artist unknown, 57th TCS, 375th TCG. This C-47 served with the 57th Squadron from December 1944, if not earlier, and saw 5th AF service until condemned and salvaged in Japan in 1947. The plane's field number had only recently been added when this photo was taken, since the original chalked-on version, for the painter's guidance, is still visible.

CARGO CUTIES

BAD (MAG)GIE, Douglas C-47, unidentified serial number, artist unknown, 57th TCS, 375th TCG. The bracketed section of *MAGGIE*'s name is noteworthy, but why it was considered necessary to present it in this way is not yet understood. This is another example of a pin-up copied from the January opening of the 1944 *Esquire Varga Calendar*, and her field number in this photo is X156.

BETTS the BEAUT, Douglas C-47, 42-92063, artist B. Balliet, 70th TCS, 433rd TCG. Received by the 70th Squadron on November 14, 1943, this C-47 must have had the pin-up painting, later signed off by the artist as his twelfth work, added soon after as the plane was transferred out on December 27 due to an accident. Returned to the 433rd ca. February 1944, she subsequently saw service with the 66th Squadron under the new name of *Pink Stuff* (q.v.).

Belle of the Isles, Douglas C-47, unidentified serial number, artist unknown, 70th TCS, 433rd TCG. When C-46s took over from C-47s as the main cargo aircraft type in 5th AF service, the field numbers of 54th Troop Carrier Wing (TCW) planes were changed to reflect that. For C-46s, just the prefixes were altered, from "XA" to "X," but for the remaining C-47s, such as *Belle of the Isles*, while they retained the "X" prefix, the number was reduced to two digits and, in some cases, an "A" suffix to make, on paper at least, the type of aircraft in use quickly determinable. This was important because the C-46 was a much-larger aircraft than the C-47, capable of greater load-carrying capability and longer range. The "A" suffix can be seen in this photo, but since the field number is not known, identification of this C-47 is not currently possible. Unit identification was possible only thanks to the artist, including the squadron number within the flourish at the end of the word *Isles*.

Betty Lou, Douglas C-47, 42-93233 (unconfirmed), 57th TCS (unconfirmed) and 58th TCS, 375th TCG. With artwork inspired by *Esquire* magazine's September 1943 Varga Girl, in 58th TCS service it is known that the field number of this C-47 was 177. One 58th TCS C-47 with this field number was serial 42-93233, received by the 5th AF in May 1944 and reportedly operated by both the 57th and 58th Squadrons. This may be that plane, but confirmation is currently lacking.

BISCUIT BOMBER, Douglas C-47, 42-92036, artist unknown, 56th TCS, 375th TCG. It was Australian troops on the ground in New Guinea who coined the term "biscuit bomber," because food drops they received were one of the most popular (and necessary) roles undertaken by 5th AF C-47s. Along the way, the term also became popular with troop carrier squadron personnel, this artwork having been added, apparently, in late 1943, when this aircraft was serving with the 55th TCS, the artist coming up with this idea of a gift-wrapped delivery being held aloft by a naked lady! In 55th TCS hands, BISCUIT BOMBER carried field number 103. This C-47 was condemned and salvaged in 1946.

BILLIE L., Douglas C-47, 42-23713, artist unknown, 66th TCS, 433rd TCG. This aircraft was written off in New Guinea following major damage in a forced landing on February 12, 1944. Its place in the squadron was later taken up by a replacement C-47 named *Ghost of Billie L* (q.v.), which took over the same squadron number and featured a similar pin-up.

Blonde Baby, Douglas C-47, 42-23588, artist unknown, 39th and 40th TCSs, 317th TCG. These two views confirm that the same name and artwork appeared on both sides of the nose of this C-47, but the tacked-on *Eva* was only on the RHS. Note also in the RHS view the repainted section, suggesting perhaps that another name had once been there. The full field number cannot be seen in this photo, but it is believed to have been 18 while with the 39th TCS and 28 while with the 40th. She left the 40th TCS in November 1943 and, like BISCUIT BOMBER, was condemned in the immediate postwar period.

BUBBLES, Douglas C-47, 42-23585, artist unknown, 39th TCS, 317th TCG. This svelte bathing beauty appeared on both sides of the nose of this C-47 and was identified as field number 19 when this photo was taken. At another stage it is known to have carried field number 15. The aircraft survived the war but was salvaged soon after.

BULBOUS ANNIE, Curtiss C-46, unidentified serial number, artist unknown, 57th TCS, 375th TCG. The shape of the C-46's fuselage probably led to this name, with the pin-up (based on the June 1943 Varga Girl pin-up) subsequently being added for good measure. Unit identification is taken from another photo of ANNIE that shows that her field number was XA151.

BURMA, Curtiss C-46, unidentified serial number, artist unknown, 8th CCS, 2nd CCG. C-46s were widely used in the CBI (China-Burma-India) theater of war, but the origin of this name was more than likely the wartime acronym for Be Undressed [and] Ready My Angel. It carried field number X706, and one source has suggested that this C-46 was 42-101047, lost in the vicinity of Hollandia on November 24, 1944, but the aircraft lost on that date was 42-101046, which, however, was operated by the 7th CCS, not the 8th.

BYE, BYE, BLUES, Douglas C-47, unidentified serial number, artist Miller (?), unit(s) unidentified. All that is known about this C-47 is that it was an A model (of which around five thousand were manufactured) and the pin-up was based on the *Esquire* October 1943 Varga Girl (another four other nose art works on C-47s based on the same Varga Girl follow). She survived frontline service to be subsequently converted to a fly-in, fly-out repair shop and was used by FEASC; her last known field number was W863. Note the artist's artistic sign-off in the space between the pin-up's back and the name; it seems to read "IT'S MILLER", but no other details are known.

Classy Chassis, Douglas C-47, unidentified serial number, artist unknown, 55th TCS, 375th TCG. Although one source has put forward serial number 43-16119 as the identity of this C-47, this cannot be correct, since that C-47 did not serve with the 5th AF. Another source has suggested 42-92812, and while that C-47 did serve with the 5th, the connection between serial number and name has yet to be proven. It's seen here with field number 104 (later X104); for another example of this popular wartime nose art name, but on a bomber, see chapter 2.

CLARA, Curtiss C-46, unidentified serial number, artist unknown, 57th TCS, 375th TCG. While the last digit of the field number in this photo is not completely visible, it would seem to be either a "6" or an "8." The 57th TCS used field numbers in the range X151 to X175, but unfortunately no other information is currently available.

The Coral Princess, Douglas C-47, 42-24410, artist unknown, 58th TCS, 375th TCG. The name of this C-47 may have been taken from a character created by US cartoonist Zack Mosley for his well-known and well-received *Smilin' Jack* newspaper strip stories. Note evidence of an earlier field number (perhaps a nonstandard 187?) since painted over. This was yet another C-47 that survived wartime service but was salvaged soon after.

COMPLETE OVERHAUL, Curtiss C-46, unidentified serial number, artist unknown, 56th TCS, 375th TCG. Despite the odd angle of this photo, the photographer still managed to capture this C-46's field number, XA129, thus allowing unit identification. C-46s began to replace C-47s in the 5th AF by October 1944; eventually 485 were received.

Cyndia, Curtiss C-46, unidentified serial number, artist unknown, 8th CCS, 2nd CCG. Little is known of *Cyndia* but the author expects that the artist responsible for this work was also responsible for *Ginger* (q.v.) and *"Squigy"* (q.v).

dE-ICER, Douglas C-47, 42-23874 (unconfirmed), artist unknown, 70th TCS and later 69th TCS (unconfirmed), both 433rd TCG. This C-47 is believed to have initially worn field number 385, and if, as thought, it was later transferred to the 69th TCS, the field number, incomplete in this photo, would have been 359. This C-47 was damaged in a landing accident on April 30, 1945, and subsequently salvaged. As to the name, see comments on similar-named B-24 *LI'L D'-ICER* in chapter 2.

DEFENSELESS VIRGIN, Douglas C-47, 42-23872, artist unknown, 69th TCS, 433rd TCG. This C-47, field number 356, which was received in Australia from the US in late August 1943, served in the SWPA until condemned in December 1944. The head adornment seems to be a flower in full bloom, which may seem odd, but when put together with the name, clearly the reference here is to "deflowering." This photo was mailed home to a family member, but a censor has cut the radar aerial out beforehand due to concerns over what he evidently believed was secret equipment.

The Dutchess, Douglas C-47, 41-38630, artist unknown, 40th TCS, 317th TCG. This C-47 was flown to Australia in October 1942 and is known to have served with the 41st TCS for much of 1943, until transferred out in October of that year. In January 1944, it was received by the 40th TCS, and that is when field number 44 and the artwork seen here (based on *Esquire* magazine's June 1943 Varga Girl) were added. Subsequently, this C-47 served with Air Transport Command in 1944–45 but was disposed of by the USAF in 1946. For her subsequent history, see chapter 7.

Ellie Mae, Douglas C-47, 42-23653 (unconfirmed), artist Delmer L. Sparrowe (unconfirmed), 46th TCS, 317th TCG, later 67th TCS, 433rd TCG. Sparrowe was an airplane mechanic, subsequently crew chief, who served with the 46th TCS in the SWPA for some eighteen months, and it was probably during 1943 that this nose art (based on the Varga Girl that appeared in the February 1942 issue of *Esquire* magazine), together with Sparrowe's wife's name, Ellie Mae, were added (according to a family member, Sparrowe "would have done that nose art"). In 46th TCS service it also carried field number 87, not yet added at the time the first photo was taken. Following the C-47's transfer to the 67th, as seen in the second photo, the field number changed, the name was painted over, but the pin-up was retained. If the serial number has been identified correctly, this C-47 survived until 1946, when it was condemned due to an accident.

"FLYING HI", Curtiss C-46, unidentified serial number, artist unknown, 8th CCS, 2nd CCG. A rare color shot of 5th AF C-46 nose art, this image is from an Eastman Kodak Minicolor print created in September 1945. The artwork was probably added in the US since it was in place prior to the addition of the field number. The 8th CCS was the first of the 2nd CCG squadrons to arrive in the SWPA, arriving in Australia on November 6, 1944, but this photo was taken later, probably in the Philippines or Okinawa.

Form-1A, Douglas C-47, 43-15477, artist unknown, 65th TCS, 433rd TCG. Form-1A (normally written Form 1-A and seen as such on a B-24 photo in chapter 2) was a US military classification that meant "fit for duty." This C-47, seen ca. late 1944–early 1945, with nose art based on an earlier Earl MacPherson pin-up, was assigned to the squadron commander, Maj. Marvin O. Calliham, whose name appears on the top line under the cockpit window (in April 1945, Calliham became group commander). While the full field number is not visible, it can be seen to be in the range X201–X209. An earlier 65th C-47 with a similar theme was *OUR FORM-1-A-LILLIAN-ETHEL* (q.v.). *Form-1A* ended the war in the Philippines and was salvaged there postwar.

FRENESI, Curtiss C-46, unidentified serial number, artist unknown, 8th CCS, 2nd CCG. To the uninitiated, this name may seem to be of foreign origin, but it is simply an abbreviated form of the term "free and easy." The field number for this C-46 with the large but inexpert pin-up was X708; the 8th CCS used field numbers in the range X691 to X720.

FRIDGID MIDGET JR., Douglas C-47 42-23954, artist unknown, 39th TCS, 317th TCG. After this C-47 was received by the 5th AF in August 1943, it appears (from a second photo seen by the author) that the pin-up was added first, while the name came later in tribute, apparently, to the original *FRIDGID MIDGET* (presumably that was the spelling), serial number 41-18658, destroyed in a Japanese bombing raid on Port Moresby on January 25, 1943. Just how long the name and artwork seen here lasted is not known; perhaps they were short lived, since this is the only photo seen by the author showing both in place. This C-47 was returned to the US mid-1944, was transferred to private ownership, and was still extant in 1962, but its fate currently remains unrecorded.

GEORGIA PEACH / TEXAS HONEY, Douglas C-47, unconfirmed serial number, artist unknown, 55th TCS, 375th TCG. These two names for the same aircraft have not been linked before, but the shared field number and similarities of the pin-up artwork on both sides have led the author to this conclusion. While other researchers have identified this aircraft as 42-23598, it is known that field number 111 was assigned to 42-32805 until at least January 1944. Given, however, that this photo is undated, once again it is not possible to be more definitive about the aircraft's identity. The nose art on another 55th TCS C-47, *LADY LUCK* (q.v.), was similar to this work but probably by a different artist.

"*Geronimo*", Douglas C-47, 41-38668 (unconfirmed), artist unknown, 22nd TCS, 374th TCG. This C-47 was originally assigned to the 39th TCS, 317th TCG, and arrived in Australia in January 1943. The 39th TCS gave up its new C-47s to the 374th TCG for service in New Guinea soon after, and Jennifer Gradidge reports in her comprehensive 2006 "DC-3" production list update (see bibliography) that it was while 41-38668 served with the 22nd TCS that the name and nose art seen here were added. The field number of this C-47 at this time was 33. Around eighteen months later, 41-38668 was one of the twelve war-weary C-47s made available by the 5th AF to the Australian Commonwealth government (via the Department of Civil Aviation) for use by Australian airlines. Further information and a photo taken in the 1960s of the former 41-38668 can be found in chapter 7.

Ghost of Billie L, Douglas C-47, unidentified serial number, artist unknown, 66th TCS, 433rd TCG. This C-47 replaced the original *BILLIE L.* (q.v.) and was given the same squadron number (237) and a pin-up along the same lines. Later, perhaps in the hands of a different squadron, the original name was painted over, and she was renamed *"Miss Carriage"* (q.v.).

"Ginger", Curtiss C-46, unidentified serial number, artist unknown, 8th CCS, 2nd CCG. It can be seen that *"Ginger"* was wearing no field number at the time this photo was taken, but she is known to have later been given squadron identification X702. The same artist responsible for this work was probably also responsible for *Cyndia* (q.v.) and *"Squigy"* (q.v.).

The Golden Horseshoe, Curtiss C-46, unidentified serial number, artist unknown, unit(s) unidentified. While this C-46 lacks a field number or any other form of identification, it has been seen in another photo in company with a XA-numbered C-46, and this photo has been included on that basis.

Gone Forever, Curtiss C-46, unidentified serial number, artist unknown, 6th CCS, 2nd CCG. The theme and pin-up style of this artwork are similar to that seen in appendix 2 on C-47 *LONESOME CHERRY*, suggesting to this author that both were painted by the same artist. The artwork on the similarly themed B-17 *Ready Betty 'Gone Forever'*, a photo of which appears in chapter 2, also featured a winged cherry.

HELL'S ANGEL 2nd, Douglas C-47, unidentified serial number, artist unknown, 46th TCS, 317th TCG. While there were no known C-47s in the 46th TCS prior to this one named *"Hell's Angel"*, Philip Brinson's history of the 317th TCG records that there was one in the 41st TCS. *HELL'S ANGEL 2nd* carried field number 85 and may have replaced *THE AMAZON* (q.v.) in 46th TCS service.

HOMESICK ANGEL, Douglas C-47, unidentified serial number, artist unknown, unit(s) unidentified. The author acquired four original photos of this artwork in the course of his research, but all that is known about the plane is that the pilot's name seems to have been a Capt. Foster, while the crew chief was TSgt. Orval E. Zwiebel. It seems likely that she ended the war on Biak, but nothing further is currently known.

HONEYMOON EXPRESS, Douglas C-47, 42-23582, artist unknown, 41st TCS, 317th TCG. Here are two photos of this C-47: the first (*above*), ca. late 1943, shortly after the Nadzab paratroop drop (note parachute symbol); the second, ca. 1945. This aircraft, which originally carried squadron number 412 (painted over by the time the first photo here was taken), later became field number 62 and, as such, featured in the 1944 Australian Department of Information film *Jungle Patrol*, which followed a group of eight Australian infantrymen flown aboard this C-47 from Port Moresby to the Ramu Valley to fight the Japanese. By July 1944, when it participated in the paratroop drop at Noemfoor, it wore field number 67, subsequently changed to X67 as shown at right. The name appeared on both sides of the aircraft, but the pin-up was only on the RHS. This C-47 was later transferred to the 46th TCS and was destroyed on the ground by enemy action in the Philippines on March 11, 1945.

NOSE ART OF THE 5TH AIR FORCE

Hot "Box", Douglas C-47, 43-15446 (unconfirmed), artist unknown, 40th TCS, 317th TCG. Often, artwork on C-46s and C-47s appeared on only one side of the nose, although, as mentioned earlier, sometimes the name was repeated. Here is a case where the name was repeated but the artworks are completely different. In the LHS view, the pin-up is sitting on a box of White Horse Rare Scotch, while the RHS pin-up, seen above, is holding what may be suntan oil or insect repellent. This C-47's field number is known to have been 43 at one time, and it is suspected that it replaced 41-18577 (*Yank's Delight*) for at least part of its 40th TCS service ca. mid-1944. It crashed on takeoff in the Philippines on August 12, 1945, and was salvaged.

HOT PANTS, Douglas C-47, 42-32840 (unconfirmed), artist Al Merkling, 55th TCS, 375th TCG. Merkling is best remembered as a member of the 20th CMS and for his extremely popular nose art on eleven of the unit's F-7s (see chapter 1 for a full list), but he was also "commissioned" by the 55th TCS to add his artistic flair to the noses of two unit C-47s, this one featuring a pin-up, while the other, named *JUNGLE BUM*, was Merkling's take on the look of a well-seasoned SWPA soldier. If the serial number quoted above is correct, this C-47 had first served with the 22nd TCS prior to being transferred to the 55th TCS ca. December 1943; the photo below right shows it in its early 55th TCS days with its earlier mission summary still in place, as well as flying-horse nose art and a two-word name, only the first word of which (*PEGASUS*) is visible. Also note evidence of an earlier field number, since painted over; the 22nd TCS used two-digit numbers in the range 26–50. As *HOT PANTS*, this C-47 seems to have enjoyed only brief SWPA service, since few photos of it with the Merkling artwork are known, and if her tail number was 232840, it was back in the US by February 1945.

Hot-to-go, Douglas C-47, 42-24403, artist unknown, 40th TCS, 317th TCG. One of only two known 5th AF C-47s with nose art copied from the January offering that appeared in the 1944 *Esquire Varga Calendar*—the other being *BAD (MAG)GIE* (q.v.), this C-47 was initially assigned to the 33rd TCS, 374th TCG, but had been transferred to the 40th TCS, 317th TCG, by January 1944, where she became field number 36. She survived the war and went on to Japan, but, somewhat surprisingly, photos of this nose art are uncommon, this one being a late addition to the collection.

HOT ROCKS, Douglas C-47, unidentified serial number, artist unknown, 40th TCS, 317th TCG. This C-47 carried field number X33. The name may seem unusual to many readers, but, according to the Merriam-Webster dictionary, a "hot rock" is a "highly skilled or daredevil airplane pilot," so, evidently, the pilots were giving themselves a pat on the back. There was a 380th BG B-24 also named *HOT ROCKS*; see chapter 2.

Ione, Douglas C-47, 42-24226, artist unknown, 40th TCS, 317th TCG. This pin-up was another based on the October 1943 *Esquire* magazine Varga Girl. In 40th TCS service, *Ione* carried field number 33 until she was replaced by another "33" (42-108928) sometime in 1944. She remained in the SWPA until around the end of the war, though, and returned to the US straight after, being disposed of in 1946 while flying with Consolidated Air Transit Inc and Consolidated Air Freight until a crash in Colombia in 1953.

"Hurkie", Douglas C-47, unidentified serial number, artist unknown, 58th TCS, 375th TCG, later 39th TCS, 317th TCG. As explained in the caption for *Belle of the Isles* (q.v.), here is another example of an "A"-suffixed field number on a C-47. Prior to X19A, this C-47 carried field number X193.

JERSEY BOUNCE, Curtiss C-46, unidentified serial number, artist unknown, 67th TCS, 433rd TCG. While only the first digit of the field number is visible in this ca. 1945 photo, it has been identified elsewhere as X318. Unfortunately, no further information is currently available, other than the fact that the C-46's name was taken from a popular wartime song.

NOSE ART OF THE 5TH AIR FORCE

JOANNE, Douglas C-47, 42-23847, artist B. Balliet, 67th TCS, 433rd TCG. According to the official record card for this aircraft, it had been received by the 5th AF only on August 25, 1943, and was condemned less than three months later due to an unspecified accident, so, not surprisingly, few photos of her seem to exist. So much so, in fact, that even during the wartime period, one could not be provided for the squadron history *Skytrain*, published in Australia for the unit in 1945.

KEEP IT UNDER YOUR HAT, Douglas C-47, unidentified serial number, artist unknown, 57th TCS, 375th TCG and 65th TCS, 433rd TCG. This C-47 had the nose art (based on a Vargas pin-up that appeared in the 1941 *Esquire Varga Calendar*) added prior to or following its assignment to the 57th TCS, 375th TCG, but the name came later. Just when this occurred is not known, but she is seen here in 65th TCS hands; while serving with the 57th TCS, her field number was 155. She survived the war and was subsequently salvaged on Biak; see a last photo in chapter 7.

LADY LUCK, Douglas C-47, unidentified serial number, artist unknown, 55th TCS, 375th TCG. As mentioned earlier, this was a popular name to accompany nose art, given that it was an easy and uncomplicated choice to come up with, and one that readily lent itself to the inclusion of a pin-up. Few photos of this nose art seem to be known, but another, taken at Townsville, does suggest that her field number at that time was 105; hence the above unit identification. The nose art on another 55th TCS C-47, *GEORGIA PEACH/TEXAS HONEY* (q.v.), was similar to this work but probably by a different artist.

Kings Cross *SHUTTLE*, Douglas C-47, 42-23617 (unconfirmed), artist unknown, 57th TCS, 375th TCG. Sydney's Kings Cross has been regarded for decades now as Sydney's, if not Australia's, most notorious "hotspot," and no doubt the influx of well-paid American servicemen there during World War II helped cement that notoriety. Bob Kelly in volume 2 of his *Allied Air Transport Operations, Southwest Pacific Area in World War II* study notes that by January 31, 1944, departing plane "flights [to Sydney from New Guinea] averaged two aircraft per day allocated among the different troop carrier squadrons." By October of that year, however, as the US forces moved northward, Australia stopped being an American leave area, and perhaps this nose art even changed as a result. Note in these two photos how the pin-up's hair color changed along the way.

CARGO CUTIES

"LADY LUCK", Douglas C-47, unidentified serial number, artist unknown, 65th TCS, 433rd TCG. Another *LADY LUCK*; the name of this C-47 is difficult to see in this photo but followed the contours of the legs above the pin-up, seemingly running out of space in the process. The origin of the artwork was a pin-up by Earl MacPherson, a more photographed version appearing on 22nd BG B-24 *"SHOO-SHOO BABY"* (see photos in chapter 2). The use of the "X" prefix with the field number dates this photo as after October 1944; it's hoped that this C-47's luck continued for the rest of her military service.

LAZY LADY, Douglas C-47, 42-23651, artist unknown, 46th TCS, 317th TCG. This C-47, field number 81 (formerly "39" of 40th TCS, and by March 1944, reportedly, 359 of the 69th TCS), another of the Nadzab paratroop drop aircraft, is seen here in a photo that was probably taken at Port Moresby on December 7, 1943, with visiting celebrities, *left to right*, including concert accordionist Andy Arcari, actor Gary Cooper, and actresses Phyllis Brooks and Una Merkel. It seems likely that *LAZY LADY* was one of the C-47s that were used to transport the concert party around northern Australia and New Guinea during its tour of US bases in November–December 1943. It was on this visit that the party added their names to the LHS of B-24 *TWIN NIFTIES II* (see photo in chapter 2). This C-47 (which featured the pin-up only on the RHS) survived the war and made it to Japan postwar but was salvaged there in 1948.

THE LONESOME ANGEL, Douglas C-47, 42-23955, artist unknown, 39th TCS, 317th TCG. This C-47 reportedly carried the name *Louise* on the RHS (whether in lowercase or uppercase is not known), and its field number was 16. It served in the SWPA for around a year and was destroyed by fire after veering off Sentani airfield, in what is now West Papua, on August 2, 1944.

LONG DISTANCE, Curtiss C-46, unidentified serial number, artist unknown, 8th CCS, 2nd CCG. Apart from the unit identification (thanks to the field number), nothing further is known about this C-46, but readers may like to compare this photo with that of the repainted, unnamed postwar C-46 in chapter 8, since both C-46s share the same decorative spiral markings on their propeller hubs.

Lovable Lou, Douglas C-47, 42-23958, artist unknown, 39th TCS, 317th TCG. Seen here wearing field number 12, this C-47 with a pin-up based on George Petty's gatefold from the September 1941 *Esquire* magazine was received by the 39th TCS in August 1943. She was transferred out, reportedly, in June 1944, and an accident toward the end of the war saw *Lou* condemned and subsequently salvaged.

Mamma-Duck, Douglas C-47, 42-24222, artist unknown, 40th TCS, 317th TCG. 40th TCS status reports included in volume 4 of *Allied Air Transport Operations, Southwest Pacific Area in World War II* list this C-47 as on hand until at least October 1, 1944. Her field number during this time was 34. Jennifer Gradidge's encyclopedic second 2006 volume on DC-3 history states that due to brake failure, *Mamma-Duck* crashed on landing at Noemfoor Island on November 20, 1944, and did not fly again.

Mary, Douglas C-47, 42-100618, artist unknown, 40th TCS, 317th TCG. This C-47 carried field number 26 and was identified on the RHS of the nose by the name *"BARBARA" ANN*. The pin-up, based on the March pin-up from the 1944 *Esquire Varga Calendar*, appeared on the LHS only. This was another C-47 that survived World War II but was condemned in 1946 and subsequently salvaged.

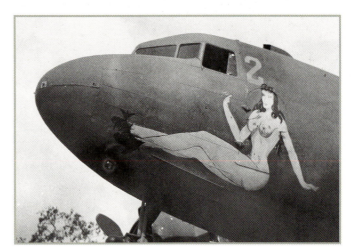

Miscellaneous, Douglas C-47, 41-7732, artist unknown, eventual unit that added artwork unidentified. This C-47 was one of the first two received in Australia, having arrived with sister ship 41-7733 and three Douglas C-39s by ship in April 1942. It was originally assigned to the 21st TCS, 374th TCG, and by late in the year was with the 22nd TCS. Assigned to the 40th TCS, 317th TCG, ca. January 1943, where it was given field number 38, by the end of 1943 it was serving with the 41st TCS as field number 66 but was subsequently transferred to the 54th TCW, which unit, it seems, identified it as field number 2. Because of its long and sterling service, flying more than two thousand hours with the 5th AF, plans were made for it to be flown back home for publicity purposes. At some point along the way, the C-47 had been named *Miscellaneous* (in reference to a typical load carried), but just on the RHS. Prior to leaving New Guinea for the Townsville Air Depot, the additional information "Veteran of S.W.P.A." was added to both sides of the nose, but, subsequently, the wording on the LHS was painted over and this poorly executed pin-up was added instead. Unsurprisingly, there was little chance of the pin-up surviving (aside from the low standard of artistry, its size and absence of clothing and the beckoning finger made it totally unacceptable), and she was roughly painted over soon after, the "Veteran of S.W.P.A." wording was reinstated, and the *Miscellaneous* name was added to the LHS (see photo in chapter 7).

MISS BEHAVIOR, Douglas C-47, unidentified serial number, artist B. Balliet, 68th or 69th TCS, 433rd TCG. The identity of this C-47 is not presently known to this author, the absence of photos of her suggesting that, perhaps, her service was limited.

Miss TREATED, Curtiss C-46, unidentified serial number, artist unknown, 5th CCS, 2nd CCG. The 2nd CCG (comprising the 5th, 6th, 7th, and 8th CCSs) was formed only in 1944 and moved to the SWPA at the end of the year with its new C-46s. In 1945, however, it played an important role in moving supplies, ammunition, personnel, and equipment to forward bases. By January 1945 the group was operating the most C-46s in the SWPA, and by September the 5th CCS could proudly claim that they "had landed at almost every military airstrip from Sydney, Australia, to Chitose, Japan." The USAAF stencil data for this plane (just visible in the bottom right hand corner) reveals it to be a D-5-CU model with a serial number beginning 42-, indicating that it would be in the serial number range of 42-96806 to 96824 or 42-101038 to 101170.

MORNIN AFTER, Douglas C-47, 43-15474, artist Stephen Potasky, 46th TCS, 317th TCG. This C-47 was flown to Australia in April 1944 and reportedly wore field numbers 94/X94 following assignment to the 46th TCS (see also *Pleiades*, which follows). It was condemned in November 1945. This is the only known example of an aircraft nose art painting by Potasky, but as squadron sign painter there may have been others. He was an accomplished landscape and portrait painter, and his obituary in 2000 indicated that he had worked as an artist-illustrator for manufacturing giant International Telephone and Telegraph for twenty-five years and later taught watercolor classes. This is another example of an artwork copied from Alberto Vargas's April 1944 *Esquire* magazine's pin-up and, according to former crew chief Frank Elston, was added in August 1944. The NMF B-17 behind is 41-24353, a survivor of early 43rd BG missions when it served with the 64th BS, later an armed transport, but by late 1944 the personal aircraft of Gen. Robert L. Eichelberger, commanding general of the 8th Army. The general named his plane *Miss Em'* after his wife, Emmaline (1888–1972), to whom he wrote daily.

"Miss Carriage", Douglas C-47, unidentified serial number, artist unknown, 5th AF unit/s unidentified, later IV ASAC Far East Air Service Command. This C-47 was originally named *The Ghost of Billie L* (q.v.) but was renamed at some later stage. Postwar, after being flown to Biak, "Miss Carriage" was salvaged. A photo of her remains at Biak can be found in chapter 7.

OUR FORM-1-A-LILLIAN-ETHEL, Douglas C-47 42-24228, artist unknown, 65th TCS, 433rd TCG. By chance, the artwork both on this C-47 and that at below left was inspired by the same pin-up: the November offering from the 1944 *Esquire Varga Calendar*. Unfortunately, however, this C-47, field number 201, was lost well beforehand, failing to arrive at Saidor on March 6, 1944. The crash site was found from the air later that year, but the remains of the passengers and four crew members could not be recovered until postwar.

OLE MAN MOE, Douglas C-47, 42-23873 (unconfirmed), artist B. Balliet, 69th TCS, 433rd TCG. This busy artwork was the artist's tribute to two supporting characters from Al Capp's *Li'l Abner* cartoon series, Ole Man Mose (note difference in spelling) and Moonbeam McSwine. If the serial number is as stated above (the stencil panel above "OLE" certainly identifies the model as a C-47A-35-DL, a block of 174 aircraft from 42-23788 to 42-23961), this aircraft did not see long service, just from late August 1943 until early January 1944. Note evidence of an earlier field number in the 450s, which were used earlier by the 69th. Below the pilot's open window appears the word "FISH," undoubtedly the nickname of the "D" flight leader, Lt. Mayhew Fishburn.

Open Date, Douglas C-47, 42-24257, artist unknown, 40th TCS, 317th TCG. This C-47 carried field number 38 while with the 40th in 1944–45. Reportedly, this C-47 also carried the name *Jenny* on the RHS (whether in lowercase or uppercase not known). It survived the war but only just, being condemned in September 1945.

PASSION WAGON, Douglas C-47, unidentified serial number, artist unknown, 58th TCS, 375th TCG. Apart from the field number, 185, and the fact that the pin-up art is based on the September pin-up from the 1943 *Esquire Varga Calendar*, nothing further is currently known about this C-47 (another C-47 with field number 185 was *SECOND HAND Fannie* [q.v.]). Note the repainted section of the nose, suggesting that some other artwork had previously existed, but it is not currently known what that may have been.

Pel, Douglas C-47, 41-18584, artist unknown, 40th TCS, 317th TCG. Research by Robert Kelly shows that this aircraft was initially named *"FLAMINGO"* and carried field number 36. As such, one of its last jobs was to bring back to "civilization" the crew of B-24 *SKY LADY* (see photo in chapter 2). These men had bailed out of their doomed aircraft and been rescued by New Guinea natives and taken to a mission station. From there, they were then flown out, one man at a time, by RAAF Tiger Moths to an airstrip accessible by larger airplanes, from where *"FLAMINGO"* brought them back to Port Moresby. A replacement "36" was received by the 40th TCS on November 12, 1943, and 41-18584 was apparently then passed on to the 54th TCW but returned to the 40th TCS in January 1944, and it may have been at that stage that the artwork and name seen here were added. The field number, although not evident in this photo, became 32, but the aircraft did not remain in the SWPA long, being returned to the US in August 1944.

Pink Stuff, Douglas C-47, 42-92063, artist B. Balliet, 66th TCS, 433rd TCG. Previously named *BETTS the BEAUT* (q.v.), following repairs after an accident on December 27, 1943, she was assigned to the 66th TCS, apparently where the new name was added. Note how carefully the old field number was painted over, so carefully, in fact, that it can be seen to have been in the 380s (the 70th TCS used field numbers in the range 376–399). Also note the X prefix added below the cockpit window. The photo is undated but suspected to have been taken on Biak. This C-47 made it to the Philippines late in the war but was condemned following the end of World War II and subsequently salvaged.

PISTOL PACKIN MAMA, Douglas C-47, 42-23662, artist Lew Straley, 40th TCS, 317th TCG. It was originally named *Annie Oakley* and given field number 84 in the 46th TCS, but the name would appear to have changed when the C-47 moved on to the 40th TCS, date unknown. In 40th TCS service, the field number (only partly visible in this photo) was X39. She made it as far as Japan for the postwar occupation but was condemned and salvaged there in 1948.

Pleiades, Douglas C-47, unidentified serial number, artist unknown, 46th TCS, 317th TCG. The name of this "heavenly body" is taken from the star cluster better known as the Seven Sisters, but little is known about this C-47's usage. It is safe to say, though, that the photo probably dates from late 1944 as the 317th TCG issued an order ca. August 1944, that its field numbers (6-99) were to be repeated under the nose in yellow numbers 18 inches high. The under-nose numbers seen in this photo, however, do appear to be a lot larger than that.

NOSE ART OF THE 5TH AIR FORCE

POPPY, Douglas C-47, 42-23493, artist unknown, 66th TCS, 433rd TCG. These two views show that *POPPY*'s artwork, seen in the close-up, was subsequently overpainted. The removal of pin-up art from 5th AF planes by order was rare, but this seems to have been one such case (another was *Shiny Sheila*, which is featured in the next chapter). The later photo was taken at Lae in March 1944. This C-47 was retired from 5th AF service in January 1945 and later saw brief service with the Philippine air force. *Lae photo AWM 071768*

Pretty Baby, Boeing B-17, 41-2665, artist unknown, 40th TCS, 317th TCG. Named after the popular ragtime-era song of the same name; the artwork was another example based on the October pin-up from the 1943 *Esquire Varga Calendar*. The 40th TCS was equipped with this B-17 only from December 1943 until August 1944, so this photo must date from that period. During this time, the field number used by this B-17 for squadron identification was "41."

PRETTY BABY, Douglas C-47, 42-93235 (unconfirmed), artist unknown, 57th TCS, 375th TCG, later 40th TCS, 317th TCG. The last of the known 5th AF planes of this name that featured nose art, *PRETTY BABY* was at Clark Field when this photo was taken, and chances are that the war was over or almost over by then. Before becoming X28 with the 40th TCS, it had been X165 in the 57th TCS. If the serial number quoted above is correct, *PRETTY BABY* was condemned and salvaged in the immediate postwar period.

Pretty LOUISE, Curtiss C-46, unidentified serial number, artist unknown, 8th CCS, 2nd TCG, later 56th TCS, 375th TCG. The original field number for *LOUISE* was X691, but she was later transferred to the 56th TCS, 375th TCG, where it was changed to XA131.

Quivering Sal, Curtiss C-46, 44-77481 (unconfirmed), artist unknown, 57th TCS, 375th TCG. If the stated serial number is correct, this C-46 was received in Australia in January 1945 and went on to see long service—until 1949—with the 5th AF, after which it was "reclaimed" (salvaged). For the vast majority of the C-46s selected for postwar use, though, once the war ended it seems that pin-up nose art was quickly done away with.

"REAREN TO GO", Curtiss C-46, unidentified serial number, artist unknown, 6th CCS, 2nd CCG, later 55th TCS, 375th TCG. Another example of a play-on-words name; while "rearen" (i.e., rearing) is stated, "rear end" is obviously implied. Perhaps surprisingly, the use of this name does not appear to have been more widespread on other aircraft to accompany pin-up art. This C-46 was involved in a collision with 28th PRS F-5 43-28960 on June 27, 1945, and probably did not fly again afterward. See photo taken after the accident in chapter 7.

REBEL'S Dream, Douglas C-47, unidentified serial number, artist unknown, 57th TCS, 375th TCG. A later photo shows that this pin-up, a version of the October page from the 1944 *Esquire Varga Calendar*, was still in place, but no longer named, whilst a new field number, A017, had been added. Field numbers A001 to A025 were used by the C-47s of the 318th TCS, 3rd Air Commando Group.

'RED'IE AND WILLING, Douglas C-47, unidentified serial number, artist unknown, unit(s) unidentified. This photo has been included on the basis that it came from a SWPA collection, and a field number may have appeared in the overpainted area behind the cockpit. The artwork is based on a Vargas pin-up that first appeared in the April 1943 issue of *Esquire* magazine, but the misspelling of "ready" and highlighting of "RED" remain unexplained.

RUSTY, Douglas C-47, 42-24256, artist unknown, 40th TCS, 317th TCG. This C-47 was assigned to the 40th TCS in October 1943 and was replaced around a year later, after she had to be condemned following what would appear to have been a landing accident.

THE RUBE, Douglas C-47, 42-23656, artist unknown, 46th TCS, 317th TCG. Although obscured in this photo, the field number worn at the time was 86. A short-lived three-digit field number, 435, was also worn at one time, and at that stage alongside the field number on the LHS, there was a parachutist mission symbol, which was probably for participation in the Nadzab airborne landing of September 5, 1943. This C-47's subsequent service with the 5th AF is unknown, but a later photo taken at Townsville shows that by then, her name had been painted out. She did survive the war and, as with *Rotation Plan*, which appears in appendix 2, went into postwar service with the Dutch naval air arm and subsequently the Indonesian air force.

SECOND HAND Fannie, Douglas C-47, 41-38731, artist unknown, 58th TCS, 375th TCG. *Fannie*, whose artwork was based on the popular June pin-up from the 1943 *Esquire Varga Calendar*, arrived in Australia in July 1943. While her field number cannot be seen in its entirety in this photo, it is known to have been 158. In September 1944 she was transferred to the Pacific Wing of Air Transport Command, at which stage the nose art was, perhaps, painted over. After surviving the war, the former SECOND HAND Fannie was disposed of in 1945 and was operated in the US until sold to Chile in 1951. It last flew in 1996 and was left at El Tepual Airport, Puerto Montt, Chile, and, as of 2021, was still there, essentially a complete airframe, being used by the airport's fire rescue section for training purposes. See "The Tale of CC-CBO" by Álvaro Romero on the Latin American Aviation Historical Society's website.

Shakes ALL OVER, Douglas C-47, 42-23705, artist unknown, 55th and 57th TCS, 375th TCG. This C-47 was delivered to the 5th AF in June 1943, and while the author has no information concerning its early service, it seems that by early 1944 it was flying with the 55th TCS as X103, and it is suspected that it was with that squadron that the nose art and name were added. Later the plane was transferred to the 57th TCS, where the name and nose art, as shown in this photo, were retained but the squadron number was changed to X163. *Shakes* went missing in bad weather on a flight from Saidor to Nadzab on July 9, 1944, and it was not until 1948 that the remains of the plane and those aboard—five crew and two passengers—were found.

"*Sleepy TIME GAL*", Curtiss C-46, 42-96786 (unconfirmed), artist unknown, 8th CCS (unconfirmed), 2nd CCG (unconfirmed). An internet search for a C-46 aircraft bearing this name revealed that the 8th CCS lost such an aircraft, serial number 42-96786, on February 28, 1945, on a flight in the Darwin area, resulting in the presumed death of her four-man crew. While not definite, it is considered most likely that this was the artwork applied to that particular plane.

SLEEPY TIME GAL, Douglas C-47, 42-100622 (unconfirmed), artist unknown, 55th TCS, 375th TCG. Known to have carried field number X107; the 55th TCS's first 107 was lost in a crash in October 1943, and *SLEEPY TIME GAL* is likely to have been its replacement. The artwork, like that on the A-20 of the same name seen in chapter 2, was based on a Gil Elvgren pin-up. This C-47 was damaged on August 12, 1945, and subsequently salvaged.

SLUT II, Douglas C-47 41-18498, artist unknown, 39th TCS, 317th TCG. This C-47 replaced an aircraft that ground-looped at Gusap on October 28, 1943, and was named after a stateside loss that occurred on December 23, 1942. Its time with the 39th TCS appears to have been limited to late 1943 and the first six or seven months of 1944 (C-47 42-93494 replaced it as field number 17 by August 1), and while it is known that it ended up with the A-20-equipped 388th BS for a while in 1945, whether that was with or without nose art is not currently known, but its unashamed boldness together with the size of the lettering used would suggest not.

SO WHAT!, Douglas C-47, unidentified serial number, artist unknown, unit(s) unidentified. While the artwork and indifference to official attitude implied by the name make this photo a worthy candidate for inclusion in this work, nothing is known about the identity of this C-47 or the unit to which it belonged. Most likely the photo was taken in 1945, but apart from that, all that can be said with certainty is that the field number, partially visible, confirms that it must have been a 5th AF aircraft.

SPEEDY STEEDE, Douglas C-47, unidentified serial number, artist unknown, unit(s) unidentified. Despite the absence of information concerning this little-photographed aircraft, it was seen and photographed (apparently at Cape Gloucester, New Guinea) by 5th AF soldier James P. Gallagher around mid-1944 (see his *With the Fifth Army Air Force: Photos from the Pacific Theater*), and this photo has been included on that basis. The pin-up is the third seen in this chapter that was based on the October 1943 Varga Girl.

"Squigy", Curtiss C-46, unidentified serial number, artist unknown, 8th CCS (unconfirmed), 2nd CCG (unconfirmed). Unit identification is on the basis that the artist responsible for this work was probably also responsible for *Cyndia* (q.v.) and *Ginger* (q.v.), both of which served with the 8th CCS. No other details on "Squigy" are currently known.

STEPPIN' OUT!, Douglas C-47, serial number 42-23xxx, artist B. Balliet (unconfirmed), 68th TCS, 433rd TCG. This is another possible Balliet work, but what is needed is a closer view that confirms the existence of his name and "job number," which are known to have reached #22 if not higher.

Stuff, Douglas C-47, 42-24225, artist unknown, 40th TCS, 317th TCG. This C-47 came to the 40th TCS around October 1943 to become field number 35, replacing 41-18577, *Yank's Delight* (q.v.). It survived the war but was condemned shortly afterward and subsequently salvaged.

"*SUCKA*", Douglas C-47, 42-32876, artist B. Balliet, 55th and 56th TCSs, 375th TCG. This was Balliet's third nose art painting; as already mentioned, he added his name and numbered each one. What is suspected to have been an earlier photo shows that the field number had then been 106, confirming service with the 55th TCS, but reportedly shortly after transfer to the 56th TCS, *"SUCKA"* was condemned due to "chronic radio and electric trouble." While in 55th TCS hands, the word "COLD" appeared above the two playing cards (*at left of pin-up*), while "TURKEY" appeared below.

SURE SKIN, Douglas C-47, 42-23860, artist B. Balliet, 68th TCS, 433rd TCG. Carrying field number 328 in this photo, *SURE SKIN* survived the war only to be lost in a midair explosion immediately afterward while serving with Far East Air Service Command (FEASC), those aboard (four crew members and twenty-six passengers) all being killed. Possibly by then, the aircraft had been stripped of camouflage, and the artwork may have been removed or changed, but details are not currently known. This artwork was the tenth completed by Balliet.

TAIL HEAVY, Douglas C-47, 42-920xxx, artist unknown, 65th TCS, 433rd TCG. These two views show the same artwork on this C-47, field number 209, at different stages. It seems from the photo above that the artist may have considered leaving this "chaplain shocker," but realizing that it would not have been seen as acceptable it was dressed up as shown at right. The partial identification of the serial number is possible because USAAF aircraft of this subtype (C-47A-DK) occupied the small serial number range 42-92024 to 42-92091. Of these, around twenty-five were received by 5th AF units, three known examples that served with the 65th being 42-92025, 42-92034, and 42-92038.

NOSE ART OF THE 5TH AIR FORCE

TAIL WIND / *Tail Wind*, Douglas C-47, unidentified serial number, artist Sgt. Joseph M. A. Woznicki, 57th TCS, 375th TCG. Another popular nose art name (see chapter 2 for other examples), and here are two photos of nose art on what is suspected to have been the same C-47, but whether or not Woznicki was responsible for both sides is not currently known. This C-47 began SWPA service using field number X158, with the X positioned below the cockpit window, but is seen here after her last field number had been painted out. No other details are known, except that the LHS pin-up was based on an Art Frahm work titled *Double Trouble*. The C-47 behind carries field number X96A.

TEXAS HELLCAT, Douglas C-47, 42-23341 (unconfirmed), artist B. Balliet, 69th TCS, 433rd TCG. Balliet completed at least three artworks for the 69th TCS: *OLE MAN MOE*, *YOUR'S*, and this one, with *TEXAS HELLCAT* being his seventeenth "commission" (of, it seems, twenty-two), not all of which have been identified. It was also a rare example of an overtly sexual pose and, for that reason, may have been short lived (see also *YOUR'S*, which follows, also by Balliet). This C-47 was returned to the US postwar and sold to Brazilian purchasers in 1947, remaining in Brazil until written off in 1968.

TEXAS HONEY / GEORGIA PEACH, Douglas C-47, unconfirmed serial number, artist unknown, 55th TCS, 375th TCG. These two names for the same aircraft have not been linked before, but the shared field number and similarities of the pin-up artwork on both sides have led the author to this conclusion. See caption for the *GEORGIA PEACH* photo for comments on the aircraft's identity.

Tokyo or BUST, Curtiss C-46, unidentified serial number, artist unknown, 57th TCS, 375th TCG. These two photos show this large nose artwork both from a distance and close-up. One of the many 5th AF personnel who photographed her was avid photographer James P. Gallagher, who recalled that it had caught his eye several times, initially in the Philippines. He included the following information about the artwork in his book *With the Fifth Army Air Force*: "Only color film could have captured its superb artwork, but film of any kind was scarce, and I had to be satisfied with black and white. 'Tokyo' appeared in a deep red, while "or Bust" glowed in primary yellow. The flesh and makeup of the painted lady were admirably natural; her hair was jet black and her sparse garb a flaming red." Note that this C-46's field number had originally been XA153 (the "A" having been added to quickly differentiate, on paper, C-46s from X-coded C-47s) but subsequently was simplified to X153 when C-46s took over from C-47s as the 5th AF's main transport aircraft type in use in 1945.

TROUBLE, Douglas C-47, unidentified serial number, artist unknown, unit(s) unidentified. This C-47 can be seen to have previously worn a field number, but other than that, nothing is currently known about it. It was up to the transferring unit to paint out or over field numbers prior to aircraft being "turned into repair depots or otherwise transferred out," but there were no such requirements for unofficial artwork.

Unnamed Boeing B-17, 41-24420, artist unknown, 58th TCS, 375th TCG. It is a little-known fact now that at the end of 1943, twelve B-17s were assigned to the 54th TCW as armed transports. Formerly serving with the 43rd BG, half were E models, the other half F models. While eleven of these twelve B-17s are believed to have continued in troop carrier service with existing nose art, this one, field number 176, was the exception. Starting out as *Caroline* (see photo in chapter 2), that nose art was changed to a painting of a helmet-wearing youngster dressed in a diaper and holding a spanner named *"G.I." Jr* (photo above; a 5th AF badge was added to the front of the oversized helmet). That nose art was, however, apparently short lived, dropped in favor of the unnamed pin-up reproduced here. The last photo shows the B-17 at Nadzab, and it may be that a pin-up also appeared on the plane's LHS, but further details are currently unknown.

Three photos of CCS Curtiss C-46s with unnamed nose art, each with an unidentified serial number, artist in each case unknown: *top*, X608 of 5th CCS, 2nd CCG; another unnamed 5th CCS C-46 with nose art with a field number using the same stenciling was X601; *above*, X659 of 6th CCS, 2nd CCG (note the nonstandard positioning of the field number in this case, much lower than seen on other C-46s or C-47s); *right*, X665 of 7th CCS, 2nd CCG.

Unnamed Curtiss C-46, unidentified serial number, artist unknown, 55th TCS, 375th TCG. Originally XA185 of the 58th TCS, 375th TCG; note the alterations in darker-colored paint, changing the field number to X105.

Unnamed Douglas C-47, 42-23614, artist unknown, 57th and 56th TCSs, 375th TCG. This "Doug" is seen here wearing field number 154 while serving with the 57th TCS; later that was changed, it is thought, to 126 while serving with the 56th TCS. It survived the war but was salvaged in the Philippines in 1948.

Unnamed Douglas C-47, unidentified serial number, artist unknown, 65th TCS, 433rd TCG. The field number of this C-47 is believed to have been X214 at the time this photo was taken; another photo of it in its last guise as X102A can be found in chapter 7. The pin-up was copied from Gil Elvgren's 1939 work titled *French Dressing*.

Unnamed Douglas C-47, 42-100479, artist unknown, 57th TCS, 375th TCG. With nose art based on the September pin-up that appeared in the 1944 *Esquire Varga Calendar*, here we have a close-up of the nose art of this C-47, field number 166 or X166. This plane was received at Brisbane at the end of November 1943 and was condemned due to an accident in January 1945.

Unnamed Douglas C-47, 42-24257, artist unknown, 40th TCS, 317th TCG. This C-47, with a pin-up based on the Varga Girl from the September 1943 issue of *Esquire* magazine, was received by the 40th TCS in October 1943 and assigned field number 38, which had been applied prior to this photo being taken but is a little difficult to see. It survived the war but was salvaged soon afterward.

Unnamed Douglas C-47, 43-30747, artist unknown, 40th TCS, 317th TCG. This lovely copy of a Vargas work from the 1942 *Esquire Varga Calendar* appeared under the pilot's window of this C-47 received by the 40th TCS in November 1943 as a replacement for *Blonde Baby* (q.v.). Although unseen in this photo, the field number carried was 28. Later named *The BLUEGRASS Baby*, this was yet another C-47 that survived the war but dropped off USAAF records soon after.

Unnamed Douglas C-47, unidentified serial number, artist unknown, 57th TCS, 375th TCG. This C-47 carried field number X153 and was later named *KENTUCKY BELLE* but is believed to have been salvaged in the Philippines, date unknown.

Unnamed Douglas C-47, 42-24407 (unconfirmed), artist unknown, 40th TCS, 317th TCG. C-47 42-24407 served with the 40th TCS throughout 1944 and into 1945, carrying field number 39, and this is likely to be that aircraft. The artwork, "winging her way through the sky," according to the Phil Stack verse that originally accompanied it, is based on the *Esquire* Varga Girl for December 1943. For another example of this pin-up on a C-47, see *THE ALBUQUERQUE QUEEN* at the start of this chapter. This C-47 survived the war and was subsequently sold to commercial interests in the Philippines.

NOSE ART OF THE 5TH AIR FORCE

Unnamed Douglas C-47, 42-24223, artist unknown, 55th TCS, 375th TCG. Two views of this aircraft show its artwork (again based on the December 1943 *Esquire* Varga Girl pin-up) in an early stage, the first presumably ca. May 1944, shortly after it was added to the squadron, and the second many months later, with the artwork long completed and an "X" prefix added to the field number. Prior to May 1944, 42-24223 served with another unit (40th TCS, 317th TCG, has been suggested but not confirmed), and a name, still partially visible in the original photo, was added to the nose, but details are lacking. This C-47 was condemned in July 1945 due to an accident and subsequently salvaged.

Unnamed Douglas C-47, unidentified serial number, artist unknown, 21st TCS, 374th TCG. The first use of W-prefixed field numbers had occurred when the 374th TCG began operating under the 5298th TCW (P) in November 1944 (this unit subsequently became the 322nd TCW little more than a month later). Interestingly, though, unofficial markings appear to have been out of favor in the 374th by this time, since this is the only example seen by the author that shows a W-prefixed C-47 from the 374th with nose art. Note how the new field number has been applied over an earlier, unfortunately unknown, previous identity.

Unnamed Douglas C-47, unidentified serial number, artist unknown, unidentified TCS, later 57th TCS, 375th TCG. This C-47 originally saw service with an unidentified TCS, using a field number ending in 9, as seen here, but was transferred to the 57th TCS later, where it served as X174. Apart from the fact that the artwork was based on the November page from the Earl MacPherson *Artist's Sketch Pad Calendar* for 1944, no further details are currently known.

Unnamed Douglas C-47, unidentified serial number, artist unknown, 56th TCS, 375th TCG. Clearly the artwork is a based on a "Queen of Hearts" theme, the artist, perhaps, considering that to name it was unnecessary. This was, apparently, one of a number of prints of this photo made available to interested parties, but the radar aerials below the cockpit have been purposely censored in case any of the prints fell into the wrong hands (unlikely by the time this photo was taken). This C-47's field number was 139.

Unnamed Douglas C-47, unidentified serial number, artist unknown, 58th TCS, 375th TCG. This may be the LHS of *Willie-B II* (q.v.), which is also known to have carried field number 182, but without a serial number, confirmation is lacking. Later, after a move to the 57th TCS, where this C-47 carried field number 155, the name *DRUNKARD'S Dream* was added in two lines below the artwork.

Unnamed Douglas C-47, unidentified serial number, artist B. Balliet, 68th TCS, 433rd TCG. As mentioned earlier, it is believed that Balliet completed twenty-two nose art paintings, and while not all of them have yet been identified, this example, so far, is the only unnamed example that has been found. Unit identification stems from another photo that shows that this C-47's field number was 327. There were at least two other nose art paintings done by Balliet for the 68th TCS: *SURE SKIN* (q.v.) and *WHOOO! The "GRAY GHOST"* (q.v.), while another possibility is *MISS BEHAVIOR*.

253

Unnamed Douglas C-47, unidentified serial number, artist unknown, unit(s) unidentified. This photo is believed to have been taken on Biak following the C-47's transfer there after frontline service. As a result, her field number and other details often found under cockpit window ledges have been painted over. No other details are currently known.

Unnamed Douglas C-47, unidentified serial number, artist unknown, unit(s) unidentified. This photo was a late addition to the project but is of a SWPA C-47 wearing a field number, although it is a little difficult to see. While the artwork was based on a naked sitting-up version of *Esquire* magazine's October 1943 Varga Girl, further details are not currently known.

WHAT'S COOKIN?, Douglas C-47, 41-38629, artist unknown, 33rd TCS, 374th TCG. With a name inspired, no doubt, by Universal Pictures' 1942 musical *What's Cookin'*, this C-47 appears to have served with the 33rd TCS until transferred out and featured the two nose art paintings seen here at different times. It is known that there was also a *WHAT'S COOKIN' 2nd* (which carried field number 82 but no pin-up, it seems), which probably replaced the original *WHAT'S COOKIN?*, but details are lacking. 41-38629 was later assigned to IV ASAC and was returned to the US in January 1945. Disposed of nine months later, it was written off following an accident while in commercial hands in Brazil in 1953.

Virgin Princess, Douglas C-47, serial number 43-15xxx, artist unknown, unit(s) unidentified. It is known that this artwork was carried on both sides of the nose of this C-47, but, according to the only photo that this author has seen of the RHS, the name was carried only on the LHS. Although the serial number on the data panel is hidden from view by the artwork, the aircraft model is a C-47A-85-DL, a block that ran from 43-15454 to 43-15632. Many of these C-47s were assigned to the 5th AF, the first of which were flown across the Pacific to Australia in April 1944. While the two photos seen by the author suggest that the field number carried began and ended in 1, no better identification is currently possible.

WHOOO! The "GRAY GHOST", Douglas C-47, 42-23863, artist B. Balliet, 68th TCS, 433rd TCG. This C-47 was assigned to the 68th TCS in August 1943 and at that time had standard olive-drab upper surfaces with lighter undersides. This photo, however, shows that a fresh, darker coat of paint was later applied, and it seems likely that the pin-up and name were spruced up at the same time, since this version is a lot lighter than the original. After less than seven months' service, though, on March 21, 1944, she swung on takeoff from Finschafen en route to Nadzab, with personnel of the 26th PRS on board, and was subsequently written off.

The WIDOW MAKER, Curtiss C-46, unidentified serial number, artist unknown, 57th TCS, 375th TCG. Although unseen in this photo, this C-46's field number was X157, which confirms its 57th TCS ownership. It is understood that this was one of the C-46s taken to Japan by the 57th postwar, but what happened to it following the unit's inactivation in March 1946 is not known. The pin-up is not holding a bladed weapon in her right hand; the photographer has lined up, probably accidentally, that hand with an under-fuselage aerial.

Willie-B II, Douglas C-47, unidentified serial number, artist unknown, 58th TCS, 375th TCG. While we have seen that most pin-up nose art was copied from popular culture of the day, the origin of this example is not currently known. Unit identification is again possible in this case because it is known that this C-47, prior to the name being added, carried field number 182. A photo of the LHS of another "182," an unnamed C-47, appears on page 253, but whether this is the same aircraft is not currently known.

Yank's Delight, Douglas C-47, 41-18577, artist unknown, 40th TCS, 317th TCG. There were enough difficulties in wartime American/Australian relations when it came to Australian women being seen in company with off-duty US military personnel without adding fuel to the fire with a highly suggestive name and artwork like this. It has been suggested that by January 1944, *Yank's Delight* was renamed *Christmas Delight*, but confirmation is lacking (on the RHS of the nose, the name BUGLE-NOSE, without artwork, appeared). This C-47 carried field number 35 until around October 1943, when it was changed to 43, and perhaps the name change, if there was one, occurred at the same time. The plane was returned to the US in August 1944, was disposed of from Ontario, Canada, in 1946, and was written off following a crash in Canada's Northwest Territories in 1951.

YOUR'S, Douglas C-47, unidentified serial number, artist B. Balliet, 69th TCS, 433rd TCG. Seemingly a full-frontal-nude artwork from a distance, at a closer viewing it can be seen that the otherwise explicit nature of this painting has been protected by adding a passing butterfly! Balliet employed a similar tactic in another of his 69th TCS artworks, *TEXAS HELLCAT* (q.v.). The pilot's name under the window ledge is Lt. B. H. Cole; Cole was "C" flight leader at the time. This C-47, then carrying field number X353, may have ended the war on Biak.

CHAPTER 5
Other Types

This chapter provides an opportunity to display some additional examples of pin-up nose art on airplanes in second-line units not already covered. Types seen for the first time in these pages include a very rare North American O-47, a Piper L-4, and three Stinson L-5s (the L-4s and L-5s were the smallest planes in the 5th AF's inventory). Making a reintroduction in this chapter are two examples of the B-17, an aircraft type that in earlier days helped make nose art popular but by 1945 was no longer a bomber, but, as seen in the heading photo, an air sea rescue aircraft that carried an airborne lifeboat. Two air-sea rescue units, the 3rd and the 6th Emergency Rescue Squadrons (ERSs), were assigned to the 5th AF in 1945, and their primary equipment was a mixture of B-17s and Canadian Vickers OA-10As, the USAAF version of the PBY-5A. Some crews, wanting to be a part of the pin-up craze, did add pin-ups to their planes, but only in a limited way. A factor here was the lack of space for unofficial names or artworks (or both) on the noses of OA-10s, the solution being that artworks appeared a little farther back on the boat hull, where there was more room; two examples follow.

Heading photo. Billie Louise, Boeing B-17, unidentified serial number, artist unknown, 6th ERS, 5th ERG. Originally invented by the British with downed bomber crews particularly in mind, the US airborne lifeboat was larger and sturdier for open-sea use and soldiered on postwar as standard long-range ASR equipment in USAF service. Also note that the unit designation, "6th E.R.S.,", has been painted on the nose radome. In 5th AF service the rescue B-17s were known as "Jukeboxes," while the other rescue aircraft in use, OA-10As, were known as "Playmates." The 6th ERS was one of the last flying squadrons to join the 5th AF, a unit history noting that "although one mission was flown in March, the squadron did not begin actual operations until April 3, [1945]."

Perhaps surprisingly, a lot of former frontline B-25s were relegated to second-line duties. As early as 1942, the 5th AF had experimented with stripping a former B-25 bomber "to transport essential materials in combat zones," and by late 1944 with veteran B-25s, particularly D models (there had been 255 B-25s in tactical units in New Guinea as of April 30, 1944, of which 141 were Ds) coming up for replacement following the assignment of sufficient numbers of the new B-25J model, lots of former frontline B-25s were pensioned off. The vast majority of these, though, were still capable of second-line duties, particularly when it came to the urgent movement of personnel from New Guinea to Australia (from Nadzab to Townsville by stripped-down B-25 was about a four-hour flight) and, on the return flight, the aforementioned transportation of "essential materials" (often fresh meat, fruit, and vegetables, and even alcohol, but fresh milk, it seems, only rarely) back to New Guinea. When units moved on to the Philippines, there was still interest by many of them in acquiring their own B-25; the 33rd TCS, for example, added one to its lineup as late as July 1945. These B-25s became known to servicemen as "fat cats," the name of a famous former 3rd BG B-25, serial number 41-12449, that had been the first to be converted and put back into use after being stripped of more than 2,000 lbs. of combat equipment.

The original B-25 with the "fat cat" name had animal nose art, but all the B-25 photos included in this chapter, along with some others in chapter 7, are likely to have been of other "fat cat" airplanes (but with pin-up nose art), the difference being that the early history of those included in this chapter is currently unknown. The odd A-20 was also used on similar duties, and photos of two of them also follow.

Coconut Queen, Canadian Vickers OA-10-A, unidentified serial number, artist unknown, 3rd ERS (unconfirmed), 5th ERG (unconfirmed). As already mentioned, lack of space on the noses of ERS OA-10s saw pin-ups added a little farther back on the plane's boat hull; the position of this Vargaesque example was on the LHS aft of the cockpit and just forward of the leading main-plane strut. It is known that this OA-10A was delivered to the SWPA in February 1945, and while the delivery crew joined the 13th AF's 2nd ERS, it seems most likely that their plane went to the 3rd ERS, which, for the most part by then, was operating from Leyte. Note here, and with *"I'LL BE SEEIN' YOU"*, which follows, that probably because of the urgent need for more OA-10-As in the Pacific, most, it seems, retained their original factory-applied white finish.

The DEFENSLESS VIRGIN MARY, North American B-25, unidentified serial number, artist unknown, unit(s) unidentified. The author has a few different photos of this unarmed B-25 and its nose art, all probably taken in the Philippines in 1945. It may be that this one belonged to a FEASC unit, but without any clues, it has been decided to leave it in this chapter, since it may have belonged to a 5th AF unit.

Edibelle, Stinson L-5, unidentified serial number, artist unknown, 157th, 159th or 160th LS (unconfirmed), 3rd ACG (if one of the aforementioned squadrons). 5th AF Stinson L-5 pin-up nose art existed, but relevant photos are difficult to find (one other follows). The 157th, 159th, and 160th Liaison Squadrons joined the fight against the Japanese in January 1945 on Luzon, and while confirmation is still pending, the author believes that there is a good chance that this L-5 belonged to one of these units. In the January–June 1945 period they flew an outstanding number of missions and were responsible for evacuating many wounded, as well as undertaking the variety of other uses that the L-5 was famous for.

OTHER TYPES

Fast Lady, North American B-25, artist Charles R. Chesnut, 22nd BG. Here is a close-up of the pin-up seen being painted in chapter 1. As mentioned at that point, however, the identity of this B-25 is, unfortunately, unknown. *Fast Lady* was last reported at Nichols Field, Manila, in September 1945.

'*In the Mood*', unidentified airplane type, unidentified serial number, artist unknown, unit(s) unidentified. This is from a 5th AF Service Command photo collection and features a copy of the September 1943 *Esquire* magazine Varga Girl; the only additional information that the author can add is that it is suspected that the photo was taken at the Townsville Air Depot. The absence of camouflage paint does suggest that the airplane may have been a second-line type.

"*I'LL BE SEEIN' YOU*", Canadian Vickers OA-10-A, 44-34056, artist unknown, 6th ERS, 5th ERG. Photographed at Kadena, Okinawa; the plane's name may have been taken from the popular film of the same name but, on the other hand, could have simply been wishful thinking, although, as mentioned already, the 6th ERS was a very late starter in the war against Japan. While this OA-10-A has previously been linked to the 2nd ERS, the photo has the original owner's writing on the back, identifying the plane as from the "6th Air Sea Rescue Squadron." Note that this artwork is on the OA-10-A's RHS; the name was repeated on the LHS but not the artwork. "*I'LL BE SEEIN' YOU*" was still in use by the 5th AF in June 1946.

LITTLE CHIEF COCKEYE, North American B-25, unidentified serial number, artist unknown, 43rd BG. While this B-25's earlier history is unknown, by early 1944 it was in the hands of the 43rd BG and being used for second-line duties. If the artwork and name seem familiar to readers, that will be because they were based on an earlier artwork named *BIG CHIEF COCKEYE*, photos of which appear in chapter 2. Another, later photo of *LITTLE CHIEF COCKEYE* (which ended the war at Nadzab) appears in appendix 3.

NOSE ART OF THE 5TH AIR FORCE

LiTTLE CHiEF, Douglas A-20, 42-54084, artist identified only as "521," 321st BS, 90th BG. These three photos show the artwork prior to and after completion, taken from similar vantage points, and a close-up of the pin-up and the boxes on which she has her feet. This A-20, which had formerly served with the 3rd, 312th, and 417th BGs, was another "fat cat" plane, and while the pin-up (wearing an A-2 flying jacket with the "Jolly Rogers" 90th BG insignia) could be only wishful thinking, spirits such as gin, apparently readily available in northeastern Australia, were undoubtedly on the shopping list. The crescent-shaped marking on the top RHS box is in fact a "C" for the US Army's Field Ration, Type C. The box is marked "AUSTRALIA" at the top and with USASOS (the abbreviation for the US Army Services of Supply branch, the usual source of all the army's day-to-day needs) below the "C." Photos of this artist's other known work, *BOOBY TRAP*, can be found in chapter 2. This A-20 ended up on Biak for salvaging.

PUG NOSE, Consolidated B-24, 41-23823, artist unknown, Headquarters V Air Force Service Command. This B-24 picked up its name while with the 90th BG (see photo in camouflage below, taken in New Guinea), but the pin-up was added only after the camouflage was stripped away in preparation for its new role as a transport with Service Command (other changes include an apparent lack of any armament, removal of the top turret, and a fairing over part of what had been the bomb aimer's Perspex panel). The pin-up in this instance was based on a Gil Elvgren artwork titled *Tree for Two*, wording that can be seen to have been retained at middle left of the close-up photo.

Queen Mary, North American B-25, unidentified serial number, artist unknown, CRTC. Although this photo was taken from a distance, it can be seen that this was another B-25 stripped of camouflage and tactical markings that, late in the war, was given a new identity and new job, in this case as the personal airplane of veteran B-25 pilot, and former 3rd BG commander, Col. John P. "Jock" Henebry after he assumed command of the 360th Air Service Group FEAF in 1945. Henebry had married his sweetheart, Mary Elizabeth "Liz" McGuire, in 1944, and the artwork on the nose of this B-25 was a likeness of her. Henebry returned home in October 1945, and this airplane was undoubtedly subsequently salvaged, probably in the Philippines, where the 360th Air Service Group had been transferred earlier in the year.

SHINY SHIELA, Douglas C-47, 41-23421, artist unknown, General Headquarters, Southwest Pacific Area [GHQ, SWPA]. This C-47 was received by the 5th AF in May 1943. Around the same time, a former KLM DC-3 being used by Gen. MacArthur was pensioned off, and 41-23421 was chosen to replace it, even using the same call sign, VHCXE (the original CXE was given call sign VHCXL instead). Noteworthy for C-47s at this time was that because it was stripped of paint and operated in natural-metal finish, which certainly made it stand out as being different (see photo below; the first VHCXE had also, apparently, been stripped of camouflage, but perhaps its use by MacArthur was limited). The *SHINY SHIELA* name (misspelled, no doubt, due to American unfamiliarity with the Australian slang term for a young woman or sweetheart) and artwork undoubtedly reflected the pride associated with the introduction of this new plane for GHQ usage, but both name and artwork were short lived, due, apparently, to official complaints. According to former pilot Henry "Hank" Godman, this C-47 was in use by GHQ for more than six months; she was subsequently replaced by a new XC-108 (VIP B-17) named *BATAAN*. Lower photo, A. A. "Bill" Penglase

SOLID STUFF, Stinson L-5, 42-98708, artist unknown, 25th LS. Although identified as a liaison squadron (LS), this unit saw service in New Guinea primarily as a rescue unit to begin with. Unit personnel began arriving at Nadzab in February 1944, and squadron pilot Jim Whitaker is seen here with his L-5 two months later after two aircrew rescues: the first, an American; the second, presumably, an Australian. It has been recorded that the artwork here, and another on the tail fin, were cut from copies of *Esquire* magazines, but the pin-up (which bears her own name, *Hussy from Houston*) looks to be too big to have come from a magazine, even if it was a gatefold. This plane's Australian connections grew stronger postwar, when it was one of four L-5s purchased in Manila for resale in Australia by the Sydney-based firm Aerial Transport Co. The former *SOLID STUFF* subsequently had four Australian owners, all from the state of Queensland, but was withdrawn from use in 1963; some parts from it were later used in the rebuild of the former 42-99470, later VH-BFR. *Gene Saltrinik via Malcolm Long*

OTHER TYPES

STORMY WEATHER, Consolidated B-24 44-40184, artist unknown, 43rd BG. This B-24 was the first NMF example to be received by the 64th BS (if not the 43rd BG) and as such had been named *SHINING EXAMPLE*, without any accompanying artwork. Damaged in action on a mission against Balikpapan, Borneo, on October 10, 1944, it was repaired and put back in service as a group transport renamed *STORMY WEATHER*, from the 1943 film of the same name about a World War I soldier who returns home and meets and falls in love with a singer unwilling to settle down. Reportedly, the film's lead actress, Lena Horne (1917–2010), was the inspiration for the pin-up painting. Note the retention of the B-24's bomb log (thirty-two missions) and a Purple Heart emblem from its earlier frontline service from May to October 1944.

Unnamed Douglas A-20, unidentified serial number, artist unknown, unit(s) unidentified. This nose art is believed to have been photographed in the Philippines, but the only other information known about the aircraft (derived from another photo) is that it featured red-and-white rudder stripes (the first A-20s built for the USAAC featured this marking, but it was officially regarded as "eliminated" in May 1942) and probably a red-colored tip to the vertical fin. There were more than one of these stripped-down, highly polished, unarmed A-20s in use (Col. Chester A. Coltharp, while CO of the 345th BG, flew one for a time in 1945, but not one with nose art, it seems), and given that they were not operated by the 13th AF, it is suspected that this example was from a 5th AF unit.

Unnamed Boeing B-17, 43-39272, artist unknown, 6th ERS, 5th ERG. As mentioned above, airborne lifeboat-equipped B-17s began to see service in the Pacific only late in the war; a brief history of the 6th ERS provided by the Air Force History Office confirms that in the first six months of the squadron's 5th AF service, beginning in March 1945, there had been fourteen occasions when airborne lifeboats had been dropped. Note the similarities in the nose art on the unnamed B-17 when compared with *Billie Louise* in the heading photo; both are on a dark background and painted below the LHS cockpit window. Clearly visible on the original print of this image is the fact that this was a B-17G model; the oft-quoted designations B-17H and SB-17G for airborne lifeboat-equipped B-17s did not come into use until postwar.

Unnamed North American O-47, 39-116, artist unknown, unit(s) unidentified. Among the collection of US airplanes that found their way to Australia in early 1942 were ten prewar O-47 three-seat battlefield observation planes. It is suspected that most, if not all, were used only for local, nonoperational flights in Australia, but one or two may have been used in a similar capacity in New Guinea. By March 1944 there were at least three left in Australia, with 39-116, seen here, being one of them, but by then they were in the hands of 5th AF Service Command at Garbutt Field, Townsville, awaiting salvage. The pin-up is based on the September 1943 *Esquire* Varga Girl.

Unnamed Stinson L-5, unidentified serial number, artist unknown, 25th LS. While most World War II nose art was elaborate, it took little effort to dress up this Stinson L-5 in New Guinea in November 1944 to give its nose some semblance of a face; the kissable lips are the most obvious addition, but eyelashes have also been added above the "eyes." While it's not of a pin-up, the author considered this photo worthy of inclusion in this chapter as a simple personalized nose marking with a female connection. The plane at right is one of the unit's Cessna UC-78s, tail number 679.

WINGED VIRGIN, Piper L-4, unidentified serial number, artist unknown, unit(s) unidentified. While the use of Piper L-4s by the 5th AF is little known, official USAAF listings indicate that there were four L-4Bs in New Guinea as of April 30, 1944, a number that was reduced to two by June 18. Both were in tactical units at the time; probably the 25th LS. A previously unpublished photo of another confirmed 5th AF L-4, named *MOBY DICK JR.*, appears in the following chapter.

CHAPTER 6
Fearsome Nose Art

While fearsome nose art was seen on some military aircraft in World War I, it was not until World War II that it became a "popular" art form. The German air force, the Luftwaffe, was the first major user of shark's-mouth markings during World War II, and, not to be outdone, Curtiss Tomahawk fighters (early model P-40s) of the RAF's Western Desert–based No. 112 Squadron followed suit ca. September 1941. This in turn led to the adoption of the same style of marking by P-40s used in China by the American Volunteer Group (AVG), with one press caption to a early photo of AVG P-40s in flight stating that "with Shark Heads painted on their planes, these 'Flying Tigers' look fearsome as they go Jap-hunting." Certainly, in early 1942, when Allied victories were few and far between, promoting the work of the AVG and their shark's-mouth (or shark's head) planes was a distraction from Pacific war woes. The prestigious and well-illustrated *Life* magazine was just one of the many AVG champions; in the March 30, 1942, issue, readers learned that the "Flying Tigers" were in Burma, while a subheading claimed that a "handful of American pilots" had shot down "300 Jap warplanes in 90 days." It was little wonder that the "Flying Tigers" and their adopted insignia became so popular.

As far as the 5th AF was concerned, early copiers of the "shark's head" marking in 1942, predictably, were some early P-39s/P-400s and P-40s received in Australia, followed later in the year by some early P-38s too, notably of the 39th FS of the 35th FG, but other types followed in 1943, particularly B-25s.

Why shark's-mouth B-25s? Well, it had been decided by around the end of 1942 to convert some from bombers to strafers, and new markings for the converted planes quickly followed, in keeping with their new image. How the B-25s were chosen for the role was explained as follows by Gen. Kenney, taken from an article he wrote titled "Air Power in the Southwest Pacific," which appeared in the June 1944 issue of the official *Air Force* magazine:

> We did not have enough forward firepower [in early 5th AF bombers] to take out the deck defensive fire that every Jap boat seemed to have. The B-17s didn't have it and it looked like too much of a job to remodel the Fortress. The A-20 had four forward-firing caliber .50s, but it didn't have much range and couldn't carry big bombs. The B-26 was going to be replaced by the B-25 in our theatre. By the process of elimination, it looked like the B-25 [would have to be used]. We took out the

Heading photo. North American B-25, unidentified serial number, artist unknown, 90th BS, 3rd BG. Of all the fearsome markings painted on the noses of aircraft during World War II, the most popular was the so-called shark's teeth. This photo, taken by 3rd BG photographer Jack Heyn at one of the Dobodura airstrips, is suspected to have been taken on November 2, 1943, after the massive raid on Rabaul by 5th AF medium and heavy bombers, but the identity of the B-25 remains unconfirmed.

bombardier, put a package of four .50s in the nose, two more packages of two guns each on each side of the fuselage, threw away the bottom turret, put some more gas in its place, balanced the plane with a little lead where necessary, and as soon as enough were ready to equip a light bombardment squadron, we started training.

The light bombardment squadron initially involved was the 90th BS, the combat log for which indicated that by January 4, 1943, eleven of its B-25s "were in Brisbane getting 8-50 cal. guns installed." While teething problems were reported, the planes were returned to the squadron progressively, and on February 16, six of them undertook their first mission, a raid on the Malahang airfield at Lae. The log called the attack "highly successful," reporting that 7,450 rounds of .50-caliber machine gun ammunition had been expended in twenty-five seconds! Just where and when the modified B-25s had the shark's-mouth markings added is not currently known, but photos show that some of the artwork (if not all) was completed by March 1943, with the 3rd BG men who produced the group souvenir volume *The Reaper's Harvest* describing the "toothy" look achieved as that of "a cumbersome shark-faced demon, spitting fire at his enemy."

This success led to more B-25 strafer conversions for other 5th AF B-25 squadrons—the 71st BS, 405th BS, 822nd BS, and 823rd BS (all of the 38th BG), and the 498th BS and 499th BS of the 345th BG, but with shark's-mouth markings already in use by the 90th BS, there was interest in coming up with other extreme-looking nose markings (mostly still based on teeth) that were different. This was not only for building esprit de corps in the squadrons, but also for adding to what *The Reaper's Harvest* describes as "the terror of low-level attack" in which all these squadrons would be involved.

On the basis of the animal chosen for the squadron nose art, the B-25 squadrons became known by the following names:

71st BS (to New Guinea, ca. October 1942)	"Wolf Pack Bomb Squadron"
405th BS (to New Guinea, ca. October 1942)	"Green Dragons Bomb Squadron"
498th BS (to New Guinea, June 1943)	"Falcons Bomb Squadron"
499th BS (to New Guinea, June 1943)	"Bats Outa Hell Bomb Squadron"
822nd BS (to New Guinea, June 1943)	"Black Panthers Bomb Squadron"
823rd BS (to New Guinea, June 1943)	"Terrible Tigers Bomb Squadron"

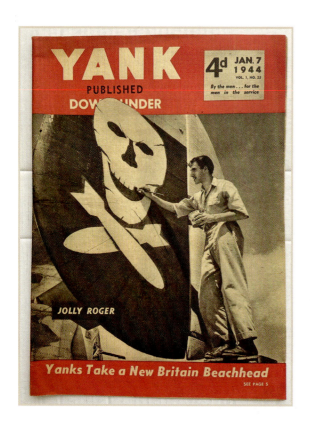

Left: The 90th BG's famous "Jolly Roger" tail insignia, which featured a grinning skull over crossed bombs (described by *Yank* magazine staff correspondent Cpl. Ralph L. Boyce in an article on the group as "the most famous trademark in this theater of war"), was designed by SSgt. Leonard H. Baer, and began appearing on 90th BG B-24 vertical fins in late 1943. The standard size of each insignia was 7 by 4 feet. *Right*: The earliest known example of a 5th AF airplane with personal markings featuring a skull was the winged skull on this North American B-25 *RITA'S WAGON* (serial number 41-30055, artist unknown, 500th BS, 345th BG), which was added ca. March 1943, prior to the squadron's movement to the SWPA. Whether or not this was an original idea is currently not known (the unofficial emblem of the 490th BS, 341st BG, 10th (later 14th) AF already in use at that time was also a winged skull), but it was only in use for a few months, not being reinstated following this B-25's conversion to strafer. As seen here soon after its arrival at Port Moresby, with no bomb log yet started, the name "MORT" below the cockpit window was the nickname of the aircraft's captain, Lt. Max H. Mortensen, one of the great 345th BG personalities, who rose from flight leader in the 500th Squadron to the position of deputy group commander by war's end.

Examples of the artwork of these units, as well as others, including the 320th BS, 90th BG (the "Moby Dick Bomb Squadron"), whose personnel considered that the size and shape of their B-24s could be said to be whalelike, follow in this chapter.

Some of these squadrons did adopt their wartime insignia as official emblems, as approved by AAF Regulation No. 35-22 of August 2, 1943, notably a "black caricatured bat" for the 499th BS (approved November 22, 1943). The "head and neck of a mythical dragon" also became the official emblem of the 405th BS, but not until 1954 (the 405th was inactivated on April 1, 1949, but reactivated on January 1, 1953).

This chapter is divided into three sections: the first (main) section deals with fearsome unit markings; second, other "toothy" nonunit markings; and, last, four examples of nose art based on other scary animal characters. Unlike much of the other nose art painted on bombers (this chapter being mainly bomber aircraft based), it is suspected that all, except one of two examples out of the more than ninety included in this chapter, were added in the SWPA.

1942 Fighters

80th FS, 8th FG

Unnamed Bell P-39 or P400, unidentified serial number, artist unknown. This squadron was in action with Airacobras from July 1942; most featured an aircraft identification letter on each side of the nose, forward of the cockpit, but this one lacks that. The surname of the soldier in the photo is Garner, but no other details are known (location, however, may be Jackson Field, Port Moresby); given that the squadron converted to P-38s beginning in early 1943, its time on P-39s/P-400s was comparatively short. A good selection of other photos of 80th FS P-39/P-400 shark's-teeth markings, all of which were different, can be found in John Stanaway's 8th FG history, *Attack & Conquer*.

39th FS, 35th FG

The 39th FS was the first P-38-equipped fighter squadron to operate in the SWPA and, while precise details are unavailable, was quick to adopt the aggressive cowling markings shown here. This enlargement is from an official photo dated November 1942, and on that basis it is the earliest view in the author's collection showing the shark's-mouth markings on the engine cowlings of a 5th AF P-38. *USAF via Malcolm Long*

1943 Bombers

13th BS, 3rd BG

P.I. JOE, North American B-25, unidentified serial number, artist unknown. As seen in this photo, some 13th BS B-25s had fearsome-looking black skulls painted around the nose guns, to give the impression, in action, that the mouth was spitting fire (the positioning of the skull was such that two guns were in the vicinity of the mouth area, the other two immediately above, to the left and right of the nose). The practice appears to have been limited, however, to the second half of 1943. *P.I. JOE* (a play on the nickname of an army enlisted man, "G.I. Joe," altered in honor of the 13th BS commanding officer, Maj. David M. Conley, who had earlier served with the 28th BS in the Philippines Islands; hence the P.I.) was one of the force of tens of the medium bombers involved in successful raids against enemy targets in the Wewak area on August 17 and 18, 1943, a story written up for the *Yank* "Down Under" edition, appearing in the issue of September 17,

although the artist's impression of the airplane left a lot to be desired. Less than two weeks later, though, *P.I. JOE* crashed on takeoff from Dobodura; see photo in chapter 7.

71st BS, 38th BG

The Scoto Kid, North American B-25, 41-12908, artist unknown. Identifiable by its 131 mission bomb log (two rows of twenty-six, one row of twenty-four, two rows of twenty, and one row of fifteen) and claims for two enemy aircraft shot down, this is definitely *The Scoto Kid* (the name appeared only on the LHS). Prior to its strafer conversion, this B-25 had been operated under the name *Mauvourneen* by the 405th BS, but from ca. August 1943 until replaced in September 1944, it was known as *The Scoto Kid* and carried the nose markings seen here. The idea of a bloodthirsty wolf's-head squadron insignia (thus the collective term "Wolf Pack" for the squadron) had been dreamed up in a San Francisco bar ca. mid-1942 and agreed to prior to the first 71st BS flights across the Pacific to Australia. The initial form it took, though, was as shown in the photo below of *TORRID TESSIE "The TERROR"* (this B-25, serial number 41-29692, survived frontline service to be converted to a "fat cat" transport renamed *TORRID TESS*; see photo and further information in chapter 7). Note, however, that it was only following the strafer conversions in Australia that the changeover to this sizable cartoonlike insignia occurred. As will be seen when comparing this image with others that appear in this chapter, of all the fearsome unit markings added to the noses of 5th AF airplanes, the 71st BS's wolf's heads seem to have been altered the least.

90th BS, 3rd BG

The AVOCA AVENGER, North American B-25, 41-30161, artist unknown. The shark's-face look seen here was added sometime in 1943, prior to the plane's conversion to a strafer, when this B-25 featured pin-up nose art and the name The VIGOROUS VIRGIN (see photo in chapter 2). At the end of November 1943, both this plane and HELLS FIRE, a photo of which follows, were transferred to the 500th BS, and in both cases the shark's face was retained. By then, though, what was left of the pin-up and The VIGOROUS VIRGIN name had gone, replaced by the "armed" duck seen here. In 500th BS hands, the B-25 was assigned to Lt. Thomas F. Tackaberry, from Avoca, Michigan, and it was Tackaberry who arranged for the new name to be added. In September 1944 the B-25 was transferred to the 498th BS for a short time but subsequently was declared war weary. When this photo was taken is not known, but the bomb log shows sixty-eight missions.

"CHATTER BOX", North American B-25, 41-13088, artist unknown. After conversion to a strafer, this B-25 was assigned to Lt. Robert D. Chatt in February 1943, if not earlier, and named "CHATTER BOX" at his request. This B-25, acknowledged as the first of the squadron's B-25s to have shark's teeth added, saw brief but eventful service with the 90th BS, participating in the Bismarck Sea Battle of March 3, 1943, but was left to the snakes and crocodiles of a swamp northwest of Port Moresby following a forced landing there on April 16. This photo is of 90th BS aircrew who flew in the Battle of the Bismarck Sea, and includes the CO, Maj. Ed Larner, *roughly middle rear, wearing his cap*; bearded Bob Chatt, CHATTER BOX's pilot, *next row down, sixth from right*; and Flying Officer Maurie Carse, RAAF, Chatt's second pilot, *second from left at rear*. A photo of the B-25 in the swamp can be found in chapter 7. *From The Reaper's Harvest (see bibliography)*

FEATHER MERCHANT, North American B-25, 41-12442, artist unknown. One of a number of new B-25s taken over from the Dutch in Brisbane in late March 1942, this aircraft participated in the Royce Mission to the Philippines before the islands fell, and subsequently flew missions in New Guinea with the 13th BS. Later converted to a strafer, in early 1943 it was assigned to the 90th BS and participated in the Battle of the Bismarck Sea on March 3, subsequently receiving the shark's-face look seen here, which became the standard squadron decoration, although it seems that each was different to some degree. *FEATHER MERCHANT* was heavily damaged after being shot up over Lae on May 25 but was eventually returned to service again. Due to the 90th BS's conversion to A-20s at the end of the year, *FEATHER MERCHANT* was transferred to the 499th BS, 345th BG, where it was repainted with that squadron's bat's-nose insignia and renamed *Miss Priority*, but after only brief frontline service it was pensioned off and stripped of armament and other unwanted hardware and paint (except for a slightly different nose insignia), and it joined the ranks of other "fat cat" fast transports in use between New Guinea and Australia. This role lasted until later in the year, when the B-25 was transferred from the 499th to a service squadron and subsequently abandoned at Tadji. For a last photo and further information, see chapter 7. A. A. "Bill" Penglase

HELLS FIRE / HELL'S FIRE, North American B-25, 41-30278, artist unknown. These two photos taken of the LHS of this B-25 show (*right*) *HELLS FIRE* while with the 90th BS (the writing below the cockpit window reads "Pilot Lt. MacLellan") after thirty-three missions, and, *below*, with a small pin-up added and the name in altered position and apostrophe added, following transfer to the 500th BS, 345th BG, in November 1943. It was in this latter guise that this B-25 and her six-man crew were lost as a result of air combat on February 9, 1944, after attempting to provide cover for the downed crew from the 500th BS's *MEXICAN SPITFIRE* (see photo in chapter 2).

MORTIMER/Mortimer, North American B-25, 41-12443. The 90th BS combat log notes on May 9, 1943, that a reporter visited the squadron that day to interview the crew chief, TSgt. Lee, on the first anniversary of this B-25's frontline service—by then it had flown over six hundred flying hours, of which more than half were combat hours, the diarist commenting that "it is a hard job to find a plane that can weather combat this long." The name *MORTIMER* was originally applied in block letters on both sides of the nose from an early date, but the teeth and eyes were added only following the B-25's conversion to a strafer, date unknown. Perhaps because of the newspaper publicity it was due to receive, *MORTIMER*'s nose was subsequently painted over and new, sharper teeth, a different-shaped eye, and a new version of the name were added, while the mission log (seventeen bomb symbols along with claims for nine enemy planes shot down and five enemy ships sunk) was moved to below the cockpit window (*photo at right*). For a last view and a later comment on this famous B-25, see chapter 7. *Top right, A. A. "Bill" Penglase*

RUNT'S ROOST, North American B-25, 41-29727. The pilot assigned to this aircraft (this occurred probably during the second quarter of 1943), Lt. Joseph Helbert, was shorter in stature than most (if not all) of his 90th BS peers, and it has been said that he was known by the nickname "Runt"; hence the name of his plane. By the end of July, Helbert had flown thirty-three missions, many of them in this aircraft. His tour of duty ended in November 1943, at which point he returned to the US, but what became of *RUNT'S ROOST* has yet to be established.

NOSE ART OF THE 5TH AIR FORCE

SPOOK II, North American B-25, 41-12969. This B-25, with somewhat of a friendly face compared with other angrier-looking aircraft in this chapter, is understood to have been initially assigned to the 13th BS but, following conversion to strafer, went to the 90th BS, where it was usually flown by the commanding officer, Maj. Ed Larner (transferred in from the 89th BS to command the 90th at the end of December 1942). The first mention of "969" in the 90th's combat log is on February 7, 1943, and more references follow, notably as a result of the Bismarck Sea battle the following month, when Larner and other 90th BS B-25 crews claimed fifteen hits on three destroyers and seven transports of the Lae convoy. Larner's daring was legendary, but his luck ran out when, while buzzing the fighter airstrip at Dobodura on April 30, 1943, *SPOOK II*'s LHS engine cut out and it suddenly crashed in flames, killing all eight men aboard.

320th BS, 90th BG

MOBY DICK, Consolidated B-24, 41-24047, artist unknown. Of this B-24, the 90th BG wartime souvenir book, *The Jolly Rogers: Southwest Pacific, 1942–1944*, said that it "was so famous that her whole unit was named after her." Not only that, but it was the first of all the other whale-mouthed 320th BS B-24s that followed, photos of some of which are also to be found in this chapter. It was flown out to Australia in November 1942 and remained in 90th BG service until October 1943, when it was returned to the US. By then the B-24 had completed sixty-five missions, a new line of thirty bomb symbols being added above that shown in the LHS photo. In the US, its frontline markings were retained initially for publicity purposes, but the teeth, at least, may have been deleted when the bomber became a trainer. *MOBY DICK* was salvaged at Searcey Field, Stillwater, Oklahoma, and had been disposed of by October 1945.

405th BS, 38th BG

Unnamed North American B-25, unidentified serial number, artist Howard Wetzel (unconfirmed). This wonderfully clear photo was taken at the Townsville Air Depot on June 15, 1943, the reason behind the photo being, no doubt, the recently installed nose gun pack (note also the rarely seen gunsight forward of the cockpit). Research for the *Sun Setters of the Southwest Pacific Area* volume established that the idea of naming the 405th BS the "Green Dragons" occurred only in May 1943, so the artwork seen here is certainly a very early version of the squadron motif, all of which were different to some degree and, in fact, altered as time went on. Note particularly in this photo the effort put in to adding scale representations to the head.

TOKYO SLEEPER, North American B-25, 41-12905, artist unknown. This B-25 was delivered to Australia in August 1942 named *ROW BINDER II TOKYO SLEEPER*, and while the *ROW BINDER II* part of the name was lost reasonably quickly (its removal on the LHS of the plane made room for the bomb log) and the rest of the name fell victim to the plane's conversion to a strafer, it continued to be known as *TOKYO SLEEPER*. The "Green Dragons" unit insignia was added ca. May 1943, and in the course of a joint 71st BS and 405th BS attack on Japanese shipping off Wewak on September 2, 1943, the crew of Lt. Roy Glover (*at right in the photo at left*), flying the *SLEEPER* at the time, were given the credit for sinking the Japanese merchantman that had been under attack at the time, the heavily laden *Nagato Maru*, part of a convoy that had arrived only earlier that day. As seen in the photo above, this B-25 ran up an extensive bomb and victory log; eventually 136 missions and a thin line of claims for enemy aircraft shot down (nine) and ships sunk (three). Its demise came at Biak, on July 24, 1944, in a crash landing; at the time it was considered to have been the oldest frontline B-25 still in service in the SWPA.

498th BS, 345th BG

Labor Pains, North American B-25, 41-30047, artist unknown. Research for the *Warpath across the Pacific* volume concluded that this B-25, one of the first assigned to the 498th, went into action in late June 1943, but that the early version of the 498th's falcon's-head nose insignia was added only in September 1943. Given that the B-25 was written off due to damage caused by enemy AA fire over Wewak on September 27, this photo, taken at Cairns, Queensland, must also date from that same month. Note in this photo the extensive and time-consuming attempt at feathering the squadron insignia and the seventeen-mission bomb log to the top right of the B-25's original artwork of a helmet-wearing youngster with rifle and bayonet, which was based on the J. C. Leyendecker (1874–1951) *Saturday Evening Post* cover artwork for the New Year's issue for 1943. Leyendecker began painting "Baby New Year" covers for the *Post* in 1907; that for 1943 was his last offering and featured the toddler wrecking Fascist symbols. *A. A. "Bill" Penglase*

The ALL-AMERICAN, North American B-25, 42-53420, artist unknown. From the second group of B-25s assigned to the 498th in August 1943, this one remained in service until April 1944, when it was transferred out to the V Bomber Command Replacement Pool. That the enemy readily identified the difference in some of these fearsome markings was evident when reports were received by the unit that its prominent, yellow-nosed B-25s had led to them being called the "yellow-nosed butchers" in some Japanese propaganda radio broadcasts; from a 5th AF perspective, high praise indeed. *From The Falcons: History of the 498th Medium Bombardment Squadron United States Army Air Corps* (see bibliography)

"RED WRATH", North American B-25, 41-30024, artist unknown. It was for good reason that the 345th BG called themselves the "Tree-top Terrors"; at left the rearward-facing tail camera in the preceding B-25 captured this and other similar views of the yellow-nosed *"RED WRATH"* behind and slightly to the side in an attack on a heavily defended enemy AA gun position near Boram Airfield on October 16, 1943. This was just part of a massed attack that day on the Boram and Wewak area by the 345th BG. This B-25 saw long 345th BG service: more than twelve months with the 498th BS, then not quite two months with the 500th BS, at which stage the falcon's head and original name and artwork (*shown above*) were painted out and replaced by a pin-up with the name *PANNELL JOB*; see photo in chapter 2. *Boram photo, USAF via Malcolm Long*

499th BS, 345th BG

"LUCKY BAT", North American B-25, 41-30058, artist John H. "Mick" Michalowski. The 499th BS's original operations officer (and later commanding officer), Capt. (later major) Julian B. Baird, recalled postwar that it was while the squadron was in training in the USA that the idea of a bomb-riding bat heading out of the flames of hell came to him as the squadron emblem. He had Michalowski add the *"LUCKY BAT"* name and an appropriate insignia to both sides of the nose of this B-25 at Waterboro AFB, South Carolina, and the design on the RHS, slightly different from that on the LHS, was later submitted to higher authority and subsequently approved as the squadron emblem. Baird subsequently flew the B-25 to Australia and later on some missions; the nickname *"the Chief"* referred to him. *"LUCKY BAT"* was subsequently converted to a strafer at the Townsville Air Depot and returned to the squadron around September or October 1943, with the converted nose and new nose markings with four .50-caliber machine guns in the bat's mouth and, as Baird put it, the bat's "wings folded back along the side." The new look is shown in the photo below. The third photo shows Lt. Howard F. Rhode with squadron signage, date and place unknown. The text on the sign reads *BATS OUTA HELL! BOMB SQUADRON*. Rhode and his crew were killed in a night-flying exercise accident on May 9, 1944, while based at Nadzab.

Unidentified BS, 38th BG

North American B-25, unidentified serial number, artist unknown. This unidentified B-25, thought to be from a 38th BG squadron since other photos that came with this one were identifiable as such, has a long snouted creature with exposed teeth as nose art. It is the only such photo seen by the author, but further information is currently not known. The location is suspected to be Durand strip (also known as Waigani and 17 Mile) at Port Moresby.

NOSE ART OF THE 5TH AIR FORCE

Unnamed North American B-25s, unidentified serial numbers, artist(s) unknown. These two different photos, taken from similar positions, show the bat nose insignia at different, although undated, stages of the squadron's history ca. 1943–44. Note the differences in everything from mouth shape, eyeball and teeth size, eyebrow emphasis, and wing shape and detail. Whether or not either of these B-25s was named is unknown, since 499th Squadron airplane names usually appeared only on the bomber's LHS.

While there were many representations of the nude female form on display in off-duty facilities throughout US military camps in the SWPA (and elsewhere), the 499th BS was so pleased with their lucky-bat nose art that this work was commissioned late in 1943 for the officers club. It featured squadron B-25s in action over the Salamaua Isthmus, scene of many squadron battles midyear (before, in fact, the lucky-bat nose art was introduced!). Having their photo taken with the artwork here are the Loverin brothers, Wes and Orlen, with Lt. Charles L. Banz sitting at right. By chance, both the Loverins were based in the Port Moresby area at the time; Orlen served with the 499th BS, while Wes was a fighter pilot with the 36th FS, 8th FG. Orlen Loverin, however, together with his copilot, navigator, twenty-four other passengers, plus a four-man crew, all lost their lives on December 19, 1943, when the 22nd TCS C-47 they were aboard traveling to Sydney exploded in midair north of Rockhampton, Queensland. The photo below is a close-up of the underside of the nose seen in the larger image, and provides a contemporaneous impression as to how the lucky-bat insignia looked below the nose.

276

1943 Fighters

39th FS, 35th FG

A fine view of squadron number 19 (unidentified serial number) and its shark's-mouth engine cowlings. The P-38 features ca. 1942-style national markings, which remained in vogue on P-38s until around mid-1943. While the photo is undated, the squadron swapped its P-38s for P-47s late in the year, a diary entry indicating that the last P-38s left on November 21, 1943.

Regina I (42-12654, squadron number 30), and *REGINA II* (unidentified serial number, squadron number 16), two of Lt. Paul M. Stanch's planes, both of which were named after his wife (an internet check indicates that Stanch married Regina C. Wright in "about 1942"), but the officer in the earlier photo, taken in January 1943, is not Stanch but Lt. Richard C. Suehr. In the course of 185 combat missions in the SWPA, Stanch claimed ten enemy aircraft shot down; in the photo of *REGINA II*, nine victory symbols can be seen (Stanch's eighth and ninth enemy aircraft claims were two "Oscars" on September 22, 1943). *Regina I, US Signal Corps 168886 via Edward Rogers*

1944–45 Bombers

13th BS, 3rd BG

SCOTCH and SODA, Douglas A-20, 42-86568, artist unknown. Worthy of a passing mention in this chapter is the reintroduction of "the Grim Reapers" unit insignia on at least some of the 13th BS's A-20s as a nose insignia in 1944. Known affectionately as "Oscar," the insignia had been seen first on SPAD fighters of the 13th Aero Squadron in 1917–18 and was officially approved in 1924. It took a back seat in the early Pacific war years, but following the use of the name for the entire 3rd BG in the B-25 era sometime in 1943 (*see sign photo*), it is thought to have been reintroduced as a nose insignia ca. February 1944 specifically for the 13th BS, by the then squadron CO, Capt. Theodore G. Fitch. This was probably in response to other fearsome nose art that Fitch saw in the SWPA. *SCOTCH and SODA* was a well-used 13th BS A-20 by the time this photo was taken, with probably more than seventy missions notched, but the four-row bomb log is hard to make out in this photo due to the camera angle. Capt. C. J. Krayenbuhl was the assigned pilot at the time.

71st BS, 38th BG

Unnamed North American B-25, unidentified serial number, artist unknown. A late-war photo of the LHS of a camouflaged 71st BS B-25 with both a pin-up and the wolf's-head "Wolf Pack" squadron insignia can be found in chapter 2 (see *Emergency STRIP*), but here is the RHS of another 71st BS strafer, noticeably different because it is in NMF. This and two other photos that appear toward the end of this chapter are the only shots in the entire volume showing frontline B-25s that are not camouflaged; there was an official instruction issued in March 1945 that decreed that A-20, A-26, and B-25 aircraft destined for use by Far East Air Force (which included the 5th AF) would continue to use camouflage, but it seems that very late in the war, some localized decisions led to a small number of B-25s being stripped of camouflage in theater.

90th BS, 3rd BG

BARRY'S BABY, Douglas A-20, 42-86768, artist unknown. The 90th BS went into action for the first time with its A-20s on December 9, 1943, but it may have taken a while for shark's-teeth noses to be added, and just how widespread the practice was is not known. Certainly, photos of shark-nosed A-20s are uncommon; only one other is included in this work (see *Butch* in chapter 2). *BARRY'S BABY* was damaged as a result of a forced landing on April 16, 1944 ("Black Sunday"), but was repaired. It was subsequently assigned to Lt. Harold R. Prince, whose name can be seen below the cockpit side window, and this may be the last photo taken of *BARRY'S BABY* since it had to be ditched at sea between the Admiralty Islands and New Guinea on May 14, 1944, due to mechanical problems. Prince did not survive the ditching; aged only twenty-three, he was already a seventy-three-mission veteran and had been serving in New Guinea for fifteen months. Note the incomplete teeth markings following the earlier nose repairs, with the lack of interest (or available time, perhaps) in reinstating them suggesting to the author that they were not regarded as highly as other fearsome squadron markings covered in this chapter.

320th BS, 90th BG

SALVO, Consolidated B-24, 42-73122, artist unknown. This great photo was one of a number taken by aerial photographer Paul S. Seamon of the 67th TCS from a C-47 after a chance encounter midflight while both planes were returning from their different missions. Their destination was probably Nadzab; the 67th TCS was based there from November 1943, while the 320th BS moved there in February 1944. Note how the teeth and mouth on this B-24 are much more detailed than the style painted on *MOBY DICK*, seen earlier, and how the upper row of teeth extends over the side of the nose turret. This may have been an interim version of the marking replaced by that seen below. The other nose art on the B-24 is a caricature of an eagle disposing of Axis leaders Hitler and Tojo. The name *SALVO* appears directly below the middle of the eagle.

Unnamed Consolidated B-24, unidentified serial number, artist unknown. This angle shows well how the mouth and teeth discussed above look from a partly side-on, partly nose-on vantage point. This photo filtered down to me from my late father's small wartime photo collection, and I suspect, therefore, that the location was Morotai Island and the date sometime in 1945, but no other details are known.

a snappin' 'n' a bitin' and unnamed Consolidated B-24, 42-72949 (*a snappin'*) and unidentified serial number, artist(s) unknown. These two photos show 320th BS B-24s with similar-style squadron markings that extend to the top of the back of the nose turret. As will be seen in the group of photos that follow, though, this style was subsequently simplified on the 320th's NMF B-24s. The named B-24 was that assigned to Lt. (later captain, then major) John W. Kline. Kline was able to keep a pet bulldog in New Guinea, and it was a likeness of this animal ripping the seat out of an enemy soldier's trousers that was initially painted on the nose of his airplane; the teeth and mouth were added later, although just when is not currently known. Kline became squadron CO from March to July 1944, and it seems likely that this photo dates from that period. As for the unnamed B-24, because of the absence of armament it is suspected that this photo was taken following the end of the war, in which case it confirms that not all the "Moby Dick" squadron B-24s were stripped of camouflage beforehand. The location is suspected to be Biak. For a photo of *a snappin' 'n' a bitin'* at Biak postwar, stripped of both its camouflage and nose art, see chapter 7.

the BOISE BRONC, and *OLD IRON SIDES*, Consolidated B-24s, 44-40728 (*BRONC*) and 42-110053 (*IRON SIDES*), artist unknown. Shot from similar angles, these two photos show some differences between the mouths painted on these two B-24s: that on *OLD IRON SIDES* is opened wider and has some bigger (and sharper?) exposed teeth, but there are fewer in the upper row and more in the lower row. Note also the red inside outline of *OLD IRON SIDES* mouth, which is absent from the *BRONC*'s mouth painting. *OLD IRON SIDES* was assigned to the 320th BS around May 1944, and *the BOISE BRONC* came later, but chances are that the mouth and teeth were added around the same time (early 1945?), since it seems that 42-110053 was originally camouflaged (this is suggested by the reapplied, simplified ID stencil, and the late addition of the name over the 142 mission bomb log. It is thought that this B-24 was credited with around 150 missions by war's end.

DISPLAY OF ARMS, Consolidated B-24, 44-41478 (unconfirmed), artist unknown. Taken at Garbutt airfield, Queensland, immediately postwar, this is the second of two photos of what the author suspects to be the same plane but from different sides, which came from the same photo album (the other photo appears in chapter 2). It is known that "478" participated in the 90th BG's last bombing mission of World War II, flown on July 24, 1945, but little more. Note that while the vertical stabilizer, rudder, and nose-top antiglare panel paintwork have suffered significant fading and wear and tear, the mouth and teeth markings still appear to be in good condition, again suggesting a more recent application.

Unnamed Consolidated B-24, unidentified serial number ending in 5 (possibly 44-42385), artist unknown. The M-model B-24s, such as this one, were the last to see wartime service, and thus this example was one of the last of 320th BS's planes to wear the "Moby Dick" squadron markings. Nevertheless, the look remains virtually the same as others in this chapter, without the red inside edging of the mouth. The serial quoted above is of the only B-24 with a serial number ending in 5 of the last six flown back to the US by the 320th BS ca. November 1945.

386th–389th BSs, 312th BG

An early and later view of the original unofficial 312th BG insignia, which undoubtedly had its origins in what was seen being added to the vertical stabilizers of the 90th BG's B-24s by the end of 1943: the so-called Jolly Roger insignia, seen earlier in this chapter. The 312th's version was confined to the nose only and, while much smaller, was painted around the forward-firing guns of their Douglas A-20s, with two guns sticking out of the eye socket areas in the skull, the other two in the top ends of the crossed bones. The nose insignia in the photo, above, was one of the first, if not the first, to be added and appeared on A-20G serial number 43-9038 that had been assigned to the 388th BS in February 1944 which later carried a pin-up named

Rough Stuff! (see photo in chapter 2). The close-up of the later version shows how the insignia evolved to a more hardened look. While the crossed bones in both photos look similar, the nose is no longer present, the mouth is bigger, and there are missing teeth and a less-than-happy look, more in keeping with what was probably the desired result. As mentioned in chapter 2, by August 1944 the 312th BG were calling itself the "ROARIN '20s," and a new group insignia was designed to promote that name, but the earlier nose tip skull marking was still in general usage, it seems.

405th BS, 38th BG

Unnamed North American B-25, 43-28025, artist unknown. A rare overall view of this B-25, which served with the 405th from September 1944 until it was lost due to engine failure and a subsequent ditching in the East China Sea on July 28, 1945. Another B-25 that was shepherding 025 back to Yontan at the time reported that one crew member survived the rough water landing and that emergency supplies were dropped, but shortage of fuel necessitated a return to base after orbiting the scene for an hour and three-quarters. When a search party returned later, there was no sign of any survivors; the fate of the six crew members remains unknown (this was the squadron's second-to-last B-25 lost with crew members killed or missing and believed killed). Note the camera nose bulge on the closest B-25. The serial number of this plane is believed to have been 43-28088, which was, indeed, a 405th BS plane in use from September 1944 until a forced landing in China on March 20, 1945. On this occasion, though, it is thought that all the crew survived.

Unnamed North American B-25s, artist(s) unknown. "Green Dragon" B-25s lined up on Yontan airfield, Okinawa, in November 1945 as the unit was preparing to move to Japan as part of the US occupation force. This view, an official photo, suggests that the squadron insignia was applied uniformly (it may have been the photographer's aim to give this impression), but a LHS view confirms that the mouth and teeth shapes on individual aircraft were not so similar after all. The second B-25 in this lineup is 44-30921, which had been assigned to the 405th only in July 1945.

498th BS, 345th BG

Unnamed North American B-25s, unidentified serial number (*right*) and 44-29597 (*above*), artist(s) unknown. Here we see two late-war photos of the impressive falcon's-head squadron insignia. Tail number 597 was assigned to the 498th BS in May 1945 and survived the war; for a postwar photo of it after conversion to a fast transport and the stripping back of its wartime paint and markings, see chapter 7.

499th BS, 345th BS

The Wilda Marie, North American B-25, 41-30016, artist unknown. Seen here in the flesh and as part of a surrender leaflet, whether the choice of this "Bats Outa Hell" B-25 for the leaflet was intentional or not is not known, but it could well have been, since it has been noted that in many cases, artwork rather than photos was used on such leaflets. This B-25 had been in 499th BS hands from around March 1943 and, prior to the addition of the bat insignia, had been named *"TIGER LADY"* (a photo of her can be found earlier in this volume). It was transferred out of the squadron in August 1944 as war weary. *Via David Hopton*

Unnamed North American B-25, 44-29600, artist unknown. Scanned from a 1945 print taken from the original K-21 camera negative of the April 6 convoy escort attack by the 345th BG off the China coast, this well-known photo was captioned as follows when it appeared in a lengthy article on the 5th AF's antishipping successes in the June 1945 issue of the official Army Air Forces confidential *Impact* magazine: "[An] Air Apache, its savage snout gleaming with warpaint, makes one of the opening bomb runs." This was the second of three vessels attacked, and, in fact, the 501st attacked first, with one B-25 scoring a direct hit amidships, which destroyed the funnel. The 499th BS was second over the target, with 43-36205 scoring another direct hit amidships, which sealed the ship's fate. The B-25 in the photo was flown by Lt. Francis A. Thompson, who had to be content with strafing the vessel since "205" was in a better position to carry out the bombing attack.

DIRTY DORA, North American B-25, 41-12971, artist unknown, and *"DIRTY DORA" II*, North American B-25, 41-30276, artist unknown. The first *DORA* (said to have been named after a certain Aussie girl from Sydney) was a 405th BS, 38th BG original that was in action in New Guinea by early 1943. It was subsequently transferred to the 71st BS and from there flown to the Townsville Air Depot for strafer conversion midyear. The photo above was probably taken at the air depot, but on an earlier occasion. In August 1943, with the modification work completed, she was assigned to the 499th BS, and, after the bat nose insignia was added, the original name was reapplied in much the same style and position as the original, but without the quotation marks. *DORA* became one of the best known of the 499th's strafers thanks to long service (until the end of August 1944, but out of action from February to April due to nosewheel repairs) and her "punchy" name. The photo showing the impressive bomb log is most likely to have been taken late in 1943; later the "lucky bat" was repainted in a lighter shade of blue, and the name was reapplied for the third time. The assigned pilot for much of *DORA*'s glory days had been Lt. (later captain) Victor W. Tatelman, who left the squadron to be sent home in March 1944. Following his return to the SWPA later in the year as a radar countermeasures (RCM) expert, it was explained in the exhaustive 345th BG history *Warpath across the Pacific* that "Tatelman convinced his superiors at 5th Air Force to let him equip a B-25 which could home in on Japanese radar sites." The B-25 he selected was 41-30276, which had been pensioned out of the 345th BG in April 1944 and then served with the 312th BG until January 1945. During that earlier period, this B-25 had been named *SIR BEETLE* and had completed more than sixty missions, after which it had been passed to a service squadron. From there it was stripped of most of its paint, although its *SIR BEETLE* name, artwork, and bomb log were retained for a while, even after an eight-gun nose conversion was completed. When the decision was made that Tatelman's old squadron, the 499th, would be responsible for "support and maintenance," though, it returned to service as its *"DIRTY DORA" II*, complete with updated lucky-bat squadron insignia as shown in the third photo.

The MARGARET HAYNE, North American B-25, 41-30274, artist unknown. Despite the photographer being more interested in capturing an informal image of the unidentified men in this late 1944 photo rather than the nose art, it also shows well the wing detail being applied to 499th B-25s at this stage. *The MARGARET HAYNE* was one of two former 38th BG D-model strafers assigned to the 499th at the end of August 1944, both of which were transferred out only weeks later (in October) following receipt of the first B-25Js. The name under the cockpit window ledge is that of assigned pilot W. P. Jenkins.

Unidentified North American B-25, unidentified serial number, artist unknown. Recognizable as a late-war B-25J model by the blind-landing antenna on the top of the nose, this would probably have been among the last of the ninety plus of these aircraft to pass through the 499th's hands in the course of the squadron's two and a half years of wartime existence. The extensive research that went into the 345th BG history *Warpath across the Pacific* concluded that postwar, "most of the aircraft were transferred out to other units, and the few that remained were pushed off the cliff at Ie Shima." This B-25 is suspected to have been one of the postwar survivors, and it may have been one of those flown to Korea in a flag-waving exercise in early September 1945 (note that armament is still fitted). Of interest regarding the markings, note that by this time, the mouth and eye/eyebrow shapes of the 499th BS's bat insignia seem to have been somewhat standardized, but there were still lots of variations to the bat's wing shape and composition. In addition, this is the only photo seen by the author showing wear and tear to the black paint that had represented the wing area. Note, too, a possibly repainted section that has partly covered the lower outline of the wing. Another variation is that there appears to be no outline to the bat's head. Midfuselage below the open cockpit window is what may be a small name, but, unfortunately, it cannot be made out.

Betty's DREAM, North American B-25, 44-30934, artist unknown. On August 19, 1945, it fell to three pairs of B-25s from the 345th BG to rendezvous with and guide two Japanese transports (the Japanese version of the DC-3 was specified, but Type 1 land-based bombers, known to the Allies as the "Betty," were used instead), making for Ie Shima with a Japanese surrender delegation on board. For the delegation, this was the first leg of their journey to Manila to arrange the Japanese surrender with the Allied powers. Also involved in the mission were a top cover of P-38s and a 6th ERS OA-10A and airborne lifeboat-equipped B-17G. The B-17 was ordered to an orbit point from which the pilot was to follow the Japanese once they passed, which, apparently, did not prove difficult, but only one pair of the B-25s found the two enemy aircraft, which were by then, reportedly, "at the wrong altitude, in the wrong place and off course!" This historic photo was taken of *Betty's DREAM* from the accompanying B-25 (unnamed 498th BS 43-28115), with one of the Japanese bombers (ordered to be painted all white and feature only green crosses as markings for ready identification) and the B-17 in the background with P-38s overhead. *Betty's DREAM* had been assigned to the 499th only in June 1945 and, in the brief time before hostilities ended, had flown twenty-two missions and claimed two enemy vessels sunk. Note across the stabilizer and rudder the striking "Air Apaches" group insignia, and above that, the airplane's prominent tail number, 0934.

500th BS, 345th BG

Unnamed North American B-25, 41-30051, artist unknown. A survivor of early 500th Squadron missions the B-25 seen in these two photos was one of three that are known to have featured sailfish as nose art. This came about thanks to the 1939 hit song, "Three Little Fishies" about three young fish who escape the wall of their dam and make it out into the open sea where danger awaited them. Three B-25 crews in training together at Savannah, Georgia, could see the parallel between this story and their own and had sailfish (a strong fighting fish rather than the baby fish in the song) painted on their planes as well as names adopted from a line from the song (the line was "Boop-Boop Dit-Tem Dot-Tem What-Tem Chu" according to the 1939 Brunswick Recording version). Perhaps because no sheet music was available, though, what should have been *BOOP BOOP* became *BOOM BOOM* as seen at top. Note also in this photo the claim for an enemy plane destroyed. That action occurred on October 12, 1943, but four days later the B-25 was damaged in the course of a massed 5th AF attack against Wewak by all four squadrons of the 345th BG. Sent south for repairs, when *BOOM BOOM* did return in early 1944 the lower photo, dated September 1944, shows how it looked, minus the sailfish and name but with a sharkmouth added. Along with two other 500th BS old-timers "51" was declared "war weary" in October 1944.

822nd BS, 38th BG

The 822nd, initially equipped with B-25Gs, flew their first mission in October 1943, but it seems unlikely that the squadron insignia, created by TSgt. Fred Miller, followed quickly, perhaps not before the beginning of 1944. These views show how that insignia, which was wrapped around the entire nose, looked on two of the more than thirty B-25Gs used by the squadron. The early example (*at right*) is 41-64837 but lacks the yellow squadron identification band across the bottom of the vertical stabilizer and rudder. The taxiing B-25 is unidentified, but its yellow squadron identifier across the bottom of the vertical stabilizer and rudder can seen to be in place.

FEARSOME NOSE ART

The photo above, although taken from a distance, still gives a good impression of how the "Black Panthers" wraparound insignia looked from ground level. *Right*, in early 1944, directly or indirectly, all former 408th BS, 22nd BG B-25Ds bombers were transferred to the 38th BG, four of them being received by the 822nd BS (two of these were *THE BEAST* and *BLONDE BOMBER*, photos of which can be found in chapter 2). This "Black Panther" is suspected to have been one of them, but it seems that because they were not strafers, they were of limited use to the squadron, and all were transferred out for second-line duties by September. Note that the unit insignia was painted below the cockpit on these planes because of the glazed nose.

With the introduction of the B-25J model, with its different spread of guns, a new style of "Black Panthers" unit insignia was designed for the space available. The photo at left is a very good close-up of that insignia on a named but unidentified camouflaged B-25J, while the slightly blurred view below (taken at Morotai) is interesting since it shows that while most 5th AF B-25s remained camouflaged, there was the odd late-war exception. This B-25 seems to have a tail number of 3919, but its identity has yet to be confirmed. Noteworthy in this photo are the black lower portion of the vertical stabilizer and rudder (a squadron identification that had originally been yellow on camouflaged 822nd BS B-25s), and the noticeably faded anti-glare panel. *Morotai photo via Ken Merrick*

823rd BS, 38th BG

Unnamed North American B-25s, 42-64853 and 42-64855, artist unknown. Two clear overall photos of these "Terrible Tigers" B-25s that served together in the 823rd BS from around April 1944 until August–September 1944 (42-64853 had earlier served with the 405th BS). Note the shooting-star insignia, probably derived from the 5th AF insignia, on the vertical stabilizer of 42-64853, and evidence of some other marking, since painted over, on the LHS rudder of 42-64855. Both B-25s were among 38th BG B-25Gs subsequently transferred to the 345th BG, with 853 going to the 498th BS and 855 to the 501st BS, but with the receipt of the first B-25Js by the 345th ca. September–October, all these older strafers were declared war weary within a short space of time.

Bugs Bunny, A B-25J-model assigned to the 823rd, ca. October 1944, for most of its wartime service this strafer featured just the name LITTLE PRINCESS De Anna on the LHS and the squadron insignia. As such, it flew at least sixty-five missions, which were recorded in groups of five in three rows of twenty, with the other five symbols being added between the nose insignia and name. Toward the end of the war, though (perhaps at the same time as the side guns were removed), the existing name was painted over, as was the bomb log, which was reproduced in a smaller area, and the B-25 returned to service as *Bugs Bunny*, as shown in this slightly blurred image. According to the research carried out for the *Sun Setters of the Southwest Pacific Area* volume, *Bugs* flew only another eight missions before the war ended.

"Mary" and *TEE-KAY*, North American B-25s, *"Mary"* unidentified serial number, *TEE-KAY* 42-64817 (unconfirmed), artists unknown. These three close-ups of named 823rd BS B-25s, showing the front and LHS of *"Mary"* and RHS of *TEE-KAY*, reveal how the work of different artists led to different results. The artist responsible for *TEE-KAY* has opted for a more simplified finish with less detail and larger but fewer teeth, while the artwork on *"Mary"* has a lot more detail, including a greater number of smaller teeth, which have been given a rough, gnashed look. If *TEE-KAY* was, indeed, 42-64817, then it is interesting to note that it was transferred to the 498th BS, 345th BG, in August 1944, where the tiger's-head artwork would have been replaced by the 498th's falcon's head.

Tiger Lilly and unnamed North American B-25, unidentified serial numbers, artist(s) unknown. These two photos were taken using the same camera and were purchased together by the author in 2011. While these are nice close-ups of the "Terrible Tigers" nose art on these two B-25s, unfortunately there is little else known about the planes. The bomb log for *Tiger Lilly* reveals thirty-seven missions, but again this does not help identify her. Learning the short surname visible under the LHS cockpit window may have helped, but a close examination of the original photo has not narrowed it down conclusively. As for the second plane, note how an old, unidentified artwork has been painted out to make way for the 823rd insignia.

Other 5th Air Force "Toothy" Nose Art

"BOB'S ROBIN", Curtiss P-40, ET196 (unconfirmed), artist unknown, 9th FS, 49th FG. This photo, taken at RAAF Station Darwin in June 1942, has been seen before but shows well the shark's-mouth painting on this P-40, which was one of the first in the SWPA so marked. This was not a squadron marking, though, just a whim on the part of the assigned pilot, Lt. Bob Vaught (his pet name for it appeared on both sides of the fuselage, adjacent to the cockpit), but in this photo it is not Vaught standing by the cockpit but a fellow squadron member, Lt. Andrew J. Reynolds. Both men survived the war and continued to serve in the USAF postwar, but they subsequently died at relatively young ages; Reynolds was fifty-nine, Vaught sixty. *Australian Department of Information*

EAGER BEAVER, Lockheed P-38, 44-23527 (unconfirmed), artist unknown, 432nd FS (unconfirmed), 475th FG. Virtually nothing is known about this P-38 and its interesting nose art, which undoubtedly was inspired by what was seen on the noses of 38th and 345th BG B-25s. It is known, though, that the 432nd FS used squadron numbers in the range 140–169, and it is on that basis that this photo has been included. *EAGER BEAVER* ended the war on Biak. *Jim Trevor*

GERALDINE, Consolidated B-24, 42-41056, artist unknown, 403rd BS, 43rd BG. After the success of the 320th BS's whale's-mouth look, there seems to have been little interest among other 5th AF B-24 squadrons in following suit in some way, but here is one exception. Named only on its LHS (she was named after the wife of pilot Lt. Robert A. Sausville, who had married his high school sweetheart, Geraldine T. Marra, in 1942), this bloodthirsty B-24 (two blood drops can be seen dripping from the mouth, a look that was replicated on the LHS) served in New Guinea from late 1943 until April 1944 and flew at least forty-five missions before being "transferred out for unknown reason." The photo was taken at Jackson's Field, Port Moresby, but the identity of the pipe-smoking crew member is not known.

MOBY DICK JR, Piper L-4, unidentified serial number, artist unknown, unit(s) unidentified. Seen in other photos mostly from the RHS and usually in company with 320th BS B-24 *MOBY DICK*, here is an LHS view of this liaison airplane; note the apparent lack of a fuselage star on this side; it did, however, have one on the RHS! Close examination of the L-4's tail similarly suggests that its USAAF serial number is also lacking. It probably belonged to a service unit, but nothing further is currently known about *MOBY DICK JR*.

Stubborn Hellion, North American B-25, 42-32314, artist unknown, 500th BS, 345th BG. This artwork must rank as one of the most innovative to appear on any 5th AF aircraft, and although a horse is not considered a fearsome animal by most people, the overall look must have still been disconcerting, to say the least, to those enemy combatants, if any, who saw it (the squadron's "Rough Raiders" tail insignia, featuring a snorting mustang head, probably influenced the choice). Just how many missions it flew in this guise is not known, but what is known is that it was in 500th BS hands for only less than four months, initially being known as *SNAFU II*, before being lost following a low-level mission against Kavieng, New Ireland, on February 15, 1944. The name *Stubborn Stallion* would have been more in keeping with the artwork than *Stubborn Hellion* (the Merriam-Webster dictionary defines a hellion as "a troublesome or mischievous person"); perhaps *Stallion* was meant?

Unnamed/unidentified Curtiss C-46s, unidentified serial numbers, artist(s) unknown, 5th CCS, 2nd CCG. As with the B-24s of the 320th BS, C-46s were considered by some as having a whalelike shape. This led the 5th CCS to adopt a caricature of a flying sperm whale (inspired, perhaps, by "Monstro," the awesome whale in Walt Disney's 1940 animated film *Pinocchio*) as its unofficial squadron emblem. The lead C-46 in this late-war squadron lineup photo taken in the Philippines featured the emblem on the RHS of its nose at one stage, while the next in line, with a field number also in the X610–619 range, can be seen to have had a whale-look mouth and teeth nose art added (there is also a name on its nose, but it is unclear what that is). Despite the apparent damage to the photo, it has been reproduced here since it is the only one seen by the author of a 5th AF C-46 so marked.

Other Fearsome Animals Used as Nose Art Subjects

"Flying Wolf", Consolidated B-24, 42-41091, artist unknown, 403rd BS, 43rd BG. A relatively new B-24 when written off in New Guinea as a result of a forced landing on December 23, 1943, the wolf in this painting was not dissimilar in style to the artwork seen on 71st BS, 38th BG B-25s. Amazingly the remains of this B-24 lay in situ in the Ramu Valley, despite scrub fires and some sporadic visits by scrap dealers, until 1991, when it became the focal point for a Liberator restoration in Australia. A deal had been struck with the owner of a Liberator fuselage there that if a wing and tailplane could be found, he would make the fuselage available for restoration. With the assistance of many parties, most importantly the RAAF, provider of the main labor resource for the project, both the main plane and horizontal stabilizer were removed from *"Flying Wolf"* that same year and received in Melbourne, Victoria, in 1992. It took some time for the fuselage to be made available; it did not follow until 1995, and the process of mating the main plane to the fuselage could begin only after a lot of cleaning and preparatory work, all by volunteers, was completed. It was a proud day for all concerned on August 15, 2000, though, when, to quote the website of the restoration group (b24australia.com), "The mostly intact bomber was dedicated before an audience of 1,100." At the time of writing (2021–22), further work is being carried out to make the Liberator (RAAF serial number A72-176) as complete as possible.

Unnamed Curtiss P-40, unidentified serial number, artist unknown, 9th FS, 49th FG. One of the fiercest-looking 5th AF nose art paintings around in 1942—albeit, it seems, for only a short time—was this fire-eating dragon on 9th FS P-40 squadron number "85." The plane belonged to Lt. George Preddy, seen here with it, and had originally been named *TARHEEL*, but after a repaint due, perhaps, to damage inflicted in air-to-air combat on June 15, the P-40 came back to the squadron with the dragon nose art, a salute to Preddy's flight commander, Capt. Joseph J. Kruzel. While serving with the 17th Pursuit Squadron (Provisional) in the Java campaign in early 1942, Kruzel had his crew chief add a fiery dragon to the nose of the P-40 he was flying at the time, and a photo taken of that became the inspiration for the later work. On July 12, 1942, though, in a four-ship training flight south of Darwin, P-40s 85 and 87 collided in midair, leading to the death of Lt. John Sauber, injuries to Lt. Preddy, and the loss of both planes. *USAF*

"SCORPION", Consolidated B-24, 41-24073, artist unknown, 319th BS, 90th BG. An uncommon choice for a nose art subject was this huge, yellow, bomb-wielding scorpion, but given that between November 1942 and February 1943 the 90th BG was based in northern Australia, where scorpions have a reputation for being larger and more venomous than in other parts of the continent, it seems likely that finding one (or more!) of these "critters" led to the decision to have one added to the nose of this B-24. *"SCORPION"* went on to serve in New Guinea until a forced landing near Finschafen on September 6, 1943; a photo of the nose after that incident can be found in the following chapter.

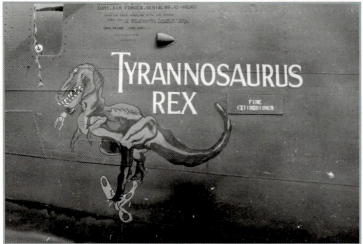

TYRANNOSAURUS REX, Consolidated B-24, 42-40363, artist unknown. 400th BS, 90th BG. Seen here early on, prior to the addition of a bomb log, this "T. Rex" survived many frontline missions to be pensioned off to the CRTC at Nadzab in 1944. It is the only 5th AF bomber known to have featured a dinosaur as nose art (at a time when dinosaurs did not enjoy the widespread popularity that they do today) and was a good example of how those who suggested and painted it saw American strength over Japanese forces (note the trampled Japanese fighter under the creature's clawed feet, and its pilot with little chance of escape). Another "Rex" nose art painting made an appearance ca. the late 1980s on a Boeing B-52 (serial number 59-2587) named *STRATOFORTRESS REX*.

CHAPTER 7
What Happened to Them All?

Factory acceptance of combat airplanes for the Army Air Forces was more than four thousand per month over the January–August 1944 period and in excess of three thousand per month from September 1944 to May 1945. With the end of the war in Europe, airplane production began to slow down, but it was thought by most observers that the war in the Pacific would go on for years. With the A-bombing of Hiroshima and Nagasaki in August 1945, though, World War II ended, and all of a sudden not only were there were huge numbers of unneeded planes requiring some form of disposal, but there were fewer service personnel to undertake work on them. That the reduced numbers of men led to more planes being junked is confirmed in the September 1945 entry for the 374th Air Service Squadron, which states, "Seven planes were returned to the Pool for salvage as not being fit to expend man hours to put them in flying condition."

Heading photo. B-25 medium bombers as far as the eye can see, photographed at Clark Field, Luzon, in March 1946, the official caption for this photo referring to them as "now excess aircraft" in storage! With no interest in them, however, they all were eventually salvaged. The closest B-25, serial number 43-27886, was a former 41st BS, 501st BG (13th AF) plane named *LET'S FACE IT* with pin-up by Jack Kellogg, based on Alberto Vargas's gatefold from the April 1944 *Esquire* magazine. Behind it, *middle of photo*, is a former 405th BS, 38th BG B-25J-6 with serial number beginning 43-28xxx, a rare survivor of that subtype, more than twenty of which had been assigned to the "Green Dragons." *Official Army Air Forces photo*

So many of the 5th AF's wartime airplane types—A-20s, B-25s and older B-24s, C-46s and C-47s, P-38s and P-47s—were phased out over 1945–46 and were later scrapped. B-24s were now considered obsolete and were to be replaced by Boeing B-29s; they quickly disappeared from the 5th's inventory, some of the better ones being flown back to the US for possible disposal but otherwise left in open-air storage at such locations as Clark Field in the Philippines and on Biak Island, in the then Dutch New Guinea, until their fate was decided.

Of all the locations, from northern Australia to Ie Shima, where the 5th AF had been based and condemned and wrecked airplanes had been left, the most famous was Nadzab, near Lae. Australian radio (and later TV) personality Keith Smith (1917–2011) had been sent to Lae prior to the end of the war to serve in an Australian Army Amenities Service radio station there and, hearing stories of stocks of beer said to have been "hastily bulldozed into the ground" at Nadzab, paid a visit to the base with friends soon after the war ended. "It was an eerie experience," he later wrote:

> The buildings were deserted, the vast landing strips silent and billions-of-dollars-worth of fighters and bombers and equipment abandoned, left high and dry by the passing tide of war.
>
> Acres and acres of spare parts, wings, fuselages, undercarts, engines, armament... hundreds of crates not even opened. Yesterday, they had been catalogued, tabulated, enumerated, serviced, and today they were so much junk, fit only for pots and pans.

After climbing inside some of the planes there, Smith and his friends got back in their jeep "without looking for the beer and quit the place. It was just another 'victory garden' illustrating the appalling waste, not of men this time, but machines" (Keith Smith, *World War II Wasn't All Hell* [Surry Hills, Australia: Hutchinson Australia, 2010], 187).

Appendix 3 provides another Australian view of Nadzab's wartime leftovers, and one particularly relevant to this study, since it was written in 1945 and concentrates on the pin-up bomber nose art seen there at the time.

As a testament to the expense and waste of war, it is hard not to think about the Consolidated B-32 story. With a production cost, as stated by the War Department, of $790,000 each, only nine reached the Pacific, of which four were written off in theater. The other five were returned to the US postwar, where they joined 119 other new and slightly used B-32s subsequently put up for disposal, but since there was no interest in them, they were later smelted down. Most used former frontline planes suffered the same ignominious end.

As mentioned in the introduction, many B-24s were also returned to the US postwar, but for those with pin-up nose art, it seems that with only a few exceptions, anything considered too risqué was cleaned up or removed completely en route. The tacit approval given to risqué nose art in theaters of war outside the US was, as *Playboy* magazine's Hugh Hefner later pointed out, "dismissed as smut on the home front."

The main location where former frontline B-24s were left postwar was Kingman Army Air Field, Arizona. In a survey of airplanes to be disposed of, carried out across America during the week of January 24, 1946, out of a total of 5,531 unwanted B-24s, 2,396 were at Kingman. Other bases where large numbers of this bomber type could be found were Altus, Oklahoma (1,272), and Walnut Ridge, Arkansas (1,148).

This chapter looks at not only some of the aircraft that made it to these "boneyards" at home and abroad, but wartime losses and other examples where the original nose art changed significantly.

a snappin' 'n' a bitin', Consolidated B-24 (see chapter 6). Stripped of camouflage and markings, proof that this was the former *a snappin' 'n' a bitin'* (now with altered "Moby Dick" whale's-mouth squadron markings) is provided by the inclusion of the last three digits of the plane's serial number on the nose. This photo, with former 43rd BG B-24 *RUPTURED FALCON* in the background still in camouflage, but now with altered name, was taken on Biak postwar. *Official Army Air Forces photo*

BACHELOR MADE, North American B-25 (see chapter 2). This former bomber with service both in the 22nd and 345th BGs went on to lose its armament and camouflage to become *HARDSHIPS 2nd*, as shown here, in late 1944 as 38th BG's "fat cat" aircraft, with an insignia combining the group's four squadrons: the 71st, 405th, 822nd, and 823rd. It was on strength of 405th BS until May 1945, subsequent fate unknown.

BAIL-OUT Belle, Consolidated B-24 (see chapter 2). The *Belle* artwork and name appeared on both sides of the nose of this B-24, as did the bomb log. Around October–November 1944, though, both bomb logs were moved farther aft, with some of the space where the log had been on the LHS being taken up by the addition of the 529th BS insignia, a young Native American brave holding a toy B-24. This B-24 was the only ship in the squadron to carry the squadron insignia like this. After its service in Australia, it has been reported that Belle flew no further missions (sixty-four missions show on the bomb log, of which website 380th.org documents sixty), and she ended the war on Biak. As can be seen, by the time this photo had been taken, her days were numbered.

Bashful, North American B-25, 41-30772, artist unknown, Headquarters Squadron, 38th BG. Official records confirm that this stripped-down late-war B-25 with the abbreviated tail number was 41-30772, which had originally served in the 22nd BG as *Bashful* (see chapter 2). Later this plane went to the 823rd BS, 38th BG, where, as mentioned previously, the pin-up was, most likely, exchanged for the "Terrible Tigers" squadron markings. 41-30772 left the 823rd ca. September 1944 and was transferred to the 3rd BG, where it became the second B-25 to take on the *"FAT CAT"* name and an almost identical look. It was transferred to Depot No. 3 in July 1945.

BAYBEE, Consolidated B-24 (see chapter 2). While taking off from Guiuan, Samar, on February 22, 1945, the nosewheel tire of this B-24 blew out, the nosewheel leg collapsed, and she ground to a halt with a damaged nose. *BAYBEE* never flew again and was salvaged soon after.

Beautiful Beast, Consolidated B-24 (see chapter 2). On August 22, 1944, this B-24 was involved in a taxiing accident at Fenton in Australia's Northern Territory, and she was subsequently stripped of parts. As late as 1951, the bare fuselage, still with a portion of her nose art in place, remained in situ but it was subsequently scrapped. *Tom Cleary*

"The Blonde Bomber", Consolidated B-24 (see chapter 2). Given the extensive collection of 90th BG nose art images presented in this volume, it is fitting that the only overall B-24 photo found by the author showing one in the process of having its camouflage and markings being removed in the field is this view, dated August 1944, of this 90th BG bomber. Despite all the work necessary, this B-24's days seem to have been numbered; she was subsequently salvaged at Nadzab, no doubt without reinstatement of the nose art. One other change readily noticeable in the photo is the addition of the last three digits of the bomber's serial number (942) on the nose turret, a late-war identification added to B-24s to make it easier to single out individual airplanes while parked.

Bread Line in '49, Consolidated B-24 (see chapter 1). This B-24 suffered a hard landing in bad weather at Yontan, Okinawa, after the end of the war (exact date unrecorded; its last officially documented flight was on August 28, 1945), resulting in a buckled nose that led to the decision to salvage it as soon as practicable. In this slightly blurred photo, the damage to the nose is evident, as is the fact that salvage has probably already occurred, while fires evident in the background from the smoke that is visible may be from fires started in connection with the 380th BG getting ready to leave the area. Documentation covering the events of this period is not readily available, but it seems that the winding up of the famous "Flying Circus" Bomb Group had occurred by the end of September 1945.

"CHATTER BOX", North American B-25 (see chapter 6). *"CHATTER BOX"* is seen here in the swamp northwest of Port Moresby after its forced landing. As the 90th's combat log put it, "088 is in good shape but the task of getting in to this desolated [*sic*] swamp and bringing the plane out would not pay for the job involved." It was officially regarded as written off soon after.

THE DRAGON AND HIS TAIL, Consolidated B-24 (see chapter 2). Three more images of this widely known artwork: the first taken probably not long before the B-24's departure for the States ca. October 1945; the second awaiting its fate at Kingman, Arizona; the third a later B-24 masquerading as this most elaborately decorated of all B-24s. Note in the first photo how not only the armament has been removed, but the top turret as well, which reduced the B-24's weight considerably and made the forward section of the bomber safer if a water ditching on the long flight home occurred. Once it arrived back safely in the US, though, it was flown to Kingman Army Air Base and went the way of all other five-thousand-plus planes there, stripped of engines and later chopped up and smelted down into pots and pans. There seemed to have been genuine attempts to save the plane because of the artwork, but as well-known aviation photographer William T. Larkins (who actually saw it) succinctly wrote in his book *Surplus World War II US Aircraft*: "It was one of the last planes to be scrapped at Kingman and requests to save it failed." While Bartigian's artwork still looks to be in good condition in the second photo, the antiglare panel on top of the nose has now almost completely faded away. The rising popularity of World War II aircraft nose art in the 1990s saw the last flying B-24J in the world (serial number 44-44052, owned and operated by the Collings Foundation of Stow, Massachusetts; see also *TONDELAYO* below), repainted just like Bartigian's original and seen in the third photo. The artwork was relatively short lived, though (from 1998 until 2005), it being a little too bold for some spectators. The B-24 has since been put back into OD camouflage and now bears the name and (inoffensive) markings of *Witchcraft*, a famous 8th AF veteran of 130 missions.

The Dutchess, Douglas C-47 (see chapter 2). Following its 1946 sale, this C-47 was operated commercially in Alaska for around four years, then purchased by the Canadian government for its Department of Transport. Operated by the Canadians until 1995, toward the end of that time in the markings of the Canadian Coast Guard, it subsequently returned to the US, where it was initially owned by Odegaard Aviation and operated under registration N1XP. Ten years later it became the centerpiece for Duggy LLC, a charity aimed at stimulating young people's interest in aviation. At the time of writing, this veteran warbird, named *Duggy* and unmissable in overall bright-yellow finish with *The Smile in the Sky* in big letters above the cabin windows, is a rare airworthy survivor of 5th AF World War II service. *Graham Hustings*

Eager Lady, Douglas A-20, 44-240, artist unknown, 388th BS, 312th BG. Photographed postwar on Biak and from the same collection of photos as *a snappin' 'n' a bitin'*, KEEP IT UNDER YOUR HAT, "Miss Carriage", and READY TEDDY, also reproduced in this chapter, this A-20, reportedly received ca. May 1945, was the last 388th BS plane to be decorated with a name and nose art. Assigned to Capt. Earl L. Storch, did *Eager Lady* participate in sixty-seven missions prior to war's end, or was the bomb log simply carried forward from Storch's earlier plane, named *Sweet Louise* (serial number 44-223), which is known to have also participated in sixty-seven missions? Note the Waco CG-4 glider in the background; many of these had been shipped to the SWPA late in the war for possible use, which, in the end, did not eventuate (78 CG-4s were being held by IV ASAC as at the end of September 1944; others ended up at Nadzab; see Sgt. Ryland's article in appendix 3). *Official Army Air Forces photo*

FEATHER MERCHANT, North American B-25 (see chapter 6). As mentioned earlier, after service with the 90th BS, this B-25 was transferred to the 499th BS, 345th BG, initially as a strafer, later (ca. early 1944) as a stripped-down "fat cat" fast transport. This photo shows the nose of this B-25 with its bat squadron markings, but with a red trailing edge added, a feature that is believed to have been unique to this plane. Its "fat cat" role lasted until later in the year, when it was transferred to a service squadron and subsequently abandoned at Tadji, then an important Allied base on the north coast of New Guinea. In 1974, thirty years later, the incomplete airframe (with a tailplane added from the wreckage of another B-25) was recovered for local display as part of an agreement to permit the export of other World War II aircraft found at Tadji.

EMBARRASSED, Consolidated B-24 (see chapter 2). Of all the former 5th AF B-24s returned home, *EMBARRASSED* was the one, it seems, that the greatest amount of effort went into decorating for what was hoped would be a stateside war bond tour. As can be seen here, the crew has been fully identified, including where they were from, a good talking point, no doubt, had this B-24 been involved in war bond flights. Note too the impromptu 380th BG badge (the BG was nicknamed by unit members "The Flying Circus"). The bomb-throwing Donald Duck cartoon character (the insignia of the 531st BS) is suspected to have been added in wartime but, again, would have made a good talking point on any postwar bond publicity flights. On the RHS of the nose, to ensure that the public knew that this B-24 had seen service with the 5th AF, a large 5th AF badge was added adjacent to the pin-up. There was no war bond tour, though; *EMBARRASSED* flew only to Kingman, Arizona, perhaps with her pin-up already removed! The photo below has been seen before but remains a memorable image showing how the scrapping of these aircraft at Kingman was proceeding ca. 1947. Note how Donald Duck's sailor suit has visibly faded after, it seems, only two summers. Another 380th BG B-24 that was decorated with crew details for her long-awaited flight home was *Shy-Chi Baby*, a photo of which follows in this chapter. *Kingman photo, Jerry McLain via Steve Birdsall*

"Geronimo", Douglas C-47 (see chapter 4). Gifted by the 5th AF to the Commonwealth government for Australian airline use, 41-38668 subsequently became one of seven of these planes converted for their new role by Australian National Airways (ANA), work that began in 1944. A contemporaneous reference noted that "the conversion involved major structural changes to the fuselage," not only to remove the large cargo doors, but to rework the floor-supporting structure and install a toilet and "buffet compartments" and front and rear baggage compartments. In addition, the fitting of interior soundproofing, trim, ventilation, and twenty-four passenger seats was also required, and, not surprisingly, with nonmilitary materials scarce, this all took time, as a result of which the conversion was not completed until March 9, 1945. Registered VH-AEO for service with ANA, by June 1946, following charter to Guinea Airways, it was transferred to Trans-Australia Airlines, serving with this airline until sold to East-West Airlines in 1975. In the meantime, the plane had been converted again, this time for use as an aerial-survey aircraft and, in January 1958, was reregistered VH-DAS in conjunction with the commencement of what was to be a long-term lease by the South Australian Department of Lands. This photo was taken by the author at Adelaide's West Beach Airport ca. 1968; little did he know at the time that he was looking at a former 5th AF C-47 (while the astrodomes seen in this photo did suggest that this "DC-3" had seen previous military service, they, in fact, had been fitted only in 1957 as part of the conversion for aerial-survey work). VH-DAS was withdrawn from use in 1976 and offered for sale again the following year. The company that purchased the aircraft, however, ceased trading in 1981, as a result of which DAS sat around in a state of disrepair until leased for inactive use in the film *Sky Pirates*, in which it was repainted in USAAF wartime markings, with a fictitious serial number and field number, and with the name *Miss Fortune*. Following filming, the damaged airframe was moved to a scrapyard in Cairns but rescued from there and subsequently moved in July 1984 to become a tourist attraction as a supposed wartime crash site. It was still there, at what is now known as the Kuranda Koala Gardens, in 2019.

"GEORGIA PEACH", Martin B-26 (see chapter 2). After limited service with the 33rd BS, this B-26 was stripped of camouflage and its earlier markings, given a complete overhaul, and passed on to the 19th BS ca. September 1943, at some point (while at the Townsville Air Depot, perhaps) picking up the name *FURY* and the panther nose art seen here. *FURY* stayed with the 19th BS, the last of the 5th AF's B-26 squadrons, until January 1944, when it was flown south again, this time for scrapping.

gunmoll 2nd, Consolidated B-24 (see chapter 2). It seems likely to the author that when the camouflage on this B-24 was removed, the LHS pin-up and name went as well, but the RHS artwork was very carefully protected from damage and retained. It is suspected that when this photo was taken, the nose had been marked "WS" (although only the "S" is visible) for "Withdrawn from Service." This appears to have been an uncommon marking, but for another fully visible example, see the photo of P-47 *MARY-E* that follows.

"HELL'S BELLE", Consolidated B-24 (see chapter 2). As mentioned earlier, *"HELL'S BELLE"* was one of the first of nine B-24s passed on to the RAAF by the 5th AF for use as crew trainers. Whether her nose art was retained when received by the RAAF on February 22, 1944, or not is not currently known, but what is known is that her total flying time to the end of 1944 was 826 hours. On a dual instruction flight from the RAAF heavy-bomber operational training unit base at Tocumwal, New South Wales, on January 11, 1945, though, while in the throes of becoming airborne, the nosewheel suddenly collapsed and the B-24 hit the end of the runway before coming to rest as shown. Despite an official Court of Inquiry into the incident that dragged on for months, the cause of the collapse was never satisfactorily resolved, and the B-24, RAAF serial number A72-8, was subsequently written off. *RAAF Official*

HERE'S HOWE, North American B-25 (see chapter 2). While it has been suggested that this B-25 was shot down in error on Boxing Day 1943, here is proof that the cockpit section was still around, probably at Nadzab, much later (this photo was taken postwar). Until the serial number of this B-25 can be established, though, further comment is speculative. *Via Malcolm Long*

HOBO QUEEN II, Consolidated B-32 (see chapter 2). For purposes of comparison, two more views of this late-war very heavy bomber: *above*, at the end of her wartime service, with mission markers and revised nose art still looking bold and bright, while at right, taken from a similar vantage point as the first, but postwar, there is evidence of a damaged nose (note stressed panels and scratched bomb log) due to nosewheel retraction or collapse, which led to her subsequent salvage and scrapping on Okinawa. At left in the second photo is another example of the late-war "Hawkeye" unit insignia (see chapter 1) on 20th Reconnaissance Squadron F-7 tail number 2328 (serial number 44-42328).

JUGGLIN' JOSIE, Consolidated B-24 (see chapter 2). This B-24 of the 530th BS was being used by the 529th BS at Darwin, Northern Territory, on July 25, 1944, in a training role when she came to grief while landing. There were no injuries, but, as a result, it seems that this B-24 became the first in the Darwin boneyard (the 529th BS was the first of the 380th BG's squadrons to be based at Darwin). *R. P. "Ron" Nicholas*

JUNGLE QUEEN, North American B-25 (see chapter 2). Nadzab's fame as a bomber boneyard grew out of visits to the area after the previous occupiers, the 360th Air Service Group FEAF, moved on to the Philippines, but it had included a substantial salvage yard long before that. Wartime photos of the salvage area at Nadzab are uncommon, but here is one from ca. 1944 showing predominantly B-25s and A-20s "out to pasture." The B-25 at far right is *JUNGLE QUEEN*.

KEEP IT UNDER YOUR HAT, Douglas C-47 (see chapter 4). Note the protective covering over the windows of what is left of this C-47 and that in the background (similar protection was afforded other airplanes kept at Biak, presumably in reserve; see the photo of the unnamed A-20 that follows). Once the war ended, though, there was little reason to retain airplanes with no future such as these two C-47s. *Official Army Air Forces photo*

LiL' DEiCER II, Martin B-26 (see chapter 2). This B-26 was transferred out of the 408th BS ca. spring 1943 and is seen here at the Townsville Air Depot, stripped of camouflage and with new nose art named *MAD GREMLIN* in place. Adjacent to the tail gunner's position on at least one side (the LHS), there was the comment *SHOOT YOU'RE FADED*, in the same style of lettering as *MAD GREMLIN* in three separate lines below a pair of dice. The word "Gremlin" was already in common usage by 1943 as a general description for the cause of an unsourced aircraft serviceability issue and in this case was used, perhaps, due to this B-26's questionable reputation. The plane may have returned to the 22nd BG for "fat cat" duties, but details are currently unknown.

LUCKY [legs], Consolidated B-24 (see chapter 2). The original leggy artwork was removed following this B-24's transfer to the RAAF and was replaced by enlarged digits 11, taken from its new serial number, A72-11. One of three former 5th AF B-24s used by the RAAF that in February 1945 were ordered to be transferred back to the USAAF, A72-11 flew as far as Cooktown, Queensland, in April en route to Biak but was grounded there with fuel and engine problems. The RAAF was tasked with repairing the aircraft but initially lacked the required parts. Later inspections indicated more work was required, but once the war ended, it was decided that instead of repairing the old bomber, it would now be salvaged in situ, this work being undertaken by personnel of No. 6 Central Recovery Depot RAAF in December 1945. There was little left by the time they finished, but the engineless incomplete hulk was reportedly then dumped at sea. *Bob Talbot*

MARY-E, Republic P-47, unidentified serial number, artist unknown, unit(s) unidentified. The "W.S." lettering has nothing to do with the nose art, simply identifying the aircraft as "Withdrawn from Service." All that can be added is that the photo was purchased from an Australian source and, therefore, is considered most likely to have been taken in New Guinea.

Miscellaneous, Douglas C-47 (see chapter 4). Flown back to the US ca. August 1944 and put to use on war bond flights to publicize the C-47's two-year, two-thousand-plus hours of 5th AF service, the large pin-up seen in chapter 4 is believed to have been applied in its last days of its time in the SWPA and is suspected to have been short lived for many reasons, as already outlined. As a result, the pin-up was quickly painted out in a very rough fashion, using a clearly darker color. The C-47 is seen here doing a low pass over one of the Douglas plants (Santa Monica?) for the benefit of its employees. Note the prominent 5th AF tail insignia (probably added to both sides), the retention of its last known field number, and the addition of mission symbols not present in the earlier photo. *Miscellaneous* was subsequently disposed of but appears to have enjoyed only brief postwar commercial use. *McDonnell Douglas*

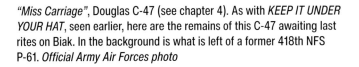

"*Miss Carriage*", Douglas C-47 (see chapter 4). As with *KEEP IT UNDER YOUR HAT*, seen earlier, here are the remains of this C-47 awaiting last rites on Biak. In the background is what is left of a former 418th NFS P-61. *Official Army Air Forces photo*

MISSIN' YOU, Consolidated B-24, 44-40399, artist unknown, 65th BS, 43rd BG. Perhaps surprisingly, this is the only known 5th AF bomber (and it was probably one of a very small number worldwide) to have expressed this sentiment. The pin-up was based on the Varga Girl that appeared in the then-latest issue of *Esquire* magazine, that of May 1944, but this B-24 served only briefly with the 43rd BG, around two months, after which its subsequent story is virtually unknown. As seen in this photo, though, it was already in an advanced stage of being salvaged in theater when this photo was taken.

Mortimer, North American B-25 (see chapter 6). On August 15, 1943, the 90th BS combat log proudly recorded that this B-25, as with *FEATHER MERCHANT* seen earlier in the chapter, originally built for the Dutch but taken over by the USAAF in Australia, and the oldest ship then in the squadron, had finally been "taken off combat status and returned to the mainland." It would seem that one of the Queensland-based air depots converted *Mortimer* for use on second-line duties, but outwardly, with the deletion of its earlier fearsome personal markings and mission and victory symbols, it became just another war-weary B-25 of largely unknown significance.

The MUSTANG, Boeing B-17 (see chapter 2). A last look at *The MUSTANG*, this time the LHS, looking very much the worse for wear after almost three years of USAAF service, most recently as a crew trainer in Kansas. This photo was taken at Albuquerque, New Mexico, where the B-17 was flown to await scrapping. Above the name *MUSTANG* can be seen a row of purple hearts, above which are a repeat of the same stencils symbolizing Japanese shipping claimed sunk (*middle*) and enemy aircraft claimed shot down (*top*), seen in the RHS photo included in chapter 2. These symbols, plus a bomb log painted on the RHS, were added to the bomber, apparently more in the interests of raising the profile of the 5th AF's role in the SWPA for the folks back home than being an accurate reflection of *The MUSTANG*'s actual combat career.

MY "Oklahoma" GAL, Boeing B-17, 41-2649, artist unknown, unit(s) unidentified. It is known that this B-17 began its USAAF service with 19th BG prior to being transferred to the 43rd BG, but it is not known to have been given a name or nose art during its time in the SWPA. As with *Ready Betty 'Gone Forever'* (see chapter 2) and, to a lesser extent, *The MUSTANG* (at left), this bomber had an exaggerated bomb log (in this case, very exaggerated, 203 missions expressed in six rows of thirty and the last of twenty-three; *The MUSTANG*'s bomb log was "only" 109 missions) and other symbols added to the LHS of the nose, and it seems likely that the nose art was added at the same time for effect! It has already been pointed out in numerous photo captions that after the war ended and bombers were returned to the US for disposal, much of the pin-up art did not survive, but planes returned during wartime such as this one would have, no doubt, been expected to have had some artwork in place, and if it did not exist already, it would not have taken too much effort to add something "appropriate"; that is, acceptable to the public at large. This photo was probably taken at Kelly Field, Texas, the enlarged "03" being the B-17's field number at the time. According to research for the 43rd BG history *Ken's Men against the Empire*, this B-17 was later transferred to a combat zone, in this case the Mediterranean, and survived the war to be salvaged after an accident at Goose Bay, Labrador.

naughty but nice, Boeing B-17 (see chapter 2). As mentioned in the caption to the wartime photo, there was only one crew member who survived the loss of this bomber—the navigator, Lt. José L. Holquin, and, with the help of the PNG Museum of Modern History's Bruce Hoy and local PNG enthusiast Brian Bennett, he revisited the crash site in 1982, with the intention of recovering remains of as many crew members as possible. Recovery of the remains did occur, but not until government assistance in 1984. On his 1982 trip, though, a damaged section of nose was turned over to reveal the pin-up picture, still mostly intact. Holquin later wrote, "How could she still look so nice after all those years?" That section of the nose was subsequently moved from the crash site and is now on display at the East New Britain Historical & Cultural Centre Kokopo Museum; this photo was taken in 2015. This is a rare example of 5th AF bomber pin-up nose art that survived World War II, albeit in a damaged state. *Mrs. Judi Ryan*

NOCTURNAL NEMESIS, Northrop P-61 (see chapter 3). This P-61 had been received by the 421st NFS in April 1944 and was written off after being damaged in a bombing raid at Tacloban in the Philippines in November. This photo, with the P-61's nose and other parts removed and sections of the side-mounted radar antenna missing, would seem to have been taken as a reminder of the pin-up artwork before the plane was unceremoniously pushed into a heap with other wrecks, an all-too-common fate for damaged airplanes on busy airstrips.

ONE TIME, Consolidated B-24, 41-11869, artist unknown, 319th BS, 90th BG. In this instance, the artwork appeared on the LHS while the name was on the RHS. This photo was taken at RAAF Station Darwin after the B-24 crash-landed there on the way home from a reconnaissance of Ambon on March 18, 1943, in the course of which it endured a running battle with enemy fighters for one hour, twenty minutes. With a damaged engine, a fire in the rear turret, guns out of action, and at least one wounded crew member, *ONE TIME* managed to reach cloud cover and make the oversea crossing without ditching, but to attempt to go farther than Darwin (the 319th's base at Fenton was not far south of Darwin) was too risky. *Les Sutton*

PANAMA HATTIE, Consolidated B-24 (see chapter 2). Given the new name and artwork seen here following her time with the 43rd BG, WELL GODDAM may have seen only limited service after transfer to the 54th TCW (assigned along with eleven other B-17s in December 1943) but was later used as a VIP transport by Gen. Paul B. Wurtsmith in his role as commanding general of V Fighter Command. Wurtsmith later commanded the 13th AF, and his B-17, by then stripped of the OD finish, was reportedly left on Okinawa, but its eventual fate is not currently known.

PETTY GAL, Consolidated B-24 (see chapter 2). As mentioned in chapter 2, this B-24 had been badly damaged as a result of being hit by antiaircraft gun fire near Formosa on May 18, 1945, but was able to be nursed back to Lingayen airfield, where, presumably, this photo was taken, although possibly months later. Note that while the name still seems bright and vibrant, almost all the artwork has become noticeably faded.

Phyllis J. of WORCESTER, Consolidated B-24 (see chapter 2). The "X" on this B-24 is likely to have sealed her fate—to be left on Biak for eventual scrapping. Note the text below the "X," perhaps more of the story why it was to be left behind, but none of it readable, given the distance away from the camera.

P.I.JOE, North American B-25 (see chapter 6). This B-25 came to grief at Dobodura on September 28, 1943, when its undercarriage collapsed prior to takeoff and the RHS propeller shattered on contact with the metal runway matting. The crew was uninjured, but one of three senior Australian army officer passengers aboard, Brigadier Roy Sutherland, was killed by part of the propeller that broke away and penetrated the fuselage. While there has been a lot of conjecture over both the identity and tail markings of this particular B-25, all that can be established from this photo for certain is that at least two thin horizontal bands were worn over the tail fin and, presumably, the rudder.

PRINCESS PAT, North American B-25, 41-30176, artist unknown, 498th BS, 345th BG. Formerly the airplane assigned to the 498th commanding officer, the then Maj. Chester A. Coltharp, PRINCESS PAT is seen here with an eighty-seven-mission bomb log and victory symbols representing four enemy aircraft claims, but minus nose guns and with a simplified falcon's-head squadron nose insignia, with just a small section of its original "neck" line remaining due to a panel replacement (the purpose of the bracket attached, in part, to that panel is not known). The B-25 had been passed to the Fifth Bomber Command Replacement Pool at Nadzab in April 1944, and it is suspected that this is where this undated photo was taken. Most likely, PRINCESS PAT ended her days there.

"RED HEADED GAL", North American B-25 (see chapter 2). Here is a close-up of the new nose art applied to this B-25 following frontline service. The artist is unknown, but note how he has the pin-up looking up to and within reach of the cockpit window. To which unit "RED HEADED GAL" was assigned at this time is not known, but reportedly she was condemned after an accident in 1945 and subsequently salvaged.

READY TEDDY, Douglas A-20, 43-21984, artist unknown, 388th BS, 312th BG. Already stripped of nosewheel, tires, and propellers, this A-20 awaits its fate on Biak Island postwar. Named *Miss Priss* after the daughter of the plane's first assigned pilot, Lt. Eugene M. Lopez, it had begun flying missions with the 388th BS late in 1944. At that stage it featured a delightful painting of a young girl holding a soft toy behind her back. When Lopez left the squadron and was replaced by Lt. John S. Young, the painting was retained but the name was changed to *Miss Pam*. When Lt. Clarence R. Schertz replaced Young as assigned pilot late in the war, though, he had the painting (except for its original red-heart background) painted out, and the pin-up shown here and new name added. Schertz's name along with that of the crew chief, SSgt. Joseph S. Wray, can be seen in this photo. Note too the 105-mission bomb log and, between the names and mission markers, symbols for six ducks, the known death toll in a damaging bird strike experienced by Lopez while returning from a mission on January 7, 1945. *Official Army Air Forces photo*

"REAREN TO GO", Curtiss C-46 (see chapter 4). Following transfer to the 55th TCS, 375th TCG, and now bearing field number X118, this C-46 was struck by out-of-control 7th AF Lockheed F-5 43-28960 on June 27, 1945. Both planes were probably subsequently written off.

RED-HOT RIDEN-HOOD III, Consolidated B-24 (see chapter 2). This B-24, which was flown to Clark Field for disposal ca. July–August 1945, is seen here more than a year later, artwork defaced, and waiting to be reduced to scrap by the acetylene torch.

"SCORPION", Consolidated B-24 (see chapter 6). Shown here more than a month after a forced landing on the coast near Finschafen, due to engine trouble, and concerns over the chances of successfully crossing the Owen Stanley Ranges, clearly "SCORPION" was never going to fly again, but the original photo caption claimed that much of the B-24 would be used again (i.e., for spare parts). While most of the nose art has been damaged beyond recognition, the bomb log is still mostly visible, and since the earlier photo was taken, the top row can be seen to have been extended to the left to show a total of thirty-three missions. The six other bomb symbols seen earlier below the three stencils, for enemy fighters claimed, are also faintly discernible. *Official Army Air Forces photo*

SITTING PRETTY, Consolidated B-24 (see chapter 2). As reported in the second of the *Ken's Men against the Empire* volumes, this B-24 suffered accidental damage on April 3, 1945, and was subsequently salvaged by the 481st Service Squadron. The photo cannot be dated precisely but is suspected to have been taken in the March–July 1945 period. The adjacent NMF B-24 is the 65th Squadron's *CAROLYN MAE*, reportedly not salvaged until September 1945. Also of interest is the oddly marked P-40 behind *SITTING PRETTY*.

Shy-Chi Baby, Consolidated B-24 (see chapter 2). This was another 531st BS B-24, like *EMBARRASSED* seen earlier in this chapter, that her end-of-war ferry crew had hoped would lead to some publicity following their arrival back home; hence the addition of their names, ranks, and crew positions (no hometowns are stated though) and bold *97 MISSIONS* statement (the last word incomplete at the time this photo was taken). Being a dressed pin-up (the author apologizes that the RHS of the photo is not clearer) meant it had a better chance of survival during the flight home, and it did subsequently stay in place, but *Shy-Chi Baby*'s fate was the same as all the others that were flown to Kingman, Arizona: the scrap heap. Note at top left, adjacent to the partial bomb log, a highlighted tribute to Lt. J. W. Kay. Kay had been *Shy-Chi Baby*'s last wartime airplane captain, who, along with four others in his crew, lost their lives flying back to Okinawa on September 8, 1945, in another B-24 after transporting former prisoners of war to Clark Field. The five men were the last of the 380th BG's more than four hundred wartime deaths.

"*SKY WITCH*", Consolidated B-24 (see chapter 2). As mentioned earlier, this B-24's last mission occurred on November 7, 1944. By then, as seen here, its OD camouflage had been removed along with its name and pin-up, which, a little surprisingly, was not replaced. On that last mission, which included searching for and finding enemy naval activity in Brunei Bay, it was badly damaged in an encounter with enemy fighters and only narrowly made it to Morotai Island, where it is suspected that this photo was taken (note that the plane is behind a rarely seen fence in this photo; clearly this was no run-of-the-mill B-24). By all accounts, "*SKY WITCH*" never flew again.

SNAFU, Consolidated B-24, 42-40513, artist unknown, 529th BS, 380th BG. As mentioned in connection with the photos of *SNAFU NO II*, this B-24 was salvaged at Fenton, Northern Territory, following its accident there on September 15, 1943, but the nose art lived on for a while at least on the stripped nose section left in the Fenton scrapyard. The RHS nose art seems to have been the most photographed, but a similar work did appear on the LHS. While the fate of the nose section is not known, a section of *SNAFU*'s rear fuselage survived the Australian outback postwar to become an exhibit in the Northern Territory Aviation Museum, now called the Darwin Aviation Museum.

SWEET TAKE-OFF, Consolidated B-24 (see chapter 2). As mentioned earlier, this B-24 stayed with the CRTC after its move to the Philippines but gained a new nose turret, name (*ELFRIEDA*), and nose identification (the last three digits of its serial number) prior to being left at Clark Field for disposal postwar, as seen here. The very neat "CAF" lettering above the pin-up was some kind of Clark Field group identification; another group identity seen at Clark on an F-7 was "AAF."

TONDELAYO, North American B-25 (see chapter 2). In 2002 the Collings Foundation, an educational foundation based in Stow, Massachusetts, that is dedicated to the preservation and public display of transportation-related history, decided to replicate the markings of TONDELAYO on their B-25 (USAF serial number 44-28932), purchased in 1985 and previously operated as *Hoosier Honey*. The completed nose art is shown below in close-up, with a view of the original from a similar angle.

SY'S HOT NUMBER, Douglas A-20, 43-9500, artist unknown, 387th BS, 312th BG. A former 417th BG A-20 transferred to the 312th BG ca. March 1944, where it was assigned to Capt. Waldo M. Simonsen (hence the name "Sy"), this airplane, with a pin-up based on a prewar George Petty artwork, was damaged in a flight line explosion at Nadzab on July 4, 1944, and not flown again. This photo is from the same collection as HERE'S HOWE, seen earlier. *Via Malcolm Long*

TORRID TESSIE "The TERROR", North American B-25 (see chapter 6). After frontline service in New Guinea with the 71st and 405th BSs of the 38th BG and later, reportedly, the 90th BS, 3rd BG, this B-25 was converted to a "fat cat" plane (work that is suspected to have been carried out at the Townsville Air Depot), and as TORRID TESS she was assigned to the 673rd BS, 417th BG, for second-line duties with this Vargas-based artwork and altered name. This B-25 was lost in New Guinea while with this squadron on May 22, 1944, along with all aboard, three crew and seven passengers; it took another fifteen years until the wreckage and remains of TESS, alias TESSIE, were found.

TRAMP, Consolidated B-24 (see chapter 2). As seen in this photo, the short-lived *TRAMP* artwork was painted over, to be replaced by a caricature of an angelic young child, named *Sandra Kay*. This was to commemorate the first-born daughter of SSgt. James P. Benton, one of the gunners in Ed Harkins's crew, born on the day they were assigned a new B-24 to fly to Australia. It was on that B-24 that the initial nose art of the angelic young child, named *CUPID* (probably in capital letters), appeared, but the crew and bomber were separated at Townsville. Posted to the 530th BS, 380th BG, around October 1943, the Harkins crew was assigned to *TRAMP*, but squadron artist Bill McBroom was asked to replace the existing artwork with something along the lines of what had appeared on the B-24 they had delivered. Harkins and crew flew *Sandra Kay* from November 1943 to June 1944, after which they were rotated home, but the name and nose art remained and was reapplied after the airplane was stripped of its original paintwork. In March 1945, *Sandra Kay* became the first 380th BG B-24 to notch one hundred missions and went on to fly more missions than any other in the bomb group. *Sandra Kay* did not survive the war, though; she was salvaged following a crash landing on Mindoro in May 1945.

Unidentified North American B-25, unidentified serial number, artist unknown, 823rd BS, 38th BG. Two photos from Australian sources; on the basis that the name discernible on the fuselage side is *HORSE*, the author initially considered that this plane with the impressive incisors was *OLD WAR HORSE*, but that G model reportedly came to grief on Saidor in April 1944, and these photos were taken much later at an boneyard on Morotai Island (this is supported by the presence of B-24 *TWO TIME* [serial number 44-40546, artist V. P. Allan, 72nd BS, 5th BG] in the second photo, since it is known that she definitely ended her days there). The 823rd also had a Morotai connection, being based there from mid-October 1944 until the end of January 1945, but its older B-25s (mainly B-25Gs) had been replaced by new B-25Js by then, so, once again, the complete story of the fate of this B-25G is currently unknown. *Photo below, RAAF Museum*

Unnamed Douglas C-47 (see chapter 4). Last seen as X214 of 65th TCS, 433rd TCG, earlier in this volume, the field number here, however, indicates that it had subsequently been transferred to the 55th TCS, 375th TCG. The 55th was based in Luzon from February 1945 until the end of the war, and it was probably here where this photo was taken. Hours flown was one of the major factors in determining whether an airplane was considered war weary or not; for C-47s, that figure seems to have been 1,500.

Unnamed Douglas A-20 (see chapter 2). This plane was previously reported as having been salvaged following a flight line explosion at Nadzab on July 4, 1944, and this photo is believed to have been taken on Biak and shows 43-9109, probably then in reserve, with pin-up still in place but with bomb log (*top left*) and former pilot and crew chief crew names (*above the pin-up's head*) painted over. As with C-47 KEEP IT UNDER YOUR HAT, seen earlier in this chapter, clearly some attempt has also been made to protect the cockpit Plexiglas from the sun's damaging rays. As in the case of that C-47, though, the end of the war meant that it was also the end of the line for reserve aircraft, and the A-20 is likely to have been salvaged soon after.

Unnamed Douglas C-47, 43-15473, artist unknown, 55th TCS, 375th TCG. This C-47, field number 103, came to grief in a built-up area near Newcastle, New South Wales, Australia, after encountering bad weather on a flight south from Archerfield, Queensland, on August 10, 1944, which necessitated making an emergency landing. The big "American bomber" caused a lot of local interest, as did its pin-up nose art, and despite police attempting to control onlookers and their use of cameras, this photo was taken and has survived. The short-lived nose art (the C-47 had been in 55th TCS use for only a few months), however, was not so lucky, and concerns over its immodest pose reportedly led to the New South Wales Police (who were keeping the crash site secure) painting it out. *Neville Hopkins via Des Hopkins / Greg and Sylvia Ray's Phototimetunnel*

Unnamed Lockheed P-38, unidentified serial number, artist unknown, 36th FS, 8th FG. A forced landing caused this (probably) unrepairable damage, and while no further details are known, it seems that the seaside-scene nose art was short lived, since other photographs of it are yet to be found. Location is probably the Philippines.

Unnamed North American B-25, 41-30227, artist unknown, 71st BS, 38th BG. The nosewheel of this "Wolf Pack" B-25, with a fifty-seven-mission bomb log, hit a drainage ditch at Dobodura while taxiing in from a mission on February 22, 1944, which caused the nosewheel to collapse and led to the heavy damage shown. It never flew again.

Unnamed North American B-25, unidentified serial number, artist unknown, 405th BS, 38th BG. The photo of this Green Dragon seemingly put out to grass was from an Australian source and, on that basis, was probably taken in New Guinea. There were at least four B-25D Green Dragon losses at Allied bases in New Guinea in 1943–44, but without a date or location it has not proved possible to be more specific about the identification of this nose section.

Unnamed Republic P-47, 42-22687, artist TSgt. W. E. White, 9th FS, 49th FG, later CRTC. This fighter crashed in the highlands of Papua New Guinea near Tauta village on April 29, 1944, in the course of a test flight. It lay there, undisturbed, with the canopy apparently closed and no remains of her pilot aboard, until found in 1979. Remarkably, as this photo shows, the artwork looked nearly as good following the wreckage's discovery as it was the day it had been applied. In 2004, the wreck was recovered and shipped to Sydney, Australia, to assist in other P-47 restorations. *Bruce Hoy*

Unnamed North American B-25, 42-64816, artist unknown, unit(s) unidentified. A former 823rd BS, 38th BG strafer that was transferred to the 498th BS, 345th BG, in August 1944, the latter unit kept it only until October, when, along with the other unpopular G and H versions, it was, it is believed, transferred back to Townsville as war weary. In this case, though, it was given a new lease of life as a "fat cat" plane for an unidentified service squadron, and the name WAR WEARY was painted on the modified nose for all to see. By this late stage of the war, though, everyone was war weary, and the B-25, which is suspected to have originally carried the 823rd Squadron's "Terrible Tigers" nose insignia, drew little interest. As a result, photos of WAR WEARY are uncommon.

Unnamed North American B-25, 42-64803, artist unknown, 822nd BS, 38th BG and 501st BS, 345th BG. This "Black Panthers" B-25G (*above*) was one of the first to see combat with the squadron in October 1943 and, according to the research carried out for the group's history volume *Sun Setters of the Southwest Pacific Area*, flew its last combat mission with the 822nd on September 2, 1944, after which it was passed on to the 501st BS, 345th BG. This photo is dated September 12, 1944 (the location is not recorded), but the B-25, despite having been transferred out of the 822nd, retains the "Black Panthers" nose marking (just visible) and features both 822nd and 501st BS tail markings (the yellow band at the base is from the 822nd, while the white band above it denotes the 501st). The *Sun Setters* volume notes that most of the bomb group's B-25Gs were transferred out around the same time, and perhaps it was because so many airplanes were involved (a figure of thirty-seven is mentioned) that the old squadron markings were not painted out. As to the fate of this particular airplane, with little interest in these 75 mm cannon-equipped B-25s at this stage of the war, it is likely that the wreck was simply hauled off to be salvaged after this incident.

Unnamed North American B-25 (see section on 1944–45 bombers, 498th BS, in chapter 6). Photographed in Japan ca. 1946–47, this is suspected to be 44-29597 (most of the tail number, 429597, is discernible on the original print) in Japan after armament and wartime markings were removed and a modified nose section was added. Official records indicate that this former strafer was salvaged ("reclaimed") in September 1947.

VICE UNLIMITED, Martin B-26, 40-1491, artist unknown, 19th BS, 22nd BG. This B-26 had earlier carried a colorful non-pin-up artwork named *MAJOR MONSOON* while serving with the 33rd BS but was renamed *VICE UNLIMITED*, and the first artwork was replaced by a small pin-up while serving with the "Silver Fleet," the 19th BS, in the second half of 1943. This photo, revealing a bomb log of fifty-eight missions, is likely to have been taken at Eagle Farm airfield, Brisbane, Queensland, home of the 81st Air Depot Group, if, as thought, this unit was responsible for salvaging these planes once they were phased out of 5th AF service. As can be seen, the name and nose art have already been removed, an early example, it would seem, of official disapproval of pin-up art found on bombers being returned to "civilization" for scrapping.

"VIRGIN ABROAD", Consolidated B-24 (see chapter 2). Here is *"VIRGIN ABROAD"*, with *PEACE OFFERING* in the background (both artworks by Raymond Hafner), as they looked (note that turret armament has been removed) immediately prior to being flown back to US following the war's end. Both B-24s ended up in huge open-air storage at Kingman, Arizona, and it is noteworthy that the artwork on *"VIRGIN ABROAD"* did remain in place until that B-24 was scrapped, but whether the same could be said for *PEACE OFFERING* is not currently known.

YANKEE GAL, Consolidated B-24 (see chapter 2). According to research for the 22nd BG history *Revenge of the Red Raiders*, this B-24 was assessed as battle damaged and salvaged in August 1944. The 22nd BG moved from Nadzab to Owi Island soon after, that action, perhaps, making easier the decision to leave *YANKEE GAL* behind.

the *WANGO WANGO BIRD*, Consolidated F-7 (see chapter 1). This slightly crazy-looking yet imposing artwork had but a short life: it was ruined along with the rest of the aircraft when it crashed on landing at Nadzab on June 18, 1944. Research by 20th CMS researcher Chuck Varney established that the *BIRD* flew only four missions altogether, the first on May 4, 1944, the last on the day it was lost.

NOSE ART OF THE 5TH AIR FORCE

We have already seen from this chapter's heading photo just how extensive the collection of unwanted former wartime aircraft at Clark Field in the Philippines was postwar. The top of page view of more "excess" planes at Clark Field is another official shot issued at the same time as the heading photo, but this time showing B-24s, C-46s, and C-47s (*rearmost*). The print's original caption this time, does, however, confirm that all were awaiting disposal. Unfortunately, given the distance of the planes from the airborne photographer, identification of individual aircraft is virtually impossible, but a "Hawkeye" (6th Reconnaissance Group) F-7 can be identified from its distinctive tail insignia out front of the second row, while the B-24 with the pyramid-shaped tail markings in the first row had belonged to the 26th BS, 11th BG, 7th AF. The two other photos here show a later stage of the cutting up and destruction of Clark Field B-24s and the fiery end of unwanted P-38s (complete with engines), a very undignified end to two of the best-known 5th AF airplane types that had formerly ruled the skies of the Pacific in 1943–45. *Aerial view, Official Army Air Forces photo*

318

CHAPTER 8
Postwar Postscript

Despite people having an unchanged attitude toward pin-up art in the immediate postwar era, the glory days of 5th AF airplane nose art were well behind by 1947–48 as the 5th settled down to its role in occupation duties, much of which centered on the reconstruction of Japan.

Few of the 5th's main wartime airplane types were even around by 1947. Cargo planes (C-46s, had, as noted in chapter 2, become the main cargo plane type in use in the Far East) were an exception, but most of those in use by 1947–48 seem to have been "cleaned up" or toned down. Other wartime types that made it to Japan early on were B-25s, a small number of B-24s (five were used by the 90th BS, 3rd BG, between December 1945 and July 1946, mainly on weather flights), F-7s, and P-38s, and while their collective service was limited, photos that follow suggest that there was no rush to change wartime nose art, which is not surprising given that some of it (on the P-38s, for example) had been added perhaps only weeks earlier.

Along with the disposal of so many wartime aircraft, it is important to note that within a year of the war's end, a new order advised that except for night fighters and exceptional cases, "camouflaging of the exterior surfaces of AAF aircraft is no longer required," and while it seems to have taken a long time for all remaining camouflaged planes to be stripped back, this directive effectively ended the wartime-era camouflage

Hi Honey!, Lockheed P-38, unidentified serial number, artist unknown, 36th FS, 8th FG. In a great overall view of a late-war 36th FS P-38 "dressed up" for occupation duties in Japan, *Hi Honey!* was photographed at Ashiya airstrip in January 1946; by the end of the year she had been salvaged there. The pin-up on this P-38 is a little hard to make out here but was based on the June 1945 Varga Girl, but with a heart background rather than a cushion as Vargas had included. The "Flying Fiends" squadron insignia (see photo in chapter 3) appears on the engine cowling.

Surprisingly, the cover of the twenty-four-page May 1946 Meiji Building 5th AF telephone directory did not feature the 5th AF's famous emblem or a traditional Japanese scene (discounting the simple waterfall drawing, which may well have been an afterthought) but was centered on this pin-up, probably based on Vargas's August 1944 calendar girl. Was it that it was still considered that a pin-up would be of greater interest to 5th AF personnel than any Japanese landmarks or natural beauties, or did the unidentified artist get his instructions wrong?

319

"standards" (see paragraph 1 of Army Air Forces TO [Technical Order] 07-1-1 of June 1946, reproduced in *USAAF Aircraft Markings and Camouflage, 1941–1947: The History of USAAF Aircraft Markings, Insignia, Camouflage, and Colors* by Robert D. Archer and Victor G. Archer).

New planes assigned to 5th AF units, such as B-25 replacement the Douglas A-26 (which, due to some early problems when trialed by the 5th AF in 1944, did not see service in the Pacific until 1946) and North American P-51s and Northrop F-15s (used only by the 8th PRS), did, in some cases have pin-ups added to them, but they were also toned down from the "no rules" days of 1945, and in one case, that of *Death's Angel II* (*photos of which follow*), was anything but glamorous. It has been said that 35th FG F-51s (the designation P-51 was changed to F-51 in 1948) still featured pin-up nose art as late as 1949, but if so, this was perhaps a last pre–Korean War hurrah, since the replacement of Far East Air Force F-51s by Lockheed F-80 jet fighters also occurred that year.

The largest airplane in Japan known to have featured nose art in the early stages of the occupation was the F-7 *LOVELY LOUISE*, seen on the opposite page. Belonging to the 20th Reconnaissance Squadron, this squadron's F-7s were replaced by Boeing B-29s/F-13s (initially of the 1st Reconnaissance Squadron, which was not a 5th AF unit, later of the 9th Squadron), but just how much nose art appeared on them is unknown (the postwar Far Eastern service of each squadron was short lived; the 9th, which was assigned to the 5th AF's 314th Composite Wing, from just June 1946 to October 1947), and it seems likely that what did exist had been wartime-applied while in the hands of the original units to which these planes had been assigned.

Other pin-up nose art on multiengine planes of the 5th AF postwar, apart from an unnamed C-46 and the bold Beech C-45 *ANXIOUS ANN* seen below, was featured on at least two B-17 ASR ships. Both B-17s are believed to have been operated by the 3rd ERS, later (1948) renamed 3rd Rescue Squadron, and later still (1950) 3rd Air Rescue Squadron. This squadron, which began service in Japan equipped with these modified B-17s, OA-10s, and C-47s, by 1947–48 added some Sikorsky R-6 helicopters (redesignated H-6 in 1948) to its

ANXIOUS ANN, Beech C-45, 44-47331, artist unknown, Headquarters Squadron, 5th AF. From the same collection as the P-51 photos that follow, these two rare views date from no earlier than 1947 (the national markings are of the design introduced in January 1947). The pin-up is yet another version of the Varga Girl that had appeared in the October 1943 issue of *Esquire* magazine. By 1947, however, Vargas was no longer working for *Esquire*, but at war with the magazine. In a contract between the two effective on January 1, 1944 (a document that Vargas did not read before signing), he was to work for ten years, six months, and to complete "not less than twenty-six (26) [drawings] during each six-month period." It was physically impossible, and while legal action seemed to take the artist's side concerning the workload required of him, the magazine was awarded control of the "Varga" name. As to this nose art painting it may have fallen out of favor with 5th AF hierarchy reasonably quickly, since no other photos of it have been seen.

STAR of ATSUGI and *RAMP TRAMP*, Boeing B-17s, unidentified serial numbers, artist unknown, 3rd ERS (unconfirmed), 314th Composite Wing. Neither of these photos is dated, but both show airborne lifeboat-equipped B-17s used in Japan. Atsugi, about 30 miles southwest of Tokyo, was the 3rd ERS's first Japanese base of operations, and the squadron's "A" Flight was still based there as of August 1, 1946, but apparently had moved elsewhere by 1947. The history of *RAMP TRAMP* is currently unknown (the use of the word "ramp" for an airplane hardstand or parking area seems to have begun in World War II and spawned a number of nose art names), but the photo is suspected to have been taken ca. 1947. USAF ASR B-17s in the Far East remained in service there until 1951.

inventory (the R-6 was essentially a development of the earlier R-4, which had been the first mass-produced helicopter in the world), and a photo of one of these, *DANCIN' DUCHESS*, can also be found here.

Given the relatively small number of photos used in this chapter, they appear below in alphabetical order of airplane manufacturer.

LOVELY LOUISE, Consolidated F-7, 44-42135, artist unknown, 20th Reconnaissance Squadron (Long Range, Photographic-RCM), 6th Reconnaissance Group (formerly 6th PRG). Given the coverage of 20th CMS nose art in chapters 1 and 2, it is fitting that one of the last photos in this study is this very clear 1946 view taken over Japan of an F-7 of the 20th Reconnaissance Squadron, the successor in title to the 20th CMS (no tail number had been applied to this F-7 at the time the photo was taken). The unit was one of the first to be involved in the ambitious War Department Post Hostilities Mapping Plan (coverage of six million square miles in three years!) but not for long as it was inactivated in June 1946. The original pin-up on which the nose art was based appears to be of the same vintage, a mirror image, it seems, of the June pin-up from the 1946 *Esquire Varga Calendar*, perhaps one of the few from that calendar to make it on to a 5th AF airplane.

Unnamed Curtiss C-46, unidentified serial number, artist unknown, unit(s) unidentified. A rare case of a pin-up on a 5th AF C-46 in the postwar period was this Vargaesque example. This C-46 is known to have been in Japan ca. 1947, the decorative spiral markings on the propeller hubs suggesting previous service with the 8th CCS (see the photo of LONG DISTANCE in chapter 4 for a similarly marked C-46; the 8th moved to Japan in September 1945 but was inactivated a short time later), but further details are lacking. Some repainted areas (along the top of the fuselage and adjacent to and in line with the bottom of the cockpit windows) are also apparent.

VAGRANT VIRGIN, Douglas A-26, unidentified serial number, artist unknown, unidentified BS, 3rd or 38th BG. Early A-26 deliveries to FEAF ca. early January 1946 included both solid-nosed A-26Bs and transparent bombardier compartment-nosed A-26Cs. Here are two views of this impressive nose art, copied from the May 1945 *Esquire* Varga Girl, on a B model. During the Korean War (1950–53), B-26 (the A-26 was redesignated B-26 in 1948) nose art had another "airing," but that was completely unrelated to these early post–World War II examples, which are suspected to have been short lived.

EMBRACEABLE You, Lockheed P-38, 44-26334, artist unknown, HQ Squadron(?), 49th FG. Lt. Col. Wallace R. Jordan, formerly a wartime executive officer and commanding officer of the 9th FS, is seen here with his airplane in Japan in the winter of 1945/46. It is thought that Jordan probably continued to use his wartime plane number (91 was a 9th FS number) for ease of recognition; it can be seen that symbols for his wartime aerial victories were also added to it. Website veteran.tributes.org notes that following his 1945 posting to the Pacific from the United States he had extensive roles in Japan "as operations officer, deputy commander, and then commander of the 49th Fighter Group." His time as group commander was limited to around February 1946, but that may have been when this photo was taken.

ATOMIC BLONDE, North American B-25, unidentified serial number, artist unknown, unidentified BS, unidentified BG. Another example of the popularity of the Atomic Blonde name post-August 1945, this *ATOMIC BLONDE* is clearly a 5th airplane, but her identity is presently not known. As with the photo above this photo was also taken in the winter of 1945/46. The name of the crew member in the photo is not known.

LADY MARGO, North American B-25, 43-36166, artist unknown, 499th BS, 345th BG. This B-25 was renamed LADY MARGO (formerly LITTLE MISS HELL II, earlier LITTLE MISS ELL II) ca. June 1945 and is seen here postwar with the last incarnation of the squadron insignia with its broad-brush approaches both to the representation of the batwing skeletal structure, now in simplified form, and matching wing outline. If this was another example of the "dressing up" of 5th AF planes for expected occupation duties, it was, again, short lived, since the comprehensive group history *Warpath across the Pacific* notes that after courier flights to Japan in September, word came through "that the unit was going to deactivate," virtually ceasing to exist by the end of October. It is known that some 499th B-25s were scrapped in Japan, and LADY MARGO may have been among them.

MY BUCK, North American B-25, 44-29590 (unconfirmed), artist unknown, 17th TRS, 71st TRG. B-25J-22 gunships such as MY BUCK had been, generally speaking, assigned to the 5th AF's B-25-equipped units by January 1945, so their wartime service was limited. Not seen in this photo, though, is that MY BUCK had a significant bomb log, sixty-plus missions, perhaps a cumulative total for a pilot with earlier service with the 17th. The artwork was based on the June 1943 Varga Girl, and what may be the artist's name appeared at bottom left of the pin-up. The 71st TRG moved to Japan in October 1945, and it was there where this photo was taken. The group's inactivation followed only a few months later; the 17th TRS was then based at Yokota. Its B-25s went the way of all but a few other 5th AF B-25s: off to the boneyard. *Claude Phoenix*

Unnamed North American B-25, unidentified serial number, artist unknown, 71st BS, 38th BG. This photo was taken at Ashiya in January 1946 by the same photographer as *Hi Honey!* seen earlier. According to the Group's history, *Sun Setters of the Southwest Pacific Area*, though, only 12 B-25s remained on hand by December 13, 1945, due to the anticipated receipt of new Douglas A-26s (*see previous page*). This fierce-looking B-25 may, therefore, have been one of the last in 5th AF service at that time. The 71st BS was inactivated in late-1946 but this was not the end of teeth being applied to some 5th AF airplanes as the 158th LS, based in Japan from around the same time as the stay of the 71st ended, subsequently adopted sharkmouth nose art as a unit insignia.

Death's Angel II, North American P-51, 44-73638, artist unknown, 7th FS, 49th FG, 314th Composite Wing. *Death's Angel II* was not like anything else seen in this volume, a weird mixture of a pin-up and the macabre. The first *Death's Angel* was a P-51 assigned to Lt. Harry M. Chapman in late 1944 while he was serving in England with the 376th FS, 361st FG, 8th AF, but why he chose the name is not currently known. Postwar, after training on jets and time as a test pilot, Chapman reverted to P-51 flying, but this time in Japan, and evidently considered that the name of his wartime fighter was worthy of another airing. Note the 7th FS's "Bunyip" squadron marking on the fuselage; this had first been seen on the rudder of 7th Squadron P-40s in 1942 and appeared on the nose of at least one P-38 (the squadron commander's plane) postwar, when the 49th FG became part of the occupation force. Chapman remained a member of the 7th Squadron until April 1949 and went on to more-senior positions, rising to the rank of brigadier general. He retired on July 1, 1974, and passed away in 2013.

FLORIDA'S BEAUTY, North American P-51, unidentified serial number, artist unknown, unidentified FS, 35th FG (unconfirmed), 314th Composite Wing. From other photos of 35th FG P-51s/F-51s in Japan in the postwar period (the P-51 designation was changed to F-51 in 1948), it seems that approval was given for minor pin-up artworks and accompanying airplane names to be added to this group's P-51s/F-51s as long as they adhered to a specific standard. That standard would appear to have been that no nudity was allowed, and each artwork and name was to be applied only to the RHS of the plane and contained within the top panel below the engine exhaust outlets. Further examples of these can be found in Larry Davis's *Planes, Names & Dames*, vol. II.

Jackie, Northrop F-15, 45-59326, artist unknown, 8th PRS, 71st Reconnaissance Group. The late-war high-flying photoreconnaissance variant of the P-61 night fighter, this was somewhat of a rarity in USAAF (subsequently USAF) service when it did begin to see service in 1947, since the end of the war had reduced production numbers down to thirty-six. Most of these were shipped to Japan, where they were operated exclusively by the 8th PRS (redesignated 8th TRS [Night Photo] in August 1948), the first two arriving at Johnson AFB from Kisarazu on June 24, 1947. Lt. Virgil Heistand, whose name can be seen on this side of 326, was one of the ferry pilots that day. This is the only example of an F-15 with a pin-up of any sort in place found by the author, and despite its size may also have been short lived. A version of Bill Hankey's diving-hawk group insignia was painted on the fin of these aircraft, and it seems that the new squadron artist may have been influenced by Hankey in other ways too; note the star over the lower case letter "i" in the name, instead of a dot, a hallmark of Hankey's earlier 8th PRS work. The 8th Squadron ceased operating F-15s (by then redesignated RF-61Cs) in early 1949.

DANCIN' DUCHESS, Sikorsky R-6, 43-45412, artist unknown, 3rd ERS / 3rd Air Rescue Squadron, 314th Composite Wing. This R-6 was assigned to FEAF in April 1947 and spent its operational life with the 3rd Squadron until salvaged in 1950. Just when (and where) the photo was taken is not currently known, but the fact that the helicopter remains in wartime OD finish suggests ca. 1947. Another R-6, serial number 43-45403, in the later orange-yellow paint scheme was decorated at Yokota AFB ca. September 1948 with a bikini-wearing pin-up named *STUPIFY'N JEANNE* as part of that year's Air Force Day air show, but that artwork is, under the circumstances, suspected to have been short lived.

APPENDIXES

APPENDIX 1
P-39 Door Art

The flatness of the automobile-style pilot's door on the Bell P-39/P400, also known as the Airacobra, lent itself to official and, subsequently, unofficial markings. The heading photo and five photos that follow are representative of such artwork, 1941–44.

JULIE, Bell P-39, unidentified serial number, artist unknown, 41st FS (unconfirmed), 35th FG. Her assigned pilot was a Lt Owen.

PHYLLIS, Bell P-39, unidentified serial number, artist unknown, 41st FS, 35th FG. From a 41st FS collection; hence the unit identification.

Bell YP-39, 40-35, artist unknown, 39th PS, 31st PG. Bob Mosher photographed the unit insignia on this early P-39 from Selfridge Field, Michigan, while it was on display in nearby Detroit on November 29, 1941. The 8th FG later inherited at least one former 39th FS (the 39th Pursuit Squadron was redesignated 39th Fighter Squadron on May 15, 1942) P-39, still with its "Cobra in the Clouds" unit insignia on the door, while based in New Guinea.

PIGEON TOED PRINCESS, Bell P-39, unidentified serial number, artist unknown, unit(s) unidentified. The soldier in the photo is unfortunately not identified.

"SOUTHERN BELLE", Bell P-39, unidentified serial number, artist unknown, 110th TRS, 71st TRG. Another example of an artwork based on the Vargas gatefold pin-up from the April 1944 edition of *Esquire* magazine; note that the name ending with the letter E at far left was not SOUTHERN BELLE but something else ending in LEE. The names forward of the artwork are those of the pilot, Lt. Thomas, and the crew chief, Sgt. Kaminski; no other details are currently known.

Unnamed Bell P-39, unidentified serial number, artist unknown, 110th TRS, 71st TRG. This was the most accurate copy of the now-well-known illusionary illustration "what's on a man's mind," and probably the only one to appear on a 5th AF fighter (for other versions, see *American Beauty* and *Big Chief Cockeye* in chapter 2). Note the start of the squadron identification number at right; it is not currently known what that was, but the 110th used numbers in the range 10–39. The pilot assigned to this particular P-39 was Lt. Jesse L. McNeill.

APPENDIX 2
Far East Air Service Command Nose Art

As will be seen from the images in this appendix, some of the boldest examples of pin-up nose art on SWPA cargo and other second-line aircraft appeared on Far East Air Service Command planes. As explained in a report by a subsidiary unit, following the creation of the Far East Air Force (Provisional) in June 1944, a Far East Air Service Command (FEASC) was activated, and "among those units assigned were the IV Air Services Area Command and the V Air Service Area Command." The assignment of aircraft to IV ASAC for the delivery of "tactical supplies" followed, and, as an example, FEASC Assignment Order No. 3, dated July 27, 1944, involved three former 13th AF C-47s. Other ASAC aircraft had previously seen service with the 5th AF, but the September 30, 1944, summary of aircraft numbers in New Guinea, mentioned elsewhere, indicates that IV ASAC had twenty-six C-47s by then (there was no mention of V ASAC at that stage), but perhaps some of these were being held for reassignment to troop carrier units. Photos of more than ten known FEASC C-47s follow, many of them in NMF (front-line C-46s and C-47s remained camouflaged), but thus far, to this author's knowledge, only one of these planes has been identified by serial number. Nose art on three "secondhand" B-25s can also be found here; given the second-line use of B-25s by tactical units, examples of which have already been seen in this book, there is no reason to suppose that FEASC did not follow suit.

This lineup of C-47s on Wama airstrip, Morotai Island, in 1945 includes at least one from FEASC, *"She'll Do Me"* (second in line in NMF). The first plane in the lineup has the number 29 on the nose and tail and is most likely from a 13th AF unit, while the third was named *The NAVAJO* and was operated by the 33rd TCS, 374th TCG. *Bert Peake*

Audrey, Douglas C-47, unidentified serial number, artist unknown, IV ASAC. Long-legged *Audrey* was loosely based on the June pin-up from the 1944 *Esquire Varga Calendar* and carried field number W807, only part of which is visible in this photo.

BOTTOM'S UP, Douglas C-47, unidentified serial number, artist unknown, IV ASAC. This artwork was copied from the February pin-up in the 1944 *Esquire Varga Calendar*. W-prefixed field numbers (as opposed to X-prefixed field numbers) appear to have been introduced in the SWPA in November 1944, and IV ASAC was evidently assigned (at least) the block W801 to W820.

"*HANGAR QUEEN*, Douglas C-47, unidentified serial number, artist unknown, IV ASAC. A "hangar queen" was a plane with serviceability issues that would have seen it, back in the US, remain in a hangar for a longer than normal time, but here the reference is probably more a case of using an air force term to popularize the nose art. The added pin-up was an updated version of one of Alberto Vargas's early works for *Esquire* magazine, his February 1941 Varga Girl; compare with the nose art on Lockheed P-38 *Shady's Lady* in chapter 3.

DREAM girl, Douglas C-47, unidentified serial number, artist unknown, unit(s) unidentified. This plane, originally named *Meat Waggin* (see photo at right, taken before the name was completed and edging/shading added), was one of a number of varied types used by a unit that called itself Atabrine Airlines, which was active in the Philippines (and probably based there) in 1945 (from April, if not earlier) and most likely a component of FEASC. A photo of a unit B-25 named *LONG ISLAND BELLE* follows.

HELEN & FLO, Douglas C-47, unidentified serial number, artist unknown, IV ASAC. This C-47 is believed to have earlier worn field number W806.

Homing Pigeon, Douglas C-47, unidentified serial number, artist unknown, IV ASAC. Earlier this C-47 is believed to have worn field number W819.

Little "*BUTCH*", Douglas C-47, unidentified serial number, artist unknown, IV ASAC

LONESOME CHERRY, Douglas C-47, unidentified serial number, artist unknown, IV ASAC. The pin-up style of this artwork and its sexual theme are similar to that seen on C-46 *Gone Forever* in chapter 4, suggesting to this author that both were painted by the same artist (at least one other work by this artist, also on a C-47, is known). The artwork on B-17 *Ready Betty 'Gone Forever',* a photo of which appears in chapter 2, also included a winged cherry.

LONG ISLAND BELLE and 'Princess Marie', North American B-25s, unidentified serial numbers, artists unknown, units unidentified. Both of these are suspected to have been ca. 1945 FEASC "supply depot ships" (the 'Princess Marie' image came from the scrapbook of a 27th Air Depot Group member), but the origins of the planes are currently unknown. Of further interest in regard to the *LONG ISLAND BELLE* B-25 is that it carried the nickname Atabrine Airlines (in capital letters) along the top of the fuselage and later had her glasshouse nose exchanged for something smaller and more aerodynamic.

Rotation Plan, Douglas C-47, 42-23537 (unconfirmed), artist unknown, IV ASAC. The USAAF's rotation plan, the replacement of time-expired combat crews, was a common subject of discussion and complaint, particularly for men in the war against Japan (by September 1944 it was expected that transport plane crews would have to fly one thousand hours, more than double the hours set down at the same time for heavy bomber crews, before they could look forward to rotation), but, as with other military terms, it lent itself to other more earthy interpretation. If the serial number stated above is correct, this C-47 was purchased in Manila by the Netherlands government postwar and saw service in the East Indies with the Dutch naval air arm, later (after Indonesian independence) the Indonesian air force.

RUGGED But RiGHT, Douglas C-47, unidentified serial number, artist unknown, IV ASAC. The name of this C-47 would appear to have been taken from a version of a bawdy traditional song, the first two lines of which are "I just called up to tell you that I'm rugged but right / A rambling woman, a gambling woman, drunk every night." In the background of this photo, probably taken at Biak, is another IV ASAC C-47, *Still Putting Out* (see the following page).

Still Putting OUT, Douglas C-47, unidentified serial number, artist unknown, IV ASAC. This C-47 had earlier worn field number 804, the positioning of which can still be clearly seen in the painted-out area (the W appeared separately above the number as per an official instruction).

"She'll Do Me" and *"She's RITE"*, Douglas C-47s, unidentified serial numbers, *"She'll Do Me"* artist unknown, *"She's RITE"* artist Lee Warren (the artist's name can be found below the right knee), V ASAC (unconfirmed) and IV ASAC. Here we have two C-47s named after Australian colloquialisms. Despite what undoubtedly seemed to young American servicemen like a term with sexual overtones, "She'll do me" simply means "That's good, I'll take it," while "She's rite" (the correct English-language spelling of the second word being "right" rather than "rite") means "Everything's all right." Apart from the names for these two C-47s, though, note that the field number on *"She'll Do Me"* is the only FEASC C-47 seen by the author with a W-prefixed field number in the 900s, while in regard to *"She's RITE"*, artist Warren added an "AFTER VARGA" acknowledgment above his name; the painting is Warren's likeness of the January 1944 Varga Girl, sans clothing and with right arm extended. Prior to the application of the IV ASAC arrowhead marking on *"She's RITE"*, this C-47 carried field number W815.

WHODUNIT? the / The 2nd, North American B-25, 42-53431, artists unknown, IV ASAC (unconfirmed). Craven and Cate, in vol. 5 of their *Army Air Forces in World War II* official history, note that IV ASAC had two depots in New Guinea, one (Depot No. 1) at Finschafen, the other (Depot No. 3) at Biak. Furthermore, "it was found necessary in January 1945 to begin an expansion of the Biak air depot to serve the Philippines." Given that the first photo seen here of this B-25, in a mixture of old and new markings, was taken at Biak, there is good reason to believe that this was another IV ASAC "depot ship" being prepared for her new role (the source of the plane, original name not known, was probably a 13th AF unit). The other photo shows the unarmed B-25 with the altered form of nose art, a big improvement in style to the first, but still very confronting to many, given social norms over the depiction of naked pregnant women (as late as 1991, so confronting was the cover image of the August edition of *Vanity Fair*, which featured an Annie Liebovitz portrait of actress Demi Moore, naked and seven months pregnant, that some magazine retailers refused to sell the magazine).

Unnamed Douglas C-47, unidentified serial number, artist unknown, unit(s) unidentified. Another copy of Gil Elvgren's popular hitchhiker pin-up artwork titled *The High Sign*, it is known that this artwork was added to the C-47 when it was still in camouflage, but the fact that it was later stripped back to natural-metal finish has led the author to include this image here, since it seems likely that the plane belonged to a FEASC unit. It is suspected that this photo was taken somewhere in the Philippines in 1945. *C. H. "Con" Kealy*

APPENDIX 3
"The Painted Ladies Of Nadzab"

This little-known article that refers to specific bomber nose art seen at Nadzab, New Guinea, late in 1945 was written by Sgt. Frank Ryland, a journalist with an Australian Army Military History field team. It was subsequently published in *Salt*, the Australian Army Education Journal, vol. 11 no. 11 (January 28, 1946):

America has certainly left its stamp on Nadzab in more ways than one. In the graveyard of planes up there in the Markham Valley is to be found evidence not only of US industrial and aerial might, but aspects of American character. Particularly evident is the accent on sex, since nine out of ten of the broken bombers in this scrap heap of American planes carry the picture of a nude or near nude, titled with saucy, suggestive, or—if one is prudish—nearly salacious names.

Strewn all over the valley are hundreds of Libs, Bostons, Mitchells, besides fighters, and the skeletons of gliders.

Take a look-see over a cross section of the insignia of some of the bombers. Disney is represented with an irate Donald Duck, bearing the name Mallet Head. There is a Mexican touch in the Gay Caballero caricature entitled Jose el Diablo (Joseph the Devil). But these two alone might be called "neuter gender." The remainder are especially feminine, and hot feminine at that.

First we have "Fertil Myrtle," who speaks for herself with her comely curves. Alongside is a lovely lass who carries the title "How'm I Doin'?," while "Satan's Sister" warmly welcomes one to the nether regions. "Pistol Packin' Momma" looks rather tough, and there is more than a hint of invitation in the nude labelled "Come and Get It!"

Cole Porter's famous song "Begin the Beguine" is the name given to a Varga type of girl, while a most lithesome lass with that come-on look in her eyes is called "Mission Belle." A beautiful dame in deshabille answers to "Sooper Dooper," while another beauty well above average is titled "About Average."

"Peter Heater" and "Twin Nifties" need no elaboration. But perhaps the cleverest in design, character and name are two composite pictures, each a work of art in itself. The first presents a nude with upraised leg, her leg forming part of Uncle Sam's nose, her body being part of his face. Surrounded with stars and stripes, this colorful emblem is titled "American Beauty"—and very nice too. The other one designed on similar lines has a nude's bended knee making the nose of Little Chief Cockeye.

Turning from the lighter side for a moment, one finds plenty to ponder on, if one's fancy runs free. The scene

A slightly blurry photo taken in late 1945 of part of the Nadzab boneyard. The area has already been well picked over, and while B-24s are the most easily recognizable airplane type present (the remains of a 90th BG example can be seen around midshot), four or five C-47 fuselages stacked together are also in the photo, while in the right foreground that is the remains of the twin booms and tail section of a P-38.

is so quiet, and devoid of all vegetation save some sparse kunai. It is eerie, almost ghostly, to walk through the "streets" of smashed bombers, pursuit planes and gliders. No birds sing in this deserted valley, nor is the hum of insects to be heard in the jungle a mile or so across the sluggish muddy Markham River. All is silence save for the occasional flap-flap of a broken piece of wing or the sad sigh of a breeze blowing through a broken, battered cockpit.

There's plenty of contrast. One Lib bears a beautiful girl called Flamin' Mamie; peppered along where the pilot used to sit is a row of Jap bullet holes. On another bomber, a bullet-shattered windscreen tells its own tragic tale of a losing fight.

Don't think all the planes' emblems are "show." Others tell of duty well done. Rows and rows of painted black bombs along the fuselage denote the number of bombing missions. Painted in red, the Rising Sun flag stands for a Jap plane brought down in actual combat, while the miniature black-painted planes beside them represent Jap planes "done over" on the ground.

All of them bring unanswerable questions to mind. Did that one fight in the vital Coral Sea battle which meant so much to Australia? And "Jungle Queen"—did that sultry lass see action in [the] Battle of the Bismarck Sea? "Bums Away" and "Bottoms Up"—what were their triumphs, and how did they meet their Waterloos? Where are the crew of "Satan's Sister" now?

All of these shattered planes were brought to this strange graveyard on huge trailers and dumped in a heap—millions of wasted labour hours, because man would not live at peace with his neighbours. Wasted, yet necessary in another sense, for without them mankind might have descended into the long dark night to barbaric ways of living.

But it is time to leave. The sinking sun shines dazzling on a silvered Lib while a camouflaged Boston blends with the darkening background of the distant jungle. Tropic night shades fall upon this graveyard of broken planes but not of broken hopes. For this mass of tangled wreckage is a mute but striking testimony to high American endeavour.

Our jeep jolts out to the kunai-lined track and we take a last look at "Flamin' Mamie" smiling at us in the rays of the setting sun.

Aircraft mentioned:

Mallet Head: Consolidated B-24, 42-41050, *MALLET HEAD*, formerly of 43rd BG

Jose el Diablo: Consolidated B-24, 42-41227, *Jose' "El Diablo"*, formerly of 90th BG. Artist unknown, it is interesting to note that author Ryland still refers to this B-24 by this name when he saw it in 1945, since it has been suggested that it was renamed after transfer to the 64th BS, 43rd BG.

Fertil Myrtle: Unidentified; the only known 5th AF B-24 with a name like this (*Firtil Myrtle*; see chapter 2) was written off in the Philippines in 1945. If not a B-24, it may have been B-25 *FERTILE MYRTLE,* the last known operator of which was the 475th FG.

How'm I Doin'?: Consolidated B-24, 42-41223, *HOW'M-I-DOIN'*, formerly of 90th BG; see chapter 2.

Satan's Sister: Consolidated B-24, 42-40680, *'SATANS* [no apostrophe] *SISTER'*, formerly of 43rd and 22nd BGs; see chapter 2.

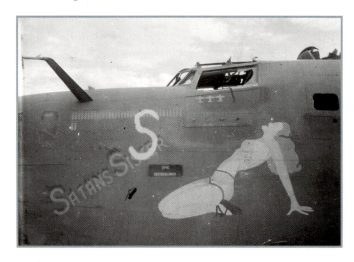

Pistol Packin' Momma: Suspected to be Consolidated B-24, 42-72787, *Pistol-Pakin Mama*, formerly of 307th BG (13th AF)

"THE PAINTED LADIES OF NADZAB"

Jungle Queen: Consolidated B-24, 42-40510, *JUNGLE QUEEN*, formerly of 43rd BG; see chapter 2.

Bums Away: Consolidated SB-24, 42-40822, *BUMS AWAY!*, formerly of 868th BS (13th AF)

Bottoms Up: Consolidated B-24, 42-40834, *BOTTOM'S UP!*, formerly of 90th BG; see chapter 2.

Come and Get It!: Consolidated B-24, 42-40941, *COME AND GET IT*, formerly of 43rd BG; see chapter 2. *Photo above, Pete Roberts*

Begin the Beguine: Consolidated B-24, 42-40650, *Begin the Beguine*, formerly of 307th BG (13th AF)

Mission Belle: Consolidated B-24, 42-40389, *Mission Belle*, formerly of 90th BG; see chapter 2.

Sooper Dooper: This is suspected to be Consolidated B-24, 42-40515, *"SOOPER DROOPER"*, formerly of 43rd BG; see chapter 2.

About Average: Consolidated B-24, 42-72777, *ABOUT AVERAGE*, formerly of 5th BG (13th AF)

Peter Heater: Consolidated B-24, 42-40917, *THE PETER HEATER*, formerly of 90th BG; see chapter 2.

Twin Nifties: Consolidated B-24, 42-40928, *TWIN NIFTIES II*, formerly of 90th BG; this spelling was only on the LHS, with *TWIN NIFTYS II* painted on the RHS; see chapter 2.

American Beauty: Consolidated F-7, 42-73045, *American Beauty*, formerly of 20th CMS; see chapter 2. *Pete Roberts*

Little Chief Cockeye: North American B-25, unidentified serial number, LITTLE CHIEF COCKEYE, formerly of 43rd BG; see chapter 5. *Pete Roberts*

Flamin' Mamie: Consolidated B-24, 41-41062, FLAMIN' MAMIE, formerly of 43rd BG; see chapter 2.

Out with the old and in with the new; one last photo to end this project. By the time this photo was taken postwar (undoubtedly at Nadzab), this incomplete B-25 was just a backdrop for the young lady in the foreground (such significant reminders of the recent past existed in situ, particularly in out-of-the-way places such as New Guinea, for many years following war's end). Although markings and insignia are not immediately apparent, a close study of this photo shows a 500th BS (345th BG) white fuselage band in place and the name of LT. F. J. GOOD below the RHS cockpit window. Good, however, was killed (along with three of his crew, his crew chief, and seven ground personnel) as a result of a bomb explosion aboard another B-25 on July 2, 1944, so this B-25 is, clearly, one from sometime earlier than that. There were no known war-weary B-25s passed over to service squadrons by the 500th Squadron in the second quarter of 1944, and only two in the third quarter of 1944, one of which was *The WAC-A-TEER* (see chapter 2), the other *JOCK JUGGLER* (name only, no nose art). Although there is no nose art on this B-25, it still may be the former *WAC-A-TEER* after strafer modifications. Note how the bomb symbols seem to be in two groupings, those at the top (number uncertain) relating, perhaps, to this B-25's 22nd BG service, while the other 26 in the bottom row could be from its service with the 345th BG.

Bibliography

General

Alfstad, Capt. William S., ed. *Pictorial Parade FEAF CRTC*. Far East Air Force Combat Replacement & Training Center, [1945].

Archer, Robert D. *The Official Monogram US Army Air Service & Air Corps Aircraft Color Guide*. Vol. 1, *1908–1941*. Sturbridge, MA: Monogram Aviation, 1995.

Archer, Robert D., and Victor G. Archer. *USAAF Aircraft Markings and Camouflage, 1941–1947: The History of USAAF Aircraft Markings, Insignia, Camouflage, and Colors*. Atglen, PA: Schiffer, 1997.

Army Air Forces Aid Society. *AAF: The Official Guide to the Army Air Forces*. New York: Pocket Books, 1944.

Austin, Reid Stewart. *Petty: The Classic Pin-Up Art of George Petty*. New York: Gramercy, 1997.

Bell, Dana. *Air Force Colors*. Vol. 1, *1926–1942*. Carrollton, TX: Squadron/Signal, 1979.

———. *Air Force Colors*. Vol. 3, *Pacific and Home Front, 1942–47*. Carrollton, TX: Squadron/Signal, 1997.

Bertrand, Neal. *Dad's War Photos: Adventures in the South Pacific*. Lafayette, LA: Cypress Cove, 2015.

Birdsall, Steve. *Flying Buccaneers: The Illustrated Story of Kenney's Fifth Air Force*. Newton Abbot, UK: David & Charles, 1978.

Campbell, John M., and Donna Campbell. *Talisman: A Collection of Nose Art*. West Chester, PA: Schiffer, 1992.

Claringbould, Michael John. *Black Sunday: When the US Fifth Air Force Lost to New Guinea Weather*. Kingston, Australia: Aerothentic, May 2000.

Claringbould, Michael John. *The Forgotten Fifth: A Photographic Chronology of the US Fifth Air Force in the Pacific in World War II*. Kingston, Australia: Aerothentic, April 1999.

Claringbould, Michael John. *Forty of the Fifth: The Life, Times and Demise of Forty US Fifth Air Force Aircraft*. Vol. 1. Melbourne, Australia: Aerothentic, 1999.

Clune, Frank. *Song of India*. Sydney, Australia: Invincible, 1946.

Collins, Max Allan. *For the Boys: The Racy Pin-Ups of World War II*. Portland, OR: Collectors, 2000.

Collins, Max Allan, and Drake Elvgren. *Elvgren: His Life & Art*. Portland, OR: Collectors, 1998.

Cooper, H. J., and O. G. Thetford. *Aircraft of the Fighting Powers*. Vol. 5. Leicester, UK: Harborough, 1944.

Costello, John. *Virtue under Fire: How World War II Changed Our Social and Sexual Attitudes*. Boston: Little, Brown, 1985.

Craven, Wesley Frank, and James Lea Cate, eds. *The Army Air Forces in World War II*. Vol. 4, *The Pacific: Guadalcanal to Saipan, August 1942 to July 1944*. Washington, DC: Office of Air Force History, 1983.

———. *The Army Air Forces in World War II*. Vol. 5, *The Pacific: Matterhorn to Nagasaki, June 1944 to August 1945*. Washington, DC: Office of Air Force History, 1983.

Darby, Charles. *Pacific Aircraft Wrecks and Where to Find Them*. Melbourne, Australia: Kookaburra Technical, 1979.

Davis, Larry. *Planes, Names, and Dames*. Vol. 1, *1940–1945*. Carrollton, TX: Squadron/Signal, 1990.

———. *Planes, Names, and Dames*. Vol. 2, *1946–1960*. Carrollton, TX: Squadron/Signal, 1993.

Deane-Butcher, W. *Fighter Squadron Doctor: 75 Squadron RAAF New Guinea, 1942*. Gordon, Australia: W. Deane-Butcher, 1989.

Dick, Gerald, ed. *Best of Paradise*. Port Moresby, Papua New Guinea: Air Niugini, 1978.

Ebbeson, Dick. *Gretel: Eighteen Year Sketch*. Pembroke, ME: East Wind, 1994.

Edgren, Gretchen. *The Playmate Book: Five Decades of Centerfolds*. Santa Monica, CA: General Publishing Group, 1996.

Elbied, Anis, and Daniel Laurelut. *The Curtiss P-40 from 1939 to 1945*. Paris: Histoire & Collections, 2002.

Ethell, Jeffrey L. *Shark's Teeth Nose Art*. Shrewsbury, UK: Airlife, 1992.

Ethell, Jeffrey L., and Clarence Simonsen. *Aircraft Nose Art from World War I to Today*. St. Paul, MN: Zenith, 2003.

Farquhar, John T. *A Need to Know: The Role of Air Force Reconnaissance in War Planning, 1945–1953*. Maxwell Air Force Base, AL: Air University Press, February 2004.

Fitch, Maj. Frederick A., Jr. *8th Air Service Group*. Privately published, [1945].

Ford, Daniel. *Flying Tigers: Claire Chennault and His American Volunteers, 1941–1942*. New York: HarperCollins / Smithsonian Books, 2007.

Gabor, Mark. *The Pin-Up: A Modest History*. London: Pan Books, 1973.

Gallagher, James P. *With the Fifth Army Air Force: Photos from the Pacific Theater*. Baltimore: Johns Hopkins University Press, 2001.

Grinker, Roy R., and John P. Spiegel. *War Neuroses*. Philadelphia: Blakiston, 1945.

Hamrick, Joseph T. *Technical Air Intelligence in the Pacific, WWII*. Cassville, MO: Joseph T. Hamrick, 2007.

Hanson, Dian, ed. *The Big Book of Breasts: The Golden Age of Natural Curves*. Cologne: Taschen, 2006.

———. *The Little Book of Pin-Up, Vargas: The War Years, 1940–1946*. Cologne: Taschen, 2015.

Henebry, Maj. Gen. John P. (USAF, Ret.). *The Grim Reapers at Work in the Pacific Theater: The Third Attack Group of the US Fifth Air Force*. Missoula, MT: Pictorial Histories, 2002.

Jones, James. *WWII*. New York: Grosset & Dunlap, 1975.

Kiser, Brett. *The Pin-Up Girls of World War II*. Orlando, FL: BearManor Media, 2012.

Laponsky, Lt. Alfred B., and TSgt. Lyle B. Quinn. *The Buccaneer* [pictorial history of the 6th Aircraft Repair Unit (Floating)]. Tokyo: Privately published, n.d.

Larkins, William T. *Surplus WWII US Aircraft*. Upland, CA: BAC, 2005.

Leder, Jane Mersky. *Thanks for the Memories: Love, Sex, and World War II*. Washington, DC: Potomac Books, 2009.

Lindbergh, Charles A. *The Wartime Journals of Charles A. Lindbergh*. New York: Harcourt, Brace, 1970.

Logan, Ian, and Henry Nield. *Classy Chassis*. London: A & W Visual Library, 1977.

Mann, Carl. *Air Heraldry*. New York: Robert M. McBride, 1944.

Marks, Roger R. *Queensland Airfields WWII: 50 Years On*. Brisbane, Australia: R. & J. Marks, 1994.

Martin, Robert J., ed. *Fifth Air Force*. Paducah, KY: Turner, 1994.

Maurer, Maurer, ed. *Air Force Combat Units of World War II*. Washington, DC: Office of Air Force History, 1983.

Potts, E. Daniel, and Annette Potts. *Yanks Down Under, 1941–1945: The American Impact on Australia*. Melbourne, Australia: Oxford University Press, 1985.

Robertson, Bruce. *Aircraft Camouflage and Markings, 1907–1954*. Marlow, UK: Harleyford, 1956.

———. *Aircraft Markings of the World, 1912–1967*. Letchworth, UK: Harleyford, 1967.

Rust, Kenn C. *Fifth Air Force Story in World War II*. Temple City, CA: Historical Aviation Album, 1973.

Rust, Kenn C., and Dana Bell. *Thirteenth Air Force Story in World War II*. Temple City, CA: Historical Aviation Album, 1981.

Sinton, Russell L. *The Menace from Moresby*. Nashville: Battery, 1989.

Smith, Keith. *World War II Wasn't All Hell*. Surry Hills, Australia: Hutchinson Australia, 2010.

Smith, R. T. *Tale of a Tiger*. Van Nuys, CA: Tiger Originals, 1986.

Stava, Robert J. *Combat Recon: 5th Air Force Images from the SW Pacific, 1943–45*. Atglen, PA: Schiffer, 2007.

Stein, Ralph. *The Pin-Up: From 1852 to Today*. New York: Crescent Books (Crown), 1984.

Swanborough, Gordon, and Peter M. Bowers. *United States Military Aircraft since 1908*. London: Putnam, 1971.

Tate, William, and Jim Meehan. *Paint Locker Magic: A History of Naval Aviation Special Markings and Artwork*. Stroud, UK: Fonthill Media, 2015.

Thetford, O. G., and C. B. Maycock. *Aircraft of the Fighting Powers*. Vol. 6. Leicester, UK: Harborough, 1945.

Valant, Gary M. *Vintage Aircraft Nose Art*. Osceola, WI: Motorbooks International, 1987.

Velasco, Gary. *Fighting Colors: The Creation of Military Aircraft Nose Art*. Paducah, KY: Turner, 2004.

Veronico, Nicholas A., Jim Dunn, and Ron Strong. *Boneyard Nose Art: US Military Aircraft Markings and Artwork*. Mechanicsburg, PA: Stackpole Books, 2013.

Walker, Randy. *More Painted Ladies: Modern Military Aircraft Nose Art & Unusual Markings*. Atglen, PA: Schiffer, 1994.

———. *Painted Ladies, Modern Military Aircraft Nose Art & Unusual Markings*. West Chester, PA: Schiffer, 1992.

US War Department [?]. *In the Eyes of the Flyers Your Planes Are Alive*. Washington, DC: US Government Printing Office, 1944.

Ward, Richard. *Sharkmouth, 1916–1945*. Reading, UK: Osprey, 1970 [?].

Watkins, Robert A. *Battle Colors*. Vol. 5, *Insignia and Aircraft Markings of the US Army Air Forces in WWII Pacific Theater of Operations*. Atglen, PA: Schiffer, 2013.

Whelan, Russell. *The Flying Tigers: The Story of the American Volunteer Group*. New York: Viking, 1942.

Wood, Alan. *Flying Visits*. London: Dennis Dobson, 1946.

Yalom, Marilyn. *A History of the Breast*. New York: Knopf, 1997.

Bomber and Recon Units

Alcorn, John S. *The Jolly Rogers: History of the 90th Bomb Group during World War II*. Temple City, CA: Historical Aviation Album, 1981.

Avery, N. L. *B-25 Mitchell: The Magnificent Medium*. St. Paul, MN: Phalanx, 1992.

Birdsall, Steve. *Log of the Liberators: An Illustrated History of the B-24*. New York: Doubleday, 1973.

———. *Pride of Seattle: The Story of the First 300 B-17Fs*. Carrollton, TX: Squadron/Signal, 1998.

Bowers, Peter M. *Fortress in the Sky*. Granada Hills, CA: Sentry Books, 1976.

Bowman, Martin. *B-17 Flying Fortress Units of the Pacific War*. Botley, UK: Osprey, 2003.

Brosius Capt. J. W., Jr., ed. *The Marauder: A Book of the 22nd Bomb Group*. Privately published, 1944.

Brown, Joe E. *Your Kids and Mine*. New York: Doubleday, Doran, 1944.

Brownstein, Herbert S. *The Swoose: Odyssey of a B-17*. Washington, DC: Smithsonian Institution Press, 1993.

Carroll, John W. *Good Fortune Flew with Me: World War II Memoirs of John W. Carroll*. Blacktown, Australia: John W. Carroll, 2001.

Casey, Maj. Gen. Hugh J. *Engineers of the Southwest Pacific, 1941–1945*. Vol. 3, *Engineer Intelligence*. Washington, DC: US Government Printing Office, 1950.

Claringbould, Michael John. *Helluva Pelican: The History, Recovery, and Restoration of a Douglas A-20G Bomber from New Guinea's Jungles*. Melbourne, Australia: Aerosian, 1996.

———. *Pacific Profiles*. Vol. 3, *Allied Medium Bombers: Douglas A-20 Havoc Series, Southwest Pacific, 1942–1944*. Kent Town, Australia: Avonmore Books, 2021.

Cundiff, Michael J. *Ten Knights in a Bar Room Missing in Action in the Southwest Pacific, 1943*. Ames: Iowa State Press, 1990.

Dakeyne, Dick, DFC. *Radar Gunner*. Coolalinga, Australia: David M. Welch, 2014.

DiMascio, Donna, with Lt. Col. David W. Ecoff Sr. (USAF, Ret.). *Descending to Go Above & Beyond* [20th CMS]. New York: Squadron, 1998.

Down Under [43rd BG]. Sydney, Australia: Privately published, 1943.

Fain, Jim, ed. *The History of the 380th Bomb Group (H) AAF, Affectionately Known as the Flying Circus*. Privately published, n.d.

Forman, Wallace R. *B-24 Nose Art Name Directory*. North Branch, MN: Specialty Press, 1996.

Galor, Walter, Don L. Evans, Harry A. Nelson, and Lawrence J. Hickey. *Revenge of the Red Raiders: The Illustrated History of the 22nd Bombardment Group during World War II*. Boulder, CO: International Historical Research Associates, 2006.

Griffith, Alan. *Consolidated Mess: The Illustrated Guide to Nose-Turreted B-24 Production Variants in USAAF Combat Service*. Petersfield, UK: MMP Books, 2012.

Hickey, Lawrence J. *Warpath across the Pacific: The Illustrated History of the 345th Bombardment Group during World War II*. Boulder, CO: International Historical Research Associates, March 1986.

Hickey, Lawrence J., with Steve Birdsall, Madison D. Jonas, Edward M. Rogers, and Osamu Tagaya. *Ken's Men against the Empire*. Vol. 1, *Prewar to October 1943, the B-17 Era* [43rd BG]. Boulder, CO: International Historical Research Associates, 2016.

Hickey, Lawrence J., Mark M. Janko, and Stuart W. Goldberg. *Sun Setters of the Southwest Pacific Area from Australia to Japan: An Illustrated History of the 38th Bombardment Group (M) 5th Air Force World War II, 1941–1946*. Boulder, CO: Forty Five Limited Liability, 2011.

Hickey, Lawrence J., and Michael H. Levy. *Rampage of the Roarin' '20s: The Illustrated History of the 312th Bombardment Group during World War II*. Boulder, CO: International Historical Research Associates, 2009.

Hickey, Lawrence J., and James T. Pettus with Osamu Tagaya, Edward M. Rogers, and Madison D. Jonas. *Ken's Men against The Empire*. Vol. 2, *October 1943 to December 1945, the B-24 Era* [43rd BG]. Boulder, CO: International Historical Research Associates, 2019.

Hickey, Lawrence J., and Edward M. Rogers with Osamu Tagaya and Madison D. Jonas. *Harvest of the Grim Reapers: The Illustrated History of the 3rd and 27th Bombardment Groups during World War II*. Vol. 1, *Prewar–December 1942*. Boulder, CO: International Historical Research Associates, 2021.

Horton, Glenn R., Jr. *The Best in the Southwest: The 380th Bomb Group in World War II*. Savage, MN: Mosie, 1995.

Horton, Glenn R., Jr. *King of the Heavies* [380th BG]. Glenn R. Horton Jr., 1983.

Houha, William F., and Conrad S. Stuntz. *Altitude Minimum: 89th Bombardment Squadron (Light) Southwest Pacific*. Sydney, Australia: Angus & Robertson, 1945.

Lever, J. A. *RAAF No. 7 OTU Tocumwal*. Koorlong, Australia: J. A. Lever, 1996

Lloyd, Alwyn T. *Liberator: America's Global Bomber*. Missoula, MT: Pictorial Histories, April 1994.

McDowell, Ernest R. *B-25 Mitchell in Action*. Warren, MI: Squadron/Signal, 1978.

Martin, Lt. Col. Charles P., Capt. Frederick L. Newmeyer Jr., Capt. Edward Mandell, and TSgt. Harold A. Larsen. *The Reaper's Harvest* [3rd Attack Group]. Privately published, n.d.

Mikesh, Robert C., and Osamu Tagaya. *Moonlight Interceptor: Japan's "Irving" Night Fighter*. Washington, DC: Smithsonian Institution Press, 1985.

Mitchell, John H. *On Wings We Conquer*. John H. Mitchell, 1990.

Nijenhuis, Wim. *Mitchell Masterpieces*. Vol. 1, *An Illustrated History of Paint Jobs on B-25s in US Service*. Odoorn, The Netherlands: Violaero, July 2017.

O'Leary, Michael. *Production Line to Frontline 4: Consolidated B-24 Liberator*. Botley, UK: Osprey, 2002.

Olson, Harlan H. *The Diary of 8th Photo Squadron New Guinea*. Privately published, 1945.

Perrone, Stephen M. *World War II B-24 "Snoopers": Low Level Antishipping Night Bombers in the Pacific Theater*. Somerdale, NJ: New Jersey Sportsmen's Guides, June 2003.

Rutter, Joseph W. *Wreaking Havoc: A Year in an A-20*. College Station: Texas A&M University Press, 2004.

Salecker, Gene Eric. *Fortress against the Sun*. Conshohocken, PA: Da Capo, 2001.

Schafer, Allan, ed. *Bombers over Grafton*. Grafton, Australia: Clarence River Historical Society, 1992.

Segal, MSgt. Jules F., ed. *The Jolly Rogers: Southwest Pacific 1942–1944* [90th BG]. Privately published, 1944.

Sinko, Benjamin A. *Echoes of the Dominator: The Tales and the Men Who Flew the B-32*. Minneapolis: Up North, 2007.

Stanaway, John, and Bob Rocker. *The Eight Ballers: The 8th Photo Reconnaissance Squadron in World War II*. Atglen, PA: Schiffer, 1999.

Sturzebecker, Russell. *The Roarin' '20s: A History of the 312th Bombardment Group, US Army Air Force, World War II*. West Chester, PA: KNA, [1976].

Vail, Lt. Richard M., ed. *Strike: The Story of the Fighting 17th* [17th Tactical Reconnaissance Squadron]. Privately published, n.d.

Wiley, Katherine Sams, ed. *The Strafin' Saints* [71st Tactical Reconnaissance Group]. Katherine Sams Wiley, n.d.

Woods, Wiley O., Jr. *Legacy of the 90th Bombardment Group*. Paducah, KY: Turner, 1994.

Wright, Capt., et al. *The Wolf Pack* [71st BS]. Privately published, n.d.

Fighter Units

Bong, Carl, and Mike O'Connor. *Ace of Aces: The Dick Bong Story*. Mesa, AZ: Champlin Fighter Museum, 1985.

Claringbould, Michael. *Pacific Profiles*. Vol. 9, *Allied Fighters: P-38 Series, South & Southwest Pacific, 1942–1944*. Kent Town, Australia: Avonmore Books, 2022.

Dooley, Ken. *Relentless Pursuit: The Untold Story of the US 5th Air Force's 39th Fighter Squadron*. Newport, RI: Pi Ken Productions, 2015.

Ferguson, S. W., and William K. Pascalis. *Protect & Avenge: The 49th Fighter Group in World War II*. Atglen, PA: Schiffer, 1996.

Góralcyk, Maciej, and Andrzej Sadło. *P-38 Lightning at War, Pt. 2*. Lublin, Poland: Kagero, 2012.

———. *Pacific Lightnings, Pt. 1*. Lublin, Poland: Kagero, 2013.

Kolln, Jeff. *The 421st Night Fighter Squadron in World War II*. Atglen, PA: Schiffer, 2001.

Kupferer, Anthony J. *The Story of the 58th Fighter Group of World War II*. New Albany, IN: Taylor, 1989.

McDowell, Ernest R. *49th Fighter Group*. Carrollton, TX: Squadron/Signal, 1989.

———. *The Thunderbolt: Republic P-47 Thunderbolt in the Pacific Theater*. Carrollton, TX: Squadron/Signal, 1999.

Pape, Garry R., and Ronald C. Harrison. *Queen of the Midnight Skies: The Story of America's Air Force Night Fighters*. West Chester, PA: Schiffer, 1992.

Stafford, Gene B. *Aces of the Southwest Pacific*. Carrollton, TX: Squadron/Signal, 1977.

Stanaway, John. *Cobra in the Clouds: Combat History of the 39th Fighter Squadron, 1940–1980*. Temple City, CA: Historical Aviation Album, 1982.

———. *Kearby's Thunderbolts: The 348th Fighter Group in World War II*. Atglen, PA: Schiffer, 1997.

———. *Possum, Clover & Hades: The 475th Fighter Group in World War II*. Atglen, PA: Schiffer, 1993.

Stanaway, John C., and Lawrence J. Hickey. *Attack & Conquer: The 8th Fighter Group in World War II*. Atglen, PA: Schiffer, 1995.

Thompson, Warren. *P-61 Black Widow Units of World War II*. Botley, UK: Osprey, 1998.

Wistrand, Capt. R. B., ed. *Pacific Sweep*. Privately published, n.d.

Yoshino, Ronald W. *Lightning Strikes: The 475th Fighter Group in the Pacific War, 1943–1945*. Manhattan, KS: Sunflower University Press, 1992.

———. *Memoirs of the 58th Fighter Group*. Privately published, 1945.

Troop Carrier and Cargo Units

Brinson, Philip R. *Among Heroes: Tales of the Jungle Skippers; A Personal History of the 317th Troop Carrier Group*. Morrisville, NC: Lulu Enterprises, 2012.

Claringbould, Michael John. *Pacific Profiles*. Vol. 7, *Allied Transports: Douglas C-47 Series South & Southwest Pacific, 1942–1945*. Kent Town, Australia: Avonmore Books, 2022.

Davis, John M., Harold G. Martin, and John A. Whittle. *Curtiss C-46 Commando*. Tonbridge, UK: Air-Britain, 1978.

Gradidge, J. M. G. *The Douglas DC-3 and Its Predecessors*. Tonbridge, UK: Air-Britain, 1984.

Gradidge, Jennifer. *The Douglas DC-1/DC-2/DC-3: The First Seventy Years*. Vol. 2. Tonbridge, UK: Air-Britain, 2006.

Harris, Capt. Collas G., ed. *Sky Train: Adventures of a Troop Carrier Squadron* [67th Troop Carrier Squadron]. Privately published, 1945.

Himber, Lt. Sheldon, ed. *On the Final with the Fifth Combat Cargo Squadron*. Privately published, n.d.

Holsoe, Maj. Torkel, ed. *Back Load* [433rd Troop Carrier Group]. Privately published, 1945.

Imparato, Col. Edward T. *374th Troop Carrier Group*. Paducah, KY: Turner, 1998.

Isby, David. *C-47/R4D Skytrain Units of the Pacific and CBI*. Botley, UK: Osprey, 2007.

Jacobson, Capt. Richard S., ed. *Moresby to Manila via Troop Carrier: True Story of 54th Troop Carrier Wing, the Third Tactical Arm of the US Army Air Forces in the Southwest Pacific.* Privately published, 1945.

Kelly, Robert H. *Allied Air Transport Operations, South West Pacific Area in WWII.* Vol. 1, *Development of Air Transport, 1903–1943.* Buderim, Australia: Robert H. Kelly, 2003.

———. *Allied Air Transport Operations, South West Pacific Area in WWII.* Vol. 2, *1943: Year of Expansion and Consolidation.* Buderim, Australia: Robert H. Kelly, 2006.

———. *Allied Air Transport Operations, South West Pacific Area in WWII.* Vol. 3, *1943: Air Transport Approaches Full Strength.* Buderim, Australia: Robert H. Kelly, 2008.

———. *Allied Air Transport Operations, South West Pacific Area in WWII.* Vol. 4, *1944: Supporting the Allied Advances.* Buderim, Australia: Robert H. Kelly, 2013.

Pennock, Capt. John H., and 2Lt. James M. Healey, eds. *The Biscuit Bomber* [57th TCS]. Privately published, n.d.

———. *V ASAC Album* [V Air Service Area Command]. Manila, Philippines: Privately published, 1945.

Other Units

Godman, Col. Henry C. (USAF, Ret.), and Cliff Dudley. *Supreme Commander.* Harrison, AR: New Leaf, 1980.

Marion, Forrest L. *That Others May Live: USAF Air Rescue in Korea.* Washington, DC: Air Force Historical Studies Office, 2004.

Websites

3rdattackgroup.org (includes 90th BS World War II Combat Log January 12, 1942–May 3, 1944).

380th.org (380th Bomb Group).

afhistory.af.mil (Air Force Historical Support Division).

b24bestweb.com (lists and, in most cases, identifies named B-24s and derivatives).

imdb.com (International Movie Data Base information).

joebaugher.com (includes a comprehensive listing of USAAS-USAAC-USAAF-USAF aircraft by serial number).

pacificwrecks.com (includes much data on Pacific war air operations, including information on individual airplanes).

varney.yolasite.com (20th Combat Mapping Squadron).

wikipedia.com (general information).

Index of Named Airplanes

USAAF airplane types are identified by designation only.

"50 CAL GAL" B-24, 187

a snappin' 'n' a bitin', B-24, 280, 296
A Touch of Texas, A-20, 37
A Wing an' 10 Prayers, B-24, 27
ACE O' SPADES, B-24, 36
ACE of [hearts], C-47, 221
ADELAIDE FEVER, B-24, 37
After Hours, B-24, 38
AIR A CUTIE, P400, 190
AIR POCKET, B-24, 39
ALBUQUERQUE QUEEN, THE, C-47, 222
ALL ALONE – AND LONELY, B-25, 39
ALL-AMERICAN, *The*, B-25, 274
AMAZON, THE, C-47, 222
American Beauty, F-7, 39, 339
AMOROUS AMAZON, A-20, 40
AMPLE LASS, C-47, 222
ANXIOUS ANN, C-45, 320
APACHE PRINCESS, B-25, 40
ART'S CART, B-24, 41
ATOM SMASHER/"ATOM SMASHER", B-24, 42
ATOMIC BLONDE, B-24, 42
ATOMIC BLONDE, B-25, 323
Audrey, C-47, 331
AVOCA AVENGER, *The*, B-25, 269

"BABY", B-24, 43
BABY BLITZ, A-20, 40
BABY GIRL, P-38, 190
BACHELOR MADE, B-25, 43
BACHELOR'S BROTHEL, B-24, 43
"Bachelor's Den", B-24, 44
BAD LANDING, C-47, 222
BAD (MAG)GIE, C-47, 223
BAIL-OUT *Belle*, B-24, 44, 297
'BAMA BELLE, P-47, 190
BAMBOO BLONDE, THE, B-29, 150
BARBARA JEAN, B-24, 44
Bare-ly Yours, P-38, 190
BARRY'S BABY, A-20, 279
Bashful, B-25, 45
Bashful Barbs, P-47, 191
Battle Weary, B-24, 45
BAYBEE, B-24, 45, 297

BEAST, THE, B-25, 46
BEAUTIFUL BEAST/Beautiful Beast, B-24, 46, 298
Belle of the Isles, C-47, 223
"Belle Wringer", B-24, 47
Bette, B-25, 47
BETTS the BEAUT, C-47, 223
BETTY, A-20, 48
Betty Lou, C-47, 223
Betty Lou, P-47, 191
Betty's Best, A-20, 48
Betty's DREAM, B-25, 285
Big Chief Cockeye/BIG CHIEF COCKEYE, B-24, 49
BILLIE L., C-47, 224
Billie Louise, B-17, 257
BISCUIT BOMBER, C-47, 224
BLACK MAGIC, B-25, 49
Black Market Babe, P-38, 191
"Black Widow", B-24, 48
BLACK WIDOW NF, P-70, 192
Blonde Baby, C-47, 224
Blonde Bomber, B-17, 50
BLONDE BOMBER, B-25, 50, 51
"Blonde Bomber, *The*", B-24, 50, 298
Blondie, B-25, 51
Bobby Anne of Texas, the, B-24, 18
"BOB'S ROBIN", P-40, 291
BOISE BRONC, B-24, 280
BOMBS TO NIP ON, B-24, 8
BOOBY TRAP, B-24, 52
BOOM BOOM, B-25, 286
BOTTOM'S UP, C-47, 332
BOTTOM'S UP!, B-24, 52
BOURBON BOXCAR, F-7, 30
Bread Line in '49, B-24, 27, 298
BUBBLES, C-47, 225
Bugs Bunny, B-25, 288
BULBOUS ANNIE, C-46, 225
BURMA, C-46, 225
BUTCH, A-20, 53
BUTCHER'S DAUGHTER, B-24, 53
BUZZZZ JOB, B-24, 53
BYE,BYE,BLUES, C-47, 225

C.O.D. KNOT FOR TOJO, B-24, 61
Cactus Kitten, B-25, 54
Calamity Jane, A-20, 54
CALIFORNIA *Sunshine*, A-20, 54
Camera Shy, F-5, 192
Career Girl, B-24, 55

345

Caroline, B-17, 55
CAROLYN MAE, B-24, 55
CARROT TOP, B-24, 56
CHANGE O Luck, B-24, 56
charmin' lady, B-25, 56
"CHATTER BOX", B-25, 269, 298
CHEROKEE STRIP, F-7, 57
Cherrie, B-24, 57
"CHICO", B-17, 57
CLARA, C-46, 226
Classy Chassis, A-20, 58
Classy Chassis, C-47, 226
COCKTAIL HOUR, B-24, 58
Coconut Queen, OA-10, 258
COME AND GET IT, B-24, 58, 339
Coming Home! SOON, B-24, 59
COMPLETE OVERHAUL, C-46, 226
Contented Lady, A-20, 59
Cookie, A-20, 59
"COOKIE", B-24, 60
Coral Princess, the, C-47, 226
CORAL QUEEN, The, B-24, 60
CRO. BAIT, P-38, 192
CROSBYS CURSE, B-24, 61
Cruisin Susan, B-24, 61
Cyndia, C-46, 227

Daddy Please, P-40, 193
DADDY'S GIRL, B-24, 62
DAISY MAE WITH A LITTLE PERSUASION, B-24, 62
DaLLy's DiLLy, B-24, 63
DANCIN' DUCHESS, R-6, 326
Dauntless "Dottie", B-24, 63
Dawn Patrol, P-40, 193
dE-ICER, C-47, 227
"Deanna's Dreamboat", B-24, 64
DEAR RITA II, P-38, 193
Death's Angel II, P-51, 325
DEFENSELESS VIRGIN, C-47, 227
DEFENSELESS VIRGIN MARY, The, B-25, 258
"DINKY", B-24, 64
DIRTY DORA, B-25, 284
"DIRTY DORA" II, B-25, 284
DIRTY GERTY/G.I. JOE, A-20, 64
DISPLAY OF ARMS, B-24, 65, 281
Dorothy Anne, The, B-24, 65
Dorothy Mae, P-40, 193
"Dottie's Double"/"DOTTIE'S DOUBLE", B-24, 65
Double Trouble, B-24, 66
DOUBLE TROUBLE, B-24, 66
DRAGON AND HIS TAIL, THE, B-24, 66, 299
"DREAM Gal", B-24, 67
Dream girl, C-47, 332
DRIP, B-24, 67
DRUNKARD'S DREAM, B-24, 68
"DUCHESS", B-24, 68
Duchess, th', B-24, 68
Duchess of Paducah, The, B-24, 69
Duggy, C-47, 300
Dutchess, The, C-47, 227

EAGER BEAVER, P-38, 291
Eager Lady, A-20, 300
Edibelle, L-5, 258
ELFRIEDA, B-24, 311
Ellie Mae, C-47, 228
"ELUSIVE-LIZZIE", B-25, 69
EMBARASSED, B-24, 69, 301
EMBRACEABLE You, P-38, 323
Emergency STRIP, B-25, 70
Empty Saddle, P-40, 194
Esquire/ESQUIRE, B-24, 70

Fast Lady, B-25, 25, 259
"FAT CAT", B-25, 297
FEATHER MERCHANT, B-25, 270, 300
FEATHERMERCHANT'S FOLLY, B-24, 71
Filthy Filbert, B-25, 71
Fire Power, B-24, 71
"FIRIN' FANNIE", B-25, 72
FIRST NIGHTER, B-24, 72
Firtil Myrtle, B-24, 72
Flak Fled Flapper, B-24, 73
FLAMIN' MAMIE, B-24, 73, 340
FLORIDA'S BEAUTY, P-51, 325
Flossie II, A-20, 73
Flying Fannie, B-24, 73
"FLYING GINNY", B-25, 74
"FLYING HI", C-46, 228
"Flying Wolf", B-24, 293
FOIL PROOF MARY, B-24, 74
FORM 1-A, B-24, 74
Form-1A, C-47, 228
FRANCIE II, A-20, 75
FREE FOR ALL!!!, B-24, 75
FRENESI, C-46, 229
FRIDGID MIDGET JR., C-47, 229
FRISCO FRANNIE, B-24, 75
FRIVOLOUS SAL, B-24, 76
Fun WASN'T IT!, P-47, 194
FURY, B-26, 302

"G.I." Jr., B-17, 248
G.I. Miss U, P-38, 194
G.I. Virgin, P-38, 195
Gallant Lady/LADY LYNN, B-24, 76
"GEORGIA PEACH", B-26, 77
GEORGIA PEACH/TEXAS HONEY, C-47, 229
GERALDINE, B-24, 291
"Geronimo", C-47, 229
GERRI, P-47, 195
Ghost of Billie L, C-47, 230
"Ginger", C-46, 230
Gladys, B-24, 77
Glamour-Puss II, P-38, 195
Gloria C II, A-20, 77
GLORIA, P-47, 196
Golden Horseshoe, The, C-46, 230
GOLDEN LADY, B-24, 78
Gone Forever, C-46, 230
GONE WITH THE WIND, B-24, 79
Good Pickin's, B-24, 79

Grade A, P-40, 196
"GRRRR", B-24, 80
gunmoll 2nd, B-24, 80, 302
Gypsy, B-24, 81
GYPSY, B-24, 81
Gypsy Rose, B-17, 81

"HANGAR QUEEN, C-47, 332
"hangover haven II", F-7, 31
HARD TO GET, A-20, 82
HARDSHIPS 2nd, B-25, 296
"Harriett", F-5, 196
HAWKEYE EXPRESS", "The, B-25, 30
HEATER, THE, B-24, 132
HEAVEN CAN WAIT, B-24, 81
Heavenly Body, B-24, 35, 81
HEAVENLY BODY, B-24, 82
HELEN & FLO, C-47, 333
HELL ON THE DOUBLE, P-38, 196
HELL'S ANGEL 2nd, C-47, 231
Hell's Belle, B-24, 83
"HELL'S BELLE", B-24, 83
HELLS FIRE/HELL'S FIRE, B-25, 270
HERE'S HOWE, B-25, 84, 303
Hi Honey!, P-38, 319
HIP PARADE, B-24, 84
HIT PARADER, B-24, 85
HIT PARADER II, B-24, 85
"HITT AND MISS", B-25, 85
HO HUM, B-24, 86
HOBO QUEEN II, B-32, 87, 303
HOMESICK ANGEL, C-47, 231
Homing Pigeon, C-47, 333
"Honey ChiLe", P-38, 197
HONEYMOON EXPRESS, C-47, 231
Hot "Box", C-47, 232
HOT BUDDY, B-24, 87
HOT PANTS, C-47, 232
HOT ROCKS, B-24, 88
HOT ROCKS, C-47, 233
HOTSEE!, B-25, 88
Hot-to-go, C-47, 233
HOW'M-I-DOIN', B-24, 88, 338
HOW'S YOUR OLE' TOMATO, B-25, 89
"Hurkie", C-47, 233
HUT-SUT, P-47, 197

"I'LL BE AROUND", B-24, 89
"I'LL BE SEEIN' YOU", OA-10, 259
I'll Be Seeing You, B-24, 16
IMPATIENT VIRGIN, B-25, 89
In The Mood, A-20, 90
'In the Mood', unidentified type, 259
Ione, C-47, 233
Island Dream, P-40, 197
ISLAND QUEEN, B-24, 90
IT AINT SO FUNNY, B-24, 24

JACK POT, B-24, 91
Jackie, F-15, 326
"Je Reviens", B-24, 90

JADED SAINT, THE, B-25, 9
JAIL BAIT, P-47, 197
Jean Creamer, P-38, 198
JERSEY BOUNCE, C-46, 233
"Jezebelle"/Jezebelle, B-24, 91
Jini, B-24, 92
JOANNE, C-47, 234
JOKER'S WILD, B-17, 33
"Juarez Whistle", B-24, 92
JUGGLIN' JOSIE, B-24, 92, 304
JULIE, P-39, 329
JUNE BRIDE, B-24, 94
JUNGLE QUEEN/JUNGLE QUEEN II, B-24, 93
JUNGLE QUEEN, B-25, 93, 304

K.O. KID, The, B-24, 94
KANSAS-CITY KITTY, B-24, 94
KAY-18, F-7, 94
KEEP IT UNDER YOUR HAT, C-47, 234, 304
"Kentucky Virgin", B-24, 94
Kings Cross SHUTTLE, C-47, 234
Kit II, P-47, 198

Labor Pains, B-25, 274
Lady from Leyte, B-24, 95
Lady GODiVA, P-47, 198
Lady is Fresh, The, B-32, 95
LADY LIL, B-25, 96
"Lady Luck", B-24, 96
LADY LUCK, C-47, 234
"LADY LUCK", B-24, 96
"LADY LUCK", C-47, 235
LADY LYNN, B-24, 76
LADY MARGO, B-25, 324
LADY ORCHID, P-47, 199
Lak-a-Nuki, A-20, 26, 97
LANA, P-47, 199
LAP DOG!, P-38, 199
LAST HORIZON, B-24, 24
LAST STRAW, The, B-17, 97
LAZY DAISY MAE, B-25, 97
LAZY LADY, C-47, 235
Lazy Lady, P-38, 199
LEMON, THE, B-24, 67
LET'S FACE IT, B-25, 295
Lewd Lady, B-25, 98
LI'L D'-ICER, B-24, 98
LI'L ROXIE RAE, B-25, 7
LIBERTY BELLE, B-24 (22nd BG), 99
LIBERTY BELLE, B-24 (43rd BG), 99
LIBERTY BELLE, B-24 (90th BG), 98
LIBERTY Belle, B-24, 99
LIBERTY BELLE II, B-24, 100
LIL BOOTSIE "ADA", P-47, 201
LiL "DAISY" CUTTER, B-24, 102
Lil De-Icer, B-25, 100
LiL' DEiCER II, B-26, 101
Lilas Marie, B-24, 101
Lilas Marie The 2nd, B-24, 101
Little Audry, B-26, 102
Little Brat, A-20, 103

Little "BUTCH", C-47, 333
"Little Butch", A-20, 103
LiTTLE CHiEF, A-20, 260
LITTLE CHIEF COCKEYE, B-25, 259, 340
"Little DOC", A-20, 103
LITTLE JODY, B-24, 103
Little Joe, F-7, 104
Little Lorraine, F-5, 200
"Little Lulu", B-24, 103
LITTLE NEL, B-25, 9
LIVE WIRE, B-24, 104
LONESOME ANGEL, THE, C-47, 235
LONESOME CHERRY, C-47, 333
LONG "DISTANCE", C-46, 235
LONG ISLAND BELLE, B-25, 334
LOUISE!, F-5, 29, 200
LOUISIANA LULLABY, B-24, 104
Lovable Lou, C-47, 236
Lovely Louise, B-24, 105
LOVELY LOUISE, F-7, 321
LUCKY [legs], B-24, 105
"LUCKY BAT", B-25, 275
LUCKY LUCILLE, B-24, 105
'Lucky Strike', B-24, 106
LUGER LUGGIN LASSIE, B-25, 106
'Luvablass', B-24, 106

MABEL'S LABELS, B-24, 107
MAD GREMLIN, B-26, 304
MAD RUSSIAN, B-24, 107
Madame Queen, B-24, 108
Mag the Hag, B-24, 108
MAID in The USA, B-24, 109
Male Call/MALE CALL, B-24, 108
Mamma-Duck, C-47, 236
Manila Calling, B-24, 109
MARGARET HAYNE, The, B-25, 285
Marge, P-38, 200
MARGIE, B-24, 109
"MARGIE", B-26, 109
Marie, A-20, 110
MARIE, B-24, 110
Marie Elena, P-38, 201
Mary, C-47, 236
"Mary", B-25, 289
MARY ANN, B-24, 110
Mary Annette, B-25, 110
MARY-E, P-47, 305
Mary "F", B-25, 111
MARY JO, The/Mary Jo, B-25, 111
Mary Joyce & Ruby, B-24, 111
Mary Liz, P-47, 201
'MARY LOU', P-40, 202
"Mary M", B-24, 112
MARY-E, P-47, 305
MAYBE?, C-47, 15
MAYFLOWER, The, B-24, 112
Meat [Waggin], C-47, 332
MEXICAN SPITFIRE, B-25, 112
MICHIGAN, B-24, 113

MICKIE'S MENACE, B-24, 113
MIDNIGHT MAMA, P-61, 202
"MILADY", B-24, 113
"Milk Wagon Express", P-40, 202
MILLIE, B-25, 50
million$Baby, B-24, 114
MILLION$BABY, B-24, 114
MIS-A-SIP, A-20, 114
Miscellaneous, C-47, 236, 305
Mischievous MARY II, A-20, 114
MISS B HAVIN, B-25, 115
Miss Bea, P-47, 202
Miss BeHaven, A-20, 115
MISS BEHAVIOR, C-47, 237
"Miss Carriage", C-47, 237, 305
Miss Charlene, B-25, 115
Miss Cheri, P-38, 203
"Miss Deed", B-24, 115
Miss Em', B-17, 237
Miss Exterminator, B-25, 116
MISS GINNY, P-38, 203
MISS GIVING, B-24, 116
MISS HAP, The, B-24, 116
Miss Jolly Roger/BOOBY TRAP, B-24, 117
Miss Kiwanis, B-24, 117
"MISS LIBERTY", B-24, 118
Miss LIBERTY BELLE, B-24, 117
Miss McCook, B-24, 118
"MISS PAT", B-25, 118
MISS POSSUM MY TEXAS GAL, A-20, 118
Miss TREATED, C-46, 237
MISSIN' YOU, B-24, 306
"Mission Belle"/Mission Belle, B-24, 119, 339
"MISSLEADING", B-24, 119
'Missouri Miss', B-24, 119
"MITCH" THE WITCH, B-25, 120
MOBY DICK, B-24, 272
MOBY DICK JR, L-4, 292
MODEST MAIDEN, B-24, 120
MONKEY BIZZ-NEZZ, B-17, 33
MONTANA MAID, B-25, 120
MORNIN AFTER, C-47, 237
MORTIMER/Mortimer, B-25, 271, 306
Mr Period, P-47, 203
"MUGGSIE", P-47, 203
MUSTANG, The, B-17, 121, 306
My Anxious Mama!, P-40, 204
MY BET, P-38, 204
MY BET III, P-38, 204
MY BUCK, B-25, 324
MY GAL Jeannie, P-38, 205
MY JOY, A-20, 120
MY "Oklahoma" GAL, B-17, 306
MY PET, P-38, 306
MYAKIN-BACK, A-20, 122

Nancy Jane, B-24, 122
naughty but nice, B-17, 121, 307
Naughty Dotty, F-5, 205
NAUGHTY MARIETTA, B-25, 123

NEAR MISS, B-25, 123
Nervous Virgin, the, A-20, 123
Net Results, B-24, 124
"*NICE PIECE*", P-38, 205
NO PEEKIN, B-25, 15
Nobody's Baby, B-24, 123
NOCTURNAL 'MISSION, B-24, 124
NOCTURNAL NEMESIS, P-61, 206, 307
Nocturnal Nuisance, P-61, 206
"*NORMA*", B-24, 126
NOT IN STOCK, B-24, 125

O'Riley's Daughter II, A-20, 125
O'Riley's Daughter, P-40, 206
Obscene Corrine, P-38, 206
OLD IRON SIDES, B-24, 280
Old Man, The, B-17, 6
OLE MAN MOE, C-47, 238
Ole' TOMATO, B-24, 126
ON "DE-FENSE", B-24, 126
ONE TIME, B-24, 307
OOOOOH! LADY, A-20, 126
Open Date, C-47, 238
Ou'r Gal, B-26, 127
"*Our Baby*", B-25, 126
OUR FORM-1-A-LILLIAN-ETHEL, C-47, 238
"*Our Gal*" II, B-25, 127
Our Gal III, B-24, 128
"*OUR HONEY*", B-24, 128
OUTA THIS WORLD, B-24, 129
OUTA' THIS WORLD, B-24, 129
OVER EXPOSED, F-7, 128

P.I. JOE, B-25, 268, 308
Pam, P-38, 207
PANAMA HATTIE, B-17, 129
PANNELL JOB, B-25, 130
Paper Doll, B-24, 130
Paper Doll, F-5, 207
PAPPY'S PASSION, B-24, 130
PAPPY'S PASSION II, B-24, 130
PASSION WAGON, C-47, 238
Passionate Patsy, P-40, 207
PATCHED UP PIECE, F-7, 23, 131
PATCHES, B-24, 131
"*PATChES*", B-24, 131
PATIENT KITTEN, B-24, 132
'*PATTY'S PIG*', B-24, 132
PAY OFF, P-39, 207
PEACE OFFERING, B-24, 132, 317
Peck's Bad Girl, P-38, 208
PEGASUS [name incomplete], C-47, 232
PEGGY'S PEGASUS, P-38, 208
Pel, C-47, 239
PETER HEATER, THE/HEATER, THE, B-24, 132
PETTY GAL, B-24, 133, 308
PHOTO JEANNE, F-7, 134
PHOTO QUEEN!, F-7, 133
Phyllis J. of WORCESTER, B-24, 134, 308
PHYLLIS, P-39, 329

PICCADILLY PRINCESS, Avro Lancaster, 15
PICKLED PEACH, B-24, 135
PIGEON TOED PRINCESS, P-39, 330
Piggy Back, F-5, 208
Pink Stuff, C-47, 239
PIONEER PEGGY, P-47, 209
PISTOL PACKIN MAMA, A-20, 135
PISTOL PACKIN MAMA, C-47, 239
PISTOL PACKIN' MAMA, B-24, 136
PISTOL PACKIN' MAMA, B-26, 137
"*PISTOL PACKIN' MAMA*", B-24, 136
"*Pistol Packin' Mama*", B-25, 137
PLEASURE BENT, B-24, 137
Pleiades, C-47, 239
POISON IVEY, B-24, 137
Polly, P-38, 209
POM POM EXPRESS, B-24, 138
POPPY, C-47, 240
Pop's Blue Ribbon, P-40, 209
Powers Girl, The, B-24, 16
Pretty Baby, B-17, 240
PRETTY BABY, B-24, 139
PRETTY BABY, C-47, 240
Pretty LOUISE, C-46, 241
Prince Valiant, B-24, 141
'*Princess Marie*', B-25, 334
PRINCESS PAT, B-25, 308
"*PROP WASH*", B-24, 138
"*PUDGY*", B-24, 140
PUG NOSE, B-24, 261
PUGNOSE PRINCESS, THE, B-24, 140
PUNJA KASI, B-24, 140
Puss & Boots, B-24, 141

Queen Ann, B-24, 140
"*Queen Hi*", B-24, 141
QUEEN MAE, B-24, 142
Queen Mary, B-25, 261
Queen o' Hearts, A-20, 142
QUEEN of HEARTS, B-24, 143
QUEEN OF HEARTS, B-24, 143
Queen Of Spades, The, A-20, 26, 143
Queen Of The CLouds/Queen of the Clouds, B-24, 144
"*QUEEN OF THE STRIP*", B-24, 144
QUEER DEAR/Queerdeer, B-24, 145
QUITCH, B-25, 144
Quivering Sal, C-46, 241

RAMP TRAMP, B-17, 321
Rangy Lil, B-24, 146
Ready Betty 'Gone Forever', B-17, 146
READY TEDDY, A-20, 309
"*READY WILLING AND ABLE*", B-24, 146
"*REAREN TO GO*", C-46, 241, 309
REBEL'S Dream, C-47, 241
RED HEADED GAL/"RED HEADED GAL", B-25, 146, 309
Red-headed Rebel, the, B-24, 146
RED-HOT RIDEN-HOOD II, B-24, 147
RED-HOT RIDEN-HOOD III, B-24, 148, 309
Redhot Ridinhood, B-24, 147

'RED'IE AND WILLING, C-47, 242
"RED WRATH", B-25, 274
Regina I, P-38, 277
REGINA II, P-38, 277
Reina del PACIFICO, B-25, 148
RIDIN' HIGH, A-20, 148
Rio Rita, B-24, 148
RIP SNORTER, the, F-7, 149
"RITA'S WAGON", B-25, 266
ROAD TO TOKYO, B-24, 150
ROARIN' ROSIE, B-24, 150
ROARING TWENTIES, THE, A-20, 149
"ROBBIE 'L", B-24, 151
Roberta and son, B-24, 71
ROSE IN BLOOM, B-25, 7
Rosy Cheeks, P-40, 209
Rotation Plan, C-47, 334
ROUGH KNIGHT/Rough Night!/Rough Knight, B-24, 151
Rough Stuff!, A-20, 152
Round Trip Ticket, B-24, 152
ROUND TRIP Ticket, B-24, 153
ROYAL FLUSH, B-24, 153
ROYAL FLUSH II, B-24, 153
Rubber Nose, P-47, 210
RUBE, THE, C-47, 242
RUBY'S RICKSHA, B-24, 153
RUGGED But RiGHT, C-47, 334
RUM AND COKE, B-24, 154
RUNT'S ROOST, B-25, 271
RUSTY, C-47, 242

"SACK", The, B-25, 155
SACK BOUND, B-24, 155
SACK-TIME SAL, P-47, 210
"Sack Time", B-24, 155
Sadie, B-24, 156
SALVO, B-24, 279
"SAN ANTONIO ROSE", P-38, 210
SAN SUSAN, A-20, 156
Sandra Kay, B-24, 313
SANDY, B-24, 156
"Satan's Angel", B-25, 157
SATAN'S BABY, B-24, 157
Satan's Secretary, B-24, 156
'SATANS SISTER', B-24, 157, 338
SCARLET HARLOT, B-25, 158
SCARLET NIGHT, P-40, 210
"SCORPION", B-24, 294, 310
SCOTCH and SODA, A-20, 278
Scoto Kid, B-25, 268
SEAFOOD MAMA, B-24, 158
SECOND HAND Fannie, C-47, 242
SEVEN DAY LEAVE, B-25, 158
Shady's Lady, P-38, 211
Shag-on, A-20, 158
Shakes ALL OVER, C-47, 243
Shamrock Sherry, B-24, 12, 159
She' Asta, B-24, 159
"She'll Do Me", C-47, 331, 335
"She's RITE", C-47, 335

SHINY SHIELA, C-47, 262
SHIRLEY ANN, B-24, 159
"SHOO-SHOO BABY", B-24, 160
Shy-Chi Baby, B-24, 160, 310
"Silver Lady", B-24, 161
SITTING PRETTY, B-24, 161, 310
"Six Bitts", B-24, 29, 162
Sixty-niner, The, P-47, 211
SKY LADY, B-24, 162
"SKY LADY", B-24, 162
"SKY WITCH", B-24, 162, 310
SLEEPY TIME/SLEEPY TIME GAL, A-20, 163
SLEEPY TIME GAL, C-47, 243
'SLEEPY TIME GAL', P-47, 211
"Sleepy TIME GAL", C-46, 243
"SLEEPY TIME GAL", B-24, 163
SLEEPY-TIME GAL, B-24, 163
Slick CHICK, P-47, 211
Slightly DANGEROUS, B-24, 164
SLIGHTLY DANGEROUS, B-24, 164
Slightly Dangerous, P-38, 212
SLOW MOTION, B-24, 164
SLUT II, C-47, 243
SMOKEY, A-20, 164
Smoky, B-25, 165
SNAFU, B-24, 311
SNAFU NO. II, B-24, 165
SNATCHER, P-38, 212
SNIPER, A-20, 165
So Inviting, P-38, 212
SO WHAT!, C-47, 244
SOLID STUFF, L-5, 262
SOONER The Better, The, P-38, 212
"SOOPER DROOPER", B-24, 166
"SOUTHERN BELLE", P-39, 330
"SPECIAL DELIVERY", B-24, 128
SPEEDY STEEDE, C-47, 244
SPINDLE SHANKS, P-40, 213
SPOOK II, B-25, 272
"SQUAW PEAK", B-24, 166
"Squigy", C-46, 244
ST LOUIS BLUES, F-7, 31
STAR DUSTER, B-24, 167
Star Eyes, B-24, 167
STAR of ATSUGI, B-17, 321
STEPPIN' OUT!, C-47, 244
Still Putting OUT, C-47, 335
STORMY WEATHER, B-24, 263
Strictly Sex, P-38, 212
STRIP POLKA, THE, B-24, 167
"Strokem Dodie", B-25, 7
Stubborn Hellion, B-25, 292
Stuff, C-47, 244
"SUCKA", C-47, 245
SULTAN'S DAUGHTER, THE, B-24, 168
SURE SKIN, C-47, 245
"SWAMP ANGEL", B-24, 168
SWEET RACKET, B-24, 168
"SWEET SIXTEEN", B-24, 168
SWEET TAKE-OFF, B-24, 169, 311

INDEX OF NAMED AIRPLANES

Sweet WILLUMS II, A-20, 169
SY'S HOT NUMBER, A-20, 312

TABU, B-24, 170
TAIL HEAVY, C-47, 245
Tail Wind, B-24, 170
TAIL WIND, B-24, 170
TAIL WIND/Tail Wind, C-47, 246
"Tail Wind", B-25, 170
TARGET FOR TONIGHT, B-24, 171
TEE-KAY, B-25, 289
"TEMPERMENTAL LADY", B-24, 171
TEMPTATION, B-24, 171
TEN Hits and a "Miss", B-24, 15
TEN KNIGHTS in a BAR ROOM, B-24, 172
"TENN." SQUIRREL HUNTER, B-24, 61
TEXAS HELLCAT, C-47, 246
TEXAS HONEY/GEORGIA PEACH, C-47, 247
Texas Pom Pom, A-20, 172
THIS ABOVE ALL, F-7, 172
Thoughts of Midnite, P-38, 213
THREE POINT LANDING, B-24, 173
"TIGER LADY", B-25, 173
Tiger Lilly, B-25, 290
'TINKIE', B-25, 173
TITIAN TEMPTRESS, B-24, 174
"TODDY"/"Toddy", B-24, 174
Tokyo or BUST, C-46, 247
TOKYO SLEEPER, B-25, 273
TONDELAYO, B-25, 175, 312
"TORRID TESSIE"/TORRID TESS, B-25, 268, 312
TRAMP, B-24, 175
TROUBLE, C-47, 248
"TUGBOAT ANNIE", B-25, 16
TWIN NIFTIES/TWIN NIFTY'S, B-24, 176
TWIN NIFTIES II/TWIN NIFTYS II, B-24, 177
TWO BOB TiLLiE, B-24, 176
TWO TIME, B-25, 313
TYRANNOSAURUS REX, B-24, 294

U.S. ANGEL, P-47, 218
UNDECIDED/Undecided, B-24, 178
"UNDECIDED", B-17, 19
UNDER EXPOSED!, F-7, 179
"Urgin Virgin" II, B-29, 15

V..._ SURE POP, B-24, 182
Vagrant Virgin, P-38, 218
VAGRANT VIRGIN, A-26, 322
VICE UNLIMITED, B-26, 317
VIGOROUS VIRGIN, The, B-25, 183
VIRGIN [crossed through], P-38, 218
"VIRGIN ABROAD", B-24, 183, 317
Virgin Princess, C-47, 255
VIRGINIA MARIE, P-38, 219
ViVACiOUS ViRGiN!, the, B-24, 183

WAC-A-TEER, The B-25, 184
WANGO WANGO BIRD, the, F-7, 32, 317
WAR WEARY, B-25, 316
WELL DEVELOPED, F-7, 184
WELL GODDAM, B-17, 308
WHAT'S COOKIN?, C-47, 254
WHITE WING, B-25, 184
Who ME?, P-47, 219
Who's Next?, B-24, 185
WHODUNIT? the/The 2nd, B-25, 336
WHOOO! The "GRAY GHOST", C-47, 255
WIDOW MAKER, The, C-46, 255
Wilda Marie, B-25, 283
Wilful Winnie, P-38, 219
Willie-B II, C-47, 256
WILLIE'S FOLLY, B-24, 185
WINDY CITY KITTY, B-24, 186
WINDY CITY KITTY [IT'S UP TO YOU], B-24, 185
"WINDY CITY RUTHIE", P-38, 220
WINGED VIRGIN, L-4, 264
WOLF PACK, B-24, 187
WOLF, the, B-24, 187

X-L-ENT, P-47, 220

Yank's Delight, C-47, 256
YANKEE DIDDL'ER, B-17, 188
YANKEE GAL, B-24, 25, 186, 188, 317
YOUR'S, C-47, 256

ZOLA, Handley-Page Halifax, 15

David Vincent has authored several books on WWII aircraft, focusing on their service with the RAAF. He has been collecting images of 5th Air Force nose art since 2004. David lives in southern Australia.